Prison Capital

Justice, Power, and Politics

Heather Ann Thompson and Rhonda Y. Williams, *editors*

EDITORIAL ADVISORY BOARD
Dan Berger
Peniel E. Joseph
Daryl Maeda
Barbara Ransby
Vicki L. Ruiz
Marc Stein

The Justice, Power, and Politics series publishes new works in history that explore the myriad struggles for justice, battles for power, and shifts in politics that have shaped the United States over time. Through the lenses of justice, power, and politics, the series seeks to broaden scholarly debates about America's past as well as to inform public discussions about its future.

A complete list of books published in Justice, Power, and Politics is available at https://uncpress.org/series/justice-power-politics.

Prison Capital

Mass Incarceration and Struggles for Abolition Democracy in Louisiana

....

LYDIA PELOT-HOBBS

The University of North Carolina Press Chapel Hill

© 2023 Lydia Pelot-Hobbs
All rights reserved
Set in Charis by Westchester Publishing Services
Manufactured in the United States of America

Library of Congress Cataloging-in-Publication Data
Names: Pelot-Hobbs, Lydia, author.
Title: Prison capital : mass incarceration and struggles for abolition
   democracy in Louisiana / Lydia Pelot-Hobbs.
Other titles: Justice, power, and politics.
Description: Chapel Hill : University of North Carolina Press, [2023] |
   Series: Justice, power, and politics | Includes bibliographical
   references and index.
Identifiers: LCCN 2023025339 | ISBN 9781469675107 (cloth ; alk. paper) |
   ISBN 9781469675114 (paperback ; alk. paper) | ISBN 9781469675121 (ebook)
Subjects: LCSH: Mass incarceration—Louisiana—History—20th century. |
   Mass incarceration—Louisiana—History—21st century. | Mass
   incarceration—Government policy—Louisiana. | Racism against
   Black people—Louisiana. | Petroleum industry and trade—Political
   aspects—Louisiana. | Capitalism—Political aspects—Louisiana. | Prison
   abolition movements—Louisiana. | Louisiana—Politics and government. |
   BISAC: SOCIAL SCIENCE / Ethnic Studies / American / General |
   SOCIAL SCIENCE / Human Geography
Classification: LCC HV9475.L2 P456 2023 | DDC 365/.9763—dc23/eng/
   20230622
LC record available at https://lccn.loc.gov/2023025339

Cover illustration: USGS topographic map of Louisiana State Penitentiary.
Courtesy of Wikimedia Commons.

For Arthur Mitchell, Hayes Williams, Lee Stevenson, Lazarus Joseph, JoAnn Johnson, Henry Glover, James Brissette, Ronald Madison, Althea Francois, Robert Goodman, Penny Proud, and too many others whose lives have been cut far too short and for the multitude of individuals, known and unknown, who have and continue to struggle for a more free Louisiana.

Contents

List of Illustrations, ix

Acknowledgments, xi

Introduction, 1

1 Decentralizing Angola, 22
  Liberal Interventions, Overcrowding Crises, and the Making of a New Era

2 Consolidating and Contesting Law-and-Order Austerity, 61

3 Jailing Louisiana, 100
  Sheriffs, Policing, and Growing Opposition

4 Carceral Disasters, 142
  Hurricane Katrina, Organized Abandonment, and Racial State Violence

5 Reconstructing the New Orleans Criminal Legal System in the Wake of Hurricane Katrina, 168

6 To Walk down the Street without Fear, 207
  Curbing Criminalization and Demanding Life in the New Orleans Tourism Economy

Conclusion, 251
Making Freedom

Notes, 265

Bibliography, 337

Index, 361

Illustrations

Figures

1.1 Harry Connick district attorney campaign ad, *Times-Picayune*, September 12, 1973, 34

1.2 "We Can't Adequately Handle Any More Prisoners" political cartoon, *Times-Picayune*, July 23, 1975, 43

1.3 "Jungle Justice" political cartoon, *States-Item*, August 22, 1974, 45

2.1 "We've Solved the Prison Overcrowding Crisis" political cartoon, *Times-Picayune*, September 24, 1989, 98

3.1 "The New Parish Prison," *States-Item*, October 23, 1977, 114

3.2 Sheriff Foti political cartoon, *Times-Picayune*, June 10, 1983, 115

3.3 "Louisiana Jails," Inside Newsletter, Louisiana Coalition on Jails and Prisons, 118

4.1 Althea Francois speaking at a post-Katrina OPP press conference, October 12, 2005, 165

5.1 OPPRC smaller jail ad, September 8, 2010, 200

6.1 BreakOUT! "Your Guide to Street Safety & Preserving Your Rights with the Police," 216

6.2 BreakOUT! #KnowYourRights social media campaign, 2013, 221

6.3 BreakOUT #BlackTransLivesMatter billboard, 2015, 240

Graphs

2.1 Louisiana unemployment rate by race, 1981–1998, 77

3.1 State prisoners held in parish jails, 1978–2004, 140

Maps

0.1a State prisons in Louisiana, 2

0.1b City and parish jails in Louisiana, 3

6.1 French Quarter Economic Development District map, 229

Tables

1.1 Louisiana budgetary growth, 1970–1975, 32
3.1 Parish jails with more than 50% bed space held by state prisoners, 1998, 112

Acknowledgments

This book is a love letter to Louisiana. It would be easy to read these pages that detail racial and gendered state violence, neoliberal restructuring, and disasters of all kinds as a denunciation of Louisiana. But that would miss the point. My critical documentation and analysis were not done to create a spectacle of suffering or to disavow Louisiana (or the broader US South) but to highlight that Louisiana deserves so much more. Louisiana has been held hostage by white supremacy and racial capitalism at the peril of countless people past and present. But other futures can still be forged. As the various antiracist organizers whose stories grace this book have articulated time and time again, Louisiana is worth fighting for. Even in the face of the crises of mass incarceration and climate calamity, Louisiana can be made into a different kind of place. It is my hope that this book can contribute something to struggles for freedom in the swamps of Louisiana and beyond.

The generosity and labors of many people made this book possible. First and foremost are the organizers, activists, and advocates who kindly shared their stories with me: kai lumumba barrow, Xochitl Bervera, Melissa Burch, Cielo Cruz, Eugene Dean, Don Everard, Naomi Farve, Nia Faulk, Jacinta Gonzalez, Shana M. griffin, Keneisha Harris, Norris Henderson, Biggy Johnston, Anthoni/Kym Johnson, Shaena Johnson, Mayaba Liebenthal, Jack Cassidy, Evelyn Lynn, Tamika Middleton, Cobella Moore, Pam Nath, Keith Nordyke, Lhundyn Palmer, Ursula Price, Milan Sherry, Andrea Slocum, Ted Quant, Bill Quigley, Jai Shavers, Checo Yancey, Wes Ware, and Arely Westley. Additional thanks go to BreakOUT! staff and members who trusted me enough to let me write about their organizing. I owe a special debt of gratitude to Norris Henderson who generously shared his stories of organizing with me repeatedly over close to fifteen years while encouraging this project from its very earliest seeds.

I was immensely fortunate to have had the shrewd attention of Ruth Wilson Gilmore on this project, letting me know when I went off course or when I hit on something important. Ruthie's critical mentorship is always anchored in the political stakes of our work—that it may clarify rather than mystify the operations of racism, capitalism, and punitive state power so that we are better equipped to strategize and organize for a more free world. Without a doubt, this book is sharper and deeper because of her guidance. In the early stages, I also benefited from the generative feedback of Eric Lott and Rupal Oza. Eric helped me think through what it means to study the US South without falling into the trap of southern exceptionalism and to understand the interplay between the cultural and material politics of racism. Rupal deepened my thinking on how a feminist analysis could be scaled up in my considerations of political economy and reminded me to always keep the particularities of Louisiana situated in global circuits of power.

This book was indelibly shaped by the classrooms and advisement of many faculty members. At the CUNY Graduate Center and the broader New York Graduate School Consortium, I had the pleasure of learning formally and informally from Herman Bennett, Kandace Chuh, Barbara Jeanne Fields, David Harvey, Cindi Katz, Setha Low, Jennifer Morgan, Frances Fox Piven, Robert Rheid-Pharr, Neil Smith (for a brief time before his untimely passing), and Nikhil Pal Singh. My work on the Angola Special Civics Project initially developed as a master's thesis at the University of New Orleans under the supportive advising of Rachel Luft, Renia Ehrenfeucht, and Elizabeth Steeby. I am particularly grateful to Rachel Luft, who in her office, home, and innumerable activist meetings modeled for me staunch antiracist and feminist research praxis in the world of post-Katrina organizing. It is with much sadness that Arnie Hirsch passed away before this book came to fruition. His work and teachings on race, urban politics, and New Orleans history are imprinted throughout these pages. I would be remiss if I did not acknowledge that it was at Oberlin College that I first learned the pleasure of critically engaged study and writing. Thank you to Gina Pérez, Meredith Raimondo, Anu Needham, and Pam Brooks for beginning me on this path.

I have been more than lucky to have found this book a home at the University of North Carolina Press. The enthusiasm and rigor with which Brandon Proia edited this book surpassed any expectations I might have had. Brandon began editing this manuscript before he was technically my editor, mixing his adept streamlining of my writing with a profound understanding of the political stakes of this work. I am also very thankful for Dawn Durante stepping in as editor at the tail end of this process to ensure a smooth production process. I thank my two anonymous reviewers for their insightful and generative feedback that strengthened this book. Rebecca Hill, who revealed herself as one of these reviewers, offered thoughtful comments that helped me better situate this story within national currents of carceral formations and grassroots organizing.

I could not have done this project without the aid of archivists at the Amistad Research Center, especially Chris Harter; the Hill Memorial Library at Louisiana State University; the Louisiana State Archives; the Louisiana Research Collection at Tulane University, particularly Sean Benjamin; the Southern Historical Collection at the University of North Carolina; the New Orleans Public Library Special Collections; and the librarians at the University of New Orleans who helped me find the *Angolite* collection that had been mis-shelved. In addition, I am thankful to Bill Quigley for joining forces with me to track down the elusive case documents of the Hayes Williams federal lawsuit and to Keith Nordyke for graciously sharing his own personal copies of Hayes Williams case materials with us. Melissa Burch and Shana M. griffin kindly shared their personal papers of abolitionist organizing in pre-Katrina New Orleans, and Critical Resistance digitized their files on Critical Resistance South so that I could use them without flying out to Oakland. Numerous Louisiana state bureaucrats answered emails and phone calls about the everyday functioning of the Louisiana state government from the taxation of mineral resources to the workings of the state bond commission.

I thank those institutions that supported this book at various points. The CUNY Graduate Center, the Oberlin College Alumni Graduate Fellowship, the Human Geography Small Grants Program, and the University of Kentucky all provided resources for my research and writing. Early on, I was provided with the priceless gift of time in an extended sabbatical from my work with AORTA. Thank you, Zhaleh Afshar, Autumn Brown, Roan Boucher, Sunny Dakota, Anisha Desai, Kate Eubank, Neily Jennings, Esteban Kelly, Bex Kwan, Marc Mascarenhas-Swan, Jenna Peters-Golden, Dana Peterson, kiran nigam, and Manju Rajendran. Many people assisted in ways big and small on this project. Christian Keeve was a delight of a research assistant whose keen attention to detail kept things moving along, allowing me the head space to actually write! Jeff Levy significantly helped this GIS-challenged geographer by making the maps featured in this book. Meaghan LaSala and Hannah Pepper were superb transcriptionists for several of the interviews I conducted. Hannah Adams, Ben Berman, and Nick Hite were always available to answer my questions regarding Louisiana law.

In the face of neoliberal austerity's assault on higher education and attacks on critical race scholarship and teaching, I was extremely privileged to have had secure academic employment while writing this book. My initial transformation of this manuscript began while a postdoctoral fellow at New York University's Prison Education Program. Executive Director Kaitlin Noss and interim faculty director Kim DaCosta were highly supportive of my work. I am especially grateful for my students at Wallkill Correctional Facility who during class breaks ardently asked questions that influenced the reframing of this book. Of the many ways the pandemic interrupted the writing of this book, I am most disappointed that we were unable to do a manuscript workshop with PEP students in the spring of 2020. I was delighted to finish this book while on the faculty of the Department of Geography and Program in African American & Africana Studies at the University of Kentucky. Starting on the tenure track during the COVID years is not how anyone imagines starting a new position, but my colleagues have been more than welcoming and supportive of this work—special thanks to Patricia Ehrkamp, Anastasia Curwood, Priscilla McCutcheon, Nari Senanayake, Rich Schein, Nick Lally, Jack Gieseking, Carol Mason, and Matt Wilson.

Numerous friends, comrades, and colleagues made the typically individualized process of writing a book feel like a part of a shared political project. Multiple interlocutors read drafts at various stages, helping me clarify my broader interventions, add nuance to my arguments, and correct my facts when more precision was necessary. Thank you for taking the time with my words: Craig Gilmore, Judah Schept, kai barrow, Wes Ware, Nathan Jessee, Dan Berger, David Stein, and Heather Berg. In addition, I was lucky to have benefited from the cutting-edge work of the constellation of scholars in and around the world of the American Studies Association's Critical Prison Studies Caucus and their feedback on portions of this work at countless conferences and invited presentations. Thank you, Dan Berger, Anne Bonds, Michelle Brown, Melissa Burch, Orisanmi Burton, Jordan Camp, Sarah Haley, Rebecca Hill, Marisol LeBrón (since our Oberlin days!), Touissant Losier, Jenna Loyd, Laura McTighe, Erica Meiners, Naomi Murakawa, Andrea Morrell, Tejasvi Nagaraja, Jack Norton, Judah Schept, Stuart Schrader, David Stein, Emily Thuma, and Tyler Wall. In addition, I have deep gratitude to be in relation to these other scholars committed to accountable scholarship on Louisiana: Siri Colom, Sarah Fouts, Nathan Jessee, and Laura McTighe. I was stretched in my thinking over the years through discussions with Chris Dixon, Jordan Flaherty, Christina Hanhardt, Christina Heatherton, Mingwei Huang, Jenny Kelly, and K-Sue Park. I am enormously thankful for David Stein, whose deep commitment to analyzing racial capitalism and the conditions of possibility for abolitionist reforms is only surpassed by his unwavering friendship.

The relationships forged at the Graduate Center have always been marked by a spirit of generosity, collective support, and radical politics. In the shadows of the Empire State Building and subsidized lunches, I was fortunate to think and scheme with Naomi Adiv, Denisse Andrade, Brenden Beck, Iemanja Brown, Bronwyn Dobchuk-Land, Chris Eng, Lauren Hudson, Hunter Jackson, Gaurav Jashnani, Malav Kanuga, Rakhee Kewada, Jenny LeRoy, Amanda Matles, Robin McGinty, Laurel Mei-Singh, Keith Miyake, Rafael Mutis, Kaitlin Noss (honorary GC student!) Marlene Nava Ramos, Christian Siener, Annie Spencer, Sam Stein, and Owen Toews. Ending up in the same cohort as Caroline Loomis was some of the best luck of graduate school. Caroline, thank you for being a steadfast friend who could seamlessly go from talking theory to giggling in the peanut gallery. Having Jack Norton to share research leads, analyze the geographic realignments of carceral power, and debate abolitionist politics over burgers has been a treasure.

Beyond the academy, many beloveds have cheered me on along the way. I am so appreciative of my New Orleans friends for believing in this project while also creating the spaces of parades and bayou picnics for me to take much-needed joyful breaks. Thank you to Hannah Adams, Hannah Pepper, Walesa Kanarek, Wes Ware, Nick Hite, Theo Hilton, Susan Sakash, Ben Berman, Kathleen Currie, Sarah Jaffe, and Casey Coleman. Thanks also go to Jenn Baumstein and David Previtali for making space in Troy for me to begin revisions on the book in earnest while overlooking the Hudson River in between ice cream and swims. I am also grateful to my parents Vickie and Mike for encouraging my voracious reading and love of school for as long as I can remember and for my sister Sarah for her dedicated support of my writing. DrewChristopher Joy is not only one of the greatest champions of my intellectual labors but is also the person I can always count on to talk about movement building with, to take Mardi Gras seriously with, and to share with me all the music I didn't even know my writing needed.

I owe so much to Byron Asher. He has been there while I researched, wrote, and rewrote every page at the same time as I was navigating the ups and downs of academic life. He helped me stay grounded through long dog walks with Ida, drives and bops throughout South Louisiana, and dedicated listening time. Thank you for believing in me and ensuring that I make time to take in the beauty this world offers. I cannot imagine this book without you.

Prison Capital

Introduction

It was not "the South," not all "the South," or most of "the South" which championed Jim Crow but actually the planter class and its political apparatus, and more importantly the capitalist sectors in London, New York, Boston, Philadelphia, and Chicago which provided the necessary support for the planter class aristocracy. Villainizing "the South" thusly ruptures the historical relationships between white racism and mercantile, agrarian, industrial, financial, and presently global capital.
—Cedric Robinson, *Forgeries of Memory and Meaning*

To accept the Southern white man's report that all the lynched are disreputable or supposed disreputable characters, is to believe the race so criminal, ignorant and bestial it must be hunted with dogs and killed like wild beasts.
—Ida B. Wells, "Bishop Tanner's Ray of Light"

If the choice were between prisons as they now are and no prisons at all, we would promptly choose the latter.
—Louisiana Coalition on Jails and Prisons, *Quarterly Report*, 1978

For most of the twentieth century, Louisiana's penal system encompassed the single Louisiana State Penitentiary (commonly known as Angola), which before 1901 had served as a site of convict leasing and a slave plantation.[1] During the 1970s, Angola entered an era of crisis. Four Black prisoners filed an extensive conditions of confinement federal lawsuit against Angola in 1971, sparking a massive crisis of legitimacy. State officials sought a resolution through an unprecedented multidecade and multiscalar project of penal expansion tied to the swings of the state's petro economy. Whereas other states under similar federal court orders in the 1970s were limited in their ability to expand penal systems because of the global hike in oil prices and the accompanied national recession, as an oil state Louisiana had surplus state revenues available for carceral expansion, in addition to federal grants through the Law Enforcement Administration Act (LEAA). Louisiana's prisons, jails, and law enforcement grew in scope and scale until the state

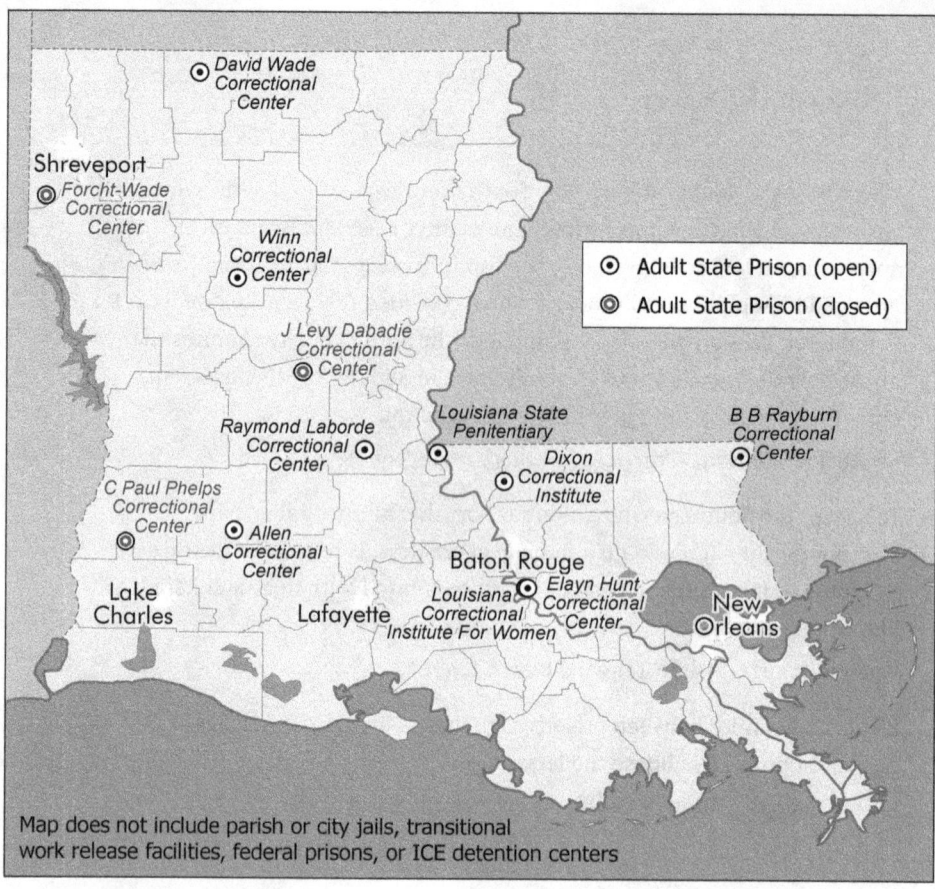

Map does not include parish or city jails, transitional work release facilities, federal prisons, or ICE detention centers

came to have the highest per capita rate of incarceration in the nation, and thus the world, for every year but one between 1998 and 2020.[2]

The 1970s marked a pivot point for the carceral state of Louisiana. A confluence of crises within and beyond the state—the ups and downs of global energy markets, the rise of national law-and-order politics, and the critiques and demands of people incarcerated in a solitary cellblock—ruptured the state's austerity approach to incarceration. This matrix of political, economic, and social forces would recur again and again: crises in the legitimacy of the carceral state; the global, national, and local economic contractions that mark neoliberalism; racist and patriarchal moral panics over "crime"; liberal federal court and policy interventions; and the collective activism of incarcerated and criminalized people. At times, these elements emerge in profound struggle; at other times they reach a kind of strategic alignment. Yet, at all times, the interplay between these material

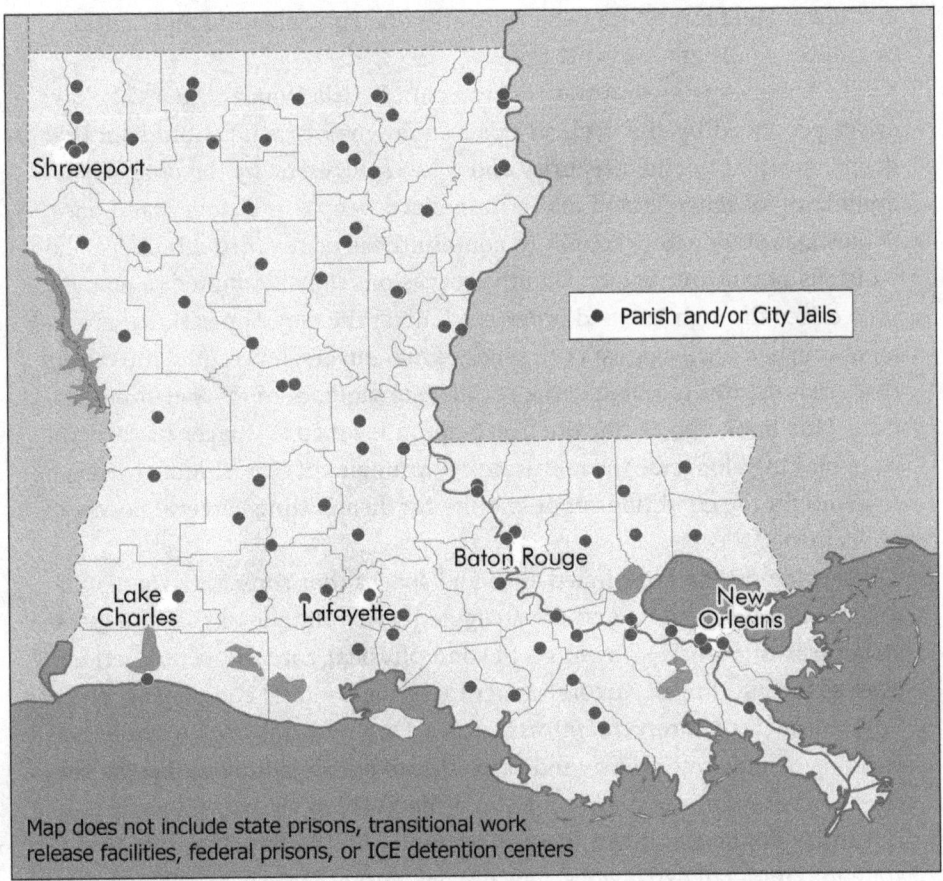

Map does not include state prisons, transitional work release facilities, federal prisons, or ICE detention centers

MAP 0.1A (*left*) Open and Closed State Prisons in Louisiana (2023) and MAP 0.1B (*right*) Parish and City Jails in Louisiana (2023). Since the initial carceral crisis that began in 1971, Louisiana's penal population has skyrocketed. In 1970, the state imprisoned 4,196 people in Angola, the Louisiana Correctional Institute for Women, and a handful of small work-release centers. At the height of the Louisiana carceral state in 2012, the state imprisoned 40,172 people in twelve state prisons, forty-one work release centers, and more than eighty jails. Black Louisianans make up two-thirds of the penal population while being only one-third of the total population of Louisiana, and they come overwhelmingly from the state's major cities, particularly New Orleans. Prepared by Jeff Levy from the University of Kentucky Pauer Center for Cartography and GIS. *Sources*: US Department of Justice, *Prisoners in 2013*, 3; Louisiana Department of Public Safety & Corrections, *Transitional Work Program Facilities*, September 16, 2014; Sakala, "Breaking Down Mass Incarceration."

and ideological forces has been central to the consolidation and contestation of the Louisiana carceral state.

The Louisiana carceral state is born out of crisis from above and below: crises produced by the cyclical ups and downs of racial capitalism that deepen inequality and insecurity and crises spurred on by the protests and organizing of incarcerated and criminalized people and their loved ones. Sometimes state actors sought to contain these crises through liberal expansions of punitive power. On other occasions they attempted to manage such crises through law and order. And along the way oppositional movements pushed back against both kinds of maneuvers, leveraging the cracks that crisis creates to unmake the racial state violence of mass criminalization. This book charts out the overlapping levers and spaces of carceral state-making alongside the multifaceted strategies of oppositional activism to highlight the conditions of possibility for dismantling carceral power in all its forms.

Focusing on the interlinked sites and spaces that constitute the Louisiana punishment regime and are struggled over reminds us that the infrastructures of punitive power go beyond physical carceral constructions, even as the building of carceral structures is an essential component. When I use the concept of *carceral infrastructure*, I am referring both to the actual building of new state prisons and expansion of parish jails alongside the passage of draconian sentencing laws and the bulking up of local prosecutorial and police power. Investments in the material infrastructures of carceral state-making—jail expansions, new prisons, surveillance cameras, cop cars, and more—are made possible by racist and patriarchal approaches to questions of violence and safety that deem displacement and confinement as fixes to the harmful and nonharmful activities categorized as "crime."

One of the primary infrastructures enabling mass incarceration in Louisiana is the intensification of multiagency and multiscalar cooperation among local, state, and federal punitive state actors—what I term *carceral cooperation*. Fully conceptualizing the drive to mass incarceration requires us to deepen our understanding of how key players in the criminal legal system across political scales and jurisdictions—Department of Corrections officials, district attorneys, federal judges, sheriffs, police departments, and Homeland Security—have coordinated their efforts to enhance the state's carceral capacity. Attending to the dynamics of carceral cooperation brings into relief that "the state" is not a singular actor or monolith. A state can be defined as a territorially bound sovereign authority, centrally administered to rule a given population through a mixture of coercion and consent—

including through a monopoly on legitimate violence—but our definition cannot end there.³

The state is never static. Louisiana is no different from any other state in that it is made up of a host of sectors and agencies both across (from the local to the national) and within scales (the Department of Corrections stands side by side with the Department of Health and Human Services). Such different institutions can be in conflict *or* alignment. What a state does and how it does it dialectically shifts in response to internal and external, material and ideological contradictions and struggles. Some state capacities grow, others shrink, certain capacities are suspended, and new ones are created.⁴ Carceral cooperation offers a conceptual means of highlighting how different state sectors are in coercive alignment yet are also riddled with fissures that activists can leverage.

Among the various new caging methods developed through carceral cooperation, one of the most significant is Louisiana's devolution of the state prison system to the parish jail system. The rise of jailing in Louisiana's carceral landscape is a key throughline in this book. Following the federal courts' 1975 implementation of population limits on Angola, state prisoners were temporarily redirected to serve their sentences in parish jails throughout the state. Rural, urban, and suburban sheriffs protested this arrangement on the ground that jails—designed for pretrial and short-term incarceration—were not fit for long-term imprisonment and sheriffs did not have the resources to shoulder this expense. State legislators first attempted to appease the powerful Louisiana Sheriffs' Association in 1976 by creating a per diem payment system in which the Department of Corrections paid sheriffs a nominal fee for each state prisoner incarcerated in their jails and by speeding up the opening of new state prisons.

As Louisiana's criminalizing regime continued to ensnare more people for longer sentences, the incarceration of state prisoners in parish jails transitioned from a provisional to a permanent arrangement. When jailed people increasingly protested and sued the state over deplorable conditions, every jail in the state was placed under the federal courts and issued new population limits—which sheriffs then leveraged to secure higher per diem rates. In the 1980s, sheriffs began to see the incarceration of state prisoners as a benefit to their departments and accompanying political machines. They began organizing to advocate that the state create new financing mechanisms for jail expansions to hold state prisoners and INS detainees, much to the displeasure of the federal courts. In turn, jailing state prisoners proved to be a viable solution to governors and state legislators who were politically committed to tough-on-crime politics but unable to afford the costs of ground-up prison construction. New Orleans sheriff Charles Foti leveraged these state arrangements to have the city replicate these funding structures on a municipal scale while colluding with law enforcement to increase the number of pretrial prisoners at the New Orleans city jail, the Orleans Parish Prison (OPP). By the time Louisiana gained the title of having the highest per capita rate of incarceration in 1998, most state prisoners were incarcerated in jails.

Even though Louisiana's ramping up of jailing alongside increased policing and imprisonment sought to manage or stabilize underlying crises, this approach instead exacerbated the systemic crises of the racial capitalist state in concert with the crises endemic to the penal system. Following the thinking of Ruth Wilson Gilmore, crisis—whether political, economic, or social in origin—is produced through the accumulation of contradictions in the social formation so that it can no longer reproduce itself. This instability is neither inherently positive nor negative but can only be resolved through the struggle of systemic change.[5] As Stuart Hall and his colleagues write in *Policing the Crisis*, the capitalist state's tendency during crises of hegemony is to turn to coercive power not as "a suspension of the 'normal' exercise of state power" but through "the increased reliance on coercive mechanisms and apparatuses already available within the normal repertoire of state power."[6] Since the 1970s, Louisiana officials have enlarged carceral power in response to a series of crises of legitimacy ranging from incarcerated people's opposition to the cruelty of prison life, to the global ascent of neoliberal austerity, and to the breaking of the levees and the drowning of New Orleans. Often, officials ramp up certain sectors of the carceral state in direct response to activist wins in other sectors—such as an increasing municipal reliance on state troopers when local law enforcement in placed under a consent decree. By expanding the state's capacity to punish, repress, contain, and displace, state actors sought to discipline those made vulnerable to heightened exploitation, dispossession, and premature death in the name of ensuring public safety and social order.

In the pages that follow, I show that the cyclical crises marking Louisiana's punishment regime are tethered to the cyclical crises of the Louisiana political economy. Consistently in competition with Mississippi for being at the very bottom of practically all US socioeconomic rankings, Louisiana residents' high levels of impoverishment and immiseration have become all too normalized in the local and national imaginary.[7] Since the 1970s, the state's development of and subsequent dependence on the extractive economies of oil and tourism have produced a series of booms and busts interwoven with the shifting demands of global racial capitalism. This seesawing at times led to windfalls of state and city revenues, while at other times it created fiscal crises. Yet in both scenarios, little to no state investments were made in the lives of Black Louisianans, who instead were repeatedly rendered as disposable to neoliberalism's stagnation of wages alongside rising unemployment, skyrocketing housing costs and neighborhood displacements, and disinvestments in life-saving infrastructures from flood protection to public hospitals.

Instead, during both prosperity and precarity, state officials repeatedly gave prisons, jails, and policing first call on public dollars and cents to contain the structural volatility of petro capitalism and to ready the ground for new accumulation schemes through criminalizing populations along lines of race, class, gender, sexuality, and age. Even though the early years of Louisiana's prison growth were marked by a carceral welfare state—state investments in prisons *alongside* investments in education, public works, and welfare—at the heart of the rise of the Louisiana carceral state is what I term *law-and-order austerity*, a bipartisan ideological and policy program whereby cuts in the social wage are coupled with carceral state endowments. Built on the dialectic between deepening economic inequality and tough-on-crime politics, criminalization has emerged as a predominant racial regime of neoliberalism.[8] In turn, punitive ideologies have justified and normalized state disinvestments in public forms of collective responsibility and care, exacerbating the "group-differentiated vulnerability to premature death" that characterizes racism, under the banner of neoliberal modernization.[9] Or, to put it more simply, mass incarceration is built on the marriage between racial state violence and organized abandonment.[10]

To say that the making of Louisiana into a carceral state is tied to its petrochemical economy is not to reduce penal expansion to a "resource curse."[11] Political power blocs and struggles, not natural resources, shape governmental decisions. However, understanding how petro capitalism articulates with the growth of carceral infrastructures is pivotal to this book. Over the course of the twentieth century, Louisiana developed its political economy on oil extraction and refinement. During the black gold rush of the 1920s, Huey Long rose to power on a populist platform that promised the people of Louisiana state investments in public works, education, and healthcare paid for by increasing taxes on oil companies.[12] Long's petro populism was modest insofar as he never called for the public ownership of the state's natural resources and the taxes that he championed were relatively limited. Yet, this petro populism still ushered in the beginning of Louisiana's fiscal dependency on oil revenues. Louisiana's petrochemical industrial complex grew in lockstep with the transition of the United States to a petroleum-based society in the wake of World War II and postwar suburbanization.[13] In this context, Louisiana's political economy developed as a form of oil welfare state, putting mineral revenues to use in broad-based yet racially differentiated state-building projects.[14] The high rates of profit possible through oil meant that, although the mineral leases and taxes levied against oil corporations were relatively low, they still translated into significant state revenue. Hence, Louisiana incentivized new rounds of oil exploration and extraction that built up the petrochemical sector, which further enriched oil capitalists at the expense of the development of a diversified political economy and the erosion of coastal wetlands.[15] Under the "extractive imperative" of the petro political economy, the capital relation was left intact and served as a barrier to transformations of power.[16]

By the 1970s, Louisiana had become economically dependent on the volatile commodity of oil. When oil prices skyrocketed in the early 1970s, the state doubled down on petrochemicals while cutting taxes on the rich and on corporations—believing oil to be a never-ending resource. These mineral revenues allowed Louisiana to take on liberal prison expansion years earlier than most other states, who were cash-strapped following the rise in oil prices. However, when oil prices dropped following the global oil glut in the 1980s, Louisiana was without a cushion to soften the blow. New Right governor David Treen leveraged the fiscal crisis to realign the state to neoliberal ends—directing dwindling state revenues and new debt schemes to punitive power while slashing social safety nets. Although politicians portrayed these choices as a pragmatic response to the unpredictability of global oil, they were political decisions that put the interests of capital over struggling Louisianians. These state policies alongside Reagan's federal austerity programs produced a massive state recession that rendered large swaths of Black Louisiana redundant to the labor market. The attendant escalation of tough-on-crime lawmaking served as a strategy of crisis containment that deepened precarity while ballooning the prison population.

Louisiana did not abandon its ties to petrochemicals even as the industry's rate of profit never returned to its previous highs. Instead, the state increasingly turned to tourism as an economic development strategy, given the persistence of state and municipal fiscal instabilities. While visitors have long been in a fixture in New Orleans, the rise of tourism followed the neoliberal push for US cities to become more entrepreneurial and service-oriented in the face of deindustrialization, shrinking tax bases, and federal cuts to municipal revenue-sharing programs.[17] City leaders increasingly marketed the city to tourists through the commodification of Black New Orleans cultural traditions—jazz, gumbo, second line parades, and more—funneling profits and revenues back to tourism while the very cultural workers the city built its image on were rendered as precarious labor.[18] Betting New Orleans's future on tourism was made possible by shifting the dominant racist geographic imaginary of New Orleans from a place of excessive danger and deviance to the kind of place that is safe, but still alluring, for family vacations, bachelorette parties, and academic conferences. Doubling down on racialized, gendered, and classed policing in tourism zones and those areas marked for tourism gentrification has displaced populations deemed a threat to the sanitized image that tourism capitalists seek to promote, thereby visibly demonstrating to outsiders the city's commitment to "public safety." Built on low-wage labor and particularly sensitive to downswings, tourism has proven that it does not fix the Crescent City's problems but exacerbates the very inequities and insecurities that push people to engage in criminalized survival strategies.

While the neoliberal racial state turns to punitive power as a tool of crisis management, the Louisiana carceral state is simultaneously battered by intertwined crises all its own. The crises that plague the penal system have been numerous: overcrowded and deplorable prison and jail conditions; scandals of police corruption, brutality, and sexualized violence; collective opposition to prison and jail siting; the exorbitant costs of mass imprisonment; and the concentration of preventable disease and death in jails and prisons.

Although these crises have little to do with the question of "crime," mainstream responses to such carceral crises have been animated by the racialized, classed, and gendered figure of "the criminal." For policy makers on the tough-on-crime end of the spectrum, these crises can be resolved by ratcheting up retributive power through passing harsher criminal penalties, increasing police and prosecutorial discretion, massively increasing the number of prison and jail beds, and implementing new surveillance technologies—in the name of deterrence. For those on the liberal reform end of the spectrum, these crises can be resolved through rehabilitation and modernization: professionalizing police, renovating and expanding carceral facilities, implementing parenting and anger management programs in prisons, and creating truancy and drug courts—in the name of correction.

Whereas tough-on-crime advocates offer no pretense of being concerned by punitive violence, liberal technocrats contend that by directing the criminal legal system to reform the "right people"—those regarded as dangerous, pathological, deviant, or all three—they not only fix individuals but also resolve the crises afflicting the penal system. In other words, reform is a strategy of carceral crisis management.[19] In reality, neither approach halts the cyclical crises of the carceral state but in fact prolongs and intensifies them because they fail to tackle the root violence of state racism and racial capitalism.

Carceral logics are sutured to state racism; in other words, the carceral state is a modality of the racial state.[20] As David Theo Goldberg elucidates, "Modern states have predicated themselves on racial differentiation, and on state-promoted and prompted racist exclusion and exploitation."[21] Anti-Black racism animates the production and extension of US punitive power; at the same time, the racial state project of criminalization is agile in its entrapment of populations not initially targeted as threats or as disposable under racial capital.[22]

As Cedric Robinson articulated, racialism is a structuring force of capitalism in that its tendency is *"not to homogenize but to differentiate—*to exaggerate regional, subcultural, and dialectical differences into 'racial' ones."[23] Under racial capitalism, racial ideologies and practices authorize the exploitation and dispossession of certain populations and places.[24] Carceral violence as a racial state practice justifies long-standing material inequalities while also facilitating capital accumulation. It takes various forms depending on the historic-geographic conjuncture: intensifying exploitation through forced productive and reproductive labor, displacing people to secure the property relation and attendant speculation schemes, regulating the labor supply through border controls, excluding criminalized people from the formal labor market, disciplining people to assent to austerity and economic precarity, and repressing labor and social movements struggling for collective liberation.[25]

The racial state's formations of carceral power are fashioned through gendered categorization and social control.[26] From the mass imprisonment of working-class and poor Black men whose masculinities are deemed a dangerous excess, to the sexual policing of trans and nonbinary people (particularly of color) for living outside the bounds of normative gender, and to the articulation of Black single mothers as breeders of criminals, criminalization as a material and ideological system reifies racialized gendered difference. At the same time, carceral power is animated through white supremacist notions of "protection"—whether of white men from Black men within prison walls or of white women from Black men in the urban sphere. Gendered power relations do not stop at the scale of the body. Patriarchal ideologies underpin conservative and liberal registers of carceral state-making: the retributive approach of "getting tough" on lawbreakers is premised on "masculinist visions of 'tough' state power," and the rehabilitative ideal is predicated on paternalistic politics.[27] Punitive power mobilizes racial and gender hierarchies and normalizes such relations.

Yet, the aggrandizement of carceral power in the face of ruptures is not inevitable. Although these periods of crises produced intensified carceral geographies, they have also formed spaces of possibility for oppositional politics, social movement formations, and coalition-building. To chart the rise of imprisonment and policing in Louisiana without attending to the myriad ways in which people organized to scale back the state's capacity to cage would be a profound mistake. Whereas elite and technocratic reformers sought to manage carceral crises through slight adjustments to the penal system, grassroots organizations anchored in the Black radical tradition fought to undo the everyday and extraordinary violence of the carceral state.[28] These strategies included incarcerated people filing conditions of confinement lawsuits, Angola activists challenging draconian sentencing laws across prison walls, community organizers building coalitions to shrink the New Orleans jail in the wake of Katrina, and queer and trans youth of color strategizing to curtail police power. Louisiana—and particularly New Orleans—has been a critical node of anticarceral movement building in the late twentieth and early twenty-first centuries.

At the core of this antiracist activism is organizing—the building of people power for transformative change by bringing together disparate people to identify how seemingly individualized problems are a product of structural forces, developing people's leadership capacities, building and deepening relationships that can withstand internal and external pressures, crafting systemic solutions to the problems that people are facing, and targeting the people and institutions that have power to make lasting change.[29] Organizing is rarely flashy or headline catching but is what Ella Baker described as "spadework," the daily commitment to showing up and tending to what needs to be done—copying fliers, knocking on doors, researching laws, facilitating meetings, taking notes—in pursuit of making a different kind of world.[30] In my analysis of grassroots organizing against carceral power, I attend to the public campaigns and protests in concert with the crucial work of organization building that is at the heart of any social movement. Although not all the organizing efforts outlined in this book achieved the outcomes they hoped for, their activism generates vital insights into the mechanisms and logics that produce mass incarceration. These efforts rework conceptions and possibilities of safety, justice, and freedom, thereby paving the way for future liberation struggles. With each new win or loss, activists refine their approach to dismantling punitive power, state racism, and racial capitalism—clarifying past misconceptions, identifying new contradictions, sharpening strategies, and heightening demands that stretch us toward new geographies of freedom.

By underscoring the significance of Louisiana antiprison and antipolicing activism, I explain how the development of the Louisiana carceral state has not only been dialectically produced through contestation but also limited through the actions of people whose stories have often gone unnoticed or been erased from the official record. The fact that the crises confronting Louisiana have been generated from above as well as from below teaches us that they can be spurred on by the everyday activism of people pushing to delegitimize and dismantle punitive governance.[31] Periods of acute political, economic, and social crises create conditions of possibility for carceral state enhancements, *as well as* for scaling back the state's punitive capacities. But neither is a given.[32]

Giving close attention to the stories of Louisiana anticarceral activism provides us with a deeper understanding of how antiracist organizing against mass criminalization has grown and shifted in the face of a capacious carceral state. One of the primary contradictions of mass incarceration is that ensnaring more and more people into the criminal legal system's web has meant that more and more people have a stake in seeing punitive power undone—expanding the potential base of people for mobilization and organization. Through organizers' successes in illuminating that criminalization is a political, not an individual issue, growing numbers of people have been drawn to antiprison and antipolicing activism as a frontline of racial, economic, and gender justice. Yet, when antiprison and antipolicing activists have made strides in shrinking the punitive arm of the state, state actors responded by updating their carceral techniques and strategies to subvert their wins such as curtailing incarcerated people's ability to file lawsuits and organize. Moreover, antiprison and antipolicing activists often have been challenged by the conundrum that the reforms they fought for, which were once seen as the liberatory edge of possibility, have at times been co-opted by the state to further extend carceral power. For example, campaigns to improve conditions of confinement are routinely leveraged by sheriffs, governors, and federal judges for jail and prison expansion.

Learning from reactionary backlash and from the political limitations of certain reforms, many organizers have come to see the politics of prison and police abolition as the only true solution to eradicate the violence of incarceration. Although it would be an overreach to state that everyone or even most people fighting mass incarceration in Louisiana are abolitionists, it is true that abolition has grown into a significant activist current. Tracking the stories of people's on-the-ground organizing reveals the rise of abolition in the late twentieth and early twenty-first centuries as not only a visionary horizon but also as a pragmatic orientation for those committed to ending the crises of policing and imprisonment. Abolitionists' actions and analysis have shifted over time in response to local conditions. After the state's turn to racial criminalization and organized abandonment of jailed people in the wake of Hurricane Katrina, activists clarified that codifying better evacuation procedures was not enough but that the jail needed to be downsized so that less people would be subjected to its catastrophic and quotidian violence. These grassroots lessons have also been informed by national activist currents while New Orleans antiprison and antipolicing struggles have reverberated outward to reshape analysis and campaigns elsewhere.

New Orleans abolitionists, in particular, have explicitly situated their activism in the southern lineage of transformative organizing against racial slavery and in the lineage of W. E. B. Du Bois's conceptualization of Black Reconstruction as an experiment in abolition democracy, in which abolition meant not only the abolition of slavery but also the creation of a society divorced from racial capitalism.[33] Hence, prison abolition includes the work of building up life-affirming economies, institutions, and cultural norms and dismantling criminalizing regimes and ending state violence.[34] This ethos of abolition democracy can be seen in the duality of demands that grassroots activists repeatedly put forth: repeal draconian sentencing laws *and* deal with the structural unemployment of Black Louisianans; shrink jails *and* invest in public mental health care; close youth prisons *and* improve schools; stop police sexual violence *and* ensure affordable housing for queer and trans Black and Latinx youth.

Reconsidering Southern Carceral Geography

To arrive at these understandings, I had to follow my research and dissuade myself of presumptions that widely circulate about imprisonment in Louisiana and, by extension, the broader US South. Too often Louisiana's standing as a leader in mass criminalization is used as evidence of the state's intrinsic backwardness—that its geography produces a temporal stagnation that places it in a forever and always premodern state. This rendering is shaped by two seemingly disparate but interlinked logics. One, anti-Black racism and colonial environmental determinism designate anywhere that Black people constitute a significant population as primitive and barbaric—keeping places like Louisiana "behind" national progress.[35] Two, the equation of "the South" with the elites who govern through white supremacist, patriarchal, and capitalist disenfranchisement, dispossession, and exploitation papers over the multitudes of peoples, politics, and dreams that make up the region. As Cedric Robinson notes in this chapter's epigraph, this formulation fails to recognize that the development of southern racism and capitalism is imbricated in national and global political and economic aims.[36]

This imagination of Louisiana as an exceptionally backward and provincial place outside national norms has influenced narratives that its criminal legal system is unlike any other. Building on long-standing ideas of the southern penal system as uniquely shaped by an incomparable culture of vengeful violence, there is a tendency to assume the state's carceral horrors are rooted in a repetition of plantation slavery and Jim Crow.[37] Although the narrative that mass incarceration is due to the rise of private prisons or corporate profiteering off imprisoned labor has been a widely debunked red herring, the Louisiana carceral state is still framed first and foremost through images of Black prisoners laboring in the fields of Angola under the watch of guards on horseback.[38] Alongside the hyperattention given to the Angola prison rodeo, this focus on extraordinary spectacles of racial state violence is inadvertently at the expense of an analysis not only of the everyday dehumanizing violence of Angola but also how the penitentiary—and the broader Louisiana penal system—has changed over time.[39]

This misreading is partially due to gaps in scholarship on the development of mass incarceration in the US South. Most work on southern punishment regimes is focused on convict leasing and chain gangs. Although this research has been vital in explaining the relationship of carceral power to Jim Crow capitalism and modernization, the reinstitution of white supremacy through gendered racial terror, and the resistance strategies of imprisoned people, this past has been often erroneously treated as explanatory for contemporary events.[40] Scholarship of the contemporary carceral state in the South continues to be outmatched by critical carceral studies scholarship on the North, the West, and the nation-writ large.[41] This gap limits our grasp of how southern ideologies, policies, and practices contributed to local, regional, and also national punitive state expansion and sidelines our understanding of southern anticarceral social movements.[42] Attending to the carceral geography of Louisiana is critical not because the state is an exception or an origin story but because it fleshes out our understanding of the contested process of making the United States into a carceral state and what it will take to abolish it.[43]

Outline of the Book

The chapters that follow chart out the contested carceral geography of Louisiana through a story of people in struggle: some trying to build out carceral state capacities in the name of safety, some trying to build out punitive infrastructure in the service of capital, and others trying to tear down penal structures in pursuit of a liberatory world.[44] Although at times the chapters engage in statewide analysis, at other times they zero in on a particular parish or neighborhood while keeping in mind how these places are situated within nested scales of political economic power.[45] New Orleans receives a significant share of attention because historically it has been the parish with the highest incarceration rate and many of the key actors in forming and contesting the Louisiana carceral state come from Orleans Parish.

Chapter 1 describes the new era of carceral crisis that began in 1971 when four Black prisoners at Angola filed the most extensive conditions of confinement lawsuit in Louisiana history. I contend that this crisis could have been managed through either scaling back or scaling up the state's carceral capacities. Although the incarcerated petitioners framed the problems through the structural violence of incarceration, the federal courts focused on overcrowding. Animated by racial liberalism and the rehabilitative ideal, state officials advocated for the decentralization of Angola: replacing it with smaller urban prisons across the state. However, when residents protested against the prison sitings and emergent law-and-order politics made mass early release politically untenable, Louisiana expanded Angola and the broader penal system, funded by a windfall of state mineral revenues after the 1973 global increases in oil prices—demonstrating how liberal reformism can facilitate carceral expansion.

Chapter 2 tracks the rise of law-and-order austerity amid the booms and busts of the oil economy in the 1980s and the attendant development of collective prisoner activism against sentences of life without parole. Governor David Treen seized on this period of crisis to push a neoliberal agenda of slashing social services while pumping limited state revenues into new carceral expansion projects above and beyond the federal court mandates—a project that became the new norm across the political spectrum. The reworking of state capacities was legitimized through racist gendered narratives, while penal expansion served to contain Black communities rendered as surplus labor. This crisis also galvanized incarcerated activists to form the Angola Special Civics Project that organized for loved ones on the outside to vote for prison reform candidates and to craft new mechanisms for early release to expand their chances at freedom.

The parish jail system soon shifted from being a temporary spatial fix for overcrowding crises to the long-term geographic solution for the Louisiana carceral state. In chapter 3, I argue that sheriffs organized to bring about this realignment of the penal system when the state's ongoing fiscal crisis made it unfeasible to build new prisons: rural sheriffs lobbied to expand their jails by increasing the number of state, federal, and Immigration and Naturalization Service (INS) prisoners behind their bars, while urban sheriffs mobilized racist fear-mongering to persuade residents to vote for jail expansion. The now 7,000-bed OPP filled up when the New Orleans Police Department adopted broken windows and community policing in the name of police reform while facilitating neoliberal redevelopment. But an emergent current of organizing informed by prison abolition arose to push back against this punitive system.

In chapter 4 I argue that the widespread criminalization and violence faced by primarily Black New Orleanians seeking to survive the state disaster of Hurricane Katrina were neither aberrations in state policy nor evidence of the state's intrinsic limitations. Rather, the abandonment of prisoners in the flooded OPP, the extrajudicial police and vigilante killings of Black men, the criminalization of storm survivors rather than providing aid, and losing thousands of imprisoned people for months in the penal system reveal how racist punitive power was at the core of the state's disaster policy. In response, grassroots organizers contended that the state's turn to racial criminalization in the Katrina crisis was a magnification of long-standing practices of the city's punishment regime. Early activist interventions explicitly framed movement demands through the legacy of Black Reconstruction and developed new organizing infrastructures for taking on punitive power.

Chapter 5 details how racial justice organizers leveraged the Katrina crisis to scale back punitive power, illuminating how acute state crises can be turned into political opportunities for undoing the carceral state. The first phase of organizing, from 2005 to 2008, was primarily led by Safe Streets/Strong Communities. Through grassroots campaigns, they overhauled the public defender system, helped create the Office of the Independent Police Monitor for greater police accountability, and began to tackle the ongoing violence of the jail. From 2008–2013 a second phase was led by the Orleans Parish Prison Reform Coalition, which waged a citywide campaign to shrink the jail from 7,500 to 1,468 beds, end the jail's municipal per diem budgetary system, and terminate the sheriff's cooperation endeavor agreement with Immigration and Customs Enforcement (ICE).

Chapter 6 examines how the policing of racialized gender and sexuality has become central to urban capital accumulation schemes and how struggles over everyday criminalization serve as a pivot point for the future of New Orleans. I trace the strategizing of the French Quarter Management District's (FQMD) Security Task Force, a leader in developing policing initiatives that regulate public space along lines of race, class, sexuality, and gender to revalorize the post-Katrina tourism economy, in juxtaposition with the activism of the organization BreakOUT! to challenge the criminalization of LGBTQ youth of color. Through a materialist Black trans feminist politics, BreakOUT! leveraged the US Department of Justice's investigations of the NOPD to curb law enforcement's everyday racialized and sexualized violence; advocated for trans and queer of color social reproduction through investments in housing, healthcare, education, and jobs; and built coalitions with Latinx workers to claim their right to life in the new New Orleans.

This book concludes with a meditation on what the development of the Louisiana carceral state teaches us about contemporary anticarceral organizing. Although many gains have been won, the ongoing dominance of neoliberalism continues to limit our ability to undo mass criminalization. I offer "abolitionist infrastructures" as a framework for organizing to dismantle carceral infrastructures.

Methods

The questions animating this book first emerged in the everyday, enlivening, and often overwhelming world of post-Katina New Orleans activism. In the spring of 2006, my mentors pushed me to spend my summer supporting antiracist organizing for a just reconstruction. I was linked up with Critical Resistance's (CR) campaign for amnesty for jailed and criminalized Katrina survivors. Although my work on the amnesty campaign was minimal at best, it was a crash course in policing and incarceration in New Orleans and what people had endured inside the flooded cells of OPP. When I returned to New Orleans in the summer of 2007 to live, a friend connected me to Safe Streets/Strong Communities, where I volunteered for the next two years doing research, media work, and other tasks as needed. Later, although not a member of the Orleans Parish Prison Reform Coalition (OPPRC), I supported their campaign for a smaller jail by signing onto public demands and attending public meetings and city council votes. Many of my ideas about carceral state development, racial capitalist crisis, and transformative organizing were initially cultivated through these spaces and relationships.

During this time, I became curious about *how* New Orleans had become an epicenter of mass incarceration. While the sentence "Louisiana is the most incarcerated place in the world" was often repeated, I wanted to know when and why had that become the case? What were the factors, conditions, and players that sent so many Louisianians—and particularly New Orleanians— to live behind bars? And what kinds of strategies had people found effective (or not) for organizing against policing and prisons? But when I went searching for answers, I kept coming up short. Books were few and far between, and most journalistic accounts parroted racist discourse that treated criminalized people as responsible for the state violence enacted against them.[46] Much of the best information came from the knowledge produced by activist organizations through grassroots research, campaign power mapping, and collective reflections on wins and losses. But still, I wanted to understand more—not as a detached researcher but as someone hopeful that such research could bolster my and others' activist efforts.

To investigate the interchange between carceral state-making, political economic conditions, and collective opposition, I conducted interdisciplinary research that included archival research, oral history interviews, and ethnographic fieldwork. Answering these questions required that I analyze official state and elite documents and perspectives in conversation with archives of oppositional movements, as well as oral history interviews and participant observation of recent antiprison and antipolicing grassroots organizing. To identify the state-level and municipal conditions under which state officials decided to expand the Louisiana punishment regime, I consulted political, economic, and legal archives that included gubernatorial and mayoral papers, the Louisiana Department of Corrections archives, state and municipal budgets, legislative documents, and federal legal rulings and reports. This archival research was fleshed out by public records requests of the Louisiana Correctional Facilities Corporation, the Louisiana Department of Corrections, and the New Orleans Police Department. In addition, I conducted six months of participant observation of public meetings concerning policing initiatives in the French Quarter to deepen my grasp of the everyday mechanisms, discourses, and decision-making that bulked up tourism policing.

Working in these archives and spaces necessitated a practice of reading against the grain of racial state violence packaged as commonsense through the narrow frameworks of constitutionality, positivism, and capitalist speculation. I read these state and elite archives and events against counter archives and extended qualitative research of multiple activist formations. I drew on newsletters, pamphlets, meeting notes, correspondence, and other ephemera to trace how people organized against the growth of the Louisiana carceral state at different historical junctures and to glean insights into the operations of carceral state-making, as committed organizers and advocates shrewdly ascertained new directions in punitive statecraft and emergent contradictions.

Invaluable to my research were the archives of Angola's prisoner newsmagazine the *Angolite*, which circulated as an uncensored prison publication between 1975 and 1994. This unusual arrangement came about as part of the liberal reforms instituted at Angola following the Hayes Williams lawsuit. As discussed by former *Angolite* editor Wilbert Rideau in his memoir, *In the Place of Justice*, Warden C. Paul Phelps (later the secretary of corrections) allowed the *Angolite* to operate as a "free press" to investigate and publish on topics ranging from clemency and parole, sexual violence within Angola, prison economics, and the activities of various prison reform and advocacy organizations. These unparalleled access and resources enabled it to do cutting-edge reporting that helped incarcerated people understand the development of mass incarceration, that informed state politicians, and was recognized through several national journalism awards.[47] The publication foregrounded a critical analysis of the state's criminal legal system during the 1970s. During the 1980s it began actively pushing against law-and-order politics, collaborating with groups such as the Angola Special Civics Project. Hence the *Angolite* serves as both a key source of historical information and a critical site to consider incarcerated writers' analysis and critiques of Louisiana's prison boom.[48]

To situate much of this archival and qualitative research, I consulted a wide range of local, regional, and national news media. In addition to helping me construct timelines of events, evaluating news media allowed me to analyze key events within public discourses about crime, policing, and prisons and to trace developments in public perception of both carceral state projects and antiprison activist endeavors. Importantly, I assessed news media not as an objective source of the "truth" but, following Stuart Hall, as another site where dominant ideologies concerning crime and safety are constructed and reproduced.[49] Hence, I often took a critical stance on the role of major media in advancing the fetishization of crime statistics, furthering racist fear-mongering, and applauding the expansion of punitive power.

In addition, I conducted oral history interviews with thirty-two people who were active in at least one, and often more, of the following social movement organizations: the Angola Special Civics Project, Critical Resistance New Orleans, Safe Streets/Strong Communities, OPPRC, and BreakOUT! I also conducted approximately eighteen months of participant observation with BreakOUT! during which I did volunteer work at the office, gave members rides, facilitated workshops, and attended protests, panels, and other events. This research was supplemented by organizational reports, pamphlets, videos, posters, and social media.[50]

Although this might sound strange, in the earliest stages of my research I did not intend to include the post-Katrina organizing I had participated in as part of this project. It seemed too emotionally close. But it quickly became clear that to leave that story out would result in an incomplete picture. Hence, in the process of researching this era, I found the lines between personal experience and research blurred, with neither fitting squarely into the container of oral history nor of ethnographic research. It was a common feature of these interviews to be asked what *I* remembered to help others jog their memories of timelines and names. Similarly, I dug through my own personal papers and emails to piece together aspects of this story in which I played a marginal part.

······

Louisiana did not hold the title of the most incarcerated place in the world for twenty years because it was stuck in the past but because it was *innova-*

tive in incorporating a range of new punitive technologies into its carceral infrastructure. Mass incarceration is a political project of modernizing punishment on an unprecedented scale. To be cutting-edge under the rubrics of racial capitalism is not to advance justice but to advance new forms of differentiated death-dealing, quick and slow. But as Louisiana activists have fought back against these innovations, they too have produced new knowledges, charting new possibilities for collective freedom.

1   Decentralizing Angola

Liberal Interventions, Overcrowding Crises, and the Making of a New Era

. . . .

> Due to a dramatic reduction in the issuance of parole and commutation of sentences, which translates into less people leaving prison, and to an increase in the amount of prisoners being sent to Angola, the prison is now packed to the seams with inmates. Angola now has 20 percent more prisoners than last year. Men are sleeping on floors and cells originally built for one are now being shared by two. Over 300 more men are warehoused in the Admissions Unit awaiting transfer to the main prison population. There are no beds for them . . . and they continue to stream in every day, with no let up in sight.
> —Wilbert Rideau, "Angola—Louisiana's Sore That Won't Heal," 1975

> The question is not whether the conditions exist but when and in what manner are these conditions to be eliminated.
> —US magistrate Frank Polozola, 1975

In 1971, four Black Angola prisoners—Arthur Mitchell, Hayes Williams, Lee Stevenson, and Lazarus Joseph—filed the most extensive conditions of confinement lawsuit in Louisiana history; it would come to be known as the *Hayes Williams* lawsuit. Although the incarcerated petitioners framed the problems of Angola through the structural violence of solitary confinement, racial segregation, toxic living conditions, and the trusty system, liberal federal judges reframed the root problem as prison overcrowding and mandated a slew of prison reforms. With prison overpopulation front and center, prison administrators, politicians, district attorneys, and activists—both behind bars and free—put forth a variety of solutions to the crisis. The dominant proposal was a reformist plan offered by the Louisiana Department of Corrections (DOC) to "decentralize" Angola by shrinking its capacity or shuttering it altogether and replacing it with smaller urban "satellite prisons." However, by decade's end the proposal to scale back Angola was abandoned in favor of planned carceral growth at Angola and beyond. Louisiana's prison population more than doubled from 4,196 in 1970 to 8,661 in 1980.[1]

When the Louisiana penal system entered a new era of crisis in the 1970s, the state chose a new path: unprecedented penal expansion. This chapter tells the story of how Louisiana turned to carceral expansion as the answer to dehumanizing prison conditions and escalating overcrowding by drawing on the twinned logics of racial liberalism and the rehabilitative ideal. With reformist penology gaining traction across the nation, Louisiana's DOC officials and the federal judges overseeing the Hayes Williams lawsuit were increasingly critical of *prison conditions* but not necessarily of the *condition of incarceration itself*—believing in the paternalistic power of rehabilitation to correct unruly Black Louisianans into proper citizens through physical incapacitation. These reformist expansions were facilitated by the welfare-state expansion politics of populist Governor Edwin Edwards and the windfall of state petro revenues following the 1973 OPEC (Organization of Petroleum Exporting Countries) oil price hike that allowed Louisiana to funnel unprecedented dollars into prison reform initiatives following the federal court mandates.

This process was not without obstacles. When residents protested the siting of new satellite prisons in their communities, law-and-order district attorneys—buttressed by the federal funds of the Law Enforcement Administration Act's (LEAA) grant program—made mass early release politically untenable. This required the state to institute new carceral strategies. To meet the federal court's mandates, officials added thousands of prison beds to Angola, opened three new rural prisons, and began to incarcerate state prisoners in parish jails in what was believed to be a temporary stopgap response to overcrowding, alongside new proposals for "controlled carceral growth." Liberal reformism served the purpose of legitimizing and planning Louisiana's carceral futures, paving the way for deeper and more brutal crises.

Formation of the Louisiana Penal System

To see how the crisis of 1971 marked a turning point in the Louisiana punishment regime requires us first to understand what came before the era of mass incarceration. A brief history of the Louisiana carceral state in the nineteenth and early to mid-twentieth centuries allows us to chart the ways in which the formation of the Louisiana penal system was intertwined with racial capitalist imperatives and contradictions while delineating the shifts in the state's 1970s turn toward mass incarceration.

In 1835, Louisiana opened the cells of the first 440-bed Louisiana State Penitentiary in Baton Rouge. The prison was built in response to Alexis de Tocqueville's publicizing the brutal conditions of the French colonial New Orleans jail built in the 1700s. Two-thirds of the prison population were US-born white men, and the remaining third were white and not-yet-white immigrant men who broke the capitalist state's social contract.[2] This racial and gendered composition of the penal system was constructed on the understanding that because only white men held the status of rights-bearing individuals, only white men's liberty could be taken away by the state. Fathers and husbands had the responsibility to discipline white women who stepped outside normative femininity, whereas private masters held the power to punish enslaved people across gender lines.[3] According to Gwendolyn Midlo Hall, planters "were reluctant to abandon their slaves to public justice because of the costs of incarceration and punishment, which were charged to the masters, to say nothing of the loss of the service of incarcerated slaves."[4]

At first, prisoners spent their time producing goods that were sold to cover the costs of the prison's upkeep.[5] However, business owners, incensed by the competition created by prison labor, petitioned the state to abolish this practice. In 1844, the Louisiana legislature prohibited the sale of prisoner-made commodities. Following this move and concerns about the cost of incarceration, the legislature adopted the practice of convict leasing.[6] The first lessors, James A. McHatton and William Pratt, turned to levee construction along the Mississippi River and other tributaries to protect planters' agricultural operations and bolster the growth of capitalist urbanization.[7] Because of the high mortality rates of levee work, Louisiana planters prohibited their slaves from doing such labor.[8] Prisoners provided a needed and cheap labor supply for this critical infrastructure.

This carceral configuration remained relatively steady until the Civil War. Convict lessors returned the prisoners back to the jurisdiction of the state, which moved all prisoners to the New Orleans city jail.[9] In May 1862, Union troops overtook Baton Rouge and significantly damaged the state prison.[10] It was not until 1867 that officials moved prisoners back into the penitentiary. By this time, the racist backlash against Emancipation was already in motion. Under Andrew Johnson's tepid regime of Presidential Reconstruction, former Confederate rebels reassumed political office and enacted Black Codes to criminalize the now-free Black population, which, in the words of Angela Davis, "simultaneously acknowledged and nullified black people's new juridical status as US citizens."[11] At this time, the New

Orleans Police Department began targeting Black New Orleanians for arrest.[12] In 1868 Louisiana imprisoned 85 white men, 203 Black men, 9 Black women, and no white women.[13]

Although Radical Reconstruction tempered this white supremacist revanchism, the penal system was still in financial crisis. When the state legislature first moved to readopt convict leasing in 1869, moderate Republican governor Henry Clay Warmouth vetoed the bill, stating that "where the lessees have absolute power over the prisoners the tendency is to work them too much and feed them too little and give no attention to their comfort and instruction."[14] But a few months later the governor agreed to a compromise bill under which convict leasing could continue, with the addendum that the Board of Control would have oversight over the prisoners' health and religious well-being and $500,000 in state bonds would be authorized for prison rebuilding.[15]

Louisiana's second adoption of convict leasing was shaped by the regional realignment of the racial capitalist state. After the Bargain of 1876, the plantation bloc in alliance with northern capitalists and New South industrialists dismantled Reconstruction to restore political and economic power to white elites. Clyde Woods documents that in Mississippi, which served as a regional model, Redeemers slashed state budgets, and "most of the funds dedicated to education, health and the disabled were eliminated. Five key state institutions were then constructed: disenfranchisement, Black Codes, the one-party state, the malapportionment of legislative districts (gerrymandering), and labor peonage."[16] Although these austerity measures undercut the gains of Reconstruction for Black and white workers alike, it was Black power that was explicitly targeted.[17] The plantation bloc overwhelmed formal Black political power, destroyed collective and cooperative systems of organization and ownership, and disorganized Black labor through racist terror.[18] It is in the context of the racist class war, which we have come to know as Jim Crow, that convict leasing became *the* primary penal structure across the South, including Louisiana.[19]

Former Confederate major Samuel James leased the growing Louisiana penal population from 1870 until his death in 1899.[20] James worked most prisoners in levee and railroad construction to meet the burgeoning demands of New South modernization.[21] Whereas the Republican state legislature attempted to curb James's power, Bourbon Democrats loosened convict leasing regulations when they ascended to state power.[22] The number of people on the lease grew due to the Bourbons' intertwined projects of widespread economic insecurity and impoverishment and the mass criminalization of the Black populace. The reenactment of the Black Codes targeted Black people to labor on the lease and gave birth to the ideology that Blackness and criminality were inherently intertwined, justifying their policing and imprisonment.[23] The Louisiana prison population grew more than threefold from 297 prisoners in 1868 to 989 prisoners, 85 percent of them Black, in 1900. This marked the first boom of the Louisiana carceral state.[24]

To capitalize on the free labor provided by the growing penal population, James purchased the plantation Angola in 1880.[25] Before long, his profits from working imprisoned people on levees, railways, and cotton farming were almost a hundred times more than the rental fees he paid to the state.[26] However, unlike in plantation slavery where enslaved people served as a source of both labor and capital to the plantocracy, under the Jim Crow political economy prisoners served only as labor—and so little care was given to their welfare.[27] Prisoners worked under brutal conditions marked by malignant neglect and corporeal violence. Their disposability was epitomized by the level of premature death that characterized James's thirty-year reign during which about three thousand people perished—approximately one person every three and half days.[28]

The Louisiana legislature abolished convict leasing at the turn of the twentieth century. Although Black and Irish workers had protested the lease as an affront to free labor and the Prison Reform Association of Louisiana pushed to end the practice because of its brutality, state officials ended leasing because they saw a revenue opportunity in prison labor that would support their antitax politics.[29] The state's abolition of the lease was coupled with its purchase of Angola to serve as its own plantation penitentiary in 1901.[30] The Board of Control, the precursor to the Department of Corrections, had as its primary goal to "first to make the convicts self-sustaining and if possible profitable to the state instead of a burden" by working prisoners on levees and farming cotton, cane, and corn.[31] It purchased adjacent plantations to expand Angola up to 18,000 acres, while the Baton Rouge prison was turned into an intake center and a prison for primarily white prisoners deemed too old or sick to work.[32]

Angola's management relied on racial and gendered divisions of living and labor. Racially segregated housing and dining areas were created to separate the minority of white prisoners.[33] And even though both Black and white prisoners were forced to work in the fields, Black men were overwhelmingly assigned to the more arduous labor conditions of the levee camps and sugar cane plantations. Imprisoned Black women were required to do a combination of work in the fields and domestic labor, while the few incarcerated white women oversaw sewing and mending work, mirroring a mixture of plantation and Jim Crow divisions of productive and reproductive labor.[34]

Although the transition to a publicly run system was lauded, contradictions quickly emerged. The state's lowering of the rate of premature death produced a steadily growing penal population (1,500 prisoners by 1905 and 1,900 prisoners by 1910) that exceeded the projected prison system expenses. Furthermore, Angola never accrued the revenue politicians hoped for. It could only generate limited revenue because private interests had successfully lobbied the state to adopt the "state-use" system whereby crops raised there could only be used within Angola or be sold to other state agencies, and not in competition with the private market.[35] Despite prison boosters' claims, financial pressures led to nominal surpluses at best that often were negated by the penal system's debts.[36] Moreover, the New Deal's Agricultural Administration Act, which directed the prison to take dozens of acres out of production, combined with mechanization decreased the number of incarcerated people needed to work on the plantation.[37] When a 1957 legislative committee pushed for an increase in penal labor as a disciplinary tool in response to prisoner unrest, the recommendation could not be implemented because of "federal agricultural regulations and quotas" and "increased use of farm machinery."[38] And when Angola administrators tried to increase industrial production, only a dozen jobs were added here and there. By 1961, only one-third of Angola's 3,240 prisoners were working in anything one could call productive labor.[39] Most importantly, prisoners were not the submissive subjects that state officials wished them to be. Time and again prisoners escaped and protested the inhumane conditions at Angola.[40]

The state responses to these carceral contradictions produced cycles of crisis and reform that would characterize the Louisiana penal system until the 1970s. Officials loathed funding the prison system, especially but not only during economic downturns. They sought to cut prison expenses by employing prisoners as "trusty guards,"[41] cutting corners on sanitary housing and decent food, overworking prisoners in the fields, and relying on floggings to increase productivity.[42] Not only were such strategies unable to cover costs but also the ongoing systematic violence of Angola led to numerous prisoner revolts. Most notoriously, in 1951, thirty-seven prisoners slashed their Achilles heels in protest of brutal working conditions.[43]

Prisoner protests had the effect of increasing public attention to inhumane conditions, leading to state investigations and a half-dozen official studies by 1960. But little was done in response to the findings and proposals made to the state legislature.[44] Adopted reforms tended to be minimal in scope, such as tinkering with prisoner classification systems, or they focused on the most egregious components of the penitentiary, such as replacing trusties with paid guards.[45] On occasion the legislature would allot additional funds for operations and renovations that included new carceral facilities for women prisoners and segregated facilities for prisoners labeled as "sex perverts."[46] But once publicity died down, state officials would again cut costs—beginning the cycle anew. At no point was the underlying violence of incarceration called into question until four prisoners sat down to sue the state for the horrors of Angola in 1971.

A New Era, A New Crisis

For much of the twentieth century, prisoner escapes from Angola were common, even constant.[47] Only the main prison was enclosed by fences and walls while the physical landscape of the Mississippi River and the Tunica woods served as carceral barriers for the prison's outer camps and vast fields. For the prisoners who worked the fields, corn and cane could serve as cover when they first ran, and the scale of the penitentiary combined with the small number of guards allowed some prisoners to get away if they were quick enough. More often than not, however, the prison chase team recaptured escapees within the penitentiary grounds or in the waters of the Mississippi.[48]

Having witnessed the limitations of this runaway strategy, Arthur Mitchell and Hayes Williams tried a different route to freedom in 1970: they attempted to slip out of the prison gates during a banquet while dressed as guests. Their plan was thwarted when, despite coordination with the guards, the nightly count was off by one. Prison officials sent Mitchell and Hayes to Angola's notorious Red Hat solitary confinement cellblock.[49]

In the Red Hat, they were locked up in pitch-black cells measuring four by six feet. Trusty guards punctuated their isolation with intermittent beatings. When they were transferred to Close Cell Restriction (CCR), they were held captive in lockdown 23 hours and 55 minutes a day. Yet within CCR, they were able to communicate with one another and began communicating with two other prisoners, a devout Muslim Lazarus Joseph and a former trusty Lee Stevenson. Instead of breaking their desire for freedom, the experience in solitary fortified their resolve. The four focused on how to transform prison conditions. As later summed up in the *Angolite*, "They reached two realities: One, if the people of Louisiana knew what was actually going on in Angola they would be shocked, and two, the way they could prove what was happening was to prove it to a federal court."[50] Following precedents set by incarcerated Nation of Islam activists, they decided to file a federal civil action lawsuit against the DOC through the Reconstruction-era 1871 Civil Rights Act that authorized people to sue states for civil rights violations.[51]

Arthur Mitchell spearheaded the lawsuit. According to former jailhouse lawyer Biggy Johnston, Mitchell was a "radical from the streets," shaped by the struggles of the 1960s.[52] Instead of focusing on a singular issue, this lawsuit would challenge the totality of the inhumane conditions that characterized incarcerated life at Angola. The four prisoners put together a case against the overlapping issues that they understood to constitute cruel and unusual punishment and civil rights violations. Their lawsuit charged that Angola was guilty of racially segregating Black and white prisoners in dorms and dining, only allowing white prisoners to be eligible for the best prison jobs, discriminating against Muslim prisoners, censoring legal mail, and relying on CCR solitary as a disciplinary tool. The medical care available was woefully inadequate, and the living and dining quarters were unsanitary. In addition, prison officials created an environment and perpetuated the trusty system that encouraged violence among prisoners. These conditions constituted Angola as a systematically racist, violent, and toxic environment that required radical change. With Hayes Williams as the lead plaintiff, the lawsuit was filed with the US Middle District of Louisiana Court in March 1971.[53]

Even as state officials balked at the lawsuit, they began to institute changes to preempt a federal ruling. On being elected governor in 1972, Edwin Edwards appointed Elayn Hunt as the new director of the DOC: she was a known liberal prison reformer and the first woman appointed to the position.[54] Hunt's appointment signaled the state's investment in prison reform born out of desires and anxieties shaped by the rise of rehabilitation-oriented penology[55] and the haunting specter of the 1971 Attica uprising.[56] Hunt pushed for a larger DOC budget to improve prison conditions and hire additional security guards to replace the trusties.[57] Hunt's efforts were backed by a handful of prison reformers in the state legislature—most notably, Representative Dorothy Mae Taylor. Over the next few years, Hunt integrated Angola's work and housing assignments; expanded its work-release programs; combined the adult, juvenile, and parole systems into one unified penal system; and closed the Red Hat.[58]

Although Hunt's reforms were aimed at Angola, her underlying goal was to decentralize the plantation penitentiary. This plan was based on the idea that Angola was a fundamentally dehumanizing space because of its mammoth size (3,000-plus beds spread over 18,000 acres) and isolated location. To create a rehabilitative environment, the plan proposed that the state open smaller "regional prisons" focused on work-release and rehabilitative programs. Moreover, siting prisons closer to cities would make it easier to hire and retain qualified staff and provide prisoners with greater access to loved ones. Under this plan, Angola would be closed altogether.[59] Hunt, backed by Governor Edwards, traveled around the state making speeches on the benefits of decentralization. The decentralization proposal gained enough traction that in 1974 the state allocated $400,000 to the DOC to conduct a study of what it would take to implement such a plan.[60] Even the president of the American Correctional Association formally endorsed the decentralization of Angola.[61]

Hunt's ability to implement immediate reforms was made possible by Louisiana's surplus mineral revenue following the 1973 global increase in oil prices. Previously, because of its racist disregard for incarcerated life, the state's approach to its penal system was characterized by systematic disinvestment. Yet, Hunt pushed to increase the DOC budget to support her reforms from $15.1 million in fiscal year 1972 to $25 million for fiscal year 1975, a jump of almost 66 percent in just three years.[62] The leap in spending was tethered to the global crises of capital of the late 1960s and 1970s. Pressures from above and below had exacerbated the contradictions of Keynesianism. The Bretton Woods monetary system fell into disarray, leading to a delinking of the US dollar from the gold standard and the abandonment of fixed exchange rates; inflation and unemployment were on the rise, productivity was in decline, and radical antiracist and anticolonial movements across the globe were challenging the legitimacy of racial capitalism.[63] At this critical conjuncture, OPEC, emboldened by the Third World Project, raised the tax rate on oil production by 70 percent to recuperate revenues that had been in decline despite soaring profits for European and US oil companies. The very next day, on October 17, 1973, Arab oil states reduced the supply of oil, followed up by an embargo on the United States, in response to Nixon's support of Israel in the Yom Kippur War and in solidarity with Palestine.[64] In a panic, US oil prices shot up fourfold, creating strains on the US economy that, coupled with the devaluation of the dollar, produced the 1973–1975 US recession.[65]

However, Louisiana was a haven for the petrochemical industry, and the OPEC oil crisis produced not a budgetary shortage but an unexpected windfall of revenue. Rich oil deposits were first discovered in Evangeline, Louisiana, in 1901 leading to intensive oil exploration and development throughout the state.[66] Over the following decades, Louisiana became a key site for oil extraction and oil industrialization. The geographic proximity of Louisiana's oil wells to the Mississippi River, along with favorable state policies, bolstered the development of the oil economy.[67] Geographer Craig Colten documented that between the 1940 and 1970 "a major infusion of federal funding during World War II enlarged processing capacity along the lower Mississippi. . . . War Production Board investment enabled construction of new artificial rubber and aviation fuel facilities, and existing refiners expanded to meet wartime demands."[68] These federal wartime investments facilitated off-shore drilling in the Louisiana Gulf in the 1940s that, along with onshore production, made Louisiana the third largest producer of crude oil in the United States.[69] Louisiana's high rate of oil extraction and processing directly contributed to the United States being the world's leading oil producer up to the 1970s.[70]

Although the Louisiana legislature first implemented severance taxes on oil in 1910, it was not until the 1970s that the legislature developed its taxation structure on the premise that oil should be Louisiana's primary source of revenue generation.[71] Beginning with Governor Huey Long in the 1920s, the state legislature passed new taxes on oil to finance state-building projects from new roads to expanding education.[72] By the 1950s, oil revenues significantly buoyed the state treasury.[73] Yet, in 1973, Louisiana began to increase oil taxes along with the general sales tax in tandem with *reductions* on income and property taxes.[74] These legislative actions intensified the state's dependence on oil revenues and attempted "to shift some of the burden of state taxation away from Louisianans to residents of other states."[75] Higher oil prices translated into larger severance taxes that greatly surpassed the rise in commodity prices. In 1973 the legislature took further advantage of oil price increases by changing how oil severance taxes were calculated from a tax based on *volume* to one based on *value*.[76] And because of the Middle East oil embargo, Louisiana was newly incentivized to intensify petrochemical extractions.[77] Oil revenues allowed Louisiana not only to cover its budgetary needs but also to have a surplus

TABLE 1.1 Louisiana budgetary growth, 1970–1975

Year	Louisiana general revenues	Combined mineral taxes (oil and gas)	DOC budget
FY 1970–1971	1,776,352,965	778,900,000	12,708,844
FY 1971–1972	1,850,928,755	914,300,000	15,138,289
FY 1972–1973	1,954,895,958	1,010,000,000	17,385,930
FY 1973–1974	2,118,910,060	1,073,000,000	20,517,742
FY 1974–1975	2,442,918,604	1,207,000,000	24,951,804

Source: Louisiana Executive Budgets

of revenue throughout the 1970s, buffering the state against the national recession (table 1.1).[78]

The growth of the DOC budget was a piece of the larger project of state-building that marked Governor Edwards's first two terms. Governing Louisiana in the tradition of Huey Long, Edwards increased expenditures for education, healthcare, AFDC payments, road building, and other public works.[79] Although expanding such state capacities was an aim of Edwards before the OPEC price hike, the oil revenue boost strengthened his plans.[80] Given the pending prisoner lawsuit, it is not surprising that the DOC would also gain increased funding amidst Louisiana's economic surpluses and pro-state expansion politics.

Even as liberal prison reform gained traction, law-and-order policing and prosecutorial power were on the rise. For instance, the New Orleans City Council approved a new policing tactic known as "stop and frisk" in spring 1967. The local press heralded this initiative as an important addition to "the war on crime."[81] The national pillar of the War on Crime was the creation of the Law Enforcement Assistance Administration (LEAA). Established through the Omnibus Crime Control and Safe Streets Act of 1968, the LEAA grant-funding program served as a mechanism for the federal government to bulk up law enforcement power at the municipal and state level. Enacted under President Johnson but notoriously championed by President Nixon, the Safe Streets Act and LEAA grants were conceived within the frame of racial liberalism that believed better police training and modernization of equipment would reduce the discretion and prejudices of law enforcement. Colorblind policing would in turn promote public safety for all.[82] However, after the rise of Black power and the 1960s urban uprisings, a coalition of Republicans and southern Dixiecrats enhanced the punitive elements of the bill as it moved through Congress.

Most notoriously, new provisions were added that allowed funds to be provided for riot control.[83]

The LEAA moved federal dollars to local criminal legal jurisdictions on a previously unthinkable scale. Much attention has been given to how the LEAA boosted the militarization of police departments.[84] This is largely an accurate assessment. Indeed, the NOPD used LEAA funds to buy a tank that it deployed against the New Orleans chapter of the Black Panthers in the fall of 1970.[85] Nevertheless, this singular focus obscures how the majority of LEAA funds went into seemingly mundane projects that built up state and municipal carceral infrastructure. In the case of New Orleans, which received 30 percent of the LEAA funds allotted to Louisiana, LEAA monies expanded everyday policing capacities by funding trainings, computer systems, and new crime labs alongside community policing programs that built consent for police power.[86]

District attorney Harry Connick leveraged LEAA funds to advance his law-and-order agenda. Elected in 1973, Harry Connick would serve as New Orleans's district attorney for the next thirty years.[87] Connick ran on a tough-on-crime platform and promised to create a new carceral cooperation anticrime body that would coordinate the efforts of the DA's office with the NOPD, the Louisiana state troopers, sheriffs' offices, and federal law enforcement agencies (figure 1.1).[88] Connick proved true to his word. A little more than a year after entering office, Connick boasted that his office "put more people on death penalties in the last 10 months than has been done in the preceding four years"[89] and created a "Career Criminal Bureau" focused on targeting "repeat offenders."[90] Connick believed the uptick in crime rates to be primarily due to the activities of so-called career criminals who were able to evade conviction because of the DA office's high caseload and the supposed abuses of defense attorneys.

The Career Criminal Bureau worked with the NOPD to screen arrests and prioritize the prosecution of individuals with prior records.[91] Key to the Career Criminal Bureau's strategy was the "constant use of the Louisiana multiple offense statutes" to enhance penalties.[92] By 1975, the LEAA allotted nearly $500 million to Connick's Career Criminal Bureau, increasing its budget to twenty times that of the DOC in 1975.[93] Within less than three years, the Career Criminal Bureau was responsible for the "disposal of 1,836 habitual offenders with an overall conviction rate of 95%," a stark contrast to the seven people who had been sentenced under the law in 1973.[94] It was so "successful" that the New Orleans Indigent Defense Office applied for LEAA funds to explicitly counteract its work.[95] Moreover,

FIGURE 1.1 Harry Connick's district attorney campaign ad, *Times-Picayune*, September 12, 1973.

two Angola jailhouse lawyers, Biggy Johnston and John McCormick, filed a racial discrimination suit against Connick for primarily prosecuting Black New Orleanians as habitual offenders.[96]

Beyond providing dollars and cents, LEAA grants produced alignments and coordination between local carceral state-makers. To receive LEAA funds, states were required to create bodies to administer its block grants. Louisiana's agency was the Louisiana Commission on Law Enforcement and the Administration of Criminal Justice (LCLE), which dispersed funds to seven geographically designated planning districts.[97] The Orleans Parish planning district was governed by the Criminal Justice Coordinating Council (CJCC).[98] Following federal guidelines, the New Orleans CJCC comprised a combination of elected officials, criminal justice professionals, and a handful of private individuals. Notably a number of the NOPD's top brass along with the criminal sheriff and district attorney sat on the CJCC.[99] In other words, the very people applying to the LEAA to enhance the carceral capacities of the state were part of the decision-making body invested with the power to decide what direction the local criminal justice system should take.[100] The CJCC's makeup reinforced the idea that the primary experts of the criminal justice system were those officials actively working to increase carceral power. Furthermore, the LEAA's federal guidelines for bodies like the CJCC shored up relationships and produced consensus between law enforcement and noncarceral officials.

Between 1971 when Mitchell, Williams, Joseph, and Stevenson filed their lawsuit and the federal court's ruling in 1975, the Louisiana criminal justice system underwent significant changes. The competing ideologies of liberal reformism and law and order were on full display within the penal system while the state was infused by new monies in response to the emerging crises of global capitalism and the beginning of the national war on crime. These contradictions and contestations would come to a head in the federal court's ruling.

The Ruling

On Monday April 28, 1975, US magistrate Frank Polozola issued the first report in the *Hayes Williams v. McKeithan* lawsuit. This report set the tone for the federal court's approach to Angola over the next several decades, especially because Polozola would replace judge Elmer West as the presiding judge in 1980. The scathing fifty-five-page report condemned the conditions in Angola in no uncertain terms. By and large, Polozola upheld the prisoners' complaints, recounting the failure of the prison to provide medical care by trained professionals, the unabashed censoring of prisoners' legal mail, the fact that the "psychiatric unit" consisted of nothing more than an overcrowded cellblock of prisoners who were let out of their cells only to shower, and the accumulation of raw sewage under the dining hall, which was then pumped into the Mississippi River. Conversely, he lauded Hunt for abolishing racial segregation and the trusty system.[101]

A principal issue of concern for Polozola, which had *not* been raised by the initial lawsuit, was overcrowding. The prison population had grown from just over three thousand prisoners when the suit was first filed to approximately four thousand prisoners, double the capacity Angola was designed for, with Black prisoners constituting 71 percent of the prison population.[102] The increase of close to one thousand prisoners in four years was a source of alarm not because more people were imprisoned but because it had produced overcrowded conditions. Polozola equated overcrowding with the recent spike in prison violence. He asserted that rampant violence among prisoners, which included 270 stabbings and 20 deaths in less than three years, was produced by a scarcity of prison guards and overpopulated facilities. Arguing that overcrowding created the situation where "the prison does not have enough cells to house those inmates who present danger to other inmates," he singled out queer prisoners as particularly dangerous in his claim that much violence stemmed from "fights involving homosexuals."[103] Even though Polozola recognized how overcrowded conditions could prove harmful, he located the root of such violence in individuals, rather than in the state's disregard for incarcerated life or its power to target a growing number of people for imprisonment.

The court's narrow conception of what constituted prison violence was further revealed by its position on solitary confinement. Solitary confinement, the precipitating issue for Mitchell, Hayes, Stevenson, and Joseph, was the only area in which Polozola did not find for the plaintiffs. It was not even part of the official investigation because of a recent case that ruled that Angola's use of solitary confinement met the minimum constitutional standards. Hence, Polozola ruled that "this issue [of solitary confinement] has been rendered moot."[104] In leaving solitary off the table, Polozola reaffirmed not only prison officials' discretion in its use but also the legitimacy of the practice itself. To the plaintiffs this was a slap in the face. They publicly challenged this argument, asking how could Polozola say nothing about Williams and Mitchell "being placed in solitary confinement for eight days in a cell with no running water, lights, faucets, toilets, shower, or bathing facilities and mattresses only at night."[105] In ignoring this issue, they highlighted that, even though Polozola's report denounced conditions at Angola, the state's concern for prisoners' health and safety had a clear limit when it came to those the prison deemed uncontrollable and thus unworthy of any semblance of care.

The crux of the report was its recommendations. While acknowledging the work of Hunt in reforming Angola, Polozola charged that more expansive prison reform was required: "No one disputes the fact that there are many conditions at Angola that must be eliminated to protect the lives and safety of the inmates incarcerated there and the civilian personnel who work at Angola. The question is not whether the conditions exist but when and in what manner are these conditions to be eliminated."[106] The question of how to alleviate such conditions was not as simple as it might at first appear. For the court, certain issues had fairly straightforward solutions. Polozola unequivocally enjoined officials from all forms of racial and religious discrimination and from censoring legal mail. In addition, he required that Angola undergo massive repairs to bring it into compliance with fire and safety standards. On the question of violence, Polozola recommended strengthening the security and surveillance of prisoners through hiring additional guards, increasing the regularity of shakedowns, purchasing new surveillance technologies, prohibiting gambling, and separating "all known homosexuals from the prison population."[107]

Yet Polozola offered the least definitive solution to the pivotal issue of overcrowding. Although he recommended the construction of temporary housing at Angola to reduce overcrowded conditions, he also stated that the problem of overcrowding required a strategic plan that considered the long-term needs of the penal system. Such a plan for Angola should begin by examining the possibility of constructing additional cells and dormitories and updating the Angola classification system.[108] However, Polozola's vision went beyond Angola and pushed for the state to study how it could implement decentralization by moving prisoners to other carceral facilities, granting more prisoners probation and parole, or even potentially building new prisons.[109]

Less than six weeks later, Judge West of the Middle District of Louisiana Court upheld Polozola's report and declared Angola to be in an "extreme public emergency." Finding Angola to "flagrantly violate basic constitutional standards" and numerous federal and state laws, West ordered a series of reforms. Generally, Judge West followed Polozola's recommendations.[110] He also added that officials were to follow all laws protecting public property and to punish prisoners who caused damage to the prison. Again, the issue of solitary confinement was elided as West ruled that the prison should continue to follow its existing procedures for punitive and administrative confinement.[111] West followed the liberal logic of Polozola in linking violence among prisoners to a lack of security and overcrowding. He mandated the expansion of Angola's security and surveillance capacities. Dangerous prisoners were ordered to be segregated from the general population, which included the immediate segregation of all "overt" homosexual prisoners.[112] When any form of assault, including sexualized violence—which for the prison constituted any form of queer sex, consensual or not—occurred between prisoners, Angola's staff were to report it to the local DA.

Finally, West ordered that the state create a comprehensive plan for the decentralization of the Louisiana penal system. However, if "complete decentralization is not absolutely assured within two years," then the state had to provide a specific timetable for building out Angola and to report on the feasibility of reducing its population either by early release or incarcerating certain classes of prisoners elsewhere.[113] Thus, if decentralization was not realized according to the court's timetable, it was likely that, rather than shuttering or shrinking, Angola would grow. Placing the possibility of carceral expansion alongside the possibility of reducing the prison population through release provided an opening for Louisiana to solve its prison crises *either* through a prison buildup or decarceration.

The West ruling once again illustrated how liberalism limited a full reckoning with prison violence. Like Polozola, West was incensed by the brutality and unlivable conditions at Angola and believed that the problems of the prison could be rectified through a modernization project. Renovating facilities to meet state standards, improving medical care, and increasing security measures would mitigate the harms created by decades of disinvestment. Yet, this push to invest in Angola was not designed to undo the institution's punishment regime. Certain practices were explicitly prohibited but only insofar as they were outside the bounds of constitutionality. Punitive practices were, in fact, enhanced in several ways—by the mandate to increase searches to the requirement that incarcerated people be subject to additional criminal charges. Underlying such actions was the dominant idea that protecting prisoners from violence meant protecting them from one another, not from the violence of the state to confine and punish.[114] It was for this reason that solitary confinement was upheld and the DOC was to institute a more regimented classification system to separate out "dangerous" prisoners deemed incapable of rehabilitation from deserving "nonviolent" prisoners capable of change.

This logic also helps explain how both West and Polozola could couple an unflinching reproach of racial segregation with the order to segregate prisoners who crossed the line of normative heterosexuality. The official antiracism of post–World War II racial liberalism was anchored in an understanding of racism in terms of individualized prejudice. The 1954 *Brown v. Board of Education* ruling, which based its critique on the psychological impacts of racial segregation, fortified this understanding at the direct expense of a materialist conception of white supremacy. This simplified rendering of Jim Crow and, by association, racism erased the Black freedom movement's assertion that racial hierarchies went hand in hand with the widespread exploitation, dispossession, and punitive power that constituted the systematic violence of the racial capitalist state.[115] By 1975 the dominance of racial liberalism made racial segregation in any facet of society, even prisons, not only illegal but also irredeemable.

Still, the courts did not find segregation as a general practice to be a problem. The prison's capacity to separate out prisoners deemed dangerous was critical to its disciplinary rule. The ease with which the court deemed "overt homosexuals" a primary cause of prison violence implicitly collapsed queerness with sexual violence. As historian Regina Kunzel has shown, during the 1960s and 1970s an outcry emerged surrounding male-on-male prison rape. The concern over this form of prison violence drew on decades of homophobic and heterosexist thinking that posited queer people as deviant and dangerous and who needed to be policed and controlled in tandem with the feminist politicization of sexualized violence.[116] However, while feminists asserted that interpersonal acts of rape and sexual assault were rooted in patriarchal power relations, the court's decision to segregate perceived homosexuals skirted this systematic analysis. The courts replaced it with one that rendered prisoner rape—a real problem at Angola—not as a product of patriarchy but as a queer phenomenon from which straight prisoners had to be protected while erasing how the prison was itself a source of sexual violence through strip and cavity searches. The ruling reinforced the long-standing practice of punishing those who refused to abide by the compulsory heterosexuality of the prison, reified queerness as an unruly danger, and again located the source of prison violence within incarcerated individuals rather than in structural conditions.

Because officials explained prison rape through the racist and gendered narrative of the hypermasculine and oversexualized "Black male rapist" preying on innocent white prisoners, the alarm around prison sexual violence was itself racialized.[117] There is evidence that such thinking shaped Polozola's findings. In an overlapping case about racial segregation at the Baton Rouge jail, attorneys with the ACLU wrote to the US Department of Justice that "Polozola recommended against a strict racially integrated ratio per cell. He said that his experience was that in a cell where you had ten (10) prisoners, if eight (8) prisoners were black and two (2) prisoners were white (as would be the case at parish prison for seventy to eighty percent of the prison population is black), *that the black prisoners would dominate the white prisoners and in many cases force homosexual acts upon them.*"[118] Integrationist mandates were undergirded by the intertwining of racist and homophobic logics. The racial liberalism embedded within the Hayes ruling did not necessitate a commitment to ending racism or state-sanctioned violence; rather it solely required that the forms racialized punishment took fit within the bounds of liberal constitutionality. The magistrate report and the subsequent federal court ruling paved the way for new prison reforms. Yet exactly how the state would meet these mandates was undetermined. The question of how to resolve the overcrowding crisis took center stage for the DOC, DAs, prisoners, and communities throughout the state.

The Prison Scramble

Competing responses to Judge West's ruling arose immediately. In the days following the court order, Governor Edwards promised to appeal the measure while also committing to reforming Angola.[119] Elayn Hunt voiced concern with the short timeline for decentralization and cautioned that investing more funds into Angola would move the state away rather than closer to shuttering the plantation penitentiary.[120] At the same time, overcrowding had reached an all-time high, with prisoners "sleeping on the floors, in the hallways, or in cots pushed within ten inches of each other. The prison has run out of beds long after it ran out of space."[121] DOC officials raised the concern that if the legislature did not soon respond to the courts, riots could ensue.[122] Incarcerated journalist Wilbert Rideau shared this sentiment, reporting that overcrowding increased prisoners' "material deprivation" that in turn led to desperation and an increase in violence.[123] For Rideau and many others locked up in Angola, the only answer to this crisis was to bulldoze Angola to the ground and to create the penal system anew through decentralization.[124]

This was not to be. Instead, the legislature prioritized passing Connick's new law-and-order package.[125] The most contentious piece of the package was a good time reduction bill, designed to prohibit people who had been convicted of armed robbery or were "habitual offenders" from accruing good time—the automatic procedure of reducing prisoners' sentences for good behavior.[126] Despite the DOC's strong opposition to the bill on the grounds that it was exactly this sort of law-and-order measure that was contributing to the overcrowding crisis, it was passed in a modified version whereby judges would have the power to determine whether a "habitual offender" was eligible for good time or not.[127]

Only the insistence of Governor Edwards compelled the legislature to respond to the federal courts. Although the state was still waiting on its appeal, Edwards recognized that it would likely fail, given the trajectory of similar federal court orders in Mississippi and Alabama.[128] The governor took action on two fronts: he pushed for the legislature to allot funding for repairs at Angola and began negotiations for the acquisition of a Caddo Parish jail to convert into a first offender prison as the first step in decentralization.[129] When the Fifth Circuit Court of Appeals upheld West's order, Edwards persuaded the legislature to appropriate $15 million for prison renovation and construction: $5 million for new construction at Angola, $5 million for a first offender prison near Shreveport, and $5 million for a first offender prison in New Orleans.[130] Tacking these projects on was easy because the state budget was still flush with oil revenue to the point that, for the third year in a row, the state was able to cover its entire construction budget with cash on hand without having to resort to debt financing through issuing bonds.[131]

However, the federal courts responded that the state was still moving too slowly.[132] West argued that state officials should do whatever it could and quickly, whether that meant applying to the LEAA for funding, holding a special legislative session, or shifting bonds from other projects to prison construction. Importantly, West stated that it was now clear that the priority was not only to decentralize the prison system but also to construct additional housing at Angola in the interim.[133] In response, Hunt flew to Washington, D.C., to urge the Louisiana congressional delegation to obtain LEAA funds for decentralization.[134] Simultaneously, Governor Edwards persuaded the legislature to give him "authority to act independently by placing the Department of Corrections among the agencies for which he can declare an emergency and spend without specific appropriations."[135] On declaring Angola to be in a state of emergency, Edwards unilaterally diverted funds from other sectors of the budget to the DOC's budget.

Opposing Satellites: NIMBYism in Practice

Even though the DOC now had a blank check with which to implement the decentralization plan, local opposition to prison siting remained a persistent obstacle. Because the state favored converting surplus state property into prisons rather than building from the ground up, the DOC was compelled to negotiate with local jurisdictions. Just as fast as DOC officials scrambled to find facilities to turn into prisons, local residents and officials scrambled to find ways of blocking such moves.[136] Hence, one of the very cruxes of the decentralization plan—that prisons should be located closer to urban centers to facilitate improved staffing, rehabilitation, and visitation— proved to be one of its downfalls as "not in my backyard" (NIMBY) politics made such siting unfeasible (figure 1.2). The central questions underlying the prison scramble became *who* had authority over surplus state lands and *what* were the ideologies that structured the terms of the debate.

The DOC first set its sights on Caddo Parish—home to Shreveport—for a satellite prison. Yet, only days after the legislature approved bonds to purchase or lease a Caddo jail, the local governing body, the parish police jury, rejected the prison conversion plan.[137] Realizing that a parish vote would not be in the DOC's favor, Hunt set her sights on a vacant, formerly Black school that closed when the school district finally desegregated in 1972. Yet, when it became evident that the Caddo Parish School Board held final authority on whether the school should be leased or sold to the DOC, hundreds of residents attended its meetings in protest.[138] When the school board voted 13–2 against accepting the state's offer of $600,000 for the site, the DOC abandoned, for the time being, the option of opening a prison in the Shreveport area.[139]

The DOC's efforts to open a prison in New Orleans were likewise halted. After learning that the DOC had purchased a nursing home in New Orleans East for $2.5 million to renovate it as a small geriatric prison, residents and politicians contested the plan.[140] Although Orleans Parish state representatives had approved $5 million bonds for prison construction in the city, they maintained they would not have done so if they had known about this particular site.[141] State representatives backed the city council in a suit against the prison that claimed the plan violated the city's zoning laws and that the state should have first attained approval from the city council. Animating the suit was the question of which state bodies had the power "to create a

FIGURE 1.2 "We Can't Adequately Handle Any More Prisoners" political cartoon, *Times-Picayune*, July 23, 1975, Capital City Press/Georges Media Group, and Baton Rouge, Louisiana.

[carceral] institution."¹⁴² The city council then voted 5–0 to amend the New Orleans Comprehensive Zoning Ordinance to explicitly state that nursing homes could not be converted into carceral facilities.¹⁴³ Before the courts ruled, the state bowed down, and Edwards suspended the plan.¹⁴⁴

Opposition to sick and elderly prisoners was not confined to Orleans Parish. The DOC's first attempt to transfer prisoners out of Angola was to move 170 prisoners in need of ongoing medical and psychiatric care to the vacant Greenwell Springs Hospital in Baton Rouge.¹⁴⁵ Yet, just days before the transfer, more than 400 Baton Rouge residents attended an oppositional mass meeting, arguing that a hospital located in a residential area should not be used to imprison "those convicted of serious criminal offenses, regardless of their physical condition."¹⁴⁶ The East Baton Rouge District Attorney's office filed an injunction against the state which asserted that the land had originally been donated to the state for a tuberculosis sanatorium and any other use was out of bounds.¹⁴⁷ Governor Edwards and parish leaders negotiated that Greenwell Springs Hospital would *temporarily* house no more than seventy ill prisoners.¹⁴⁸

The DOC also looked to use decommissioned military property for satellite prisons. Members of the Calcasieu Parish police jury in southwest Louisiana reached out to the state to propose using a former air force base as a first offender minimum security prison.¹⁴⁹ The DOC took up the proposal and included the base in its decentralization plan.¹⁵⁰ However, mounting resistance to siting a prison in the parish grew, abetted by the fact that the base was not under the jurisdiction of the pro-prison Calcasieu police jury but the more antagonistic Lake Charles City Council. The plan was squashed when the council unanimously voted against prison conversion.¹⁵¹ Less than two weeks later, Hunt offered up another option that avoided the local opposition problem: converting a World War II navy ship into a floating prison. She asserted that the prison ship would be an ideal site for "non-violent" prisoners to learn maritime vocational skills.¹⁵² But the LEAA refused to fund the plan because it was both prohibitively expensive and security would not be strong enough to "prevent a mutiny followed by a ship takeover."¹⁵³

Although the idea of a prison ship was always a reach, Hunt's proposal was made in the midst of massive local opposition to new prisons and the ticking clock of the court orders. Almost as soon as the DOC found a potential facility for a satellite prison, residents found a means of blocking the plan or at least making it so difficult to implement that the DOC dropped it. As one editorial aptly articulated, much of the resistance was fundamentally based in the conundrum that people "want the satellite prisons—but not here."¹⁵⁴

FIGURE 1.3 "Jungle Justice" political cartoon, *States-Item*, August 22, 1974, Capital City Press/Georges Media Group, and Baton Rouge, Louisiana.

Competing Ideologies of Decentralization

Although the strategies that locales used to stop prisons varied, the ideologies undergirding such opposition were remarkably consistent. Most prominent was residents' assertion that a prison would put their community at risk of dangerous criminals.[155] Central to this position was the claim that people did not want "another Angola" in their communities.[156] This rhetoric pointed to what Angola had come to represent, particularly for white Louisianans: a place overflowing with dangerous Black men who frequently were able to escape. The imagined danger posed by current and future prisoners was typically racialized and urbanized. Political cartoons depicted Angola as an overcrowded site of "jungle justice,"[157] and letters to the editor argued that prisons brought "city problems" to where they did not belong (figure 1.3). In one letter, a man wrote, "I moved here to raise my children away from the city atmosphere, the problems generated by people who don't care, who can't control themselves, much less their children."[158] Cities—particularly New Orleans, which was routinely cited as "producing" more than 50 percent of Angola's population—and urban residents were signified as uncontrollable and lawless places and people that prisons transported

Decentralizing Angola   45

into rural parishes, disrupting law-abiding residents' tranquility and safety.[159] This racially coded sociospatial logic was rooted in and extended the notion of Black people and places as sites of danger to be avoided, contained, and controlled, along with erasing how the bulking up of the New Orleans criminal legal system produced such skewed statistics.[160]

The DOC's argument that the satellite prisons would be minimum security facilities and would imprison only first offenders did not assuage locals' fears. At one public meeting in Shreveport, a resident refuted the idea that first offenders were somehow safer by stating, "The term 'first offender' keeps cropping up. They were all first offenders one time."[161] Moreover a *Red River Journal* columnist wrote that he refused to have the prison crisis "stampede me into accepting any additional non-violent, no-hardcore convicts into my neighborhood."[162] By disavowing the idea that "first offenders" and "non-violent" constituted a special class of prisoner, these statements served to undercut the DOC's claims and to reinforce the idea of incarcerated people as always an already dangerous segment of the population in need of confinement. In addition, residents called into question the DOC's promises of only housing "non-violent, first offenders" by declaring that even if a prison was opened as minimum security, "We don't know what kind of institution it might become."[163]

Finally, people protested new prisons on the belief that they would harm their local economy. Overlapping the concern about protecting public safety was the concern of protecting racial capital investments. Homeowners regularly protested the opening of nearby prisons on the grounds that they would lower their property values—implicitly seeking to maintain the principle of racial segregation that underpinned the property relation.[164] Local governing bodies voted against prisons on the grounds that carceral facilities would limit economic development in the city or parish. Officials reiterated concerns that a nearby prison would dissuade companies from opening new businesses and keep tourists from vising their communities.[165] Furthermore, people raised concerns that appropriating millions to prisons reduced the state funds available for social services such as education.[166]

Amplifying the NIMBY response to satellite prisons, numerous people contended that the ideal site for new prison construction was Angola itself. Joining with residents looking to subvert plans for prisons near their homes, several politicians challenged the decentralization plan by arguing for expanding Angola into a mega-prison of 10,000 beds.[167] In one letter to the editor, state senator Paul Forshee wrote that there was already "ample space" to "decentralize" on the grounds of Angola's 18,000 acres and that expanding Angola could potentially enable more of the plantation lands to be cultivated.[168]

Governor Edwards, Elayn Hunt, and other state officials attempted to counter such oppositional rhetoric and actions by shifting the terms of public debate. State officials brought the specter of prison riots into the conversation by reminding the public that if the overcrowded conditions at Angola continued, the state would be primed to have an "Attica situation."[169] Furthermore Hunt appealed to people's sense of civic duty in reiterating that urban satellite prisons were critical for prison reform. They believed that most opposition was based in fear and that as people learned the facts they would welcome prisons.[170] In this spirit, Hunt even suggested making pins that read, "I want a prison in my backyard."[171] The last major pro-prison argument maintained that prisons would provide an economic boost by bringing in jobs and revenue.[172] Through this triad of fearmongering, appeals to good citizenry, and economic incentives, state officials sought to win the consent of the public for decentralization.

Although the state's decentralization arguments did not sway everyone, they did influence segments of the population. Their influence is most visible in the extent to which the major Louisiana newspapers were pro-decentralization. The mainstream media largely reproduced the liberal arguments for decentralization by arguing for the need to disentangle the state from the problems long associated with Angola and insisting on the urgency of meeting the mandates of the court order.[173] Pro-prison letters to the editor contended that bringing a prison to the area would "offer another source of employment, more revenue for the area, help build up the community, and bring in new blood to the area."[174] In some locales, these pro-prison sentiments gained enough traction that people campaigned *for* a prison. In Lafayette, people argued for supporting the building of a rehabilitative prison on reformist grounds, whereas in Bossier City parish officials offered land for a satellite prison to boost the local economy.[175] Although neither site worked out, these offers signaled fissures in what had first appeared as a united, NIMBY bloc.

And even though residents opposed to satellite prisons and pro-decentralization officials and residents publicly clashed, their positions on the prison crisis aligned more than first appeared. Although the "where" and "how" were up for debate, both groups trafficked in the assumption that the primary, if not the only, solution to the court orders was to build out the Louisiana penal system. Whether people were arguing for a larger Angola to keep prisoners out of their backyards or asserting the need to create a decentralized satellite prison system to separate out "classes" of prisoners in the service of rehabilitative programs, all agreed that the principal role of the penal system was to keep criminals from running "loose in the streets."

However, this frame, while dominant, was by no means totalizing. In the free world, a few individuals expressed explicit critiques of incarceration. The primary source of opposition was the Louisiana chapter of the Southern Coalition on Jails and Prison—a grassroots regional organization focused on reforming prison and jail conditions to ensure the rights of prisoners, halting new prison construction, abolishing capital punishment, and developing alternatives to incarceration. A leader of the Louisiana Coalition of Jails and Prisons (LCJP), John Vodicka argued in response to the decentralization debate that "prisons, old or new, small or large, simply don't work. They do not 'rehabilitate.' Instead, prisons brutalize their occupants, deprive those incarcerated of their dignity and self-esteem while at the same time strengthening inmates' criminality. . . . I would rather see Angola quickly decentralized and the states [sic] large penal institutions and jails abolished altogether."[176] For the LCJP, decentralization was a strategy that targeted the fundamental dehumanization of the current penal system.

Inside Angola, incarcerated men also challenged the underlying notion of the decentralization debates—that prisoners were objects to be debated over versus subjects with their own opinions and visions for their future. In their letters to the editor, imprisoned people objected to the fear-mongering portrayals of themselves as nothing more than "mad dog killers, thieves, and rapists."[177] The Angola Lifers' Association pointed out that even the decentralization plan was too narrow because it "says little for the future of the lifers and the men serving long sentences." Its focus on first offenders was not "just one more correctional progress that would pass them by"; it was a strategy that reinforced the state's hierarchal classification of state prisoners that reified long-termers' criminality and foreclosed the possibility of their freedom.[178] Instead, the state needed to approach the overcrowding crisis through a structural analysis that interrogated the interrelationship of skyrocketing incarceration rates and unemployment.[179]

The Struggle to Open Dixon Correctional Institute

Within the back-and-forth of the frenzied prison scramble, the DOC managed to open one new prison in the first year of the court order. The conversion of the East Louisiana State Hospital into Dixon Correctional was an uphill battle that encapsulated the debates surrounding prison proposals.

When the state announced the plan to convert vacant sections of the East Louisiana State Hospital into a prison in July 1975, state officials estimated that the "facilities would be readied to accept 450 to 750 prisoners within 10 days to three weeks."[180] However, the outcry from residents began almost immediately. East Feliciana Parish residents opposed the prison because they believed it would decrease public safety. Given their proximity to Angola, they feared the region would become seen as a "dumping ground" for prisoners that would depress local property values.[181] When local opposition did not impede the DOC's plans, the residents, the Louisiana Association of Mental Health, and the AFL-CIO filed a lawsuit against the DOC. The suit argued that the transfer of prisoners to a hospital violated state law and would be a threat to the hospital's mental health patients.[182] Together with the lawsuit, local officials toyed with the idea of passing new land use regulations to thwart the prison.[183] Yet, at the same time, more than one thousand residents came out in favor of a prison as an economic development strategy.[184] With a split constituency, the police jury chose not to take any steps for or against the prison.[185]

District Judge Bennett issued an injunction against transferring prisoners to vacant buildings at the state hospital and prohibited the governor from financing the conversion without legislative approval.[186] The judge believed it was unconstitutional for the DOC to overspend its budget in times of emergency.[187] He maintained there was no need for a new prison because there was plenty of space at Angola.[188] Central to the ruling was the question of political authority and legitimacy. Who could make decisions about property transfers, what were the rules governing state departments' appropriations, and fundamentally, how much power did the executive branch hold? Whether Bennett's ruling stuck or was overruled was pivotal not only in this case but also to the overall court order. Along with the state's appeal of the injunction, it requested that Judge West intervene in the hopes he could compel the injunction to be lifted.[189] Although West did not press the state courts, he made it known that if the state Supreme Court did not lift the injunction, he would mandate that Governor Edwards call an emergency legislative session on the prison crisis.[190]

Making front-page news, the state Supreme Court overturned the injunction and ruled that it was within the jurisdiction of the governor and the DOC to buy property and for the DOC to use its budget for correctional projects beyond Angola.[191] With the court's blessing, the DOC proceeded with the prison plans.[192] On April 1, 1976, the 400-bed Dixon Correctional Institute opened up as Louisiana's first-ever medium-security prison.[193]

Displacing the Overcrowding Crisis to Jails

Meanwhile, law-and-order legislation and prosecutions exacerbated the overcrowding crisis. When Governor Edwards announced that he had fast-tracked the parole hearings of two hundred prisoners to create bed space, Connick lambasted the plan, writing that the DOC was "more vitally concerned about the problems of criminals in Angola than about the problems caused by criminals to the citizens of this community. This overconcern for the convict is shown by utilizing every conceivable means available—often regardless of the consequences—to release inmates."[194] To delegitimize early release as a potential response to overcrowding, Connick fought Orleans Parish early releases that he deemed a threat to the public.[195] Moreover, new mandatory minimums funneled more Louisianans into the already bloated criminal legal system. Second-degree murder now carried a minimum sentence of forty years, and anyone found guilty of illegally carrying a firearm would be subject to sentences of three to ten years.[196] Sentences that seemed impossible a few years earlier, such as a twenty-three-year-old being sentenced to 150 years for armed robbery, were now commonplace. As one criminal court judge noted, curtailed judicial discretion forced him "to give higher sentences than he thought were just."[197]

The prolonged process of finding sites for new prisons along with law-and-order politicking worsened the overcrowding pressures not only on Angola but also on jails throughout the state. When Governor Edwards declared Angola to be in a state of emergency, he froze any new admissions to the prison. With sheriffs barred from sending sentenced individuals to Angola, jails across the state overflowed. In New Orleans the issue came to a head with the old Orleans Parish Prison holding more than 960 prisoners in a space designed for 450 and the jail's House of Detention having over 30 people sleeping on the floor. To rectify the problem, NOPD superintendent Clarence Giarrusso pushed for city officials to release those imprisoned on misdemeanors.[198] Instead, Lieutenant Governor Fitzmorris amended the previous declaration to allow convicted individuals from Orleans Parish to be locked up at Angola.[199] But this decision was superseded by Judge West, who reiterated that Angola's population must shrink to 2,641.[200] New Orleans Sheriff Foti expressed frustration with this order, claiming that being forced to house state prisoners at the jail would cause multiple problems from increasing its own overcrowding to rising expenses.[201] When OPP's population soared above one thousand, the New Orleans City Council diverted $125,000 from the NOPD's budget to cover the jail's operating costs.[202]

The state could not ignore that jails from Caddo Parish to Lafayette were at or beyond capacity.[203] With sheriffs' agitation growing, the DOC and Judge West offered them the ability to "swap out" prisoners convicted of violent crimes from their jails in exchange for minimum-security prisoners from Angola.[204] This action, although framed as meeting public safety concerns, was just a shell game between the DOC and the parish jail system. It did not resolve the crisis but, as one prison reformer noted, merely "decentralize[d] the problem."[205] As Angola's population neared the mandated cap, the underlying crisis was displaced to parish jails.

With now more than one thousand state prisoners locked up in jails, parish officials pressed the state to provide them with additional financial resources. The Policy Jury Association of Louisiana passed a resolution asking the DOC to reduce its reliance on parish jails and for per diem reimbursements for the state prisoners they were required to hold.[206] Turning around the argument made to localities to build satellite prisons, the association argued to the new DOC secretary C. Paul Phelps[207] that to do anything else could create "another Attica situation." Phelps reiterated that the DOC's next steps depended on the bills passed in the upcoming legislative session.[208] Although the courts permitted the DOC to accept new prisoners at Angola after Dixon was opened, the root problem was still not fixed. Angola was projected to be over capacity again in just a few months.[209]

Thus began the overcrowding cycle that would characterize the Louisiana penal system for the following decades: as prisons filled to capacity, state prisoners would be scattered to parish jails throughout Louisiana while state officials would scramble to find ways to renovate and build out carceral facilities within the federal court's guidelines. For a moment, overcrowding would be contained until the everyday churning of the punitive criminal legal system sent new swaths of the population to prison to begin the cycle anew.

The 1976 Legislative Sessions: Decentralized Growth

As the regular 1976 legislative session began, a bloc of state senators were setting their sights on passing legislation that would give local jurisdictions veto power over prison siting.[210] This goal proved beyond their reach: all they could pass was a "resolution to 'urge and request' the DOC not to expand in any parish without prior support of local governing bodies."[211] Yet the legislature was able to pass a law that required the DOC to appropriate a per diem rate of $4.50 per state prisoner housed in a parish jail for longer than fifteen days.[212] Although this was a lower rate than first proposed, per diems did ease some of the financial pressures on sheriffs for the presumed temporary arrangement.

This new per diem system was just one small piece of a broader budgetary leap for the DOC, whose officials lobbied to increase their operating budget by 50 percent from $29 million to $45 million and to receive $80 million for new prison construction to meet the federal mandates.[213] As in the past several years, the aggrandizement of the DOC budget was financially feasible and aligned with the government's state-building commitments. Despite growing economic pressures caused by rising inflation and declining oil productivity, the state was still benefiting from oil revenue surpluses that were being used not only for the DOC's budget requests but also to expand education, healthcare, welfare, and other social services.[214]

Even more significant than the record growth of the DOC budget was how the capital outlay funds—the state budget dedicated to capital construction—were to be distributed through a "modified decentralization plan." Although state representatives were unable to gain veto power over siting satellite prisons, this did not mean that local opposition was ignored. The state was forced to scale back the decentralization plan. While Edwards announced that the state would "not be able to accomplish one of the primary goals of the decentralization plan—getting prison facilities out of isolated rural areas,"[215] Phelps reported to staff at the *Angolite* that given the high costs of building new prisons, Angola would not be closed as Hunt had championed.[216] Instead, Governor Edwards presented to the legislature a "modified decentralization plan" in which the DOC would add 1,400 beds to Angola to bring its carceral capacity up to 4,000 people while also expanding the Louisiana Correctional Institute for Women and work-release facilities. In addition, three new prisons would be built, one of which would be a diagnostic center to classify prisoners as they entered the penal system, to be named the Elayn Hunt Correctional Center.[217]

The Louisiana Coalition on Jails and Prisons contended that the expansion plan went above what West had mandated. They instead pushed for a moratorium on prison construction, arguing that building new prisons would be a self-defeating reform because they were likely to replicate dehumanizing conditions.[218] Yet such a viewpoint had little influence, and the legislature easily passed the decentralized prison expansion plan. Only a few months later when Judge West ordered the state to move faster, Governor Edwards called an emergency legislative session to approve another 800 beds for Angola.[219] In just a few months, the state increased Louisiana's carceral capacity by 3,876 beds, nearly doubling its prisoner population from 1970.[220]

The 1976 legislative season closed with Louisiana set on a different decentralization path than the one imagined earlier: it did not reduce the state's reliance on incarceration but instead expanded the penal system through decentralization. However, this was not the end of the state's liberal carceral planning. To implement West's order that Louisiana create a comprehensive long-range plan for the penal system, the 1976 legislature created two commissions charged with making reform recommendations for the state: the Governor's Pardon, Parole, and Rehabilitation Commission and the Prison System Study Commission.

Planning Louisiana's Carceral Future

The short-lived Governor's Pardon, Parole, and Rehabilitation Commission (GPPRC) was tasked with analyzing the state's approach to the penal system to provide guidance on how it should be reformed for "effective and workable rehabilitation."[221] Noted prison reformer Reverend James Stovall of Baton Rouge chaired it and set the tenor of its work. For Rev. Stovall, the purpose of the commission was not only to offer recommendations but also to provide a framework for understanding the prison crisis that countered tough-on-crime politics. Mixing psychological and structural arguments, Stovall argued that crime was rooted in persistent racial injustice, violence learned from the Vietnam War, widespread unemployment and underemployment, and disillusionment with the government after Watergate.[222]

The GPPRC pushed for expanding and standardizing probation, parole, and clemency eligibility alongside investing in robust rehabilitation programs. Of central concern was how recent tough-on-crime legislation had restricted probation and parole, thereby limiting prisoners' access to rehabilitative programming.[223] As of July 1977, the state's work-release facilities were largely vacant because of the more stringent requirements.[224] Commission members argued that locking up more people who had fewer opportunities for release subjected an inordinate amount of people to the degrading experience of incarceration, which was both antithetical to rehabilitation and expensive.[225] Their recommendations aligned with DOC secretary C. Paul Phelps's repeated refrain that 50 percent of Louisiana prisoners could be released tomorrow in their recommendations to widen the usage of probation and parole.[226] In 1978 the GPPRC recommended that the state repeal all parole and work-release restrictions and pass a "second offender probation bill" that would allow judges to sentence people convicted of a second felony to probation.[227] Coupled with these proposals were recommendations for greater standardization and regulation of who was deemed fit for parole and clemency. On the heels of a scandal linked to Governor Edwards that the pardon board was making backroom deals with prisoners' attorneys, the GPPRC advocated for the parole and pardon board to adopt new guidelines modeled after the US Parole Commissions point system that used a formula that quantified "risk factors" so that parole decisions were not based on political connections or arbitrary feelings.[228] Yet the GPPRC was not interested in eradicating parole limitations entirely. Insofar as parole officials followed standard procedures, the GPPRC agreed they were legitimated to decide whether someone should live and die behind bars. Furthermore, they proposed the creation of supervised clemency, which was similar to parole, in which the state could *revoke* one's commutation.[229]

The GPPRC was unable to make meaningful headway on even these moderate recommendations. Arguing it was already exceedingly difficult to send someone to Angola, the Louisiana District Attorneys Association asserted that its prisoners therefore had to be the worst offenders and as such "can never be rehabilitated."[230] Therefore, rehabilitation was an unachievable goal, leaving, "only the objectives of deterrence, incapacitation, and punishment as viable functions of the system."[231] The association advocated that the state legislature not only keep current restrictions on parole and probation eligibility but also *extend* restrictions so that people only became eligible for parole after serving two-thirds of their sentence, instead of the current standard of one-third time.[232] Recognizing the forces aligned against them, GPPRC members pivoted their attention to recidivism. They proposed creating a new community-based "clearinghouse" for formerly incarcerated persons in the greater New Orleans area as a hub for reentry services that would help alleviate barriers to employment for formerly incarcerated people.[233] Even this project was unable to come to fruition, with the legislature unwilling to earmark $130,000 for the clearinghouse from the DOC's $80 million 1979–1980 budget.[234] Not a single GPPRC recommendation became law.

Concurrently, the Louisiana Prison System Study Commission developed a twenty-five-year master plan for the state's penal system.[235] This generally liberal commission, active from 1976–1980, included Democratic and Republication state legislators, civil rights leaders, prison reform activists, and DOC officials, with staff support from the New York City-based Ehrenkrantz Group and the Wharton School of Business.[236] Funded primarily through LEAA grants, the commission was charged with studying the Louisiana penal system and recommending a plan for Louisiana's carceral future to meet the federal court's mandates and avoid future lawsuits.[237]

The commission unveiled its final report in May 1978. In a move somewhat rare in the technocratic planning world, the report began with an historical assessment of the current crisis within a longer arc of Louisiana's prison crises. Whereas "historical austerity as a rule"[238] produced previous crises, the current crisis was marked by the increasing costs of the skyrocketing penal population. It noted that in 1973 the Louisiana prison population stood at 3,550, which had nearly doubled at the time of the report to almost 7,000. If current trends continued, Louisiana would face "a shortage of at least 1,100 beds by 1982, despite the recent expenditures of $165 million to create new facilities" and raise the number of state prison beds to 8,500. Therefore, the goal of their study was "to reduce the costs associated with this growth without additional risk to the public."[239]

The grammar that the prison population *will grow* critically structured the commission's assessment of future possible reforms. As Judah Schept has shown, the discourses that surround carceral planning projects are not merely descriptive but also create "the certainty that it purportedly reflects."[240] The commission's grammar of growth illuminates that its orientation was not to shrink or even maintain the current prison population but instead how to plan for "controlled prison growth" in the face of what was deemed as an otherwise uncontrollable future.[241]

To this end, the Prison System Study Commission outlined five options for the Louisiana penal system. First was the "Continuation of Current Practices," which presumed that the current functioning of the DOC was adequate and could continue.²⁴² Second was the "Continuum of Care," which would introduce a more rigid classification system of prisoners and carceral facilities from maximum-security prisons to prerelease institutions. Underlying this option was the idea that a more stratified classification system based on behavior and time to release would promote rehabilitation and reduce costs.²⁴³ The third option offered was the "Parish Participation System" under which the DOC would contract with local jurisdictions to develop a community-based carceral system. "Less serious offenders" would be imprisoned in "local prisons," and more "serious offenders" would be kept secure in existing state prisons.²⁴⁴ Fourth was "Alternatives to Incarceration," which would increase financial sanctions and the size of supervision programs. The enlargement of such a shadow carceral apparatus over "total incarceration" would save tax dollars and better serve the reintegration of "offenders" into law-abiding society.²⁴⁵ The fifth option the commission explored was "Curtailment of Construction" that would set "a ceiling on the future construction of state correctional facilities, relying instead on planned alternatives."²⁴⁶

After assessing the "cost" and "risk" of these plans, the commission recommended the Continuum of Care, Alternatives to Incarceration, and the Parish Participation System options as fitting with their commitments to liberal reformism. It maintained that the Continuation of Current Practices had proven to be expensive and failed to provide enough sufficient controls and that the Curtailing of Construction, although cost saving, was not flexible enough to accommodate future prison growth.²⁴⁷ In contrast, the Continuum of Care option aligned with national trends to reform prisons through greater administrative categorization and standardization, whereas the Alternatives to Incarceration approach's emphasis on expanding probation matched the goals of the state's reformist DOC officials while also being vague and capacious enough to be broadly agreeable.²⁴⁸

Of all the plans outlined, the Prison System Study Commission most vigorously advocated for the Parish Participation System. Over the next year, the commission, along with the GPPRC, advocated for passage of the Community Corrections Act that would create a state-subsidized, parish jail-based correctional system in the spirit of the initial decentralization proposal. Their lobbying brochure, "Solving the Prison Problem: A Way to Save $48 Million and Avoid Court Orders," detailed how the Community Corrections Act would "allow the state to shape the future of corrections, free from pressures of overcrowding, spiraling costs, and court orders" by modernizing jails with state funds to house state prisoners while keeping them under local control. This would, in turn, reduce pressure to build new state prisons and save taxpayers' dollars.[249] Moreover, with an increasing number of parish jails under their own court orders, the commission believed this plan would bring both the DOC and jail system back into compliance.[250] Despite the commission's efforts, however, the Community Corrections Act did not pass. Instead, the state allocated $30 million for new jail construction for those parishes under court orders.[251]

The narrowness of the Prison System Study Commission's report is noteworthy given glimpses throughout its final report of what a broader analysis might have offered. Scattered throughout the report are remarks concerning the disproportionate incarceration of Black people and rising unemployment rates, hinting that the growth of the prison population might be due to structural factors and not individual pathologies.[252] Contradictory analyses can be seen in the report's discussion of law breaking. While the commission warned that draconian laws contributed to the growth of the prison population, the criminal justice "offender flow diagram," intended to show readers the process through which someone ends up in prison, begins with "the incident" (as when a crime is witnessed) without any mention of the political process under which a behavior is labeled a crime. The commission simultaneously naturalized what constituted a crime *and* pointed to the political production of criminal punishment.[253]

Indeed, the commission's analysis of prison growth primarily relied on statistical modeling of demographic shifts in relation to age.[254] Prison growth was misconstrued as a natural phenomenon rather than as a product of political, economic, and social conditions created by people's decisions. As Clyde Woods has written, "This is one of the characteristic features of positivism as a methodology" in that "policy can be advocated solely on the basis of statistical correlations. . . . Issues such as social, economic, and cultural justice are categorically excluded, and policy recommendations become just as random and subjective as the variables selected."[255] The commission's methodological choices were shaped and motivated by their own overarching goals. Their impetus and sense of urgency were not grounded in the plight of incarcerated people but instead in making the Louisiana prison system financially sustainable and politically viable.

By the close of the 1970s, both commissions had run their course. Taken together they illustrate the persistent limitations of liberal reformism and the increasing difficulty of getting liberal reforms through the legislature. On the one hand were the foreclosed imaginations of the members of both commissions, which prevented them from seeing that those deemed criminal could be released outside of a parole or probation system. To the members, formerly imprisoned people needed supervisory rehabilitation that could only be conducted through a "community" or shadow carceral apparatus. Decarceration was inconceivable for both commissions. On the other hand, external pressures not only in the form of the antagonism of state legislators but also in how the scope of their work was defined limited the commissions. As the Louisiana Prison Study Commission noted in its report, the prison system is "only one component at the end of the line in the criminal justice system, and therefore at the mercy of conditions dictated by other components in the system."[256] The siloing of what constituted legitimate areas for these bodies to interrogate profoundly limited both commissions' recommendations, even when they gestured to racial injustice and unemployment as playing a role in the Louisiana prison crisis.

Even though these commissions were formed a few years after the initial court ruling, in many respects they were already too late on the scene. As prisoners writing for the *Angolite* asserted, there was little hope that these bodies' recommendations could lead to transformative reforms because the state had already made its choices clear by planning new prisons and deciding to "pour $40 million into making Angola the biggest penitentiary in the nation—BEFORE the Commission even studies the problem, let alone arrive at any conclusions. Apparently, the legislature has already made up its collective mind as to what course corrections is to take, regardless of what the Commission comes up with."[257]

· · · · · ·

The 1970s marked a watershed moment in the Louisiana penal system. The accumulated pressures and contradictions of the liberal racial state produced a qualitatively different carceral crisis than that which had characterized Angola during the first decades of the twentieth century. The end result was the decentralization of the penal crisis in Louisiana's new prisons and dozens of parish jails facilitated by massive revenue surpluses generated from the 1970s global oil crisis.

The carceral ideologies underpinning both liberal reformism and tough-on-crime politics shaped Louisiana's path to unprecedented carceral state-building. Just as significant as the rise and solidification of law-and-order ideology in state politics over the course of the decade was how the liberalism embedded in the decentralization plan and the federal court orders reified the necessity of imprisonment. Even though both Magistrate Polozola and Judge West were aghast at conditions at Angola, the federal court rulings were anchored in liberal individualist conceptions of violence and were only concerned with aligning the penal system with constitutional standards. The court's interventions were not only unable but also uninterested in either undoing carceral logics or competing with the rising tide of law-and-order politics. Solely verifying the existence of everyday carceral violence does not equate to alleviating said violence. Indeed, state-sanctioned punitive violence rooted in racist and patriarchal approaches to "safety" was extended through the court's facilitation of the penal system's growth and mandating that new punitive practices from shakedowns to queer segregation be implemented at Angola and elsewhere. Moreover, proponents of the decentralization plan and the rehabilitative ideal trafficked in similar individualistic framings of crime and violence in their repeated fetishization of classification systems and their production of the figure of the "first offender" as the primary, if not only, prisoner capable of rehabilitation and release. Perhaps most importantly, in advocating for decentralization primarily on geographic terms—the need for prisons to be in urban arenas and built on a smaller scale—rather than on ethical grounds against the structural violence of imprisonment, the plan was able to be converted to an argument for housing state prisoners in parish jails. The debates on the prison crisis between liberal prison reformers and those tough on crime left little space to consider decarceration or other alternatives to carceral state-building. The solutions to "fix" the Louisiana prison crisis hinged not on imagining a freer world but on imagining and planning for carceral futures.

Back at Angola where the crisis first emerged, prisoners were still busy finding new avenues to freedom. Reforms were in full swing with renovations afoot to ease overcrowding. More than three hundred prison guards and scores of medical personnel were added to the prison's staff.[258] Official interpersonal violence was down with stabbings and killings among prisoners at a record low. To many, the federal mandates were a definitive success, yet the fundamental structural violence of incarceration remained. The modernization of security from the purchase of walkie-talkies to the creation of tactical squads further hindered escape attempts.[259] Queer and nonheteronormative prisoners throughout the prison system were subject to intensified surveillance and segregation in the name of protecting heterosexual prisoners from sexualized violence.[260] Of the 1,400 beds added onto Angola, 200 were dedicated to Camp J, a maximum-security solitary camp that replaced the notorious Red Hat solitary cellblock where Mitchell and Hayes were first sent after their escape attempt. The Angola administration opened Camp J earlier than planned and filled it to capacity in the summer of 1977 to break a 700-plus prisoner work stoppage protesting the state legislature's seemingly unending passage of tough-on-crime laws and the ongoing assaults on pardon and parole.[261] Despite the media coverage of the strike and the clear retributive deployment of Camp J, the federal courts had no comment.[262]

Yet while the disciplinary turn to solitary broke the strike, it did not break people's commitment to freedom. Even as the 1980s witnessed the further entrenchment of tough-on-crime politics, prisoners at Angola did not give up but instead collectivized their struggles as they devised new strategies to curb the violence of the Louisiana carceral state.

2   Consolidating and Contesting Law-and-Order Austerity

. . . .

The extent of violent crime today makes swift and sure punishment even more important than ever before. We will do everything we can to give law enforcement officers the tools they need to crack down on lawlessness in our communities.

—Governor Dave Treen, speech to Louisiana Sheriffs' Association, 1982

As the year 1982 progressed, Louisiana, one of the wealthiest states in the nation only two years before, found itself running out of money to meet state operating expenses. With the state relying upon its domestic oil and gas industry for 40 percent of its revenue, the flow of dollars into its tax coffers dropped dramatically. Continuing federal budget cuts only compounded the shortage of revenue. The lack of sufficient monies soon impacted state governmental operations, forcing Governor Treen to impose a hiring freeze on new state employees. That wouldn't be enough. By Fall 1982, the state's unemployment compensation system bankrupted from the sheer weight of having to pay out benefits to so many jobless Louisianans.

—*Angolite*, 1983

We don't want to run the pen. We want to leave the pen!

—Kenneth "Biggy" Johnston

When a New Orleans district attorney charged Hayes Williams with murder and armed robbery in 1967, his lawyer advised him to take a plea bargain to avoid the death penalty. Williams did not want to plead guilty for offenses he did not commit, but his lawyer assured his family that, if he did so, he would not serve longer than ten years and six months. By the time he told his story to the *Angolite* in 1991, he had been imprisoned at Angola for twenty-three years. "None of us realized the way the Louisiana criminal justice system actually works," he said, "so my mother begged me to plead guilty. I still can't ever say no to my mother."[1] Even then, he was unsure whether he would ever again walk out the prison gates.

By doubling down on state racism and passing harsher sentencing laws throughout the 1980s, the legislature spurred rapid growth in the number of people being locked up. In 1978 the Louisiana Prison System Study Commission predicted that the state's prison population would hit 9,600 by 1982.[2] Yet by 1982 the state's incarceration of its residents not only surpassed this prediction but by the decade's end the Louisiana Department of Public Safety & Corrections (DPSC) locked up 17,343 people.[3] By 1990 over two thousand people in Louisiana were serving a life sentence without parole, constituting 18.4 percent of people serving such a sentence nationwide. With an additional two thousand people serving a sentence long enough to be tantamount to life, close to one-quarter of those in the Louisiana penal system had little hope of release in their lifetime.[4] Whereas the *Angolite* once referred to "long-termers" and "lifers" as those serving more than ten years, throughout the 1980s multidecade sentences and death by imprisonment became commonplace—serving as a reminder that what has been defined as a long or even life sentence is not a given but has shifted over time.[5] Even Louisiana's 1990 Governor's Corrections Plan noted that this jump in state incarceration rates could only be "partially explained by increases in the state crime rate," raising the question: What else propelled this punitive surge?[6] Answering that question is the goal of this chapter.

During the 1980s, law-and-order politics and policies replaced liberal prison reform. With the watchwords of the day switching from "rehabilitation" and "reform" to "lawlessness" and "punishment," state officials consolidated punitive state governance. Key to the ballooning of the Louisiana prison population during this decade were lengthened prison sentences, restrictions placed on parole and good time, and the law-and-order politicization of clemency.

Neoliberal state realignments were central to this intensification and legitimization of tough-on-crime policies, which hinged on the adoption of austerity politics by law-and-order Republican governor David Treen after the global oil slump. Global oil price hikes of the 1970s and early 1980s had buffered Louisiana from the national recession. But when mineral taxes plummeted, they combined with an ideological refusal to raise taxes on the rich to produce a statewide economic crisis marked by skyrocketing unemployment and massive reductions in state services. This shaped the conditions under which state officials chose certain paths over others.

Under the mandates of the federal courts, the DOC was protected from austerity measures. In fact, to accelerate carceral expansion, Treen directed the remaining funds from the beleaguered state budget into the penal system beyond what was required to meet the demands of the federal courts.[7] Carceral state-building was the one arena where so-called fiscal responsibility was trumped as state monies and institutional capacities were redirected from life-affirming polices such as education and flood protections to the death-dealing programs of punitive infrastructures. State authorities implemented new methods of debt financing to sidestep democratic opposition to penal state enhancements.

The suturing of social wage disinvestments to punitive state investments structurally remade the racial capitalist state in ways that endured far beyond Treen's 1979–1983 tenure. His promotion of law-and-order austerity through leveraging economic crisis to push forth draconian policies mirrored similar state realignments nationally and helped produce this shift to the "anti-state state" across political levels.[8] This reworking of state capacities was legitimized through racist gendered narratives that portrayed white women as victims who needed to be protected from Black men who were threats to be contained. Tracking the interchange between carceral developments and capitalist organized abandonment reveals how Louisiana penal expansion at this conjuncture served to target and contain Black communities, which were rendered as surplus labor via the oil bust through intensified imprisonment. At the same time, reductions in state services in favor of law-and-order infrastructure imperiled almost all Louisianans.

The passage of tough-on-crime legislation and the ballooning of the state's penal system were not quietly accepted. Incarcerated people at Angola found themselves subjected to harsher sentencing laws that almost completely foreclosed the possibility of release. Refusing to give up their dreams of freedom, imprisoned activists formed the Angola Special Civics Project. In contrast to earlier incarcerated organizers who were primarily concerned with changing conditions within Angola, organizers with the Civics Project focused on finding avenues out of the prison altogether. Through a combination of research, political education, electoral organizing, and coalition-building, Civics Project members leveraged the dialectical interplay of political threats and opportunities to attain new mechanisms for early release. The Civics Project's collective struggle for freedom illuminates how an era of crisis can be turned into an era of possibility.

Accelerating Law and Order: The Treen Administration

The Louisiana 1979 gubernatorial election was both symptomatic of and propelled a rightward realignment of state power. The field was wide open with ten candidates running: eight Democrats, one Republican, and one Socialist. At first, there was no clear front-runner. Under the Louisiana nonpartisan open primary system, an unlimited number of individuals are eligible to run under any party and win the election outright by securing more than 50 percent of the vote. If no one receives a majority, the two candidates who receive the most votes enter a runoff election, regardless of the political parties they occupy. The 1979 election was the first time this election format had been used in a governor's race without an incumbent.[9]

The Louisiana Republican Party leveraged this electoral structure to capture state power for the first time since the disputed 1872 Louisiana governor's race and the subsequent dismantling of Reconstruction.[10] Tapped for this political moment was David Treen, a US congressman from the New Orleans suburb of Metairie, the primary conservative base of the state.[11] Treen had chaired the Louisiana States' Rights Party in the early 1960s and had mounted a gubernatorial campaign against Edwards in 1972.[12] Part of the New Right's multiscalar strategy to slowly but surely build political power and influence, Treen ran on pro-business fiscal conservatism, along with pledges to work with the predominantly Democratic state legislature.[13] In direct contrast to the flamboyant personalities of Louisiana's famously populist politicians from Huey Long to Edwin Edwards, Treen cultivated a reserved and distant persona while mobilizing conservatives.[14] With Treen winning the most votes but not achieving a majority in the primary, the second spot in the runoff was hotly contested by a recount between centrist Lieutenant Governor James Fitzmorris and pro-labor Louis Lambert, who was backed by the state's Black political organizations.[15] By the time Lambert secured a place in the runoff, Treen had already built significant support. In the final election, Treen squeaked out a win with less than a 9,000- vote lead over Lambert.[16]

The Louisiana carceral crisis was reconceptualized during this election cycle. Previous concerns regarding overcrowding were transformed into a crisis of public safety. Although the recent prison expansions had relieved some pressure, the state's unceasing carceral machinery ensured that conditions would remain crowded.[17] Even though the DOC was the fifth-largest sector of the state's budget, every gubernatorial candidate campaigned to increase carceral funding. Whether promising new prisons or more law enforcement, candidates overwhelmingly cast themselves as tough-on-crime, with the pardoning process coming to the fore for criticism.[18] While most candidates focused on eliminating impropriety, Treen reframed the issue as the overuse of pardons and pledged that, if elected governor, clemency would become "quite rare."[19]

Punitive Governance

Treen's promise troubled prisoners at Angola who already were concerned by the hardening of prison sentences during the 1970s.[20] Historically, the Louisiana prison system was lenient in its early release guidelines.[21] From 1886 until 1914, individuals with life sentences were eligible for release after serving fifteen years in prison. In 1916, the legislature created the Board of Parole and gave it the authority to parole lifers after a minimum of five years in prison.[22] Beginning in 1926, the Board of Pardons automatically reviewed all people incarcerated with a life sentence for a pardon after serving ten and a half years.[23] Although release was conditioned on approval by the prison's general manager (later the warden), in practice those serving life sentences with good behavior could count on being released under the "10/6" law.[24] In a 1971 ruling converting a death row prisoner's sentence to life imprisonment, Louisiana Supreme Court justice Joe Sanders stated that a life sentence "really means imprisonment for only ten years and six months. No true life sentence exists in Louisiana."[25] Incoming prisoners carried this understanding of the law. According to Kenneth "Biggy" Johnston, it was "understood that you do ten years and six months on life" when he was sentenced to life in prison in 1972.[26] Yet, after a few years of state legislators chipping away at what had been standard Louisiana legal practice for a half-century, Johnston soon found himself, like hundreds around him, locked away for more than twenty years and counting.

On June 29, 1972, the US Supreme Court abolished the death penalty, voiding all death sentences across the nation. In response, the Louisiana Supreme Court resentenced all former death row prisoners to life imprisonment.[27] Fearful of the political ramifications of paroling former death row prisoners, the Louisiana legislature began to restrict parole eligibility during the 1973 legislative session. Then it eliminated the automatic pardon review at ten years and six months from the new 1974 Louisiana constitution, implementing a more stringent review process. In 1979, the Louisiana legislature repealed the "10/6 law" with retroactive effect—making Louisiana one of the first states in the nation to solely use so-called natural life or "life without parole" in life sentencing.[28] At the same time, New Orleans DA Harry Connick mobilized his Career Criminal Bureau staff to recommend that the parole board deny releases. Connick credited the program with the drastic decrease in paroles granted to so-called repeat offenders from Orleans Parish from 42.5 to 10.7 percent throughout the 1970s.[29] Pardons from the governor were now the primary mechanism to attain freedom for a growing number of incarcerated Louisianans.

Treen kept his promise. Even as prisons and jails were bursting at the seams, Treen instituted an unofficial moratorium on clemency in his first year in office.[30] The following year he granted nine commutations in response to criticism.[31] This was in sharp contrast to Edwards who had granted clemency to 2,218 people between 1972 and 1980.[32] As former Angola lifer Norris Henderson recalled, "Nobody's moving cause everybody's following the mandate of the governor," fueling hopelessness.[33] In addition, Treen's Governor's Commission on Criminal Justice championed an extensive anticrime package for the 1981 legislative session. The legislative package included millions of dollars to accelerate adult and juvenile prison construction and to enlarge the state police so it could target drugs. The commission also recommended making bail more difficult to obtain and parole easier to revoke. As noted by the *Angolite*, "The proposals face[d] little opposition" and easily passed the legislature.[34]

In addition, Treen reinforced and multiplied carceral cooperation initiatives across the state. Early into his governorship he developed a new multiagency initiative involving sheriffs, state police, and municipal police to combat the vice crimes of drugs, gambling, and, in particular, to crack down on, sex work from rural St. Landry Parish to the French Quarter.[35] Perhaps most noteworthy was Treen's creation of a new source of state criminal justice aid after the LEAA was disbanded: this agency, which had funneled millions of tax dollars into law enforcement expansion during the late 1960s and 1970s, had been declared a failure at the federal level and so was phased out.[36] To replace the LEAA, Treen initiated a program to aid local criminal justice systems as part of his 1981 anticrime legislative package. In its first year, the program issued $2.5 million to localities to expand criminal justice initiatives.[37] What had once been an experiment in punitive state enlargement had become established as an essential element of state governance.

The Treen administration's expansion of punitive policies was mirrored in the hardening of a more punitive regime within state prisons. Even though the liberal reformers running the state's penal system under Edwards did not eradicate the brutality and bleakness of the state's punishment regime, they did offer a modicum of checks against the vindictive policies and practices that had previously governed the state prison system.[38] For instance

DOC secretary C. Paul Phelps directly petitioned Treen to veto "excessive" sentences passed by the legislature on the grounds that they would exacerbate overcrowding.[39] After getting consistent pushback from Phelps, Treen replaced him with John T. King, a businessman-turned state bureaucrat.[40] When questioned about his credentials for this position, King asserted that his business background provided more than enough experience: "The principles of management are the same whether you're making chocolate chip cookies or incarcerating people."[41]

King tightened up control in the prisons, including curtailing the freedom of press that the *Angolite* staff had benefited from since 1976 under the framework of the rehabilitative ideal.[42] In the words of *Angolite* editor Wilbert Rideau, "The new regime restricted content on all prison publications. Department of Corrections headquarters shut off its flow of information to the *Angolite*, canceled equipment purchases, curtailed supply orders, and put our staff under investigation."[43] Although King partially restored the newspaper staff's editorial power, cutting its budget by 40 percent limited its scope. Additionally, Angola warden Maggio prohibited the Louisiana Coalition of Jails and Prisons (LCJP) newsletter "Inside" on the grounds that its coverage of a prisoner work slowdown was "inflammatory" and encouraged prisoners to unionize. This decision was upheld by Polozola who had been appointed to replace Judge West.[44] These actions, combined with the assaults on parole and clemency, produced a period of hopelessness and attendant violence among incarcerated people.

Outside the prison walls, New Orleans officials simultaneously stoked and took advantage of residents' fears of rising crime to increase urban law-and-order.[45] New Orleans politicians urged the hiring of armed security guards in public housing and deploying state police in the city to buttress the NOPD.[46] The state poured funds into expanding the Youth Study Center, the euphemistically named Orleans Parish juvenile detention center, at the same time as it withheld federal funds from youth jobs programs.[47] These moves were championed not only by conservatives but also by liberals and progressives including New Orleans's first Black mayor, Ernest "Dutch" Morial, and even some civil rights activists as tough-on-crime politics came to dominate what constituted public safety in the political imaginary.

The expansion of criminalization was embedded in the demands of the New Orleans tourist economy. After the racial integration of public schools and federal subsidization of suburban development, New Orleans, like cities across the nation, experienced a significant outflow of white middle-class residents from the city to the surrounding suburbs in the 1960s. This white flight was not only preceded by a capital flight but also intensified it. The shrinking white middle class corresponded to a shrinking tax base for the city—leaving the municipal government cash-strapped. With manufacturing and shipping jobs in decline, city officials and elites turned to tourism as the primary economic development strategy.[48] Even though city leaders had been promoting tourism since soon after World War II, it was not until the 1970s and 1980s that New Orleans was remade as principally a tourist economy. The city invested major tax dollars in tourist infrastructure from the construction of mega-projects such as the New Orleans Convention Center to the branding and commodification of local Black culture.[49] During the early 1980s, the city and state appropriated tens of millions of dollars to razing and remaking the city's Warehouse District for the 1984 Louisiana World's Fair, a major tourist gentrification project that boosters hoped would be an economic boom not only for New Orleans but also for the state.[50] The projection of the city's image as a friendly and safe place to visit became paramount.

News circulating that New Orleans was rife with street violence was cause for concern not only in the abstract but also when it led convention groups to cancel their meetings. For example, the Chemical Manufacturers Association called off its conference due to "extreme concern for the public safety of our members and guests."[51] Mayor Dutch Morial prioritized more cops walking the streets, raising the NOPD budget from $36.3 million in 1978 to $53.4 million in 1982, while DA Harry Connick worked with the NOPD to increase policing in advance of the 1984 Louisiana World's Fair.[52] These policing efforts were just one example of how the city enlarged law enforcement resources to assuage moral crime panics, even as the city's official crime rate was actually in decline during the early 1980s.[53]

Parish Jails as the Overcrowding Fix, Again

These punitive measures further entrenched the crisis of prison and jail overcrowding. Overcrowding had become such a norm that the brief periods when the system was *not* overcrowded became newsworthy.[54] Even as the state built three new prisons, with a fourth in the works and more than a thousand beds added to prisons since the Fifth Circuit upheld Judge West's 1975 ruling, draconian sentencing enhancements meant that overcrowded conditions continued to plague the DOC. For instance, Dixon, the first new prison opened in response to the court orders, quickly became overcrowded. Although designed based on the decentralization model of 500-bed rehabilitation-focused prisons, by the spring of 1982, Dixon imprisoned 823 people. To make space for an additional dormitory, prison administrators sacrificed the prison library.[55] *Angolite* journalists argued against popular claims that the swelling prison population was due to rising crime and that the only fix was prison expansion. They outlined that the skyrocketing number of people locked up was due to mandatory sentences and the curbing of parole and pardons. They urged Louisiana to follow the lead of states, such as Texas, that were turning to mass parole to resolve their own overcrowding crises.[56]

Instead of early release, however, the state opted to lean even harder on the parish jail system. To the dismay of sheriffs, the number of state prisoners held in jails grew to 1,100 by 1980. Even with the state increasing the per diem payment for housing state prisoners from $4.50 to $18.25 per day, sheriffs were not satisfied. They argued that jails were not designed to house people serving extended sentences, and even if they were, they did not have the space.[57] The strain imposed by jailing state prisoners worsened already deplorable jail conditions that had been marked by rampant premature deaths. Prisoners filed dozens of lawsuits against jails, leading to jail after jail being placed under court orders.[58] The sheriffs' ire came to a head in the spring of 1980 when Orleans Parish sheriff Charles Foti sent buses containing 150 state prisoners to the newly opened Hunt Correctional Center and left them in its parking lot.[59]

Sheriff Foti's stunt, together with the court orders, propelled the state to innovate the "70/30 program" for financing jail expansion.[60] At first, Treen convinced Judge Polozola to increase the state prisons' population limits to reduce the number of people in jails, which also served to "send a message to judges . . . that they can give criminals maximum sentences without concern of [overcrowding]."[61] But this was not enough. Treen worked with the legislature to create a mechanism to fund parish jails' renovations and expansions. The state would cover 70 percent of the capital costs for new jail construction, while parishes would cover the remaining 30 percent either through general obligation bonds, cash on hand, or "soft matches," such as providing the land for new jails. This arrangement shifted the primary financial responsibility for capital costs from the local level to the state, which enabled parishes to move ahead on jail construction without taking on debt. It also enabled sheriffs to avoid local votes on bond measures that had the potential to spur opposition to building new jails. In the program's first year, $35 million was earmarked from the state's capital outlay budget for ten of the parish jails under court orders.⁶² Within a year of the program, the Louisiana Sheriff's Association petitioned Treen to expand Angola again *and* for additional state aid for new jails.⁶³ In 1981, the state legislature appropriated another $38.5 million for jail building in eleven more parishes to make a total of twenty-one parishes, or one-third of Louisiana parishes, participating in the 70/30 program.⁶⁴

The source of much of this money for jail building was the state's spiking oil revenues. After a few years of slight declines, the 1979 oil shock produced another petro revenue windfall. The increased valuation of oil led to a rush of new leases on oil lands, producing a boom in revenue from signing bonuses in the early 1980s.⁶⁵ Treen decided that, rather than appropriating the funds to the social wage, they would be better put to use in carceral state-making. All oil bonuses that exceeded projections were allocated to parish jail construction.⁶⁶ Additionally, oil and gas revenues held in the state's mineral income trust fund were earmarked in 1981 to extend lines of credit to capital construction projects, which were largely for carceral construction.⁶⁷ Hence, the 70/30 program allowed localities to avoid incurring significant debt while still building new jails, and oil revenues provided the means for the state to continue to build jails and prisons with limited concern for their costs.

Within just two years, Governor Treen had significantly intensified the Louisiana punishment regime. Even as imprisoned *Angolite* writers pushed back against criminalizing tough-on-crime narratives and the LCJP argued that shiny new jail renovations would do nothing to end the atrocities of imprisonment, the law-and-order framework continued to gain ground. The Treen administration's commitment to punishment was exemplified by comments made to President Reagan's staff on the success of Treen's criminal justice program. Treen's investment in the carceral arm of the state was made "not out of a desire to make life easier for these convicts, but to make sure that no judge feels compelled to release somebody back into society who should not be there just because prisons are overcrowded."⁶⁸ This commitment would prove unshakable even as Louisiana faced an unprecedented fiscal crisis.

Oil Booms and Busts, Prison Booms and Booms

Falling oil prices in 1982 drove the state into a tailspin. Oil revenues had shielded Louisiana from the national recession during the 1970s, but its reliance on oil revenues left the state particularly vulnerable to the 1982 recession.[69] Following Reagan's deregulation of the oil industry in 1981, Louisiana's oil and gas severance tax revenue hit the then all-time high of $803,146,949. But oil prices quickly began to fall from a high of $70 a barrel in 1981 to $29 a barrel in 1983 in response to a growing oil glut caused by overproduction and shrinking demand.[70] Having overestimated revenues for the first time in years, the state suddenly faced a massive revenue shortfall.

Despite state bureaucrats warning for years of the impending end to this oil boom, the state had become more, not less, dependent on the petrochemical economy. Similar to the economic development tendencies of oil-producing nation-states worldwide, Louisiana's political economy had become sutured to and narrowed by the oil economy. Because of the high rate of capital accumulation possible through the commodification of energy sources and the accompanying high rates of revenue via taxes on related industries, neither private interests nor the Louisiana government had prioritized other forms of economic development.[71] Between 1973 and 1983 one-third to one-half of the state's revenues came from mineral taxes.[72]

The precarity of Louisiana tying its political economy to the volatile commodity of oil, rather than diversifying its economic base, was exacerbated by the rise of New Right antitax politics. On entering office, Treen championed a flat 30 percent personal income tax cut. Even though this tax reform, modeled on the national Kemp-Roth Bill, was promoted as a gain to all, in actuality it ensured that the rich were the primary benefactors, while the state as a whole lost $100 million in revenue in the tax cut's first year alone.[73] This reduction in state revenue was soon joined on the national level by Reagan's Economic Recovery Tax Act of 1981, the largest tax cut in US history, along with Reagan's cuts to the federal revenue-sharing program with state and local governments, which produced alarming contractions in the Louisiana budget.[74] Treen seized the crisis as an opportunity for austerity.

Carceral Growth amidst Austerity

Even though Treen ran on a platform of fiscal conservatism, so long as the state was flush, it was hard to justify substantial cuts to state services, given the widespread support of state expansion that had occurred under his predecessor Edwin Edwards. When the state started scrambling for resources, however, Treen leveraged the economic crisis to restructure the state toward neoliberal ends. Treen cut $270 million from the state budget in the 1982 legislative session, affecting almost every state department, including a 25 percent cut to the Department of Labor.[75] Upon further deficits and the state's unemployment compensation program going broke, Treen called a special legislative session while also issuing an executive order for 4.4 percent cuts across the board.[76] Treen's actions were shaped by a 1974 state constitution prohibition on deficit spending.[77]

The following year proved even more dire. For the first time since World War II, Louisiana "suffered a decline in revenue collections from prior years."[78] As outlined in the 1983–1984 executive budget, Louisiana's falling revenues were tied both to shifts in the global oil market and to national economic restructuring: increasingly, "employment and economic activity is being absorbed by the service sector while the 'smokestack' industries cannot provide the same number of jobs they once did."[79] With escalating unemployment and the lowest per capita income in the nation, Treen did not attempt to raise revenue or marshal resources to buffer the devastation the recession was having on people's lives. Instead, Treen cut another $120 million from critical state services in 1983.[80] These policy measures ensured that what had begun as a fiscal crisis would become a manufactured economic crisis.

Yet, carceral state-building was the one arena in which so-called fiscal responsibility did not apply. The DOC did not suffer cuts but rather received a 23 percent budgetary boost during the first years of the recession.[81] Its persistent prioritization over other state departments was shaped both by the mandates of Judge Polozola that prohibited the state from cutting certain DOC baselines *and* the pro-prison politics of Treen. When revenue shortages first became apparent, Treen announced that the state would not finance any new local projects, including the 70/30 jail program, because of the Federal Reserve's sky-high interest rates following the Volcker Shock.[82] Unable to afford new penal construction, the DOC implemented double bunking—doubling the number of prisons in cells and dormitories—even though the practice went against the court's mandates. When Polozola learned of this action, he unleashed his rage at Treen and King.[83] Treen dismissed Polozola's concern that overcrowding would increase prison violence, arguing that "these are criminals, people convicted of violent crimes. The taxpayers of the state should not give them such perfect protection that nothing is going to happen to the prisoners."[84]

Prisoners pushed back against double-bunking as a dehumanizing practice that demonstrated the state's disregard for incarcerated life. Michael Savoy, locked up in the Louisiana Correctional and Industrial School, sued the state for "forcing as many as 60 prisoners to be housed in units designed for 45."[85] The *Angolite* asserted the state's creation of "an institutional environment conducive to violence on the official premise that a certain level of violence is acceptable" was no less than a total assault on imprisoned people.[86] Treen's contention that prisoners deserved state-produced lateral violence taken to its logical conclusion was to "simply pass legislation requiring the expeditious execution before an inexpensive firing squad of all these people in prison. That's precisely the manner in which the Nazi's [sic] dealt with overcrowding in their concentration camps."[87] In articulating connections between overcrowded prisons and fascist regimes, *Angolite* writers teased out how the debate surrounding double-bunking was a racial debate about the value and disposability of incarcerated peoples' lives.[88]

However, prisoners' arguments did not sway Polozola or Treen as they worked to find a compromise. Polozola advocated for the state to expand the penal system.[89] The state fast tracked millions of dollars to speed up the opening of Washington Correctional Center. When interest rates dropped, the Louisiana Bond Commission issued new bonds from Citibank, The First Boston Corporation, and the boutique investment firm Howard, Weil, Labouisse, and Friedrichs, Inc. to expand existing prisons while deprioritizing hospitals and universities. These prison projects alone increased Louisiana's bonded indebtedness to a record high of close to $1 billion which taxpayers would be paying off into the 1990s.[90] Treen also expanded the state's jailing archipelago through the reallocation of public works funds into jail construction. In addition state leaders created a new mechanism for jail expansion. Sheriffs were given the power to put new sales taxes on their parish ballots to finance "law enforcement districts," or, in other words, to fund jail projects.[91] Moreover, harkening to the logic of the slave ship, Treen contended that a recent Texas court ruling provided legitimacy for debunking against prior court standards that required "excessive amounts of space per prisoner," and emphasized that the state would save millions. Polozola reversed his position, expanding the state's carceral capacity from 9,500 to 12,000 prison beds by the end of 1983.[92]

People across the ideological spectrum critiqued Governor Treen's staunch support for the carceral state while disinvesting in the social wage. The *Winnfield Parish Enterprise* newspaper in northern Louisiana published an editorial which argued that exempting the DOC from budget cuts while instituting "cuts to higher education suggest a serious defect in the establishment of governmental priorities."[93] *The Angolite* explicated that local and national cutbacks in tandem with prison building served to undermine the gains of the civil rights era.[94] Black communities were both disciplined via the growing penal system and through the dismantling of recently expanded welfare state commitments. By the spring of 1983, even some Republican state legislators began asking, "When does this end? How long will Corrections have the first call on the state treasury?"[95]

The Louisiana Coalition on Jails and Prisons not only opposed prison expansion in the face of economic crisis but asserted that prison reforms would be more fiscally responsible. They contended that to deal with overcrowding officials should implement early releases, Governor Treen should sign the hundreds of clemency recommendations on his desk, and the legislature should implement sentencing reforms to roll pack the longer mandatory sentences passed in recent years.[96] In arguing for these modest alternatives to prison growth, the LCJP belied the notion that only through double-bunking could the DPSC save money. Rather, they revealed that even more financially sound options were possible. It was politics not economics that made such actions inconceivable. Yet, Treen would not budge, even when DPSC staff proposed that Treen authorize similar measures.[97]

Victims' Rights as Tough on Crime

The fiscal crisis did not temper Treen's allegiance to a tough-on-crime ideology. Even before oil tax revenues plummeted, the Louisiana Senate Committee on Revenue and Fiscal Affairs raised concerns about the breakneck speed of prison population growth. Naming stiffer prison sentences as propelling penal growth and the alarming expenses of prison construction, the committee requested that Treen formulate a more financially conservative solution.[98] True to form, Treen committed "to accelerate our prison construction program."[99] Although incarcerated journalists at the *Angolite* predicted that the state would turn away from law-and-order ideology given the fiscal crunch, this was not to be the case. After the passage of a new series of anticrime measures, Treen proclaimed, "The barbarous nature of today's violent crime makes swift and sure punishment even more important than ever before. . . . Many of these new laws build upon our accomplishments of 1980 and 1981 to speed up conviction and punishment."[100]

Officials championing victims' rights and moving the fight against gender-based violence to the criminal legal system were key parts of this tough-on-crime agenda. One of the long-term impacts of the LEAA, in the words of Marie Gottshalk, was the production of "a very particular kind of victims' movement, one that viewed the rights of victims as a zero-sum game predicated on tougher penalties for offenders."[101] Under the LEAA was the creation of victims' rights programs to enlist more people in the "war against crime," which reinforced the narrative that society had become too soft on criminals, leaving victims of crime without significant redress. Such patriarchal "get tough" narratives underlay national- and state-level victims' rights initiatives and the passage of more draconian sentencing in the early 1980s.[102]

Reframing sexual interpersonal violence as a victims' rights issue was central to this law-and-order strategy. During the 1970s and 1980s, radical feminists demanded that sexual violence be taken seriously as a political issue. Increasingly, state agencies across the nation offered feminist antiviolence organizations redress through punitive state expansion. For example, in the 1970s the Baton Rouge Stop Rape Crisis Center was ordered by DA Ossie Brown to withhold services from survivors if they did not file police reports.[103] This strategy splintered antiviolence feminist movements, pitting those who understood sexualized violence to be rooted in patriarchal domination and control—and thus requiring systemic change—against those who were persuaded that the best way to address sexual violence was through aligning with law enforcement to attain legitimacy and resources. Such carceral feminist politics gained traction in mainstream antiviolence advocacy and served to justify law-and-order measures as a benevolent force rather than as an extension of the state's own capacities for punitive violence.[104] Yet many women of color and white antiracist antiviolence activists were critical of such policy proposals—such as mandatory arrests for those suspected of domestic violence—insofar as they were skeptical that law enforcement could be leveraged toward feminist or antiracist ends.[105] Indeed, the failure of such carceral feminist approaches to stem sexual violence not only belied the myth of punitive deterrence. It also illuminated how carceral feminism as an ideology and a practice could not stop violence because it is predicated on patriarchal and racist approaches to safety and violence whereby "safety" is achieved through fighting interpersonal violence with state violence, rather than addressing the root causes of harm.

Aligning with this carceral feminist turn, Treen kicked off the 1982 legislative session with a "victims' rights awareness" week. Trafficking in the racist and false notion that Louisiana prioritized the special treatment of criminals (coded as Black men) over victims (coded as white women), Treen announced the formation of a law enforcement task force on violence against women and the creation of a crime victims' reparation fund to which prisoners would be required to pay restitution—a precursor to the federal 1984

Victims of Crime Act.[106] Echoes of lynching narratives reverberated in Treen's promotion of these programs. The governor declared, "We are launching a crusade to apprehend, arrest, convict, and put behind bars these despicable animals that prey upon our wives, daughters, and mothers, inflicting the horrible incalculable damage of rape."[107] Dehumanizing perpetrators of sexualized violence as "despicable animals" evoked gendered Jim Crow-era racism. Since the antilynching writings of Ida B. Wells, antiracist and feminist scholars have shown how, after Emancipation, white southerners created the figure of the Black male rapist as a hypersexual beast to justify lynchings and reassert white supremacist and patriarchal power over the region. In such formulations, women—constructed as white—were in need of protection from such dehumanized, thus racialized, subjects due to their familial relations with white men such as Governor Treen. Black women were absent in this equation as either survivors of sexual violence or as subjects deserving of state protection.[108] In his championing of victims' rights, Treen reinforced such racist narratives disguised as gender justice.[109] In couching carceral feminism as a commitment to women's safety and protection, Treen elided how his austerity budgets' disinvestment in healthcare, education, and welfare undermined the security of women and the social reproduction of Louisiana communities amid the deepening recession.

The Contradictions of Surplus Populations:
The Failures of Prisoner Labor

Treen's capacity to develop the penal system as he desired had limits, however. The oil bust was not only an economic crisis to be leveraged for neoliberal restructuring but generated oppositional forces in the labor market that had ramifications for prison expansion. From 1973 to 1981, the oil boom had created a significant increase in jobs: "Employment in the oil and gas industry more than doubled, from 47,000 to 101,000 workers."[110] This growth spurred other sectors of the economy through the "job multiplier effect" so that for every job created in the Louisiana refinery industry, 7.6 additional jobs were created in other sectors.[111] However, this multiplier effect worked in the negative during the 1980s. More than 150,000 jobs disappeared from the Louisiana economy between 1982 and 1985.[112] Because so much of the Louisiana economy was based on oil and gas, there was no sector that was strong enough to cushion the fall of the petrochemical industry. Unemployment ballooned to 12.8 percent, leaving

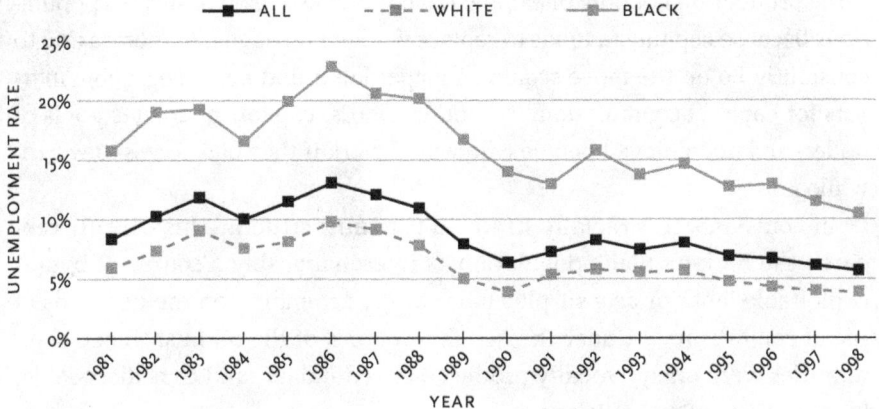

GRAPH 2.1 Louisiana unemployment rate by race, 1981–1998. Source: Bureau of Labor Statistics.

one in eight workers jobless and less than 60 percent labor force participation in Louisiana by the summer of 1983.[113]

The recession hit Black workers especially hard (graph 2.1). Even during the oil boom, Black Louisianians benefited less than their white counterparts. In the peak oil economy year of 1981, unemployment in Black Louisiana was almost three times what it was for white Louisianans. During the recession, Black unemployment was at least double white unemployment rates, reaching higher than 20 percent in some years.[114] Although the recession idled Black men in Louisiana at greater numbers than Black women, Black women in Louisiana suffered labor redundancy close to their male counterparts at an average of 18.7 percent—the highest in the nation.[115]

Treen's responses to this staggering recession and mass joblessness remained unabashed austerity combined with an ideological refusal to institute progressive taxation.[116] Instead of job programs or increased welfare support, Treen gave struggling Louisianans more prison and jail beds.[117] Even though these policies immiserated residents across race, gender, and geography, they particularly eviscerated urban Black communities who were produced as both economically precarious and as increasingly criminalized subjects. The prioritization of the carceral state over the welfare state represented not an arbitrary abandonment of certain segments of the populations but instead a targeted realignment of state resources to meet the contradictions of racial capitalism. At the core of racial capitalism is the production of inequality. As Marx explained, central to the capital relation is the production not only of exploited labor but also relative surplus populations because capitalism tends to replace workers through automation and to constantly be on the move seeking cheaper labor and new geographic markets for capital accumulation.[118] In other words, capitalism creates pools of under- and unemployed people who would work if they had access to worthwhile jobs.[119]

In Louisiana, this racially stratified capitalist structure historically rendered the region's Black population as interchangeably a source of hyperexploitable labor or as a surplus labor force, depending on the demands of racial capitalism.[120] Under the neoliberal crisis of the oil bust, Black communities were unequivocally produced as redundant, and thus disposable, labor within 1980s Louisiana.

Yet, surplus populations are not merely docile subjects in waiting. Christian Parenti aptly notes that "capitalism always creates surplus populations, needs surplus populations, yet faces the threat of political, aesthetic or cultural disruption from those populations."[121] Elites repeatedly expand the punitive reach of the state to repress and keep at bay surplus populations who are understood as having the potential to rebel.[122] Louisiana's law-and-order officials positioned impoverished and working-class Black communities, particularly young Black men whose masculinities they deemed to be in violent excess, as threats needing to be managed and contained through targeted policing, prosecution, and imprisonment. Moreover, the policing and prosecution crackdown in New Orleans penalized people for turning to extralegal survival strategies after they were structurally abandoned by the labor market. By the mid-1980s, this dialectic of disposability and criminalization led to the imprisonment of more than 10,000 Black Louisianans, mostly men from poor and working-class backgrounds—constituting 72 percent of the state prison population.[123]

Yet, incarcerating so many people was an extremely expensive state project. Despite Treen's redirecting of funds into carceral construction, the overall decline in state revenues required cost-cutting measures. These savings were most readily produced by cuts to prison operations and the turn to cheap prefabricated structures to expand prisons. Yet Treen's administration also advocated for prisoners themselves to build new prisons or renovate old ones through an "inmate labor bill." The bill would lift prohibitions on prisoners working on state construction that organized labor had previously won.[124]

The inmate labor bill captivated public debate. The New Orleans *Times-Picayune* supported the plan,[125] whereas unions protested it as "unconscionable," given that prison labor would "keep the unemployed from being able to secure employment."[126] The LCJP characterized the bill as permitting "slave labor" and argued that if Treen was so concerned about costs, he could sign the 310 pardons sitting on his desk.[127]

Prisoners were split on the issue. At first, the *Angolite* came out in support of the bill, believing it would provide a welcome form of job training and in opposition to organized labor's argument that prisoners were incapable of doing quality work. Yet as debate on the bill wore on, the *Angolite* offered a more mixed viewpoint, reflecting growing opposition among imprisoned people.[128] One prisoner, Lionel McGruder, maintained that given their long sentences, any skills gained on the inside had little chance of bettering their lives on release. Instead, the inmate labor bill would just allow "a few inmates an opportunity to build their own tomb."[129] Legislators were also closely divided. Despite Treen's vociferous support, the bill was narrowly defeated in both the 1981 and 1982 legislative session and did not even make it out of committee in 1983.[130] With jobs scarce and in high demand, politicians had trouble justifying the passage of laws that took any work away from free people.[131]

The inmate labor bill's failure points to a critical contradiction that Treen failed to foresee. The state recession produced mounting unemployment that entangled more people in the tentacles of the penal system. Treen's building up of the carceral state served as his primary strategy to manage such racialized and gendered surplus populations. But because of the recession, the state was short on funds for carceral construction projects, and so Treen attempted to save costs by turning to prisoner labor. Yet, this proposal was politically unviable *because* unemployment was so high. Although Treen's anti-state state policies ushered in neoliberal governance, the contradictions of capital surpassed the scale of his power. The conditions of possibility for certain carceral projects were foreclosed, not despite the state's economic crisis and realignment, *but because of it*.

The failure of the inmate labor bill reflected a qualitative shift from the early Jim Crow era when racist forced labor was a guiding logic of the prison system to the neoliberal rise of mass incarceration. As discussed in chapter 1, over the course of the twentieth century, prisoners at Angola increasingly were assigned work outside "productive" prison industries. Instead, prisoners were occupied with the reproductive labor of the prison: working in the laundry, the kitchen, maintenance, groundskeeping, and clerical work to keep the prison's operations humming along.[132] With a decreasing percentage of incarcerated people at Angola working on the farm, prison administrators attempted to expand the number of people engaged in more "industrial" work.[133] Although such enterprises never consisted of more than a few dozen people, they provided a small savings to the state and were heralded as job training. For these reasons, the DOC included agricultural and light industrial operations in the newly opened prisons. But, like Angola, only a small percentage of incarcerated people were involved in such enterprises.[134]

By the early 1980s, prison industrial and agricultural projects often proved to be an expense to the state, rather than a source of savings. Even though Treen's Commission on Criminal Justice initially recommended increasing the number of prisoners working in the Department of Agribusiness, this recommendation was scrapped because overall such programs had not been "economical."[135] Indeed, the state ended a slew of agribusiness programs for this reason. First the coffee-roasting operation at St. Gabriel women's prison was shuttered in 1981.[136] Soon after, the *Angolite* reported,

> The $3 million swinery operation established a year ago at Wade Correctional Institute has been shut down and its stock in the process of being sold because it proved unprofitable. . . . The legislators were also informed that the agri-business division had abandoned a 5,000-tree pecan grove project at Hunt Correctional Center because almost half the trees have died with the remainder in bad condition. The legislators also learned that the beef herd at the Louisiana Correctional and Industrial School at DeQuincy is in the process of being sold, sometimes at below-cost prices, in order to generate money to be able to put a crop in.[137]

Unsuccessful prison enterprises and demands for jobs undercut the Treen administration's prison labor goals. In fact, the growth of solitary confinement exemplified how the state's march toward mass incarceration was marked not by forced labor but by forced idleness.

Penal Politics: Treen versus Edwards

By the time reelection season rolled around, the economic devastation had rendered Treen's electoral prospects uncertain. State revenues plummeted to such lows that he placed a moratorium on new construction, including jails, and instituted another round of budget cuts.[138] In addition, after spending a term out of office, popular former governor Edwin Edwards was again eligible to make a run on the governor's mansion. The Treen campaign positioned Governor Treen as the no-nonsense fiscally responsible candidate against Edwards as the outlandish, corrupt, womanizing candidate. Edwards's comeback campaign emphasized the state's economic prosperity under his governorship and his flamboyant, charismatic leadership. Edwards did not shy away from his scandal-ridden history but pointed to the fact that his popularity knew almost no limits in his infamous quip, "The only way I can lose this election is if I'm caught in bed with either a dead girl or a live boy."[139] Polls showed that for many Louisianans corruption and a prosperous economy were a better combination than good government and economic crisis.

To mobilize voters, Treen returned to the issue of pardons. Shoring up his standing as the law-and-order candidate, Treen attacked Edwards for pardoning 1,181 people during his last term in office compared to Treen's record of only pardoning 34 people.[140] Through this racially coded attack, Treen called into question not only Edwards's commitment to public safety but also the legitimacy of governors' exercise of the power of the pardon. This strategy fortified tough-on-crime positions on early release as commonsense. But just as this antipardon campaign strategy was picking up steam, the unthinkable happened. Edwards's brother, attorney Nolan Edwards, was murdered by his own legal client whom Edwards had pardoned. In the wake of this tragedy, Treen's campaign tempered the attack on the former governor's pardon record.[141]

Being tough on crime proved insufficient to win Treen a second term. Winning only a majority in two of Louisiana's sixty-four parishes, Treen did worse in his reelection bid than when he ran as a token Republican against Edwards in 1972.[142] The *Angolite* and the Lifers' Association rejoiced at the return of Edwards and his reappointment of liberal reformers, including reappointing C. Paul Phelps as Department of Public Safety and Corrections (DPSC) secretary.[143] They were hopeful that early release, not just prison expansion, would be back on the table as a solution to overcrowding.[144] But even though the liberal ideologies underlying Edwards's approach to the prison crisis diverged from Treen's law-and-order approach, the pursuit of prison building surpassed partisan politics.

Debt over Democracy: Prison-Financing Schemes

After winning election, Edwards faced the same fiscal challenges that had defined Treen's tenure. Bond measures for jail expansion, even at reduced costs, were not as easy to pass as officials hoped when crafting the 70/30 parish jail program. Although in some places, local officials and residents were convinced of the unsubstantiated notion that prisons and jails would be an economic boost, in other places residents fought penal projects. The recession deepened residents' economic precarity and antitax sentiments, leading residents to vote down bond measures for jail and prison projects across the state. Meanwhile state officials berated residents for voting against new jail taxes and blamed them for the increase in people being released because of jail overcrowding.[145] Difficulties in jail expansion forced the state to devise new methods for penal expansion.

During Treen's administration, finance capitalists eager for more bond deals had introduced the idea of the state using lease revenue bonds (LRBs) to finance prison construction. In 1983, attorney Fred L. Chevalier of the firm McCollister, McCleary, Fazio, & Holliday, which had routinely served as the underwriters' counsel for state bond sales, wrote Governor Treen "to acquaint [him] with a tax exempt financing technique which is beginning to be used in other parts of the country for the financing of jails and other correctional facilities."[146] Chevalier went on to explain that through LRBs, which had been designed for revenue-generating state projects such as toll bridges, the state could create a nonprofit corporation that would have the capacity to issue bonds to finance carceral construction. Louisiana would then lease the prison facility from the financing nonprofit through rental payments that would be covered through the state's already existing general fund and not through any actual prison-related revenue generation. In his letter, Chevalier conceded that the state would not save any money by using LRBs, over the more common general obligation bonds (GOBs), for prison construction because LRBs tended to have higher interest rates.[147] LRBs' main advantage was that they allowed the state to sidestep democratic opposition to carceral state expansion. In contrast to GOBs, which have the full faith and credit of the government behind them, LRBs have a clause written into them that they can be canceled on a year-to-year basis—putting them outside the state's official definition of public debt.[148] Thus, LRBs, unlike GOBs, could be issued for prison construction without the state having to first gain two-thirds legislative approval *or* have a local tax election.[149] In other words, the state could push through new prison projects without consideration of its residents' views, in exchange for a higher cost of servicing debt.

Although Treen favored the LRB proposal, it was Edwards who put this debt-financing scheme into motion.[150] He did so because local resistance to new taxes for carceral construction showed no signs of letting up and close to three thousand state prisoners were overfilling the jails.[151] In 1985 Edwards established the Louisiana Correctional Facilities Corporation (LCFC) to implement LRB prison financing for three new medium-security state prisons. His childhood friend Rep. Raymond Laborde of Marksville championed the bill to form the LCFC as the nonprofit that would issue LRBs.[152] The bill was cosponsored by state legislators across the political spectrum from those in the Huey Long tradition to the emerging Black Democratic political bloc to conservative Democrats who would soon switch to the Republican Party. Legislators backed the bill because of their alignment with Edwards, their belief that mega-projects would jumpstart local economic growth, their pro-prison politics, or a combination of those factors.[153] Six backers, including Laborde, represented the parishes where the state intended to build the new prisons: Avoyelles, Allen, and Winn.

Edwards authorized the LCFC to finance the development of three new state prisons and to start plans for two more. All five potential prisons were to be leased to the DPSC, and the first three were to imprison upward of 2,500 people.[154] By the end of the year, the LCFC had issued just over $155 million in LRBs to the First National Bank of Minneapolis to finance the building and planning of the new prisons.[155] Given the financially riskier nature of the LRBs, only $104 million went to financing prison expansion. The remaining $51 million was paid to the various finance capitalists—from the bond underwriters, to the insurers, and the assorted law firms involved in the bond deal, including the law firm that originally alerted the state to this prison-financing tactic.[156]

Although the state's turn to LRB financing attempted to mute opposition to prison projects, antagonists still emerged. The *Angolite* blasted the plan for being antidemocratic. They publicized to their readers that "the tax-paying public will have no input regarding the proposed new prisons" at the direct "expense of the poor, the aged, the ill and disadvantaged."[157] Rev. James Stovall, still active with the Louisiana Interchurch Conference, and Jane Bankston, the corrections chairperson of the League of Women Voters of Louisiana, demanded a halt to the bond sale. In a letter to Governor Edwards, they argued that "at this time when state agencies are planning for a 22% cut in their budgets with hospitals and other vital institutions closing down, it is almost inconceivable to think that the decision has been made to take the most expensive route towards handling the prison overcrowding situation."[158] Moreover, Stovall wrote that many of the legislators backing this prison expansion plan were doing so for "the wrong reason . . .

to provide jobs" for their constituents, specifically for Edwards's and Rep. Laborde's home parish of Avoyelles.[159] He argued that Louisiana could not afford the multiplying of the state's prisons and warned that attempting to solve unemployment by taking on expensive prison debt was "like a person who tries to nourish his body by eating his fingers."[160] However, Stovall and Bankston's efforts, including their lobbying for legislation to void the bond sale in 1986, were to no avail.[161] The state proceeded with buying the land for the new prisons by the end of 1986.[162]

Organizing for Freedom: The Angola Special Civics Project

Even while faced with the relentless passage of draconian laws and an expanding penal system, individuals locked away at Angola refused to give up hope for freedom. Whereas previous generations of prisoners at Angola had individually petitioned the governor and parole board for release, the restrictions placed on such mechanisms pushed prisoners to develop new strategies that converted individualistic tactics to collective efforts. Having the shared memory of a different era in the state's penal system and believing it could change again, Angola activists formed the Angola Special Civics Project in 1986.

Conditions of Possibility for Prisoner Organizing

The Angola Special Civics Project, commonly referred to as the Civics Project, did not emerge out of thin air: the dialectical interplay of political threats and openings produced the conditions of possibility for prisoners to establish it.[163] Lawmakers lengthening prison sentences, restricting parole and clemency, reducing prisoners' ability to receive good time, and eliminating parole for entire classes of prisoners served as a motivating threat to imprisoned individuals.[164] Angola Special Civics Project cofounder Norris Henderson recalls the dramatic changes: "By 1979, they had abolished all benefits around life sentences. No more parole, no probation, no suspension of sentence around life sentences so life actually became life. So, the challenge to us now became: our numbers are growing astronomically, we just kind of went from a handful of lifers in the prison to all of a sudden 'boom' everybody has life now. . . . Something is wrong with this picture."[165] When Henderson was first incarcerated in the early 1970s, he was one of a few lifers inside Angola. In 1972, there were 193 men serving "natural" life sentences. By 1982 those numbers had increased to

1,084—consisting of one-third of those serving life without parole in the entire United States.[166] These moves fueled hopelessness as scores and scores of people began to fear dying behind prison walls.

This period also generated a key political opening for those inside seeking new methods of release: the appointment of reformist prison administrators to leadership roles in the state penal system following the Hayes Williams lawsuit. Sociologist James M. Jasper explains that "opportunities matter most to movements that have few of them, that are severely repressed."[167] As incarcerated individuals, the members of the Angola Special Civics Project lived highly regulated lives; therefore, relatively minimal opportunities, which were taken for granted by the outside world, had an enormous impact on their organizing. Edwards's reappointment of reformist DOC officials meant the lifting of restraints placed on *Angolite* reporting and that prisoners were again allowed to hold large events that outside supporters could attend.[168] These small openings afforded critical space for imprisoned people to cultivate relationships, develop shared analyses, and craft strategies to gain their freedom. Prison administrators' relative tolerance would prove to be fertile ground for prisoner organizing.

Earlier percolations of prisoner activism set the stage for the Civics Project. Before the Hayes Williams lawsuit, the Angola law library staff was, in the words of Biggy Johnston, "lily white." However, in response to that lawsuit, the prison administration integrated the all-white law library, along with the staff of the *Angolite* and the classification department.[169] The first beneficiary of integrating the law library was Biggy Johnston, who was assigned to the law library following his high score on the prison's aptitude test.[170] However, frustrated by the restrictions on the number of prisoners allowed in the law library at a time, Johnston filed a joint lawsuit to allow greater prisoner access to the library. After winning the suit, Johnston began teaching law classes where he educated other prisoners in "what postconviction was all about and how they could possibly use it to get out of prison."[171] The law library was also a space of relationship building where amid the stacks of Westlaw books the founders of the Angola Special Civics Project, Biggy Johnston and Norris Henderson, would meet.[172]

The law library provided valuable resources to use in challenging broader realignments in the criminal legal system. Johnston and other lifers began filing legal challenges to the retroactive repeal of the 10/6 law.[173] Several people who had accepted a guilty plea bargain under the promise that a life sentence meant serving only ten years and six months challenged their convictions on the argument that the state had broken its plea bargain. In response, the federal courts issued contradictory rulings that upheld most people's convictions while overturning a few.[174] Such mixed rulings gave lifers hope that they had a chance for freedom. Unfortunately, in February 1985 the Louisiana Supreme Court decided that the new life without parole sentencing laws were applicable to all lifers, regardless of the statute in force when they were sentenced.[175]

Under these conditions, the Angola Lifers' Association went through a heightened politicization process. Originally formed as a social club, the Lifers' Association members became sharply aware of the rise of tough-on-crime ideology when their own 10/6 dates came and went without release and then as "minimum servitude times moved from 10 years and six months, to 20 years, then 40 years, then mandatory life."[176] According to lifer Eddie Hall, "This caused us to change our goals and policies from one of socializing to the business of just trying to get out of this place . . . toward becoming more knitted together as a group and find the information and the facts we need to get out."[177] Although this "business" primarily took the form of helping one another on their individual cases, it was done in a framework that any single release could create a precedent that would make the path to freedom easier for others.[178]

Moreover, the increasing numbers of lifers in Angola pushed Lifers' Association members to question why so many people were serving life. During the early 1980s, Chairman Andrew Joseph initiated an informal study at Angola into why 75 percent of lifers were "poor, uneducated, and black."[179] At the core of its findings was that, although on paper life sentencing was race-neutral, in reality, prosecutorial discretion allowed DAs to racially discriminate in charging only certain individuals with crimes that carried life sentences. White defendants were almost always able to plea down first-degree murder charges to manslaughter, an option rarely given to Black defendants.[180] Joseph concluded that life without parole statutes were "infected with a sophisticated kind of racism" so that

> Blacks today before a court of law are in much the same situation they were in during the days of the Ku Klux Klan—the only difference is that today many of the racists wear black robes instead of white ones. We find that all that was accomplished during the civil rights era has been lost or drastically reduced by federal cutbacks, yet the president says more must be spent to build more prisons. When you talk about building more prisons, you're talking about putting Blacks in them at a disproportionate rate.[181]

Developing an analysis of how colorblind law-and-order life sentencing was in fact a racist state project pivoted the Lifers' toward a structural understanding of their imprisonment.

Furthermore, under the leadership of editor Wilbert Rideau, the *Angolite* became a key oppositional tool for imprisoned people by publicizing what was happening in the state legislature and within the DPSC. *Angolite* reporters addressed and mobilized two audiences: (1) imprisoned people at Angola and beyond and (2) the general public, including state officials. For instance, Biggy Johnston wrote a legal column for imprisoned people working on appeals that gave updates regarding the status of 10/6 and other legislative actions.[182] Furthermore, to sway public opinion, the *Angolite* placed fact-driven reporting on policing, prosecution, and imprisonment alongside narratives on the struggles of incarcerated life. These articles publicized the fallacies of notions of rising crime and lawlessness and humanized incarcerated people as deserving of release.

The *Angolite* also profiled individuals serving life without parole or practical life sentences to call attention to their cases and to demonstrate how life without parole manufactured the problem of the state's imprisonment of scores of elderly people.[183] This publicity strategy hearkened back to Governor Earl Long's Forgotten Man Committee of the 1950s, which had been charged with finding prisoners the state had lost in the system; subsequently 107 men were released. In response to the *Angolite* articles, Edwards created a new Forgotten Man Committee to identify problems with prisoner release mechanisms and to make recommendations to rectify these issues. However, after the committee recommended that the state expand parole and good time, major newspapers and law-and-order politicians denounced these reforms, ensuring that they failed to become state policy.[184]

Even though the prison administration permitted prisoners to develop certain types of oppositional spaces, it did not permit all prisoner organizations. The DPSC barred the NAACP from establishing a chapter at Angola in 1981. Warden Frank Blackburn made this decision based on his belief that that:

> [Although] the NAACP poses as a self-help group with specific orientation towards blacks . . . with respect to prisons, they would become adversary in nature such as the ACLU. For example, their work in other prisons has spilled over into the political arena. Should we allow the NAACP to function within this penitentiary, they would be entitled to establish chapters in all prisons under the

jurisdiction of the Louisiana Department of Corrections and the next step would be prisoner unions.[185]

This concern that the NAACP would foment collective agitation among Black prisoners, through lawsuits or unionization campaigns, indicated how officials' tolerance of prisoners' activism was limited when they believed it would target them. But when collective organizing was aimed at elected officials, the prison administration would prove to be surprisingly lenient.

Collectivizing Freedom: The Angola Special Civics Project

Despite prisoners' hope that Edwards's election would bring relief, their avenues to freedom continued to be restricted. Prisoner morale was so low that there was speculation that Angola was on the verge of a riot. In the words of Civics Project co-founder Norris Henderson, "All the things they measure were ripe at Angola. I mean hopelessness was there. Nobody was going home, people with long sentences. You name it. It was evident in Angola. So at this time, we, me and some other guys, started thinking about what we can do to change, *not necessarily our conditions, but our circumstances.*"[186] Having witnessed the limitations of conditions of confinement lawsuits, Henderson and Johnston decided that their goal was *not* to improve conditions inside Angola but rather to strategize how to get out of prison altogether. With 10/6 dead and the lifer population ballooning, lifers recognized that they needed to collectively organize for freedom. Having closely followed prison riots elsewhere, activists identified that, at the worst, riots brought increased repression, while at the best they brought better conditions, but either way everyone was still behind bars.[187] With this knowledge, Johnston and Henderson decided on a different route out of prison through the formation of the Angola Special Civics Project.

With Edwards's 1987 reelection campaign on the horizon, the Angola Special Civics Project's first campaign targeted the governor's race. Based on their experiences under different governors, they identified elected state officials, not prison administrators, as the real sites of power. Although Edwards's politics were not ideal, they were significantly better than what they had experienced with a Republican governor, especially regarding clemency. Thus, the Civics Project decided to organize their friends and families on the outside to vote as a bloc for Edwards. This strategy would keep a more sympathetic governor in office while also demonstrating the prisoners' political power—which they would leverage for future demands.[188]

Making the Civics Project a forceful reality required building a membership. Each of the cofounders' specific leadership styles drew people into the project. Johnston's legal experience teaching classes and winning appeals had gained him the status as a "legal genius."[189] He began recruiting folks from his law classes to join the effort. And Norris Henderson's commitment to always speaking out against injustice had earned him the respect of prisoners across race and religion—no small feat in an environment deeply structured by prison politics.[190] Former Civics Project member Eugene Dean recalls that he "just got fully involved in it because of Norris's reputation."[191] According to Henderson, "The combination of us, I think made us the thing that sang. . . . The guy that could pull people together and the guy who had the legal wherewithal to make something happen."[192]

An important leader whom Henderson and Johnston brought into the project was Checo Yancy, who drew on his experience working for the Clerk of Court and the Election Commission in Orleans Parish to give people a political education in electoral organizing.[193] The Civics Project mapped out the precincts across the state and identified in which districts prisoners had family and friends.[194] At this time, the Louisiana penal system had a population of approximately 15,000, and Angola had a population of more than 4,000.[195] Even though the state's carceral expansion sought to remove and contain large segments of the population from society, this strategy had a contradictory effect. More people locked up meant a larger slice of the population had a loved one behind bars—which, in turn, brought into sharp relief the injustice of the criminal legal system to a growing number of people. Members of the Civics Project figured that if they could get even a fraction of prisoners involved in organizing their friends and families to vote, they could sway the election.

In July 1987 the *Angolite* publicized the Civics Project's organizing strategy through a public service announcement. It outlined the significance of the governor's race and urged prisoners to encourage their family and friends on the outside to vote as a prison reform bloc: "Instead of letting the vote of our people be influenced and misguided by local and state leaders who probably don't give a damn about us, let's do it ourselves. Let's utilize the votes of our people to express ourselves in this year's state elections. We have a golden opportunity to perhaps impact the outcome of some tight races, and subsequently, our own destiny."[196] Mobilizing to determine their own futures through organizing contested the very disenfranchisement the penal system sought to impose.

In August 1987, free world activists joined up with the Angola Special Civics Project. New Orleans organizer Ted Quant of the Loyola University Institute for Human Relations attended a Civics Project meeting at Angola. When he walked into the meeting room, the walls were covered with charts and graphs. He remembers, "They had these magnificent graphs—how much it costs to incarcerate, how many people in prison, how many family members, what it would mean if a certain number of those people voted."[197] During the meeting, members detailed their plan for outside allies to organize as a bloc to flip the governor's race and put prison reform on the agenda. By the end of the presentation, Quant had decided to join them.[198]

With only a few months until the election, the Civics Project went into high gear. Members focused on setting up networks of their loved ones outside the prison by reaching out to family members through a letter-writing campaign. They made fliers about the importance of the governor's campaign both to mail out and to give to prisoners working in visiting area concession stands to hand out on the sly if someone did not feel comfortable directly talking to a visitor.[199] Moreover, they set up organizing committees based on where people were from to build networks and pool resources.[200] In New Orleans, Quant coordinated outreach to family members and friends while also reaching out to community organizations that already had relationships with currently or formerly incarcerated people, including resident council leadership from the C. J. Peete and Lafitte public housing projects.[201] Inside and outside, activists leveraged election organizing as an opportunity to draw attention to the social and economic costs of expanding the Louisiana prison system while shrinking the state's social services. They saw in the election an opportunity to put structural prison reform on the table.

From the beginning, the Civics Project made clear that incarcerated people should be in leadership of prison reform organizing.[202] As Civics Project leaders explained, because prisoners were already disempowered and silenced through the criminal legal system, replicating those dynamics through the organizing process would contribute to their continued subordination. Prisoners identified the issues and envisioned the strategy: there was no one better to lead them to freedom but themselves. At the same time, there was a role for *everyone* not despite but because of their differing social locations. Being held captive inside Angola meant they were cut off from certain information about the outside world. Therefore, outside activists had vital information to share that could strengthen the campaign. Allies were not asked to indiscriminately agree with incarcerated leaders' ideas but to work in mutual partnership to push the group forward. Romanticizing prisoners would not contribute to their freedom.[203]

A few weeks before the election, the Civics Project and the New Orleans group each held press conferences on the same day. In the morning, the New Orleans group declared, "We believe that [the criminal justice system] has failed us, in large part, because politicians find it expedient to court votes by demagogically riding the law-and-order bandwagon, calling for bigger jails and longer sentences while cutting funds for education, drug rehabilitation, and other programs that would reduce crime."[204] After the press conference, they distributed leaflets encouraging people to vote in the upcoming election and support their prison reform platform: expanding parole eligibility, shortening sentences, creating alternatives to incarceration, and providing educational programs geared at successful reentry.[205] That afternoon, the Civics Project and other prisoner organizations held a press conference at Angola announcing their aim to generate a voting bloc of their families and friends to flip the election and to serve as a long-term counter to the law-and-order bloc dominating Louisiana politics.[206]

However, neither press conference stated which candidate the Civics Project was supporting. Civics Project leaders believed they would give their law-and-order opponents ammunition to use against their favored candidate if they announced their choice too early; therefore, they planned to keep secret who they were voting for until Election Day. Furthermore, the Civics Project decided not to put into play their voting bloc until the runoff election, when they would have the greatest opportunity to be the deciding factor—and, they hoped, compelling Edwards to support prison reform once he won on their support.[207]

Unfortunately, before the runoff occurred, the election was over. Even amid corruption charges, Edwards was still considered the candidate to beat. But then Buddy Roemer, a conservative Democrat from Bossier City running a campaign premised on good government, law-and-order, and austerity, began winning endorsements.[208] With oil prices continuing to drop in response to OPEC abandoning its former price system, Edwards was confronted with an ongoing fiscal crisis. Rather than championing progressive tax reform, Edwards turned to the same kind of budget cuts and unemployment he had critiqued Treen for.[209] Without economic prosperity to buffer him against critics, Edwards was unable to spring back from his most recent corruption trial, despite his acquittal.[210] After Roemer came in first and Edwards second in the primary, Edwards shocked everyone by dropping out of the runoff.[211] The Civics Project was never given a chance to see whether their electoral strategy would work, disheartening Angola activists.[212]

Return of Crisis and Reformulation of the Civics Project

Governor Buddy Roemer entered office in March 1988 committing to "professionalize" and "depoliticize" the Louisiana clemency process. He ignored virtually all pardon recommendations, paroling fewer than thirty people from Angola during his first year in office.[213] Desperation at Angola increased as suicides, stabbings, murders, and attempted escapes steadily grew. Attempted escapees explained their actions by stating they had given up hope of ever getting out of prison.[214]

On June 21, 1989, Judge Polozola declared Angola to be once again in a "state of emergency."[215] Blaming the rise of violence on prison mismanagement and understaffing caused by the state's fiscal crisis, Polozola appointed former Angola warden Ross Maggio Jr. as the court's "expert" charged with investigating whether it was adhering to constitutional standards and the federal court's consent decrees.[216] Polozola threatened that if things did not shape up at Angola, he would place the entire penal system under federal receivership.[217] The following day, the DPSC announced it would hire more security officers, purchase metal detectors, and intensify searches for weapons and drugs. On that same day, Roemer held a press conference to assert that his policies were not responsible for the violence at Angola and to maintain his stance on clemency. The *Angolite* reported, "That night another Angola inmate hung himself."[218]

With media fixated on the crisis at Angola and Polozola pushing for reforms, Roemer instituted some slight changes. Belying his previous promises, he did pardon a handful of long-termers on July 1, 1989.[219] To comply with Polozola, the state also created new mental health units within Angola. Thus, the state responded to Angola's suicide crisis not through addressing the root cause of incarcerated people's depression—their unfreedom—but through managing them through psychiatric drugs and therapy so that they could better cope with their grim conditions.[220]

Deflated after the aborted Edwards campaign, the Civics Project's momentum stalled. Still, the Civics Project was not over. During 1988 and 1989, its leaders assessed their earlier work. First, they evaluated their base of support within Angola. Although they had amassed significant support from organizations such as the Lifers' Association and the *Angolite*, some prisoners still were reluctant to get involved. Some people believed the Civics Project was a Black-only organization, while others believed it was only for lifers. The Civics Project leadership recognized that they needed to democratize their organizational structure if they were to create a truly collective prisoner movement. They decided to rebuild by having membership intentionally represent various groupings at Angola—the different cellblocks and camps, geographic areas of Louisiana, and various types of sentences and convictions. Having forty members representing an intentional cross-section of perspectives would help them most effectively organize the rest of the prison.[221] Democratizing the organizational structure in this way was, according to Henderson, "probably the greatest decision we made to engage other folks because then the support of everybody in the prison just took off."[222]

Next the Civics Project worked to deepen the collective nature of the organization. They solidified a new structure with Henderson and Johnston remaining the chair and cochair, respectively, of the project and created five committees to carry out the organization's work: the Correspondence Committee, Legal Research Committee, Vital Statistics Committee, Distribution Committee, and the Current Events Committee.[223] Within the committee structure, it was imperative that all members felt valued and respected, whether researching legislation or stuffing envelopes. This structure facilitated the development of an organizational culture whereby members understood the interdependence of their fates under the Louisiana punishment regime. Or as Yancy remembers articulating, "We're in the same boat. If I put a hole in the boat, we're all gonna sink. . . . You got a life sentence, I got a life sentence, but we're gonna work together."[224]

In addition to deepening its democratic structure and solidarity, the Civics Project wanted to change how the outside world perceived them. Members knew that sectors of the public viewed them as illegitimate political actors because of their criminalized status, which was doubled in the dominant imaginary because they were primarily Black individuals serving long prison terms for offenses often categorized as violent. Within this context, members felt compelled to challenge the notion that their criminalized status rendered them as somehow less than human and undeserving of release. Toward these ends, Checo Yancy spearheaded a "public relations" program in which prisoners organized fundraising drives for causes unrelated to criminal justice: "We gave to sickle cell, and muscular dystrophy and all these organizations. We wanted people to know that prisoners are humans too."²²⁵ Although this move to prove themselves as worthy was fraught insofar as it had the potential to reinforce the idea that one's right to freedom was predicated on good deeds, it also was an example of how respectability politics could be strategically deployed within a constricted ideological terrain to refute the foundational logic—Black prisoners as less than human—of carceral regimes.

Back at square one following Roemer's election, the Civics Project refocused on its core issue: life sentencing. They began by conducting a ten-state study comparing Louisiana's sentencing laws to other states. Members of the Correspondence Committee sent out questionnaires to prison administrations in Texas, Pennsylvania, Michigan, Illinois, Florida, and other states; then the Legal Research Committee analyzed the responses. They learned that Louisiana had more people in the aggregate serving life without parole sentences than any other state.²²⁶ With this information they "began using the weapons that were available to [them], and the weapons that were available were the law."²²⁷

The Civics Project leadership drafted an alternative to the current life-sentencing legislation. They decided it was important that there be a mechanism for release available to all "natural" and "practical" lifers through expanding parole eligibility. Deciding how much time someone should serve before becoming parole eligible became one of the organization's biggest internal fights. Questions emerged such as the following: "What kind of restrictions are we putting on ourselves? When do we say we are eligible to get out of this place? And that became a real struggle. Who are you to decide how long I'm going to stay inside? That went back and forth until we took a consensus of what was going on around the country."²²⁸ Civics Project members were persuaded that their best chance for undoing life without parole was to craft legislation that reproduced the concept that certain convictions "required" longer sentences. Many members of the Civics Project supported using other states' legislation as their proposed policy baseline, even though every state had recently implemented harsher sentencing laws. Still, for other members, making distinctions based on convictions felt arbitrary and contrary to their desires for immediate release. Eventually the Civics Project decided to support a graduated parole eligibility proposal differentiated by people's convictions because they believed it was politically viable and therefore most likely to benefit the collective whole.²²⁹

After months of work, the Civics Project unveiled its report "Analysis of Louisiana's Sentencing and Parole Laws and Proposed Legislative Alternatives" at a symposium at Angola. They presented their research on the state's life sentencing laws and made the case for their proposed graduated parole eligibility legislation to a broad cross-section of attorneys, outside activists, judges, corrections officials, educators, media, and a member of the state legislature.

One of the concepts the Civics Project members drew on in their argument for expanding parole was the notion of "criminal menopause." This idea, coined by law professor John Turley of Tulane's Program for Older Prisoners, held that people aged out of committing crimes by their forties. The Civics Project found this idea appealing in that it legitimized their claims that incarcerated people were not a perennial threat to society and thus should be considered eligible for parole.[230] The Civics Project's turn to this theory was not without its own set of contradictions. The idea of criminal menopause drew simple correlations between age and criminal status, which reified ideas of criminal behavior as innate in certain types of people, rather than as socially constructed or produced. At the same time, the gendered naming of the term as a form of "menopause" inadvertently, yet fittingly, spoke to how the state's punitive infrastructure sought to criminalize and contain certain masculinities to limit their reproduction in society. Although the Civics Project's use of this concept illuminated the extent to which even politically engaged prisoners can internalize dominant ideologies on criminality, it also highlighted the limits and stakes of liberal criminology, especially of those seeking to shape reform efforts.

The Angola Special Civics Project's report was an organizing tool aimed at lawmakers. Hoping to sway political opinion on the issue of life without parole sentencing, they mailed copies to every state legislator.[231] In attendance at the symposium was state representative Naomi Farve of New Orleans's Ninth Ward. In her role as a state representative, she attended Lifers' Association meetings where she heard about the Civics Project's proposed legislation. Believing that people should have a second chance, she announced at the symposium that she would introduce the bill in the next legislative session.[232] Farve began the work of championing House Bill 1709 to end life without parole sentencing.

At the same time, the Civics Project's members knew that their families and friends on the outside needed to be involved in a formal organization. They initially considered partnering with the Texas-based prison reform organization, Citizens United for the Rehabilitation of Errants, but moved on when they realized that it primarily focused on conditions of confinement and did not respect the freedom strategies of incarcerated activists.[233] Instead, the Civics Project founded the Louisiana Coalition in Support of

Penal Reform (LCSPR) as a grassroots organization within which outside allies could build political leverage in solidarity with imprisoned activists. Building off the tactics used in creating a voting bloc in the recent gubernatorial election, the Civics Project supported the development of seven chapters across the state.[234] The Civics Project emphasized to the LCSPR that they were organizing to create legal structures that would collectively benefit incarcerated people rather than specific individuals.[235] The LCSPR organized voting blocs and supported the passage of House Bill 1709.[236] They held informational meetings in their members' home communities, wrote letters to the *Angolite* encouraging free readers to join their efforts, and explained the structural issues of the Louisiana criminal legal system to passengers on the buses to Angola between New Orleans and Baton Rouge.[237] In addition, they organized lobby days and coordinated phone banks to state legislators.[238]

While the LCSPR was organizing to build political leverage for prison reform, Representative Farve was working to get the bill out of committee. After more than a year of unsuccessfully trying to get the legislation to the floor, she was offered a compromise—to pass amended legislation. The amended legislation would make people parole eligible after serving twenty years and reaching forty-five years of age, but only for "practical lifers" or those serving "numbered" terms such as 50, 99, or 399 years. Anyone serving a natural life sentence would be excluded.[239] She brought the option to the Angola Special Civics Project to decide whether to accept the amended bill, even though it would not apply to most of their membership. Yancy summed up the thought process of the Civics Project: "Well, selfishly we could have said no, but it wouldn't have affected anybody. Sometimes you can be on the cutting edge of change, and it doesn't affect you but you're helping somebody else. Plus, it was another way for us to sell maybe our next project, maybe our next issue. The legislature is going to say, 'Ok these guys are reasonable. I can work with them, and they can work with us.'"[240] Civics Project members decided that denying legislation that would allow anyone to get out would be against their purpose.[241] Winning this piece of legislation, which became known as the "20/45 law," seemed like a victory that could be a scaffold for fighting for even greater parole eligibility. Once the legislation passed, imprisoned activists rejoiced, deepening their sense of hope that further change was on the way.[242]

However, this was not to be the case. The passage of the "20/45 law" became the high point for the Angola Special Civics Project. While the Civics Project and the LCSPR continued to push for parole eligibility and organized as voting blocs around state and local elections, the political openings that had once afforded them the structures for organizing began to close.[243] First, the era of reformist officials came to an end. In the 1992 gubernatorial race between Edwin Edwards and former Ku Klux Klan leader David Duke, Edwards committed to appointing more conservative prison administrators in exchange for the votes of the state's prison employees.[244] After Edwards appointed Burl Cain as Angola's warden in 1995, Cain limited the scope and freedom of the *Angolite* and increased restrictions on organizing.[245] Moreover, even as Civics Project leadership focused on collective struggle, they continued to work on their individual cases. Beginning with Biggy Johnston's parole in 1993, key leaders began going home, some directly through the 20/45 law.[246] Although this did not signal a formal end to the Civics Project, the organization lost significant capacity by the mid-1990s. Over time, the era of the 10/6 life sentence became forgotten from the collective memory of Louisiana prisoners. Increasingly, the people housed at Angola only knew an institution with thousands of lifers who had no expectation of release within their lifetime.

● ● ● ● ● ●

In the early 1990s, *Angolite* journalists Wilbert Rideau and Ron Wikberg reflected,

> Louisiana had only three adult facilities in 1975. Today, there are twelve prisons, holding 14,200 prisoners with an additional 4,300 housed in local jails because of lack of space. Louisiana currently enjoys the dubious distinction of having the third-highest incarceration rate in the country, topped only by Nevada and South Carolina. The state is broke and basic social and educational needs of the citizenry are not being met. The prisoners? They still hang themselves.[247]

With more than two thousand people serving life without parole, Louisiana then had the longest average sentence in the nation at 14.4 years, a leap from 2.25 years just over a decade earlier. The prison population boom was interlaced with the spiraling of harsh sentencing laws while the politicization of clemency led governors across party lines to restrict their use of pardons for decades (figure 2.1).[248]

The reordering of punitive governance that Louisiana underwent in the 1980s echoed aspects of Jim Crow state realignments from a century before: geographically targeted racist and gendered policing, the hardening of criminal legal sentencing procedures, and the adoption of austerity

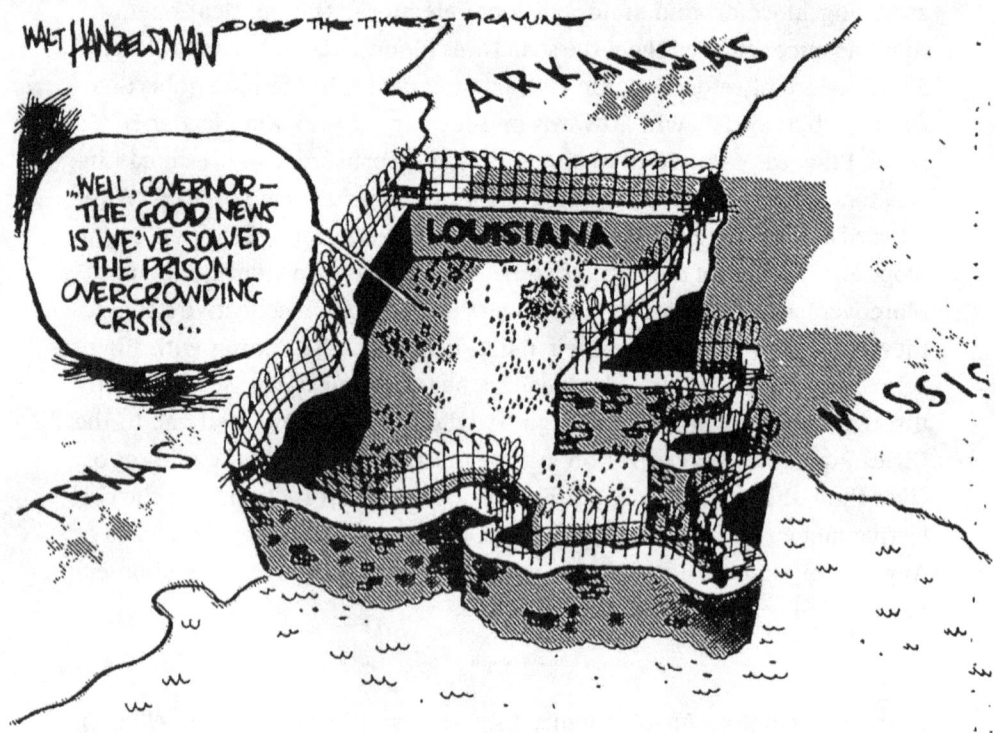

FIGURE 2.1 "We've Solved the Prison Overcrowding Crisis" political cartoon, *Times-Picayune*, September 24, 1989, Capital City Press/Georges Media Group, and Baton Rouge, Louisiana.

budgets. Yet the law-and-order austerity regime was not a mere repetition of the past. The state no longer expanded its carceral capacities to quickly work to death the state's Black working class as it had with convict leasing and the Jim Crow punishment regime. Instead, it caged thousands of predominantly Black working-class and poor men, rendered as surplus, to slowly die by life imprisonment.

The people sentenced to life behind bars were not abstract avatars but real people with desires for freedom. Although there was opposition in the outside world to the tough-on-crime measures—from the activism of the Louisiana Coalition on Jails and Prisons, to the petitions of the League of Women Voters, to the voting down of jail bonds across the state—it was the collective organizing of imprisoned people at Angola that had the most purchase at this conjuncture. Prisoners leveraged this moment of crisis to form the Angola Special Civics Project. By seeking to create tangible improvements in the lives of imprisoned people not through bettering prison conditions but by creating new avenues out of the prison, the Civics Project crafted new methods of early release that positively affected untold numbers of people across Louisiana. Their efforts revealed that the carceral state was not a monolith but was full of friction and fissures that could be targets of pressure. Through forming coalitions with outside allies, the Civics Project combined electoral organizing, political education, and the drafting of new legislation to both create new mechanisms for release and foster a movement for structural prison reform. In challenging "lock 'em up and throw away the key" politics, they refuted the carceral logics that deemed them disposable.

Even as the Angola Special Civics Project made gains, new prisons continued to be erected. On November 29, 1990, Allen Correctional Center opened in Kinder, Louisiana. It, along with the recently opened Winn Correctional Institute and Avoyelles Correctional Center (soon to be renamed for prison booster Rep. Laborde), were the last state prisons to be built through the lease revenue bond financing plot. At the time of Allen's opening, *Angolite* writers raised concerns about the fact that Allen, like Winn, would operate as a privately managed prison. Fearful that this was the new direction of carceral expansion, Angola journalists raised the alarm that the profit motive of privatization would produce overcrowded and brutal conditions and would accelerate the growth of the penal system.[249] This was, however, not to be the case. Allen would be not one of the first privately run state prisons but instead the last state stand-alone prison constructed in Louisiana. It would not be through privatization but rather through an expanded use of parish jails to incarcerate state prisoners that Louisiana would double its prison population over the course of the 1990s. All the while, new forms of oppositional activism would emerge and take hold against this penal state formation in one of the primary nexuses of the Louisiana punishment regime, New Orleans.

3 Jailing Louisiana
Sheriffs, Policing, and Growing Opposition

Louisiana is by far the nation's leader in the percentage of state prisoners housed in parish and city jails. From the sheriffs' standpoint, the benefits are many. Because parish jails typically are assigned healthy, well-behaved prisoners, they can house them for much less than $22 a day while keeping the extra money as profit. By running their jails on tight budgets, some sheriffs are making thousands and even millions of dollars and are using the money to help finance their own law-enforcement operations, such as buying new police cars and hiring more deputies.

Others have used the income to build or expand jails without asking taxpayers for more money and have pleased voters by often using inmates on work details in their parishes. Even Foti is a convert. He built two new jails in the 1990s, and Orleans Parish now houses more state prisoners than any parish in the state—more than 2,300 out of about 7,100 prisoners.

—Martha Carr, *Times-Picayune*

The atrocities of the prison system often seem pale when compared to what goes on in the nearly 100 jails and local lockups, at least one of which is located within minutes of every single person in the state of Louisiana.

—Louisiana Coalition on Jails and Prisons

We therefore propose a brick by brick, top to bottom, bottom to top, north to south and east to west rebuilding of the New Orleans Police Department that has as its goals putting more officers on the street and locking up every criminal who preys upon citizens or visitors in our city.

—Mayor Marc Morial's Plan for Crime Prevention & Reform, 1993

The Critical Resistance South Conference put Louisiana and the Southern region on the map—making visible the regional's long history of abolition organizing, challenging violent policies of policing and imprisonment, and creating oppositional frameworks to Louisiana's infamous distinction as the most incarcerated place in the world.

—Shana M. griffin

On the morning of October 19, 1993, reporters and city officials clustered together for a first glimpse of the largest expansion of Orleans Parish Prison (OPP) in history. The "campus-style" structures consisted of thousands of feet of reinforced concrete and steel, computerized glass-enclosed guard bridges, and motorized doors decorated by aqua trim. With the addition of 2,140 beds, OPP was now the largest carceral facility in the state with 7,140 jail beds. Criminal Court clerk Ed Lombard joked at the press conference that OPP, almost two thousand beds larger than Angola with enough jail space to lock up one in every seventy New Orleanians, "is the new housing plan of the future."[1]

Behind this massive jail construction stood Sheriff Charles Foti, the reigning patriarch of OPP. Under Sheriff Foti, the jail had grown tenfold, and he was joined by sheriffs across Louisiana in a massive jailing project. By the turn of the twenty-first century, local, state, federal, and immigrant prisoners filled Louisiana's jails to the brim. For those within, life was brutal. The Louisiana Coalition on Jails and Prisons long argued that "Louisiana jails can be justifiably labeled Louisiana's 'worst punishment,'" because they frequently had higher rates of premature death than Louisiana's prisons.[2] By 1998 when Louisiana gained the title of being the most incarcerated state in the nation, more than half of state prisoners were incarcerated in jails.

The 1990s were the key decade for the transformation of parish jails into a newly emboldened carceral archipelago. As this chapter will show, after being used as a temporary spatial fix to penal overcrowding, parish jails during that decade became the long-term geographic solution for the Louisiana carceral state.[3] The lack of political will to release state prisoners, combined with budgetary shortages and sheriffs increasingly seeing state prisoner per diems as a benefit, produced the context for sheriffs to collectively organize for statewide jail enlargement. In building up their jails, sheriffs built up their political power, ensuring their continued election to this coveted political office. However, unaccustomed as they were to reporting to anyone, sheriffs came into conflict with Judge Polozola regularly during this decade. Nonetheless, the state's carceral maneuvers frequently trumped Polozola's distaste for the growing role of jails in the Louisiana carceral state.

Rural and urban jails followed diverging paths. Rural sheriffs enlarged their jailing kingdoms through newly codified carceral cooperation endeavor agreements between sheriffs and the Department of Public Safety & Corrections (DPSC) and the Immigration and Naturalization Service (INS) to imprison a mix of state, federal, and immigrant prisoners. Sheriffs in urban areas leveraged fears of crime and political largess to pass municipal bonds to fund jail expansions. Although Sheriff Foti's OPP also incarcerated state prisoners and INS detainees, the largest share of people jailed there were pretrial prisoners unable to make bail.[4]

The intensification of high-profile and everyday policing produced OPP's population explosion. In response to high profile corruption and brutality charges against the NOPD, Mayor Marc Morial and NOPD superintendent Richard Pennington enacted a series of policing reforms. Under the banner of professionalizing and modernizing the NOPD, law enforcement was expanded under the banner of community and broken windows policing. Ideologically and financially bolstered by President Bill Clinton's 1994 crime bill, the "Pennington Plan" serves as an object lesson of consent-building for policing and a key turning point in Louisiana's march to mass incarceration. Based on a racist and patriarchal geographic imagination of which people and places were a danger to neoliberal restructuring, the Pennington Plan produced disorder as police arrested unprecedented numbers of young, Black, working-class New Orleanians.

The expansion of Louisiana's carceral infrastructure generated growing opposition at the turn of the millennium. As grassroots activists highlighted an epidemic of premature deaths inside OPP, prison abolition began to gain ground as an activist orientation for antiracist and feminist organizers. New Orleans abolitionists linked up with the national prison abolition organization Critical Resistance to host the 2003 Critical Resistance (CR) South conference. Working together, organizers publicized the impacts of mass incarceration in Louisiana; built relationships with local, regional, and national activists; and developed a deeper analysis of the roots of policing and imprisonment. CR South lay the groundwork for combating a new period of punitive power that would be ushered in after August 29, 2005.

Statewide Jail Expansions

State officials leveraged Judge Polozola's declaration of a new state of emergency at Angola in the summer of 1989 to realign the Louisiana carceral state toward jailing. Although the precipitating issue was violence in Angola, overcrowding once again underpinned the crisis. This fit into the seesaw of overcrowding between state prisons and parish jails since the enactment of the federal court's mandates. To comply with the federal court's initial population limits on state prisons in 1975, sheriffs were expected to shoulder overflow state prisoners in their jails. To appease the sheriffs who disliked this arrangement, state officials instituted a per diem revenue payment system between the DPSC and sheriffs' departments in the 1970s, then the 70/30 program to partially cover jail construction costs, and inventing law enforcement sales-taxing districts in the 1980s. Through these programs, individual parish jails added between 27 to 54 beds, which totaled hundreds of new jailing bed space throughout the state.[5] Yet, even these expansions were outpaced by the rates of arrest and prosecution—leading to more overcrowding.

A growing number of jailed Louisianians filed conditions of confinement lawsuits in response. Horrific conditions plagued jails from prisoners dying of heat exhaustion in disciplinary "hot boxes," to extreme medical neglect, to regular guard beatings.[6] When federal courts found jail after jail to be in violation of the Eighth Amendment, Judge Polozola consolidated the cases and placed every Louisiana jail under the Hayes Williams court order in 1981. Polozola ordered sheriffs to submit monthly reports on the number of guards employed, prisoner violence, consensual and nonconsensual sex among prisoners, escapes, riots, hunger strikes, and deaths. Population limits were placed on every jail in the state.[7]

Yet the population limits were more flexible than they appeared on paper. In addition to raising population caps when jails were expanded, sheriffs conspired to pack more people into jails with Polozola's backing. For instance, Polozola overruled Acadia Legal Services and the ACLU when they petitioned against the Lafayette jail's conversion of the exercise room into a dorm to increase the jail's capacity.[8] This case revealed that Polozola's reform consultant, former Angola warden C. Paul Phelps, was "pushing a 'shadow jail population' concept" with Polozola's approval. "Both Orleans and Jefferson Parish had set up so called 'drunk tanks' and . . . the populations in those facilities were not counted in the parish jail population limits, at least for the first 72 hours of incarceration. He urged Lafayette to establish a similar facility."[9] By developing shadow jailing spaces, federal actors created mechanisms for sheriffs to quietly enlarge jails. This turn to drunk tanks did not undermine the court's authority so much as it confirmed the extent to which it was committed to jail growth, with little concern given to the people being jailed.

The 1980s War on Drugs worsened jail overcrowding. In response to the Reagan administration's passage of the Anti-Drug Abuse Acts of 1986 and 1988, New Orleans created drug courts, which served to speed up drug convictions, and the state legislature passed a stringent package of antidrug laws.[10] Moreover, Polozola consistently approved temporary lifting of jail caps for mass arrests in the War on Drugs. These moves exacerbated overcrowding to the point that, in at least one case, the only place to incarcerate one hundred drug arrestees in an Orleans Parish roundup was in a bus.[11]

Overcrowding was not the only way in which federal oversight failed to curtail the everyday state violence of jail life. The Louisiana Coalition of Jails and Prisons (LCJP) reported that forty-three people perished behind jail bars between 1980 and 1982.[12] The ACLU continued to receive reports regularly from people incarcerated in jails of sexual violence, neglect, and discrimination. One prisoner locked up in the Jefferson Parish jail wrote the ACLU about the categorical exclusion of prisoners deemed queer from work assignments, which, in turn, precluded those prisoners from accruing good time.[13]

The LCJP reflected that, even though they had initially advocated for federal court interventions, they could not ignore this troubling pattern of jail expansion: "Scores of parishes are now planning to build—or have built— new jails, a direct result of the conditions litigation. Instead of examining alternatives to increasing incarceration, instead of finding release mechanisms for those who are nonviolent or first offenders, parishes are seemingly determined to continue a policy of over-incarceration. . . . Jail—in most Louisiana parishes—still remains a punishment of first resort."[14] In critiquing this unintended consequence of conditions of confinement litigation, the LCJP argued that the state chose not to respond to deplorable jails through decarceration but by reifying the officially unrecognized yet systemic racial violence of caging.

After Judge Polozola's 1989 declaration of a state of emergency for Angola, jail overcrowding hit a new peak. Although he did not have qualms about temporarily overcrowding pretrial prisoners, the judge was angered when overcrowded conditions directly affected state prisoners. Overcrowding was so dire that the state legislature passed a measure allowing state prisoners to replace their incentive pay with double good time. Even though one thousand state prisoners gained early release through this program and the Avoyelles state prison opened early, the jails' incarceration of state prisoners hit a new record of 4,491 people in the summer of 1989.[15] To appease Polozola, DPSC coordinated a prisoner swap with Orleans Parish, taking one hundred state prisoners from OPP who were serving longer than ten years in exchange for one hundred work-release prisoners with upcoming release dates.[16] In a flip from earlier rulings, the very next day Judge Polozola ordered the DPSC to move hundreds of state prisoners *from* parish jails *into* the state prison system.[17] Governor Roemer approved more beds at Angola and sped up the opening of the Winn prison to relieve jail overcrowding.[18] And the state legislature created yet another taxing authority for sheriffs to expand their jails.[19]

Yet, state officials knew that all these measures were only a partial stopgap. The *Times-Picayune* reported that even after the large transfer of state prisoners from jails, 1,500 state prisoners remained in jails in the New Orleans area:

> Jefferson Parish, no beds available; houses 93 state inmates, 573 others. Orleans Parish, no beds available, houses 1,292 state prisoners, 2,315 others. Plaquemines Parish, no vacancies, houses 25 state prisoners, 81 others. St. Bernard Parish, two vacancies, houses 30 state inmates, 51 others. St. Charles Parish, 39 vacancies, houses 32 state inmates, 50 others. St. John the Baptist Parish, four vacancies, houses 11 state inmates, 43 others. St. Tammany Parish, three vacancies, houses 40 state inmates, 126 others. Slidell jail, no vacancies, houses five state inmates, no others.[20]

In spring 1990, Governor Roemer released *The Governor's Corrections Plan: A Balanced and Comprehensive Approach*, which outlined carceral innovations under the rubric of reform. Asserting that the ongoing overcrowding crisis signaled that prison expansion was counterproductive for "break[ing] the cycle of crime,"[21] the plan promoted reforms in sentencing, community sanctions and supervision, and juvenile justice.[22] Many of the recommendations advocated beefing up the shadow carceral state infrastructure, such as halfway houses and "community-based residential facilities" for parole violators.[23]

Dominating *The Governor's Corrections Plan* were Roemer's financial concerns. Limits imposed by finance capital meant that Louisiana could not afford to construct new state prisons. According to the report, "Louisiana's bond rating (Baa1) is the second lowest of any state that issues general obligation bonds. As a result, the state must pay a higher rate of interest on the bonds it issues." Not only was it costly to take out debt for capital construction but the low bond rating was also partially the result of the state's rampant debt spending, including the prison building spree, during the 1980s. To improve the state's bonding rating, Roemer would need to implement a new debt reduction plan "that will satisfy the New York financial community and boost the state's bond ratings." This included *canceling* the two new Louisiana Correctional Facilities Corporation (LCFC)-financed prisons because "prison construction has contributed significantly to the state's long-term debt." Given the negative impacts such projects would have on financial institutions' perceptions of and, hence, bond ratings for, the state, "Louisiana simply cannot afford to keep building prison facilities."[24]

Yet, rather than advocating decarceration, *The Governor's Corrections Plan* proposed deliberately increasing the state's reliance on jails by entering into cooperative endeavor agreements with sheriffs. The Rapides Parish jail, which would serve as a pilot program, would incarcerate four hundred state offenders for five years beginning July 1, 1991. Contracting with the Rapides Parish sheriff had several advantages. The state would save money because it would not have to appropriate construction costs, and the DPSC would save on operating expenses since the per diem rate paid to sheriffs was lower than the average daily cost of incarcerating someone in a state prison. This arrangement was also flexible in that the contract was only a five-year commitment.[25] The plan contended that this arrangement would be a boom for localities by repeating sheriffs' arguments that they had "frankly, become financially dependent upon state funds for the housing of state prisoners."[26] Removing state prisoners from jails would put sheriffs in a financial crisis, and therefore the best path forward was to expand the state's use of jailing infrastructure. Finally, following a proposal from the Louisiana Sheriffs' Association, the plan stated that if the pilot program was successful the cooperative endeavor agreement could be replicated with other localities.[27]

Missing from the plan was any discussion of its impacts on imprisoned people. There was no mention of how imprisoning more people in parish jails meant stripping even more people of the nominal rehabilitation programs offered in state prisons. By reducing incarcerated people's lives to the state's financial savings, *The Governor's Corrections Plan* revealed how even minimal reforms were predicated on the notion that there existed an irredeemable class of predominantly Black Louisianians that the state had no plans for other than to exile behind bars.

Yet these new carceral innovations were not enough for Judge Polozola. In response to *The Governor's Corrections Plan* the state legislature allotted $250,000 to the new state sentencing commission to revamp sentencing laws, $2.8 million dollars to beef up probation and parole, $15 million to expand prison bed space, and $1.77 million to expand halfway houses.[28] Just days after the legislative session, Judge Polozola demanded that state officials "advise the court . . . why the 14.6 million dollars in state bond money available for corrections capital construction cannot be used to expand the existing state prisons by 1,200 to 2,000 beds."[29] The unencumbered bonds being referred to were none other than the remaining monies from the LCFC

1985 bond sale. With the three LCFC-financed state prisons built at lower costs than anticipated, and the plans for the two remaining LCFC prisons canceled by Roemer to rein in debt-service, the remaining $14.6 million from the initial bond sale was left in limbo. Polozola pushed the Roemer administration to "stretch" the remaining balance to add on 576 beds to the three prisons built by LCFC financing: Avoyelles, Allen, and Winn.[30]

Yet, Roemer's plan required voter approval. To expand the parish's jail capacity under the governor's plan, the Rapides Parish sheriff proposed a one-cent sales tax to convert two hospital buildings into space for six hundred jail beds. Even though this lease was approved by Governor Roemer and the Department of Health and Hospitals, Rapides Parish voters had a different opinion. Residents voted down the sales tax, making null and void the state-level approvals for the cooperative endeavor agreement.[31]

The failure of the Rapides Parish sales tax spoke to a larger set of issues for jails at the turn of the decade. The rural voters of Rapides Parish were joined by voters of other rural, urban, and suburban parishes across the state in refusing to pass tax increases for expanded jail complexes.[32] In the few cases where jail bonds did pass, it was frequently only on the third, fourth, or fifth attempt of local officials cajoling their constituents.[33] As with previous bond defeats, opposition to jail taxes did not necessarily indicate the residents were opposed to jails. But it did suggest that funneling tax dollars to jails over other state endeavors was rarely a priority for Louisianans. Caddo Parish sheriff Hathaway theorized this challenge as rooted in the problem that voters "want people locked up but they don't want to pay for it."[34]

In a few places, sheriffs responded to their proposals' rejection by voters by slashing their jail capacity. After a jail tax was voted down in Iberia Parish, the sheriff "reduce[d] the jail population to a total of 130 incarcerated adult male inmates instead of the 260 for which we were authorized." The sheriff requested that Polozola *cut* Iberia Parish's official population limits, which Polozola refused to do, stating that it was beyond his jurisdiction.[35] However, sheriffs rarely attempted to diminish their parishes' penal capacity. Instead, they primarily mobilized individually and collectively through the Louisiana Sheriffs' Association to find new carceral strategies after jail tax defeats.

This was a significant reversal of sheriffs' initial protests against the mandate that they incarcerate overflow state prisoners in 1975. Beginning in West Feliciana Parish, home to Angola, local sheriffs began *requesting* that the state send them more prisoners during the 1980s.[36] With parishes short on revenue because of the state's oil recession, local governments cut their budgets, and the DPSC's per diem system increasingly covered a substantial portion of sheriffs' operating expenses. Over time, sheriffs grew dependent on this source of revenue—especially as local governments came to expect the DPSC to supplement sheriffs' budgets.[37] The more jail space available for state prisoners, the larger the potential revenue stream for sheriffs, which in turn further augmented their power.

This is not to say that sheriffs' power came from financially profiting directly from these state–parish relationships. However, given near-total authority to determine how the funds were spent, sheriffs used these state monies to increase jail staff and purchase punitive equipment and technologies, shoring up their political standing and growing their political bloc. This was the true benefit of local jail growth for sheriffs.[38]

Although sheriffs in Louisiana held a powerful position with very limited accountability to state officials or agencies, Judge Polozola did place limits on their scope of authority. Averse to using jails as the solution to overcrowding, Judge Polozola often sparred with the sheriffs. This conflict came to a head around the jailing of INS prisoners. In the late 1980s Sheriff Belt of Avoyelles Parish (among others) began accepting federal prisoners from Washington, D.C., and immigrant detainees from INS without permission from Polozola. Following the wave of Mariel boatlift immigrants from Cuba to South Florida in 1980, President Reagan reactivated INS's stagnant policy of imprisoning unauthorized migrants, reinterpreting it to make imprisonment mandatory. While the federal government was building out the United States' immigration detention apparatus, INS contracted with thousands of local jails to incarcerate immigrants.[39] When Polozola expressed outrage at sheriffs taking in INS detainees and prisoners from the nation's capital while overcrowding precluded them from incarcerating Louisiana's state prisoners, the sheriffs justified their decision by stating the federal government's per diem of $40 a day was more than twice the state's rate.[40] Lafayette Parish sheriff Don Breaux asserted he would go broke if forced to remove the immigrant prisoners from his jail, and Sheriff Belt argued that immigration detention pulled Avoyelles out of bankruptcy.[41]

Unimpressed, Polozola issued an injunction against sheriffs holding INS or DC prisoners in Louisiana on the grounds of the overcrowding crisis.[42] Although not explicit in Polozola's injunction, it is also probable that his decision was influenced by a riot staged by Mariel Cuban immigrant prisoners at Louisiana's Oakdale Detention Center in 1987. At Oakdale, incarcerated migrants protested forced repatriation and prison conditions by burning down ten of the prison's fourteen buildings and taking hostages for over a week. At the end of the standoff, immigrant prisoners did not win any changes to their immigration statuses, and the Oakdale immigrant prison was rebuilt stronger than ever.[43] After the Oakdale uprising the federal government asked Sheriff Belt to detain 200 of the former Oakdale INS prisoners.[44] Polozola's injunction was likely attached to fears about potential immigrant detainee uprisings along similar lines.

The Louisiana Sheriffs' Association appealed Polozola's injunction.[45] They argued that incarcerating INS and DC prisoners at the higher per diem rate did not exacerbate overcrowding but benefited the state in that federal funds could "finance the building of enough prison beds to house additional Louisiana prisoners."[46] They convinced the Fifth District Court of Appeals that incarcerating federal prisoners did not undermine population limits and therefore was not a direct threat to the federal court orders.[47] Under this ruling, sheriffs were permitted to incarcerate immigrant and DC prisoners as long as they obtained written permission from Polozola.[48]

Having won their appeal to imprison INS and DC prisoners in their jails, the Louisiana Sheriffs' Association reanimated the cooperative endeavor agreement proposal. Although jail millages—voter-approved property taxes dedicated to the sheriff's department—were difficult to pass in urban areas, they often succeeded after multiple attempts, whereas they almost always failed in rural and suburban parishes.[49] The Louisiana Sheriffs' Association saw this conundrum as an opening for state-level action.

During the 1992 legislative session, the Louisiana Sheriffs' Association convinced the legislature to increase the per diem rate to $21 and to create cooperative endeavor agreements with DPSC through Act 394. Under this bill, in the case where a parish was required to renovate or increase the size of their jails to incarcerate state prisoners, the state was responsible for covering said debt service through an additional per diem of $7 per day until the debt was repaid.[50] Because the debt was paid through the per diem system, the jail expansions did not undermine Louisiana's bond rating.

Act 394 set in motion a wave of jail expansions. A slew of primarily rural parishes entered into this remodeled form of carceral cooperation.[51] Most cooperative endeavor agreements went *beyond* the official law in providing sheriffs not only with jail financing but also a commitment that DPSC would "maintain at all times a population of not less than 40% of the aggregate jail capacity" of a parish's jail.[52] This arrangement surpassed the 70/30 program in promising a baseline of state revenue through the now-guaranteed state prisoner per diems, on top of covering capital construction costs over the ten- to twenty-year lengths of the contracts. Furthermore, because this arrangement did not increase local taxes, voters had less power to shut down jail expansions. DPSC secretary Stalder summed up this arrangement this way: "We don't consider that temporary space; we consider it a partnership."[53] Between 1992 and 1994 almost five thousand beds were added to local jails.[54] No longer was there any pretense that housing state prisoners in parish jails was a temporary spatial fix: instead, it was the long-term geographic solution for the Louisiana penal system.

The cooperation endeavor agreement quickly became the new norm for the Louisiana criminal justice system, and for a time, the situation seemed calm. Yet, following a cluster of jail conditions complaints and, in response, state emergency allocations of funds to sheriffs, Polozola proclaimed that the cooperative endeavor agreements eroded state prisoners' constitutional rights. He ordered the state to move state prisoners from jails and the DPSC to establish regulations for jails incarcerating state prisoners.[55] The removal of state prisoners from jails would also "free space . . . which would permit law enforcement personnel to arrest and detain pending trial dangerous criminals."[56] To prevent the removal of state prisoners from jails, the DPSC and the Louisiana Sheriffs' Association developed mandatory jail guidelines and committed that all sheriffs would strictly abide by them. Polozola begrudgingly accepted this proposal with the stipulation that jails undergo more frequent inspections. If jails failed to meet the guidelines, they would be prohibited from incarcerating state prisoners.[57]

Just a year later, it appeared as if this punitive spatial strategy had reached its limits. While there had been hope that the prison population would stabilize, the opposite occurred. In 1993 alone, the state legislature increased the maximum penalty for manslaughter from forty to ninety-nine years, established the crime of "looting," authorized more restrictive bail standards, and instituted more sanctions on those convicted for sex offenses.[58] The bloated penal system had less than one thousand open prison beds. On the verge of another state of emergency, Polozola was troubled that Louisiana did not "have enough bed space to accommodate what the Legislature has been doing" and that jail abuses were on the rise, including sheriffs ignoring state law by having prisoners work for private establishments.[59] The DPSC responded by double bunking and hurrying jail expansions, but Polozola was not satisfied.[60] He issued yet another order for the state plan to build new prisons and asked whether Louisiana had applied for prison construction funds through the recently passed 1994 Clinton crime bill.[61]

The DPSC sought to alleviate Judge Polozola's concerns by continuing to double bunk and refurbishing a former Caddo Parish jail as a geriatric prison.⁶² But when the Louisiana Sheriffs' Association managed to block the legislature from appropriating $5 million to DPSC, thereby maintaining the growing reliance on parish jails, Polozola rescinded a previous order that had conditionally released nine of the state prisons from the court's mandates. State officials commenced a round of in-fighting about who was to blame for this turn of events.⁶³ The parish jail incarceration experiment appeared frozen for the foreseeable future.⁶⁴

But then, on September 26, 1996, Judge Polozola and recently elected Governor Mike Foster revealed that they had been negotiating about how to release most of the penal system from the Hayes Williams court order. These negotiations were instigated following the US Congress's passage of the Prison Litigation Reform Act, which served both to curtail prisoners from filing conditions of confinement lawsuits and to make it easier to terminate court orders over penal systems.⁶⁵ Polozola agreed to end his supervision of every jail, work-release center, juvenile prison, and adult prison, except for Angola, by April 1, 1997, on the conditions that prisons meet the American Correctional Association's accreditation standards, that the state "attempt" to increase bed space in prisons, and that, when possible, prisoners serving fifteen or more years be incarcerated in prisons. Jails, however, could continue to incarcerate state prisoners as the DPSC saw fit. If any violations were found in the coming months, the court order would not be extended.⁶⁶ With little fanfare, Louisiana's dependence on parish jails was permitted to grow without the oversight of Judge Polozola.

Three years after state officials brokered this agreement, the *Times-Picayune* published a front-page story on the rise of jails as the linchpin of the Louisiana carceral regime. The article noted that forty of the state's sixty-four parishes had at least one-third of their jail capacity filled with state prisoners, with twenty-two holding 50 percent or more state prisoners (table 3.1). Sheriff Belt of Avoyelles incarcerated one thousand state prisoners in his jail complex and had become the third-largest employer in Avoyelles. More than 4,500 new jail beds were in the works across the state through the cooperative endeavor agreement.⁶⁷ Along with Louisiana state revenue, federal funds from the Clinton crime bill partially financed these new jail beds for state prisoners.⁶⁸ There was no sign of retreat from this carceral cooperation infrastructure.

TABLE 3.1 Parish jails with more than 50% bed space held by state prisoners, 1998

Parish	Jail beds held by state prisoners
Acadia	71%
Avoyelles	71%
Caldwell	96%
Concordia	88%
East Carroll	91%
Evangeline	66%
Franklin	72%
Iberia	61%
Madison	88%
Morehouse	72%
Natchitoches	79%
Richland	81%
Riverbend	100%
Sabine	54%
St. Helena	60%
St. John the Baptist	74%
St. Martin	73%
Tensas	94%
Union	57%
Vernon	77%
West Carrol	78%
Winn	53%

Source: Bureau of Justice Statistics as Reported in *Times-Picayune*.

Fortress Foti: The Expansion of Orleans Parish Prison

It is unlikely that the New Orleanians who first elected Charles C. Foti Jr. as the Orleans Parish sheriff in 1974 could have imagined that he would govern the city jail for the next thirty years. Nicknamed as "little Napoleon" and described by employees as a "student of Machiavelli," Foti had an infamous quest for power.[69] Known for his penchant for cigars, pinball, and the blue-and-gold macaw named Max kept in the sheriffs' office, Foti was a polarizing figure lauded by those who favored his development of OPP and denounced by prisoners and advocates for the abhorrent jail conditions that made him the most-sued sheriff in the nation.[70]

Far more than any other sheriff in Louisiana, Foti agitated for his jail's growth. Before he was elected to office, the city had committed to building a shiny new ten-story jail through a mix of municipal bonds, state funds, and grants from the Law Enforcement Administration Act (LEAA) to satisfy a court order issued in response to a 1969 federal lawsuit over unconstitutional conditions.⁷¹ The new jail was extolled as "one of the most modern prisons in the nation," and the original plan of having the new jail replace the older one was scrapped in favor of keeping both open in response to overcrowding. While media championed Foti's oversight of OPP as a success story of rehabilitation-focused reform, city bureaucrats voiced concern that the jail's growth to 1,200 beds was "sapping the city budget" and providing Foti with outsized political leverage.⁷² Meanwhile, Foti hoped that a third building might yet be added onto the OPP complex, although such growth was, at the time, "really pie in the sky."⁷³ In fact, over the next five years, OPP would grow by almost one thousand beds.⁷⁴ Using state funds to convert a firehouse and a former hotel into jail space, Foti transformed the once single-building city jail into a sprawling complex (figure 3.1).⁷⁵

After OPP was brought under the Hayes Williams court order with the rest of the state's jails in 1981, Foti negotiated with Judge Polozola for a higher jail cap. Unlike elsewhere, Polozola's first ruling was to *raise* the jail's limit by almost six hundred beds, influenced by Foti's assertion that NOPD officers had become less aggressive due to a lack of jail space.⁷⁶ Less than a year later, Polozola increased OPP's population by another three hundred beds, with the stipulation that Foti hire another thirty-five to forty-seven guards.⁷⁷

By the summer of 1983, OPP had surpassed its maximum population of three thousand prisoners because of rising arrests, stiffer sentences, and an increase in state prisoners. Foti erected an "emergency detention center" in the form of a 100-bed "tent city" (Figure 3.2). When the tent city was announced, nearby residents held a meeting with Foti to express their concerns. They then presented a petition signed by dozens of neighbors outlining their position. In addition to outlining the danger of potential escapes, the petition also stated, "It's the feeling of the people of this area if these people are non-violent or non-threatening they should be released to do community service on the weekends and taken off the taxpayers roll."⁷⁸ Despite their mobilization in support of alternative means of managing overcrowding, the neighbors' demands were not met. Even the initial verbal commitment from Foti that he would remove the "tents 90 days from June 7, 1983," did not materialize.⁷⁹ The OPP tent city remained, expanding to four hundred beds over the next decade.

However, Foti was not always eager to incarcerate state prisoners. Along with negotiating for the tent city, Foti drafted a bill that would allow sheriffs to declare an emergency whenever jail populations exceeded Polozola's limits. This emergency would trigger sheriffs' ability to grant early release

FIGURE 3.1 "The New Parish Prison," *States-Item*, October 23, 1977, Capital City Press/Georges Media Group, and Baton Rouge, Louisiana.

FIGURE 3.2 Sheriff Foti political cartoon, *Times-Picayune*, June 10, 1983, Capital City Press/Georges Media Group, and Baton Rouge, Louisiana.

not only to defendants or those serving municipal charges but also to people serving state sentences. With backing from the Louisiana Sheriffs' Association, the bill easily passed the state legislature.[80] This policy became controversial because Foti would use early release not only to stay within the federal court mandates but also to manipulate public opinion for his own carceral aims.

As the sheriff's staff more than quadrupled to eight hundred employees with OPP's expansion and the federal court's reform mandates, Foti used his large department as a kind of political machine.[81] Although his deputies could not legally campaign for him, Foti mobilized them to campaign for jail expansion millages and other taxes that directly funded the sheriff's office.[82] Foti ingratiated himself to the public by assigning his deputies to oversee numerous work-release centers and "community programs" that he created. In the words of community activist Don Everard, "Foti was a master at basically using his resources to make people feel good about the sheriff's office."[83] Taking an expansive view of the state law that allowed willing prisoners to labor on public works projects, Foti assigned people to do "beautification projects" that ran the gamut from cleaning up after Mardi Gras parades to painting war memorial murals.[84] The definition of "public works" was stretched to include catering local high school graduations, running a meals on wheels program, and holding an annual Thanksgiving meal for seniors. In addition, deputies provided free transportation services for religious organizations and free security for Tulane University sporting events.[85] Although Foti's use of jail labor occasionally came under public scrutiny, these programs were favorably regarded and the source of puff pieces in the *Times-Picayune*.[86] His prisoner work projects served as consent-building for Foti's reign over OPP.

Still, Foti did not gain everyone's favor. One of the major sources of conflict between the New Orleans City Council and Sheriff Foti was his deliberate obfuscation of accounting records. From the time Foti entered office in 1974, he refused to provide New Orleans city officials with detailed information on his spending. Frustrations at Foti's murky budgetary practices reached a fever pitch during the 1980s when his office would routinely claim it was out of funds midway through the year and would threaten to shut down OPP if his budget was not increased. He evaded requests from city councilors on his financial records by claiming that such books did not exist because he had "no use for past records,"[87] nor was the sheriff's office obliged to provide such information. His adamant refusals raised further questions for the city council, including how much of his budget was going to programs that appeared to be primarily about building political patronage.[88] Yet, city council was unable to compel Foti to furnish his accounting documents; the LCJP was just as unsuccessful when it sued Foti for his financial records.[89]

All the while, the mainstream media habitually amplified Foti's talking points and praised his implementation of rehabilitation programs that ranged from a boxing gym to a women's gospel choir.[90] Even articles critiquing his actions complimented his office. In a *Times-Picayune* editorial by Iris Kelso ostensibly about the need to audit Foti's finances, Kelso emphasized that the desires for financial transparency did not undercut her support for the sheriff: "Here's the obligatory bow toward what Sheriff Foti accomplished as criminal sheriff. Foti has taken Parish Prison, an institution nobody knew what to do about, and put it into shape. . . . Foti has made humane conditions for prisoners when many people would just as soon see all criminals executed."[91] Upholding the narrative that Foti was a successful reformer obfuscated that hiding financial information could be tied to broader punitive violence.

Behind the veneer of respectability and rehabilitation that Foti tried to uphold, the people incarcerated at OPP reported the everyday and extraordinary violence that defined his governance of it. Foti prohibited Muslim prisoners from following their religious tenets while promoting Christian-focused programming.[92] The jail failed to provide adequate medical care to the point that guards ignored a prisoner's stroke.[93] Queer prisoners, confined to a homosexual cellblock, reported that they were denied water for weeks and only had access to ice through trading cigarettes or engaging in coerced sexual activity with guards.[94] Within the tent city, prisoners testified that they were not provided with blankets, showers, or operable toilets.[95] Despite Foti's publicity to the contrary, less than 10 percent of people incarcerated at OPP participated in programs, with people mostly confined to idle time and television as the jail's primary official "activity."[96] The deputies also regularly beat prisoners who spoke out about unconstitutional jail conditions.[97]

Although OPP prisoners persistently lodged complaints, as predominantly Black people who were doubly demonized as criminals, their plight rarely elicited public attention or support other than from the LCJP and ACLU. After a particularly brutal beating of five prisoners and a hunger strike by two of the beating survivors, the LCJP, through newsletter articles and organizing pickets outside the jail in the early 1980s, tried to get the FBI to investigate Foti's dehumanizing reign (figure 3.3).[98] However, the Louisiana chapter of the Southern Coalition of Jails and Prisons fizzled out by the mid-1980s, without any similar organization to take its place in agitating on behalf of imprisoned people at OPP and for decarceration in New Orleans for many years.

After the LCJP disbanded, the Louisiana ACLU provided prisoners at OPP with legal support. In 1989 it filed a lawsuit on behalf of a multigender group of state prisoners serving time at OPP. Their claim focused not only on OPP's reprehensible conditions of confinement but also argued that serving a prison sentence there was fundamentally a crueler punishment than doing time in a state prison, in that jails did not provide the kinds of educational, vocational, or addiction programming found in state prisons.[99] The courts would later reject this claim.

Sheriff Foti took advantage of the overcrowding state of emergency in 1989 to expand his jailing empire. He pushed for two new jail millages: one to finance the addition of 1,500 beds to the OPP complex, including a jail for

FIGURE 3.3 "Louisiana Jails," "Inside" newsletter. Louisiana Coalition on Jails and Prisons. Southern Coalition on Jails and Prisons Records (04655), Southern Historical Collection at Wilson Special Collections Library, University of North Carolina at Chapel Hill.

the mentally ill and a jail for juveniles, and the other to provide $8.5 million dollars for jail operating expenses for the next two decades.[100] Foti advocated for these proposed taxes on three primary grounds. First, the overcrowding of OPP showed no signs of letting up due to the growing number of state prisoners and the War on Drugs. The second was that Foti's office and the courts had been so underfunded that the city council had affixed an "$8 public safety fee on monthly water bills . . . to keep the criminal justice system afloat."[101] Foti argued that the two new millages would preclude emergency measures and provide the criminal justice system with a steady revenue source.

Foti's third and most prominent argument for the jail taxes was that he would be forced to release thousands of people if they were not approved. After issuing this threat, Foti implemented a policy of not incarcerating people arrested on municipal offenses and began releasing people on state charges to manage population limits.[102] Foti further preyed on voters' fears of crime by distributing a report that his office had released 11,000 people in the first three quarters of 1989 due to a lack of jail space, creatively using statistics to assert that 44 percent of those released would soon be rearrested.[103] Taking the campaign into neighborhoods throughout the city, sheriff's deputies distributed fliers detailing recent crimes in their areas to bring home the issue.[104] To clinch matters, Foti orchestrated a dramatic mass release days before the election. He alerted television stations that he was about to release more than fifty defendants and pronounced that the millage vote was "a referendum on whether we want to keep them in jail."[105] As one TV reporter recounted, Foti's deputies "told us where to go and we got great pictures. It made quite an impact. We got phone calls like crazy from people wanting to know why the prisoners had been released."[106] The media, even Foti's critics, largely followed his intended script.[107]

Despite Foti's efforts and the media's amplification of his rhetoric, voters turned out to defeat both millages on October 7, 1989. The millage dedicated to jail expansion narrowly failed by only 327 votes, whereas the millage to provide the sheriff's office with ongoing operations revenue failed by the much larger margin of 6,893 votes.[108] Although these results indicated that in at least some corners public trust of Foti's oversight of the jail was waning, pollsters reported that the defeat was largely symptomatic of "voter reluctance to add property taxes in New Orleans."[109]

Within a month of the failed jail millages, Foti moved ahead with a similar tax proposal. This time around, Foti only proposed one millage for a $34 million OPP expansion, removing the more contentious jail operations millage.[110] Although the Bureau of Governmental Research, Chamber of Commerce, Business Council, and *Times-Picayune* opposed the millage due to a generalized opposition to property taxes, the lion's share of the city's criminal justice officials, including a number of judges running for reelection, endorsed the measure.[111] In a reversal of the previous election results, the millage passed by 56 percent or by more than 12,000 votes.[112]

When some critics argued that Foti did not have the operational funding to run a jail complex of this magnitude, he filed papers in federal court claiming that the city intentionally underfunded his department. He argued that the city was undermining his ability to meet the federal mandates; instead of allotting funding through a flat yearly budget, the city should follow the state's lead and institute a per diem system for municipal prisoners.[113] The courts agreed, ordering the city of New Orleans to implement a per diem budget arrangement for the sheriff's office.[114] Starting on January 1, 1991, the municipal per diem, which was justified as necessary to avoid inhumane conditions, in fact created a new financial incentive for the Orleans Parish Sheriffs' Office to cage more people for longer stretches of time.

Although Foti never entered into a DPSC cooperative endeavor agreement, this does not mean Foti was not interested in expanding OPP's capacity for state prisoners.[115] He attempted to further entrench his office in the incarceration of state prisoners twice in the early 1990s. First, during the debate about how DPSC should use the $14.6 million in unencumbered LCFC lease revenue bonds, Foti advocated that the state appropriate the bond money to *his* office to build a 992-bed facility for state prisoners.[116] Although the state did not grant him these funds, Foti did not give up. When Edwards was reelected as governor, Foti proposed that the state expand prisoner localization through a system in which sheriffs would house "all state prisoners from their parish with sentences under 5 years." This would solve overcrowding and allow "inmates with shorter sentences to be incarcerated as close to their home as possible in order to maintain contact with their families, and upon release be more easily re-integrated into the community."[117]

Although never implemented, parts of these proposals were incorporated into the rationales for the DPSC's cooperative endeavor agreements with parish jails a year later and framed city politicians' justifications for continually allocating funds to OPP. Although Foti's office gained revenue from incarcerated state and INS prisoners, he amassed enough city dollars from millages and the municipal per diem that OPP did not need to enter into a cooperative endeavor agreement. By 1992, the Orleans Parish Sheriff Office's operating budget was almost $41 million, with $13.6 million from state and federal per diem payments and $24 million from the city.[118] Even though Foti would spend the next decade lobbying to lock up more INS prisoners, state prisoners from nearby Jefferson Parish, and youth prisoners from the juvenile justice system, OPP filled to capacity primarily through increases in municipal arrestees following the implementation of policing reforms by mayor Marc Morial and NOPD superintendent Richard Pennington.[119]

Arresting the City: The Perniciousness of Policing Reforms

Despite Foti's forecast that OPP's population would increase, by the 1993 ribbon cutting for the 7,000 plus-bed jail, its population—which included more than 1,500 state, federal, and immigrant prisoners and 540 prisoners from Jefferson Parish—stabilized at around 5,000. This is not to suggest that its jail population was "natural" but rather that the interchange between longer sentences and more frequent arrests, along with some early releases and a declining official street crime rate, produced somewhat of an equilibrium. Foti even told reporters that they should not be misled into thinking that "since we have 7,000 beds that we're going to fill them. Because we're not."[120] When reporters questioned why Foti had then pushed for this expansion, he claimed that OPP's expansion was essential for jail management.[121]

Nevertheless, OPP's population would hit seven thousand over the next few years, even as the overall official crime rate would decline. In the mid- to late 1990s, New Orleans Mayor Marc Morial and NOPD Superintendent Richard Pennington sought to manage moral panics about crime and the crises of NOPD legitimacy and economic contractions through the dual projects of liberal police reform and neoliberal urban redevelopment. Leveraging the federal material and ideological resources of the Clinton crime bill, Superintendent Pennington rebuilt consent for policing through professionalizing the NOPD. In doing so, punitive power was expanded to target those whom city officials and sectors of the public imagined, in the words of Judah Schept, as a growing "jailable population" for New Orleans.[122] Through law-and-order austerity, predominantly Black working-class and poor people were increasingly displaced from geographic zones of racialized poverty or speculative tourism development to be frequently contained in OPP.

In the early 1990s, New Orleans law enforcement launched a wave of police busts. With jail construction alleviating overcrowding concerns, Sheriff Foti and DA Connick collaborated to clamp down on "lawlessness."[123] Whereas police crackdowns in the 1980s were primarily directed at drug offenders, these sweeps targeted people who had outstanding warrants or had violated the terms of their parole or probation. In the first months of 1991, the NOPD, Orleans and Jefferson sheriffs' deputies, state troopers, and

US marshals joined forces in "Operation Crime Sweep." In its first two weekends, more than 450 people were arrested across eight parishes, of whom more than 350 people were booked at OPP.[124] These raids advanced the false notion that people awaiting trial on bond or serving probation or parole fostered a dangerous environment in New Orleans. With little attention given to the minimal infractions that constituted most parole or probation violations or that most people did not breach the conditions of their constrained freedom, these mass arrests cemented the idea that laws and judges were too lenient even as the criminal justice system grew harsher. Rather that fomenting a sense of public safety, these high-profile police sweeps escalated public concerns about street crime.

Local media exacerbated the public's fears about crime. Sensationalist stories with eye-catching headlines such as "Murder Rate in N.O. Exceeds One a Day," "Tragedy Marks a Night of Crime," and "When Will It All End?" positioned New Orleans as exceptionally violent.[125] Such articles tended to amplify police narratives that located the crisis as originating within Black working-class neighborhoods. For instance, the central thrust of one article was a recapitulation of the NOPD's argument that uncontrolled "Black on Black crime" in New Orleans public housing was boosted by its residents' refusal to cooperate with the NOPD. Even though such criminal activity was geographically contained, it threatened to spill over and infect whiter, wealthier neighborhoods.[126] This racist rhetoric blamed the very people who were disproportionally losing loved ones to interpersonal violence while making clear that, for the state, such violence was only a concern insofar as it threatened white elite interests. In addition, a local PBS affiliate introduced "Saving Our Streets," a prime-time show featuring sheriffs, police chiefs, and district attorneys imploring residents to join the fight against crime, with a hotline for viewers to call to connect with victims' rights and anticrime groups after each show.[127]

Key to rising fears of violence was a moral panic about juvenile crime. While white supremacist ideology had long positioned Black children as unworthy of the protection of the status of childhood, during the 1980s and 1990s, tough-on-crime politics supercharged such ideas. Anti-Black ideas about the rise of juvenile "super predators" circulated across the nation from the racist social science of Charles Murray to speeches by First Lady Hillary Clinton.[128] During jail expansion debates, Foti and juvenile judges asserted that youth rapists and robbers were set free because juvenile prisons were at capacity. Officials contended that there existed a new breed of young "chronic offenders who have no fear of punishment."[129] In a letter to the editor published in the *Times-Picayune,* a resident of suburban Metairie wrote that it was "time to see the enemy clearly and take a stand" because "the problem of today is killing in the streets. The problem is not racism. The problem is not recreation or jobs. The problem is not even cocaine addiction. . . . The problem is the kid enticed every day by big money, really big money, and status, killer status with his young peers."[130] Given this framing of youth lawbreakers as two-dimensional enemies motivated by ego and greed, the only option for restoring social order was intensified punishment. At the 1991 New Orleans City Crime Summit, city officials committed to increasing the number of youths incarcerated at OPP.[131]

Although popular opinion and city policy were driven by perceptions that crime was out of control, New Orleans was experiencing an overall *decline* in crime, with the exception of homicides. A 1993 study conducted by the International Association of Chiefs of Police (IACP) documented that recent years had seen between a three to twenty-five percent decline in the "serious crimes" of rape, robbery, burglary, and auto theft and similar drops in "lesser crimes" such as pickpocketing and the ambiguous offense of "criminal mischief."[132] In contrast to dominant notions of New Orleans being one of the most dangerous cities in America, the IACP documented that as of 1992 the New Orleans crime rate was surpassed by cities such as Seattle, Atlanta, and Kansas City.[133] Furthermore, the widely publicized upsurge in homicides was less linear than popularly suggested. Recent years had witnessed a fluctuation in homicide rates from 306 murders in 1990 to 346 in 1991 to 279 in 1992.[134] Overall, homicides accounted for less than 1 percent of official city crime.[135] The *Times-Picayune* even noted drops in the homicide rate and the "surprising" fact that New Orleans was statistically safer than Baton Rouge.[136]

Local statistics were in sync with a national decline in the crime rate during the 1990s. No simple answer existed as to why crime was dropping in New Orleans, or anywhere else for that matter.[137] Yet rather than admit this issue was murky, criminal justice officials tended to float self-serving and unfounded explanations. For example, Foti posited that the crime decline occurred because he was planning to build a larger jail as part of his argument that the city should maintain its level of support of OPP.[138] The NOPD heralded the 1992 dip in homicides as due to community policing in public housing, asserting this proved the need to double down on such strategies.[139] As murders started to climb again, the NOPD's solution was to urge increased funding for community policing.[140] Whether crime was officially up or down, the answer remained more cops on the street and more people locked up.

By the 1994 mayoral elections, crime topped the polls as the leading issue for voters,[141] though it was coupled with a distrust of the city government and a perception of the NOPD as corrupt.[142] Elected officials received countless complaints about NOPD officers' misconduct and brutality from residents and tourists alike. For the mayoral candidates, proving their commitment to public safety necessitated a commitment to transforming the NOPD as an institution. The rise of the broken windows theory as the silver bullet of urban law enforcement fundamentally shaped their approach to public safety.

Broken windows policing was first presented in a 1982 article in *The Atlantic* by George L. Kelling of the right-wing think tank, the Manhattan Institute, and racist political scientist James Q. Wilson. Kelling and Wilson drew on a controversial 1969 experiment conducted by Stanford psychologist Philip Zimbardo to posit that, in areas where the built environment showed signs of disrepair (the quintessential broken window), people are emboldened to engage in unseemly public behavior—such as loitering, public drunkenness, panhandling, sex work, and solicitation—which escalates to more harmful activity such as robbery and homicide.[143] They argued that neighborhoods that fail to enact informal social control invite criminality, and thus intensified police presence is warranted to stop small-scale infractions from escalating into more dangerous ones. To restore order and control, law enforcement should take a page from the pre-civil rights policing social contract where residents consented to harsh and at times violent policing as a means of reasserting state authority against lawless criminals.[144]

Borrowing from Jim Crow-era policing that operated to restrict Black public life, broken windows policing regulates public spaces to meet white middle-class norms. Policing public space serves to sanitize urban environments of populations (people of color, youth, the homeless, under- and unemployed people, queer and trans people, and sex workers) deemed a threat to gentrification.[145] This form of policing depends on police "arresting people on meaningless charges," often solely based on the criterion that "they look suspicious," thereby reifying criminalizing logics rooted in racialism.[146] Moreover, the emphasis on primarily small scale behaviors and transgressions infractions discounts macro-level analysis or interventions in favor of policing racialized poverty.[147]

Cities often adopted broken windows policing under the framework of community policing. Developed as a liberal reformist response to the 1960s urban uprisings, community policing touts the importance of more cops walking the beat to proactively protect public order,[148] based on the fantasy that "if the police just get to know the community, crime will go down and police racism will dwindle," as Stuart Schrader has written. Elites routinely promoted broken windows through community policing as a form of redress for police violence. The very malleability of the term "community" and its taken-for-granted positive associations (even though the concept is predicated on exclusion) paper over the inherent violence of policing.[149] Their melding together in policy discourse points to how policing projects are predicated both on the reformist rebranding of law enforcement and the reworking of spatial policing strategies as a consent-building project for the bulking up of police power.

Following the lead of New York City mayor Rudy Giuliani, countless police departments instituted broken windows policing in the 1990s, aided by a massive infusion of federal funds from the Clinton administration.[150] Within the landmark 1994 Violent Crime Control and Law Enforcement Act was the Community Oriented Policing Services (COPS) program that earmarked $8.8 billion for grants to put 100,000 more police on US streets through community policing.[151] Although Clinton's crime bill had not been passed by the time of New Orleans mayor's race, it was already shaping local law enforcement. Even before its passage, City Councilman Joseph Giarrusso Sr. wrote then-senator Joe Biden (well-known architect of the crime bill) to ask for an allotment of the federal funding for the NOPD to escalate its use of stop-and-frisk tactics to reduce gun violence.[152]

The 1994 mayoral race was also shaped by the deep economic crises plaguing the Crescent City. Like other cities, the rise of Black urban political power in New Orleans coincided with massive federal disinvestment in cities, ongoing white flight that shrank the city's property tax base, and global economic restructuring that produced deindustrialization and a reorientation toward a service-centered economy.[153] The fiscal contractions from the state's oil bust had hit the city particularly hard. Forty thousand jobs and seventy thousand residents left New Orleans during the 1980s, while state discretionary funds appropriated to New Orleans decreased from $27.8 million to $6.9 million.[154] The median income for New Orleans households was 26 percent lower than the national average and 39 percent lower than the surrounding parishes, with one-third of households making less than $10,000 a year.[155] The 1970s building of the Superdome and the financial catastrophe of the 1984 New Orleans World's Fair had left the city with a heavy debt burden and negative bond ratings, and state courts had prevented the state from generating much-needed revenue by ruling that a progressive wage tax violated the state's constitutional ban on local income taxes.[156] When combined with declining property values, this meant that New Orleans's primary source of revenue was a regressive sales tax, the highest in the nation, that disproportionally burdened poor and working-class residents.[157]

In the face of these deep economic problems, candidates championed tourism development and public–private partnerships as solutions. Such economic development strategies were the very same ones that had deepened racialized economic inequality over the preceding decades. Politicians' promotion of mega-projects like the Superdome had served to boost the tourism economy while funneling public dollars into private capital with little benefit to residents. Neoliberal urbanism was ascendant.[158]

The twinned promises of fighting crime and economic development enabled Marc Morial to become the next mayor of New Orleans.[159] Morial had been brought up in New Orleans politics as the son of the city's first Black mayor, Ernest "Dutch" Morial. Marc Morial's campaign asserted, "Companies refuse to relocate here because of their employees' fear about crime in this city. Tourists' concerns about crime and public safety can have an enormous detrimental impact on our city."[160] The relationship between capital investments and policing had previously been more tacit, in the 1990s it became much more explicit. In 1991, the New Orleans Business Council established a Crime Committee to develop strategies for "out-of-control crime," and the New Orleans Criminal Justice Coordinating Council added seats for business leaders.[161] One of Morial's first actions as mayor was the creation of a "Tourism Crime Task Force."[162] Reducing street crime and neoliberal redevelopment went hand in hand insofar as policing public spaces was understood as critical to speculative development and the gentrification of Black working-class and poor neighborhoods was viewed as an opportunity to reduce crime.

Morial's approach to public safety was molded by a racist and classist geographic imaginary of which people and places were a threat to New Orleans. His administration was particularly concerned about juveniles with arrests records and those who lived in "public housing developments and other low income areas," *especially* "children of female headed households" who were believed to be predisposed to criminal behavior.[163] This barely coded articulation of Black working-class and poor people and places as sources of disorder and violence trafficked in old logics that equated Blackness with criminality, as well as the patriarchal racist notion popularized by Daniel Patrick Moynihan in his "study" *The Negro Family* that Black children without strong father figures were more likely to be delinquent lawbreakers.[164] Morial advocated for the end of HUD's policy of one-for-one replacement in its new HOPE VI public housing redevelopment program. In other words, he advocated shrinking the city's public housing stock and displacing predominantly poor Black female-headed families from their homes in the name of public safety.[165]

Morial identified the erosion of NOPD's legitimacy as responsible for the department's inability to attain public cooperation. From his perspective, distrust of the NOPD stemmed from the absence of strong leadership and the low educational requirements to become a police officer, which led to the hiring of unprofessional, unqualified, and at times corrupt police officers.[166] Passing new taxes for NOPD pay increases was difficult, while voters approved millages for private neighborhood security districts.[167] However, the Morial administration contended that residents "want a partnership" with the NOPD.[168] Morial encouraged it to strengthen its burgeoning relationship with the church alliance All Congregations Together to "increase[e] community support for policing."[169] Police reforms would enable the NOPD to bring together residents, social services, and businesses to fight "the crime issue as a war."[170]

In his first one hundred days, Morial launched the Morial Administration Crime Initiatives (MAC I) as the murder rate jumped to the highest in the nation.[171] He reassigned one hundred cops from desks to the streets and secured $1.26 million from the 1994 crime bill to hire twenty-three new police officers. New Orleanians were recruited into community policing through an extensive network of neighborhood watch groups and the integration of taxi drivers into a volunteer watch dog program. In addition, Morial sponsored the "revitalization" of blighted neighborhoods and began talks with HUD about redeveloping the St. Thomas projects.[172] At the center of MAC I, however, was youth crime prevention. Morial implemented the most stringent juvenile curfew in the nation. Youth found after curfew were to be held in a new curfew detention center run by Sheriff Foti. In the law's first year, there were almost four thousand curfew detentions.[173] MAC I also included the expansion of youth recreation services and the formation of a summer jobs program for 1,300 young people. Although residents welcomed the investment, the $500,000 of largely privately raised funds for summer programs was dwarfed by the more than $80 million of tax revenue allocated to the NOPD.[174] In tying youth jobs and recreation to youth policing, MAC I branded itself as good for communities while shoring up the notion that New Orleans youth were criminals in the making.

Following a national search, Morial appointed Richard Pennington, a police veteran from Washington, D.C., as police chief just as the NOPD's crisis of legitimacy hit new heights.[175] In the days leading up to Pennington's inauguration, New Orleanian Kim Groves had filed a brutality complaint with Internal Affairs against officer Len Davis. Unknown to her, Davis ran an NOPD drug ring and was alerted to Groves's complaint. In response, Davis put a hit on Groves: she was murdered one day after filing her complaint. Before long an FBI investigation uncovered the NOPD-orchestrated killing of Groves, heightening calls to root out police corruption and violence.[176]

Soon after entering office, Superintendent Pennington unveiled his multifaceted Pennington Plan to reform the NOPD by "curtailing our crime epidemic, restoring public confidence and bringing dignity, respect, and integrity back."[177] The first piece of this plan was the creation of the FBI-supported Public Integrity Division (PID) to replace the disgraced Internal Affairs division, the formation of the Police Early Warning System (PEWS) to track citizen complaints, and the establishment of stricter standards for the hiring and promotion of police officers.[178] The second part of the plan was "comprehensive community policing" in public housing and in the Lower Ninth Ward and the creation of a citywide community policing unit. The third set of reforms aimed at professionalizing the NOPD by providing training in areas ranging from customer service to interrogation techniques and forensic science. In addition, Pennington expanded the homicide division by 40 percent. Furthermore, police were limited in the number of hours they could work outside details and were prohibited from working security at bars. The final piece of the Pennington Plan was boosting morale. All NOPD officers were to receive a 5 percent pay increase—their first raise in eight years.[179] The Pennington Plan strove to clean up and professionalize the NOPD to bolster its capacity to make both low- and high-level arrests.

The PID quickly began to investigate police officers, and by August 1995, Pennington had suspended 135 and terminated 29 officers while 21 cops resigned under investigation.[180] Pennington also convinced the legislature to pass a law that kept law enforcement personnel from expunging complaints from their records.[181] In addition to making strides in changing the NOPD's public image, Pennington enacted an expansive community policing program. Through a $4 million grant from the Clinton COPS program, Pennington hired more officers, increased overtime, and purchased new equipment. Three new policing substations were opened in public housing complexes.[182] Pennington also deployed NOPD officers to playgrounds in Black neighborhoods.[183] In 1995, community policing initiatives were responsible for 2,556 adult arrests, 493 youth arrests, and 9,500 stop and frisks.[184] Everyday community policing was coupled with the continuation of NOPD collaboration with state and federal law enforcement on high-profile raids in public housing.[185]

Pennington also used COPS funds to build consent for intensified policing practices within Black working-class neighborhoods. The NOPD launched "Operation Chill Out" in housing projects to provide water activities for children.[186] At the same time, the NOPD heavily recruited people to sign up for "crime-fighting training" and to join neighborhood watch groups. Between 1995 and 1996, the neighborhoods participating in the community policing initiative "Night Out against Crime" jumped from 56 to 220, and New Orleans won first place in citizen participation from the National Association of Town Watch.[187]

In addition to policing Black working-class spaces, Pennington intensified police saturation of areas marked for incorporation into the tourist economy. The lower Decatur section of the French Quarter, the music club strip of Frenchmen Street in the adjacent Marigny neighborhood, and the business improvement Downtown Development District between the French Quarter and Convention Center were soon crawling with law enforcement.[188] The uptick in street patrols not only came from Pennington but also was called for by property and business owners. The Downtown Development District initiated antigraffiti campaigns and agitated for police sweeps of homeless encampments and fencing off public parks to push out panhandling that they viewed as a stepping-stone to robbery.[189] After a slight rise in armed robberies, French Quarter residents and businesses pushed for a greater law enforcement presence in the neighborhood. Pennington deployed more sheriffs' deputies and state troopers "to demonstrate that the French Quarter, the economic bloodline of the city, is safe."[190] This policing strategy visibly marked to residents and tourists alike that the city was clamping down on disorder.

Having secured public approval for his crackdown on corruption, Pennington had the political capital to forge ahead with the second phase of the Pennington Plan: expanding the NOPD's reach.[191] An infusion of private funds through the creation of the New Orleans Police Foundation allowed

Pennington to hire the New York-based Linder Maple Group to develop reforms based on their work with Giuliani's New York Police Department.[192] First, the consultants recommended that NOPD adopt CompStat, a system that through statistical and geographic data tracks complaints and arrests to identify "hot spots" for policing while holding districts to quantitative policing goals.[193] The second recommendation was to decentralize the NOPD structure to give commanders greater power and accountability. Most importantly, they encouraged an aggressive recruitment campaign to bolster the size of the NOPD from 1,285 to 1,700 cops.[194]

Although city leaders supported this round of policing reforms in the abstract, the cost gave them pause. Morial's policies had not translated into economic prosperity for the city overall. Although the NOPD continued to receive federal COPS grants, the shortage of municipal revenue constrained Morial's ability to fully back Pennington's plan. Not wanting to cut other city services or to gamble on a millage vote, few revenue options were available. Initially Morial and the city council did not include the $14 million requested for NOPD expansion in the 1997 budget.[195]

But then, less than two weeks after the budget was approved, fourteen homicides occurred in one week. The city elite accused Morial of being soft on crime, while his political adversary, Republican governor Mike Foster, asserted that the residency requirement for police officers and the attack on police corruption were partially to blame. In response, Morial gave a major address charting out his crime-fighting plan. First he blamed crime on weak parenting and urged parents to fulfill their "responsibility to give love, guidance, and discipline." Second, he announced that NOPD forces would be supplemented by sheriffs' deputies and the state police. Third, Morial shared that he was asking judges not to grant probation to violent offenders and that he would ask the state to allocate $1 million for more probation officers to crack down on parolees more effectively.[196] What was not announced but was churning in the background was Morial's and the city council's search for another $10 million for new NOPD hires and increased police pay. These pay raises were funded by raising the franchise fee on the city's electric company Entergy. The company then passed along this fee to residents through their utility bills, which made it an earmarked source of revenue that worked as an unofficial tax.[197] With a budget of $100 million, the NOPD accounted for one-quarter of the city's general budget.[198] By August of 1997, its force stood at 1,548 officers.[199]

The NOPD buildup was joined by another key punitive state enhancement shaped by the Clinton crime bill: it limited federal grants to those penal systems that required people incarcerated for violent offenses to serve a "substantial portion"—ideally 85 percent—of their sentences. In 1995, DA Harry Connick succeeded in getting the Louisiana legislature to pass a truth-in-sentencing law that followed these draconian guidelines and would take effect in 1997.[200] Limiting DPSC's capacity to exercise early releases, along with the NOPD's merciless surge in arrests, intensified the swelling of the penal system at both the state and local levels.

By the time that Morial ran for reelection in 1998, his first term was widely viewed as a success. Although budget shortages meant it would be several more years before the NOPD hit 1,700 officers, Morial had made a name for himself as able to reform a corrupt police department and reduce crime.[201] A public opinion poll by the University of New Orleans found that most residents identified Pennington's policing reforms to be the greatest feat of the mayor's first term. The percentage of residents with positive feelings toward the NOPD increased from 19 to 42 percent between 1993 and 1997. For the first time in the University of New Orleans polling history, more residents believed crime to be in decline than on the rise.[202] This local approval was joined by national praise from the media, and President Clinton applauded the city's stringent youth curfew as a national model.[203]

Yet the policing reforms' impacts on crime rates were uneven. City crime rates were in decline *prior* to Morial's election. While homicides did decrease after 1995, offenses labeled "violent crime" and "property crime" were trending downward as early as 1990.[204] Research by Kevin Unter showed there was little to no significant correlation between implementing broken windows and community policing tactics and the drop in crime. According to Unter (who set out to *prove* the successes of these policing reforms), increasing the number of NOPD officers and implementing CompStat had a *negative* correlation with "violent crime." In other words, it was more likely that violence would go up, not down, after their implementation.[205] Under these reforms youth arrests exploded from just under three thousand in 1993 to about ten thousand in 1998.[206] Ensnaring predominantly Black youth into the criminal legal system occurred even though most residents did not favor the youth curfew.[207]

Under Morial and Pennington, the NOPD's arrest rate skyrocketed. Municipal arrests jumped from 20,000 to almost 35,000, traffic arrests increased from 4,500 to 11,00, and drug arrests rose from just under 4,000 to more than 7,000 between 1994 and 1998.[208] Despite Foti's earlier assertion that he did not want the expanded OPP to be filled up, by 1998 it was at

93 percent capacity, locking up an average of 6,670 people a day—the vast majority of whom were arrested on municipal-level offenses. With Pennington's implementation of even tougher zero- tolerance broken windows policing in 2001, arrests skyrocketed further until hitting a peak in 2004. Not only was New Orleans the eighth highest per capita jailer in the nation as of 1998, but Louisiana also became the state with the highest per capita rate of incarceration in the United States.[209]

Rising Opposition to New Orleans's Punishment Regime

By 1996, the city's punitive practices had spurred some New Orleanians to question the status quo. DA Harry Connick faced a challenger, Morris Reed, powered by the low approval rate of Connick among Black New Orleanians. Reed argued that Connick's office employed racial discrimination and refused to prosecute cases of police brutality.[210] Although Connick won the election, his habitual racist fear-mongering did not hold the same purchase it once had.

Of all of New Orleans's punitive infrastructure, nothing garnered as much opposition as the jail.[211] Jailed people petitioned the city council to deny Foti's budget requests given the terrible medical care and food at OPP.[212] Reports of misconduct and violence by sheriff deputies appeared with increasing frequency in New Orleans papers: they barged into people's homes without warrants and frequently threatened sex workers at gunpoint to have sex with them or be thrown in jail.[213] Accounts of deputies sexually assaulting women at OPP served as a reminder of the ethos of patriarchal invincibility that structured punitive power.[214]

As part of a report on the jailing of migrants, immigration rights advocates with Human Rights Watch, Amnesty International, and the Catholic Legal Immigration Network investigated conditions for INS detainees held at OPP. Initially Foti, like sheriffs throughout the nation, obstructed their investigation by denying access to tours or legal visits.[215] After litigation forced the INS to compel Foti's compliance, Human Rights Watch released a report confirming that "some of the most disturbing and consistent complaints of inhumane conditions came from the detainees at Orleans Parish Prison."[216] Atrocious medical care, barriers to legal representation, and almost nonexistent interpreting support marked everyday life for the 500-plus immigrant detainees. As one immigrant put it, "I don't know what to do—they make our lives miserable in here and we cannot say anything because I see they beat people. Even right now, I'm writing this letter, but I'm scared if they find out they are going to give me more hard time."²¹⁷ Although Human Rights Watch recommended reforms of the abysmal conditions, their main takeaway was that "local jails are inappropriate places to hold asylum seekers and immigrants."²¹⁸ Foti and the INS disputed the findings, but the media highlighted the impacts of Foti's practices on jailed immigrants' lives.²¹⁹

Imprisoned immigrants were not the only victims of inadequate medical care. On April 3, 1999, the NOPD picked up JoAnn Johnson, a twenty-one-year-old Black working-class mother in her neighborhood of Algiers. She told the NOPD officers that she was diabetic and requested that they allow her to retrieve her medication from her home before being taken to lock up. Officers told her, "Fuck your medication. We don't have time for that." Three days later she died from a diabetic attack.

Johnson's family asserted that the NOPD preventing her from retrieving medication, the courts setting unreasonable bail, and the sheriff's office failure to monitor her health led to her preventable death. Even the coroner posited that the stress of being incarcerated likely aggravated her blood sugar levels.²²⁰ Her family filed a wrongful death lawsuit against the NOPD and the sheriff's office—naming JoAnn Johnson's abuse as institutionalized.²²¹ Her family and other supporters held a small rally outside the jail calling for Foti's resignation.²²²

Johnson's death and her family's mobilization sparked investigations into Foti and OPP. For the first time in years, the *Times Picayune* began seriously criticizing Foti.²²³ Even Mayor Morial admonished Sheriff Foti for not publicly facing questions about the jail's medical treatment.²²⁴ Moreover, within days of the Johnson family lawsuit, the FBI announced a probe into whether Johnson's civil rights were violated.²²⁵ In turn, the ACLU's National Prison Project filed new motions on the status of medical care in OPP under the assumption that Foti was in violation of the Hamilton consent decree.²²⁶ Not limiting their complaint to diabetic treatment, the ACLU charged that incarcerated women were routinely forced to give birth in shackles and were denied treatment for conditions such as ovarian cancer.²²⁷ Amnesty International joined the chorus of complaints in calling on Foti to end the tortuous practice of using stun belts on OPP prisoners during transport. Amnesty reported that HIV-positive prisoners who did not consent to wearing stun belts were "denied transportation and thus urgent medical care."²²⁸

Families and their supporters increasingly challenged Foti's disregard for incarcerated life, and protests regularly were held outside Foti's office in the summer of 1999. One short-lived group, the Screaming Mothers of New

Orleans, asserted that at least sixteen people had died from being denied medical care within OPP over the past decade.[229] The JoAnn Johnson Justice Committee instigated a Foti recall petition that collected 30,000 signatures.[230] Another group of families who had lost loved ones inside OPP filed a lawsuit contending that not only was the medical care inadequate but the sheriff's office also systematically delayed the release of prisoners twelve to seventy-two hours after their official release and refused to offer municipal good time. These practices kept people from accessing medical treatment while the sheriff's office collected extra per diem monies from their extended incarceration.[231]

Although this activism garnered public attention, it was unable to meaningfully weaken Foti's power. The JoAnn Johnson Justice Committee did not collect the 85,000 signatures needed for a Foti recall ballot measure. The city settled with the families of those who had died from medical neglect and opted to open a miniature emergency room within OPP, a reform that served only to expand Foti's reach and funding.[232] But the questions that these lawsuits, petitions, and protests raised proved enduring. When voters rejected Foti's proposed bond measure to expand OPP by another 600 beds in fall 1999, among the reasons circulating for voting against it was that it was unethical to expand such an inhumane institution.[233]

Around this time, another constellation of grassroots activism emerged that questioned the very necessity of imprisonment and policing. Meeting through different channels in the city from the high school creative writing program, Students at the Center, to the classrooms of the University of New Orleans, to the anarchist punk house Nowe Miasto, a multiracial cohort of activists came together to organize under an explicitly prison abolitionist framework. They shared a politics marked by a nonsectarian blend of Black feminism, anarchism, and Zapatismo, a part of what Chris Dixon has termed the "anti-authoritarian current" that characterized a new generation of North American transformative politics at the turn of the twenty-first century.[234] One of their major inspirations was the Black Panther Party (BPP). Many of these young activists sought out former members of the New Orleans BBP chapter Althea Francois and Malik Rahim for political guidance and joined the political prisoner campaign to free the Angola Three when the support committee was reestablished in 1998.[235] They were also influenced by the Juvenile Justice Project of Louisiana's (JJPL) campaign to shut down the Tallulah youth prison because of its abhorrent conditions. JJPL's campaign offered a vision of engaging in antiprison struggles without reinforcing the state's carceral capacities.[236]

How to organize in ways that did not shore up the penal system was a critical question for them as prison abolitionists, *not* as prisoner reformers. As a liberatory political project, prison abolition is both a strategy and a goal for transforming society: to end the state's capacity to cage, punish, and repress and to fundamentally remake the material conditions that give rise to prisons as the catchall solution to complex political, economic, and social problems.[237] One of the central assertions of prison abolition is that attempts to reform the prison system have often had the unintended consequence of buttressing and extending carceral power, and therefore the only logical way to end the state's punitive violence is to completely abolish it.[238]

The rise of interest in prison abolition in New Orleans in the late 1990s corresponded with a national resurgence of prison abolition within radical circles. Although prison abolition was a robust strand within Black liberation struggles in the late 1960s and 1970s, there was a quieting of abolitionist politics within leftist organizing during the 1980s and early 1990s.[239] However, prison abolition attracted greater interest after the 1998 conference, Critical Resistance: Beyond the Prison Industrial Complex, which was held at UC Berkeley. It drew more than three thousand attendees, surpassing organizers' expectations. The energy of the conference was harnessed into the formation of Critical Resistance (CR) as a national organization headquartered in Oakland. The success of the conference demonstrated the appeal of abolition while also popularizing prison abolition throughout national circuits of grassroots organizing.[240]

For activists in New Orleans, the politics of abolition both spoke to the intensive criminalization, policing, and imprisonment that people witnessed and aligned with this network of activists' broader antiracist, feminist, and anticapitalist politics. For instance, Melissa Burch remembers that abolition was "exactly what I was looking for coming back from Chiapas and wanting to think about the equivalent . . . what would true social transformation look like in the US, and how might you build it."[241] In addition, prison abolition aligned with their Black feminist and women of color feminist politics. For Black feminist Shana M. griffin, there was a clear connection between prison abolitionists' analysis of state violence and the national and local work she was involved in with INCITE! Women of Color Against Violence. INCITE! placed gender-based violence in a framework that examined the relationship of reproductive and domestic violence to militarism, detention, and law enforcement and took an expansive view on questions of safety.[242]

With prison abolition as a central pillar of their political orientation, this cohort of activists formed and participated in a series of small, overlapping antiprison collective organizations. One of the primary collectives was Education Not Incarceration (ENI), centered on the claim that "we should have money for youth education and not put young people in prisons."[243] ENI engaged in a variety of political work—holding political education film screenings, conducting a book drive for the library of the Louisiana Correctional Institute for Women—St. Gabriel, and supporting the political work of the Angola Lifers' Association.[244] The overlapping memberships of ENI, the National Coalition to Free the Angola 3, and the New Orleans Prison Organizing Resource Center (NO PORC) embodied a politics not of competition but of collaboration in this burgeoning moment of radical antiprison activism.[245]

The creation of the New Orleans Prison Coalition formalized this commitment to interconnected organizing. It developed out of the work of Community Labor United (CLU), a local coalition organized by older Black Marxist activists and SNCC veterans including Curtis Muhammad and John O'Neal. CLU aimed to unite community and labor struggles and serve as a space for Left experimentation. ENI members' participation in CLU inspired them to form the Prison Coalition as an intentional alliance. Although most of these groups were truly grassroots with little to no funds or staffing support, the coalition created an infrastructure that enhanced their collective capacity to take on larger political projects.

One of the major projects of the coalition was hosting the Critical Resistance South conference in spring 2003. ENI activists had attended the 2001 CR East Conference in New York and then became involved with organizing a southern regional conference. Melissa Burch of ENI and Althea Francois, who was a main force behind NO PORC and the National Coalition to Free the Angola 3, attended the initial planning session for CR South at the Highlander Center in Tennessee. Holding a southern conference furthered CR national leadership's goal of providing organizing resources to a region that had less access to social movement infrastructure and funding than New York and California. While national and regional CR members and affiliates provided programming and logistical support, much of the vision and organizing of Critical Resistance South came from the New Orleans Prison Coalition. Burch was hired as the full-time CR South local coordinator to provide on-the-ground capacity.

New Orleans activists saw hosting CR South as an organizing opportunity—it would bring attention to the contours of the prison industrial complex in the South and deepen activism in New Orleans and the region. As Shana M. griffin recalls, there continued to be a "lack of attention" to the US South in abolitionist analyses of US prisons.[246] CR South organizers endeavored to bring visibility not only to "the South's history but also the South as it was at that moment."[247] Local activists were excited to share the lessons of the campaign to shut down the Tallulah youth prison and the gains being won by the National Coalition to Free the Angola 3.[248] New Orleans organizers hoped to deepen conversations about what southern struggles could teach about "movement work in general."[249]

CR South organizers wove community organizing principles into the outreach process. Conference organizers aimed to bring together a wide grassroots base of both politically connected and "less formally organized people": young people, family and friends of people locked up, artists, religious folks, and others concerned about the growth of the penal system.[250] To that end, relationship building was vital to fostering excitement and participation in the conference. Early in the planning process, the organizers developed an extensive outreach list. From there, Melissa Burch started systematically

> calling people up on the phone, trying to talk to them. . . . It wasn't pre-email, but emailing people definitely wasn't a main way of trying to reach them. Then, at some point, or at multiple points, I went on the road. . . . That was really critical, again, for having face-to-face conversations with people, not only just because face-to-face conversations are more likely to get someone to attend an event, but [because] the emphasis was always on organizing. . . . So the whole point was to begin building relationships that would continue through and beyond the conference, and that would continue to be a source of strength and connection.[251]

This investment in relationship building was mirrored in the local outreach process. Conference organizers decided that CR South would have the biggest local impact if held in Black community spaces. So, the entire conference was rooted in the historic Black neighborhood of Treme. The Treme Community Center was the main site of the conference. Craig Elementary School, located just across the street, was the primary place for conference workshops. Nearby churches served as locales for overflow workshops and film screenings. Yet the relationship to these places did not begin and end with using their space. Craig Elementary students made art, and Treme Center coordinator and civil rights veteran Jerome Smith was part of the conference opening event. The historic Black Catholic church St. Augustine offered their space for an interfaith breakfast on Sunday morning.[252] Local outreach included talking to people on buses, at bail bonds places, and by door knocking in the Treme, public housing, and other neighborhoods targeted for policing. As former CR organizer Tamika Middleton recalls, these conversations were not only about publicizing the conference but also about creating space to "talk about abolition and talk about the prison industrial complex without saying any of those words."[253] When someone was not home, organizers left a door knocker that read, "Know someone in prison? Know someone who's been harassed by the police? Looking for real solutions to the problems in our communities? Come to CR South."[254] Outreach was not a purely transactional tactic but an opportunity for politicizing the individualized experiences of arrest and incarceration.

Like at previous CR conferences, attendance at CR South exceeded organizers' expectations. More than three thousand people participated in the events over the weekend of April 4–6, 2003. At the opening press conference, Craig Elementary students unfurled the banner they had made that read, "Why Are So Many of Our Loved Ones in Prison?" and the Treme Sidewalk Steppers and New Birth Brass Band closed the convergence. Programming was intentionally inclusive and expansive, reflecting the nonsectarian orientation of CR South in which a range of leftist political tendencies were accepted into the big tent of the conference—including even prison reformers.[255] Workshops covered a wide range of topics such as "Prisons: New Forms of Environmental Racism," "Wrongful Conviction in the Deep South," and "INCITE-ing the Movement: Women of Color Organizing to End State and Personal Violence."[256] A significant portion of the programming focused on Louisiana, including a session on the 1811 Louisiana slave revolt, a workshop where Wilbert Rideau called in to discuss the history of the *Angolite*, and one in which former Angola Three political prisoner Robert King Wilkerson outlined the next stages of the Free the Angola 3 campaign.[257] For Burch, the most successful element of the conference was "the simultaneous involvement of former prisoners, family members, faith based organizers, academics. . . . all of these really different kinds of people and organizers coming together."[258] CR South was a site of antiprison movement-building at which people made connections, developed a shared analysis, and saw their work as part of something bigger than themselves.[259]

CR South's impact, however, went beyond the space of the conference. One of its most powerful outcomes was how it inserted new narratives around policing and imprisonment. The media team saw their work as going beyond publicizing the conference: it sought to decouple the notions of crime and punishment in local, regional, and national news. Foregrounding that prisons did not lead to greater public safety and that the billions spent on mass incarceration would be better reinvested in education, healthcare, and local economies, the CR South media group succeeded in getting news articles published in mainstream, Black, and alternative newspapers in New Orleans, Baton Rouge, Atlanta, and Miami and conducted almost twenty news and radio interviews across the region. An *Associated Press* article on the structural factors that made the South the region with the highest per capita incarceration rate in the nation ran in more than seventy newspapers across the United States.[260]

Furthermore, Burch contends that the abolitionist politics of the conference "helped to challenge a lot of the stigma and shame associated with imprisonment."[261] When the Craig Elementary School principal was first contacted, she did not want to advertise that many of her students had family in prison. But by the time the conference was held, the principal was unapologetic in talking to the media about the harms created by having students' parents imprisoned.[262] CR South's reframing of incarceration as a political problem rather than an individual failure "took what was a prior community or community-specific or family problem and made it a political one."[263]

CR South also extended activists' political analysis of mass incarceration in the South. Shana M. griffin recalls, "The Critical Resistance South Conference put Louisiana and the Southern region on the map—making visible the regional's long history of abolition organizing, challenging violent policies of policing and imprisonment, and creating oppositional frameworks to Louisiana's infamous distinction as the most incarcerated place in the world."[264] The conference not only heightened awareness about conditions being faced in the Gulf South but also enhanced people's understanding of the prison industrial complex as a multifaceted system—helping activists see the connections between their different campaigns. Burch stated, "It was now understood that all of those struggles were linked and that they were part of something bigger."[265] Although it would be a stretch to say that CR South made prison abolition "the" political framework guiding activism, it did increase abolition's legitimacy in the region.[266]

・・・・・・

At the turn of the twenty-first century, the Louisiana punishment regime was reoriented to the parish jail system. The state's adoption of carceral cooperation endeavor agreements dramatically increased the number of state prisoners locked in parish jails from 4,493 in 1990 to 17,469 in 2004

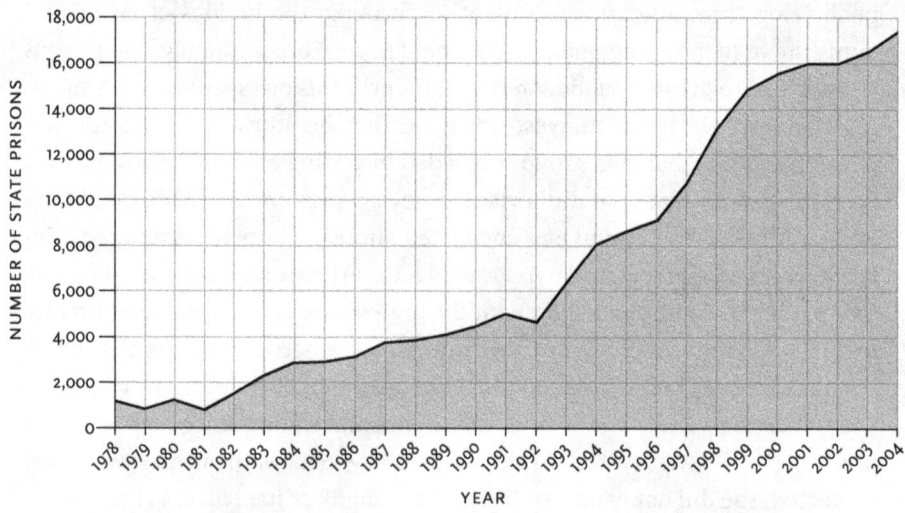

GRAPH 3.1 State prisoners held in parish jails, 1978–2004. Sources: Governor's Corrections Plan, 1990; Prison Policy Initiative.

(graph 3.1). Even the last concrete addition to the DPSC, a geriatric and special needs satellite prison under the umbrella of the David Wade Correctional Center, had originally served as a jail for Caddo Parish.[267] The spatial realignment of the Louisiana penal system was so thorough that it became commonplace for people to refer to jails as "local prisons."

This geographic restructuring of the state's penal system did not occur solely to meet DPSC budgetary shortages. Sheriffs organized to increase the number of state prisoners, along with federal and INS prisoners, incarcerated in their jails to bolster their departments' revenue and their power, and once the federal courts finally released Louisiana from the Hayes Williams consent decree, sheriffs had few limits on how many state prisoners they could jail. In this period, New Orleans became a focal point of the Louisiana criminal legal system. Sheriff Charles Foti expanded OPP almost tenfold over thirty years with minimal accountability. Yet it was not until the convergence of Mayor Morial's neoliberal urban policies and NOPD Superintendent Pennington's policing reforms that OPP's population soared above seven thousand. The embrace of broken windows and community policing was supported through the Clinton administration's COPS program. NOPD's federal funding jumped from $298,508 to $8.4 million between 1990 and 2000.[268] Between 1985 and 2004, the annual number of people booked into OPP more than doubled from 46,000 to 94,981 with two-thirds of those arrested on municipal, traffic, or juvenile charges.[269] For the first time in years, the average age of the prison population was getting younger, while 7,000 to 8,000 of the people entering the penal system each year were technical or waived parole violators.[270]

Yet, after long-standing media silence on the violence endemic to OPP, grassroots opposition contested the routinized death and disease at the jail and the broader state-sanctioned violence of the carceral state. Rallies and petitions coincided with a new current of radical abolitionist activism. What had been unthinkable just a few years earlier had been made thinkable.

In the years leading up to Hurricane Katrina, political shifts altered the landscape of the New Orleans criminal legal system. In addition to Judge Polozola releasing OPP from the Hayes Williams consent decree, Harry Connick did not seek reelection as district attorney for the first time in thirty years, and Charles Foti decided to leave the position of Orleans Parish sheriff to run for Louisiana attorney general in 2003. In the 2002 New Orleans mayoral race, Richard Pennington was the front-runner candidate until Cox Cable executive C. Ray Nagin received the bulk of endorsements—including from the city's police union who never forgave Pennington for firing cops. After his defeat, Pennington moved on to the Atlanta Police Department.

In these years, organizers and activists continued to build political power slowly but surely in New Orleans. JJPL shuttered the Tallulah youth prison, spurring the creation of the new grassroots nonprofit Friends and Families of Louisiana's Incarcerated Children. The New Orleans Critical Resistance chapter facilitated political education around the prison-industrial complex and began strategizing to create "harm-free zones" in the city to model what safety without police could be like. Norris Henderson of the Angola Special Civics Project had his conviction overturned in 2003 and founded the organization VOTE (initially for Voice of the Ex-Offender later renamed to Voice of the Experienced) to organize formerly incarcerated people. INCITE! Women of Color Against Violence held their national conference in the Treme in the spring of 2005—in many ways informed by the CR South community-based convergence—that fortified local activists' connections with national movements and organizations. And a small group of people initiated the Orleans Parish Prison Reform Coalition to pressure the newly elected sheriff Marlin Gusman to make meaningful reforms to the city's jail. A new era of possibility was opening just as the floodwaters tried to wash it away.

4   Carceral Disasters

Hurricane Katrina, Organized Abandonment, and Racial State Violence

· ·

If they enslaved us
Why would they save us?
If they put us in chains
Why would they save us from a hurricane?

—Post-Katrina Chant

They tell you what they want, show you what they want you to see
But they don't let you know what's really going on
Make it look like a lotta stealing going on
Boy them cops is killas in my home
Nigga shot dead in the middle of the street
I ain't no thief, I'm just trying to eat
Man fuck the police and President (Georgia) Bush

—Lil Wayne, "Georgia . . . Bush" 2006

Hurricane Katrina neither created nor defines New Orleans. To reduce New Orleans to the more than fifty breaks in the levee system that generated the federal flood erases the centuries of insurgent struggles and patriarchal racial capitalist state developments that produced the Crescent City.[1] And while it would be misleading to reread all the history leading up to August 29, 2005, as a rehearsal for Hurricane Katrina, it is also true that the accumulation of state actions and inactions at the local, state, and federal level *did* pave the way for the organized abandonment of New Orleans and the subsequent neoliberal remaking of the city.[2] This organized abandonment of New Orleans included not only state and city officials leaving people to the floodwaters for days but the policy decisions that allowed this crisis to happen, from lack of federal investments in levees and other flood protections to state officials' refusal to plan for evacuation transportation for carless residents. The way that law enforcement, Sheriff Marlin Gusman, and the Department of Public Safety & Corrections (DPSC) responded to the storm and its long aftermath was not so much a breakdown of the criminal justice system, as many have argued, but an intensified continuation. These individuals and institutions deployed the same carceral practices guided by the logic that Black life is always a criminalized threat to be disposed of by abandonment, caging, or individualized killings.[3]

After the state disaster that was Hurricane Katrina engulfed the city, Black New Orleanians seeking survival were met by criminalization and violence. This chapter maintains that this was neither an aberration in state policy nor evidence of the state's intrinsic limitations. Rather, arresting starving and sunburnt survivors rather than providing them with food and shelter, the extrajudicial police and vigilante killings of Black men, the abandonment of jailed people in the flooded Orleans Parish Prison (OPP), and the total disregard for the thousands of incarcerated people lost for months in the state's prison and parish jail system are stark testimony to the reality that racist punitive power was at the core of the state's disaster policy. Widespread media coverage that spread racist rumors of lawless New Orleanians looting and shooting at first responders legitimized this racial state violence. As Clyde Woods reminds us, "Hegemonic neo-liberal discourse seamlessly deployed plantation and white supremacist representations to define African Americans as cannibals, looters, rapists, and insurgents. Those who built New Orleans over the course of three centuries were instantaneously declared unworthy of returning of their city."[4]

Yet local and national activists saw amidst the wreckage an opportunity for organizing a different future for New Orleans. Hurricane Katrina not only exacerbated the crises within the New Orleans criminal legal system but also produced a crack in the foundation of carceral logics that provided a space of possibility to collectively organize. As the horrors of the NOPD and OPP became known, racial justice organizers articulated that the disaster of Katrina was not natural but instead was produced by the state's racial criminalization and organized abandonment of New Orleans. In doing so, they contended that the crisis confronting the criminal legal system was built on decades of municipal and state investment in jailing and policing at the cost of providing for residents' daily needs. A growing number of prison reformers and abolitionists explicitly framed the movement needed at this moment through the legacy of Black Reconstruction and the Black internationalist tradition of human rights. Using this framework and engaging in emergent action around OPP, organizers developed the movement-building infrastructure for taking on the New Orleans carceral state in the first five years after the flood.

Organizing in Disaster Time

Before diving into the particularities of punitive state violence and grassroots reconstruction activism in the aftermath of Hurricane Katrina, I want to step back and discuss the affective contours of organizing in the years right after the flood.[5] The language and memories of burnout and trauma permeated my interviews with organizers who were present in those first months and years after the storm, as well as in my own recollections of participating in reconstruction organizing. The heartbreak and devastation of the floods, living in a city that was still very much a disaster zone, and organizing against the unrelenting governmental attempts to remake New Orleans into a whiter and wealthier city combined to produce a certain kind of temporality of everyday life.

The struggles surrounding policing and incarceration were only one piece of a much broader movement fighting on many fronts from housing to education to labor to healthcare and for the human rights of internally displaced people to return home and be part of a just reconstruction of the Gulf Coast. It is hard to describe to folks who were not there how what I call "disaster time" felt like. Although the process of recovery was (and is) slow, it is also true that so much happened in the first years after the storm that, in many regards, time simultaneously sped up. The conditions on the ground constantly shifted as state decisions either were made at a breakneck pace or government jurisdictions and responsibilities quickly shifted (without much rhyme or reason) to the point that it was extremely difficult to determine who had decision-making power. You would go to a meeting one week, and the next week the strategies that had been decided on no longer made sense. Weeks and months felt like years. There was a sense of always needing to be on alert for whatever the state's next move would be in its project of keeping Black poor and working-class communities from returning home. As former Safe Streets/Strong Communities organizer Ursula Price recalls, "You rested for a second, and you missed ten things, and we couldn't stop to do planning or reflection or anything like that because things were happening so fast. It was also just challenging that people rightfully needed things—they needed healing, they needed material resources, they needed some time. And yet, we just didn't have it, and we had to keep going anyway."[6] It was not just the opaqueness of government "recovery" processes that made it difficult to collectively apply pressure: it was the quickness of it all. This was especially challenging in a place marked by a long-held refusal to abide by the logics of racial capitalist clock time.

Extensive energy was also swallowed up by people's own needs to rebuild their homes and lives—to say nothing of the psychological and physical toll it took to live and work in a place where moldy, rotting refrigerators littered the streets, military police in Humvees roamed the roads, and empty houses branded by their "Katrina X's" and flood marks filled the landscape for months into years. Former Safe Streets/Strong Communities codirector Xochitl Bervera remembers, "People didn't have homes. I lost my home. We were working out of cars. Or we would go to Evelyn's. She didn't have running water. So, we'd have to take a shower at the gas station next door."[7]

Somehow organizers were able to maintain a frenzied pace in their organizing efforts. It verges on cliché for activists to talk about the trap of falling into crisis-mode organizing, but collectively building political momentum amid acute crisis is a different matter altogether. Activists shared a profound sense that the window for pushing for systemic change and keeping repressive state policies at bay was short. In meeting after meeting, it was repeated that how things played out in this period would dictate the future of the city. Norris Henderson recalls that people thought they probably only had a few months "to try and get some traction around some criminal justice reform."[8] And so they threw themselves into overlapping campaigns with multipronged strategies over and over again. In my interviews, community organizers repeatedly shared that although they were proud of the agility of their work and the amount they accomplished, it was also unbelievable how much they took on. "What were we thinking?" emerged as a common refrain.

This sense of the moment's importance infused the broader activist community as well. Organizers throughout the nation—especially those from the Black Left—recognized the struggles in New Orleans as critical for the national struggle against neoliberal racial capitalism and sought to flank local activism. The spectacle of Black suffering broadcast on televisions and reported in newspapers across the globe made the centrality of Hurricane Katrina to Black politics readily apparent. The speed at which the Bush administration pushed forth a recovery agenda aimed at privatizing public housing and schools, eliminating affirmative action policies from federal labor contracts, and increasing the militarization of law enforcement signaled the state's plans to permanently displace Black New Orleanians. Black activists and antiracist comrades across the nation—many with ties to local organizations such as Community Labor United, Critical Resistance, and INCITE! Women of Color Against Violence—organized conference calls and summits to figure out what could be done; one strategy was the founding of Black Left organizations such as the People's Hurricane Relief Fund. Katrina solidarity organizing developed from the perspective that New Orleans was ground zero of national experiments to ramp up and expand neoliberal urbanism and advance white supremacy. The 2007 US Social Forum in Atlanta dedicated one of its handful of plenaries to "Gulf Coast Reconstruction in the Post-Katrina Era."[9] What was won or lost in New Orleans would have reverberations for antiracist struggles throughout the nation.[10]

Disaster solidarity was not without its frictions. Not only did the involvement of out-of-town activists often put more on the plates of already overburdened locals but it was also often difficult for those activists from elsewhere to comprehend the affective and material conditions of postdisaster organizing. When local organizers cried and expressed grief, out-of-town organizers routinely responded with frustration, not compassion. At a national strategy session, Critical Resistance (CR) organizer kai lumumba barrow recalls that New York activists were angered that New Orleanians were skeptical of their idea to hold a march in the city in December 2005. Barrow recounts being outraged at overhearing, "I came here to build a movement, not to be crying and praying and shit. These people don't know what they want."[11] Although it is unsurprising that the Katrina crisis produced heightened emotions, it was disheartening to local organizers that people seeking to be in solidarity with them repeatedly suggested their trauma was inconvenient and that they were incapable of leading their own movements.

Almost everyone describes organizing during this era as overwhelming. People worked nonstop. People barely slept. People got sick. People frequently smoked and drank too much. People were not always their best selves to one another. Tensions often ran high, just as much in the areas where victories emerged as in the areas dominated by loss. Even though there were conversations about PTSD and secondary trauma, the material conditions with which people were struggling made it challenging to integrate those tools into their organizing.[12] Moreover, in the highly gendered context of postdisaster organizing, the masculinist ability to work nonstop was rewarded, whereas the slower and steadier work of caretaking was routinely seen as evidence of not being serious about movement work.[13]

Still, there was joy. There was a profound sense of being connected to something much larger than any of us and a sense of being in movement. That we were not only in the lineage of the Black radical tradition and abolition democracy but that we also were a small part of propelling it forward in new ways. That it was possible to make different kinds of futures for New Orleans, the Gulf Coast, and the broader United States. For me to write about this period is both to return to a sense of possibility and collectivity and to excavate a sorrow that was too much to be fully felt in those fast-paced, busy times.[14]

Looming over this narrative of grassroots antipolice and antijail organizing successes are the massive losses incurred in other movement sectors in the first few years after the storm. By and large, neoliberal state projects succeeded in severely dismantling what was left of the New Orleans welfare state and displacing upward of 100,000 Black New Orleanians.[15] Following Rachel Luft, I contend that these state actions and inactions constituted not only a project of racial capitalist restructuring but also a deeply patriarchal state project, which Luft terms "racialized disaster patriarchy." Not only did Black women experience higher rates of displacement than other groups but also the dismantling of welfare state capacities constituted an attack on the social reproduction of New Orleans.[16] The breaking of the teachers' union through mass firings and the charterization of the New Orleans public school system, combined with the closure of New Orleans's public Charity Hospital, ensured that thousands of New Orleanians, largely Black women, lost their steady jobs as teachers and healthcare providers, forcing them to seek work elsewhere and never returning home.[17] Similarly, the fight against the shuttering and bulldozing of the "big four" public housing developments, under the federal government's neoliberal HOPE VI housing program, was killed by a New Orleans City Council vote. On December 20, 2007, it unanimously voted to demolish 4,500 units of viable public housing stock, explicitly displacing the Black female-headed households that made up the bulk of public housing residents and exacerbating the post-Katrina housing crisis. Simultaneously the NOPD maced and tasered protesters (me included) who were contesting the demolition of public housing. This police action revealed the ease with which the city turned to state violence to repress local social movements demanding the human right to housing and the right of return.[18]

These post-Katrina struggles, although distinct from the organizing around policing and imprisonment, also importantly intersected with it. The membership of antijail and antipolicing organizations overlapped with the membership of other racial and economic justice organizations, and staff organizers were often involved in multiple political organizations.[19] Not only did criminal justice reform organizers and activists routinely make connections between the *locking out* of Black residents from post-Katrina jobs and housing and the *locking in* of others within the criminal legal system but they also integrated lessons from those defeats into later struggles. Reckoning with the displacement of Black communities from New Orleans after the storm requires that we reckon with the massive displacement of Black New Orleanians through criminalization and incarceration in the decades preceding the hurricane.

The Disaster of State Racial Violence

The flooding of New Orleans was anything but natural. The 2005 hurricane season was the most active on record, fueled by climate-change–induced rising sea-surface temperatures in the Atlantic.[20] When Hurricane Katrina made landfall in New Orleans, it was a Category 3 hurricane, significantly weakened from when it first hit the Gulf Coast as a Category 5 storm.[21] Decades of federal and state disinvestment in flood protection were exacerbated by the coastal erosion of Louisiana's wetlands that had historically served as a natural buffer to storm surges. The petrochemical industry's dredging of canals and laying of pipelines during the oil boom years, alongside the rapid expansion of off-shore drilling in the Gulf of Mexico to meet global oil demands in the 1990s, had wreaked havoc on coastal ecosystems.[22] The 33,000 miles of pipeline crisscrossing the coast at the time of the storm were accompanied by the loss of 1,525 square miles of wetlands from 1956 to 2000.[23] Petro capitalism made Louisiana vulnerable twice over: once, through the increase in carbon emissions that produce climate change, and second, through the destruction of Louisiana's natural barriers to tropical storms.

City and state leaders failed to adequately prepare as Hurricane Katrina made its way through the Gulf of Mexico. Mayor Ray Nagin did not declare a mandatory evacuation for the city until August 28, a day before Katrina made landfall. Yet this declaration meant little to the thousands of New Orleanians without cars or places to go. At the last minute, the city opened the Superdome as a shelter of last resort. Many understandably chose to ride out the hurricane in their own homes.[24]

For those who stayed in the city, the first impression of Hurricane Katrina was that the city had been spared—but then the levees broke. Within hours, 80 percent of New Orleans was inundated with water, with reported heights of flooding upward of twenty feet and floodwaters *settling* over ten feet in some areas.[25] Innumerable people fought to save themselves and others by chopping through roofs, waving makeshift signs, rescuing one another by boat, and sharing the food and water they had. The official death toll of Hurricane Katrina in Louisiana was 1,440, with the majority Black and from New Orleans.[26] The Bush administration's malignantly slow response was summed up by the refrain that "they left us here to die" and stamped this moment as "Black people's 9/11."[27]

Criminalization was the state's immediate disaster response. The National Guardsmen searched people seeking shelter in the Superdome and Convention Center. Mayor Ray Nagin instructed the NOPD to stop its search-and-rescue mission on August 31 (while most of the city was still flooded) to begin arresting "lawless" survivors.[28] Although it is true that many NOPD officers deserted their posts, it is also true that local law enforcement received a boost in manpower from Louisiana state troopers; federal law enforcement from the ATF, FBI SWAT, the Drug Enforcement Administration, US marshals, and Immigration and Customs Enforcement; and other states' law enforcement personnel. These entities were charged with restoring law-and-order to Orleans Parish and tracking down persons deemed a concern—specifically sex offenders.[29] In the ten days after the levees broke, law enforcement arrested around 250 people, most of whom were seeking supplies or a way out of town: "178, were for looting; 26 for possession of stolen vehicles, 20 for resisting arrest, 14 for theft and 9 for attempted murder. A few were arrested on misdemeanors such as disturbing the peace."[30] The quickness with which the federal government deployed law enforcement was in stark contrast to the slowness with which supplies such as food, water, and medical care were distributed.[31]

The state's prioritization of law-and-order was made evident when a temporary jail was the first post-Katrina infrastructure project. Given OPP's severe flooding, the city did not have a functioning carceral facility. DPSC and Sheriff Gusman then refashioned the joint New Orleans Greyhound and Amtrak station into a 750-bed temporary jail referred to interchangeably as "Camp Greyhound," "Camp Amtrak," or "Angola South."[32] Angola warden Burl Cain remarked, "This is a real start to rebuilding this city, this jail."[33] As Ruth Wilson Gilmore notes, "The elites didn't start by burying the dead or feeding the living, but they did close a port—a bus station—in order to lock up as many people as possible whose exit from the city had not yet been accomplished through dispersal or death."[34] Although the media framed Camp Greyhound as vital for keeping the streets safe, the real role of the jail was epitomized by the "crime" committed by the first person locked up there: a man who was arrested after he "drove up in a stolen Enterprise rental car to buy a bus ticket."[35]

Stories circulating that Black New Orleanians had devolved into a subhuman state of violence and disregard for private property justified the primacy of policing. In a widely reported interview with Oprah Winfrey, Mayor Ray Nagin claimed that "animalistic" "gang members" were committing mass murders in the Superdome. NOPD superintendent Eddie Compass declared that New Orleanians were shooting at police and other first responders and that in the Superdome "we had little babies getting raped."[36] Although these reports were later discredited, these type of stories rapidly produced a racist and classist commonsense about Katrina survivors as unworthy of government aid.[37] As a congressional report would later note, the media amplification of such anti-Black rhetoric delayed rescue and relief efforts as FEMA employees turned back from New Orleans because of security concerns.[38]

Moreover, media recast Black Katrina survivors searching for provisions as violent thieves.[39] NOPD officers reported to CNN that no one in the city "was safe from bands of young men who were attacking people and attempting to rape women."[40] The racist logic that New Orleans had turned into a space of uncivilized urban warfare underpinned Governor Kathleen Blanco infamous announcement that she was sending 300 Arkansas National Guardsmen "fresh back from Iraq" to New Orleans, and "they have M-16s, and they're locked and loaded. . . . I have one message for these hoodlums: These troops know how to shoot and kill, and they are more than willing to do so if necessary, and I expect they will."[41] Blanco's statement was joined by NOPD captain James Scott's declaration: "We have authority by martial law to shoot looters."[42]

Militarized law enforcement's centrality to the state's emergency disaster response was not invented on the spot but was built into the Louisiana's disaster governance plans dating back decades. At the heart of Louisiana's 1974 Disaster Act was the state's need to prepare not only for hurricanes and tornadoes but also for the "man-made" disasters of "riots" and "paramilitary action." That bill bolstered the governor's ability to militarize state power and strengthen the state police during disasters.[43] The intertwining of disaster preparedness with coercive state capacities is more fully spelled out in a state police procedural manual for disasters. It outlines how to prepare for "antisocial or violent acts" aimed at transforming "the existing system."[44] Whether the disaster is "Radical/racial conflict," "Jail/Prisons Disorders," "Labor Problems," "Industrial accident" or "natural disasters," the state troopers' role is the same—to serve as "an equipped paramilitary force" to protect Louisianans' life and property.[45] To meet this goal, state troopers are to reestablish social control and containment through a broad range of actions: providing first aid, instituting crowd control, preventing looting, and conducting mass arrests.[46] Thus, the state of Louisiana's response to Hurricane Katrina through the lens of a racialized civil riot that needed to be contained and controlled at all costs was not a deviation from previous state policy but followed the state's disaster program that made policing central to any and all disasters.

In the months that followed, state and federal officials cooperated to ramp up law enforcement as a recovery program. Mayor Ray Nagin requested that Governor Blanco extend the emergency deployment of Louisiana National Guard and state troopers "to prevent further looting . . . and to give residents of the area an increased sense of security by their visibility and contact."[47] The National Guard would roll the streets of New Orleans for more than three years after Hurricane Katrina, although they were more likely to be found policing broken taillights than preventing violence. US state attorney of eastern Louisiana Jim Letten coordinated with US attorney general Alberto Gonzalez to deploy FBI, DEA, and ATF agents and US marshals to supplement the NOPD's targeting of violent crime and to police undocumented immigrants who were recruited to rebuild the city.[48] The deployment of emergency law enforcement became an everyday part of New Orleans policing.

With racist narratives and policies licensing law enforcement impunity, it is no wonder that extrajudicial killings of Black men by vigilantes and police darkened the days after the storm. In the majority-white New Orleans neighborhood of Algiers Point, which did not flood because of its location on the West Bank of the Mississippi River, white residents seized on the crisis to form a militia under the guise of protecting white property. As investigative journalist A.C. Thompson reported three years later,

> A group of white residents, convinced that crime would arrive with the human exodus, sought to seal off the area, blocking the roads in and out of the neighborhood by dragging lumber and downed trees into the streets. They stockpiled handguns, assault rifles, shotguns and at least one Uzi and began patrolling the streets in pickup trucks and SUVs. The newly formed militia, a loose band of about 15 to 30 residents, most of them men, all of them white, was looking for thieves, outlaws or, as one member put it, anyone who simply "didn't belong."[49]

During these patrols, vigilantes gunned down Black men seeking refuge. Donnell Herrington was on his way to a National Guard evacuation point with his family when he was shot in the throat and back by a trio of white men with shotguns. When he saw another pair of white men driving by, he signaled for help. But instead of offering support, they told him, "Get away from this truck, nigger. We're not gonna help you. We're liable to kill you ourselves."[50] Thompson's extensive research uncovered that Herrington was one of eleven Black men shot by white vigilantes, with four people found dead due to suspicious causes around Algiers Point.[51]

Yet, calling forth the words of Ida B. Wells a century earlier, "the killing of a few Negroes more or less by irresponsible mobs does not cut much figure in Louisiana."[52] Although Herrington attempted to make a police report, the NOPD did not even take a written statement.[53] The lack of official attention given to Herrington and others who tried to hold the vigilantes accountable for their extralegal racist violence is particularly stunning given that the members of this neighborhood militia did not try to hide their identities. Several of the militia men—Vinnie Pervel, Nathan Roper, and Wayne Janak—felt invincible enough to speak with Thompson on the record. Although they never admitted that they shot anyone, they recounted how others shot Black men assumed to be "looters" and "thugs." In addition, they said that police told them, "If *they're* breaking in your property, do what you gotta do and leave [the bodies] on the side of the road."[54] White property rights superseded Black life.

Even more brazen conversations among white supremacists are captured in the documentary, *Welcome to New Orleans*. In one scene, two white men boast about murdering Black men. Wayne Janak brags at a barbeque about how "it was great! It was like pheasant season in South Dakota. If it moved, you shot it." He then explains that Algiers Point is "not a pussy community" and that they were not going to allow "them" to "go into a white woman's home and tell her you are going to take it over."[55] According to Thompson, the unedited footage continued the conversation with Janak stating that as a Chicago-born man, this moment transformed him: "I am no longer a Yankee. I earned my [southern] wings." A nearby white woman then chimes in, "He understands the n-word now."[56] Although former Black Panther and Algiers resident Malik Rahim widely spoke out against the vigilante violence and others struggled to get the NOPD to open an investigation of vigilante shootings, no meaningful inquiry was ever conducted.

The NOPD's lack of attention to white supremacist vigilante violence against Black storm survivors is not surprising given that police officers were involved in covering up their own racist Katrina killings. These police cover-ups were ignored by local and national media until A.C. Thompson investigated the most infamous killing in 2008. Henry Glover, a thirty-one-year-old Black resident, was shot through the chest as he walked with a friend through an Algiers strip mall on September 2, 2005. Family members and a random driver passing by, William Tanner, rushed him to the nearby temporary NOPD base for medical aid. Rather than providing care, NOPD officers handcuffed those helping Glover, called them looters, and beat them senseless while Glover was bleeding out in the back of their car. The police commandeered their car and drove off with Glover still in the backseat. Later the car was found on a levee charred to its core, with Glover's body practically reduced to ash. The city coroner ruled the death "unclassified," and the NOPD refused to investigate the death.[57] A federal investigation following Thompson's story revealed that NOPD officer David Warren shot Glover in the back and then beat Glovers' companions and burned the car to cover up the killing.[58]

But the NOPD did far more than cover up a single murder. Survivors retell that while walking across the Danziger Bridge, looking for supplies and family members on the morning of September 4, 2005, they were ambushed without warning by unidentified police in a Budget rental truck. Some people attempted to shield themselves from a hailstorm of bullets, while others attempted to run to safety. When the smoke cleared, six people had been shot and two were dead. The police shot teenage Lesha Bartholomew four times in the leg, and her mother Susan's arm was partially blasted off. Her husband Leonard sustained shots to his head, back, and left heel. The NOPD shot a fourth man, Jose Holmes Jr., twice in the abdomen and killed his friend James Brissette by seven gunshots. On the other side of the bridge were two brothers, Ronald Madison and Lance Madison, who were headed home after attempting to visit their mother in New Orleans East. When the shooting began, they fled from the bridge to a motel just before Ronald Madison—a mentally disabled forty-year-old—was killed by shots to his back.[59]

The NOPD orchestrated an extensive cover-up of the Danziger Bridge shootings to protect the department. The time at which the police arrived at the bridge was known based on reports of shots fired, but it soon became apparent that the initial reports did not match reality. Moments after Lance Madison watched the police kill his brother, he was arrested by the NOPD on falsified charges of eight counts of attempted murder of a police officer. Over the next several weeks, the state shuffled Madison, like hundreds of others, around the state's carceral archipelago of jails and prisons to limit his ability to testify. Along with locking up Lance Madison, the NOPD swiftly crafted a story that the Danziger Bridge shooting was in self-defense against a group of looters who were shooting at a group of contractors. Police reports were falsified, the bridge was not swept for evidence until October 26, a gun was planted, and two witnesses were invented to corroborate the police officers' story. A federal investigation years later confirmed that the conspiracy to hide the NOPD's wrongdoing was an open secret that was known throughout the department.[60]

Local media repeated the NOPD's reports and ignored the stories of survivors. In doing so they further produced a national commonsense about Black New Orleans flood survivors as out of control and only controllable by state violence.[61] The *Times-Picayune*'s first report on the Danziger Bridge shooting read, in full, "New Orleans police officers sent up a cheer Sunday with a report that their colleagues had engaged in a shootout with an armed group on Danziger Bridge in eastern New Orleans, with none of the cops hit and five of the suspected marauders wounded. No word was available on the condition of the wounded."[62] Articles published in the following days reiterated that the group at Danziger were "carrying guns," which is to claim that they brought their deaths on themselves.[63]

The phenomenon of news parroting the police's statements, while not unique to the aftermath of Katrina, had a very powerful effect on perceptions of New Orleans survivors as a criminal threat and law enforcement as heroes. The Associated Press picked up the *Times-Picayune*'s initial coverage on the Danziger Bridge shooting and followed the NOPD's narrative of the events. Local newspapers from St. Louis to San Juan republished the Associated Press's story.[64] On CNN, NOPD deputy chief Warren Riley stated, "When [the police officers] got out of the van, they approached the subjects who were several, several feet away, who fired on the police officers. The officers returned fire, striking four of the subjects immediately."[65] MSNBC news anchor Rita Cosby reiterated the notion that poststorm violence was rooted in the behavior of ungrateful brutes: "These are folks just doing construction work, just trying to help out, and these thugs are unfortunately taking advantage of a very bad situation."[66]

The racist portrayal of New Orleanians as criminal menaces shaped the reception that displaced Katrina survivors experienced in other locales. The power of the script of Black New Orleanians as dangerous came from how easily it fit into long-standing portrayals of New Orleans as a national epicenter of street violence. Neighboring Jefferson Parish sheriff Harry Lee and Gretna police chief Arthur Lawson blockaded the Crescent City Connection Bridge over the Mississippi River, one of the main routes out of the city, to keep Katrina survivors out of majority-white suburban Gretna. Jefferson Parish law enforcement turned back survivors seeking dry ground on the West Bank of the Mississippi River by repeatedly firing shots above their heads. Gretna's mayor justified this callous action by maintaining they needed to protect their residents from New Orleans's "criminal element."[67] This was not the first time that Jefferson Parish officials racially partitioned space in the name of law-and-order. In the late 1980s, they erected barriers at the boundary line between a Black New Orleans neighborhood and a white Jefferson Parish neighborhood to keep out "criminals from New Orleans."[68] Katrina survivors displaced to other cities across the nation found themselves subject to the belief that they were escalating the crime rates in their new locales. Displaced Black New Orleanians having so many dire needs were reframed as being a criminalized problem almost anywhere they went.

The police violence enacted against Katrina survivors was mirrored by the abandonment and violence experienced by prisoners within OPP. This brutality mimicked the everyday violence prisoners were subjected to under the new sheriff Marlin Gusman. Formerly the chief administration officer under Mayor Marc Morial, Gusman was elected as Orleans Parish sheriff after Charles Foti left the position to become the state attorney general in the fall of 2004. As the first Black sheriff elected in Orleans Parish, there was some hope that Gusman would run the jail with more humanity than his predecessor. Instead Gusman followed Foti's template: refusing transparency, showing little concern for incarcerated life, and trying to expand the jail whenever he could.

Sheriff Marlin Gusman's main response to the impending hurricane was to squeeze more prisoners into the jail. Mayor Nagin declared a mandatory evacuation for the city, but OPP prisoners and staff were excluded from the order. When the DPSC offered to assist local sheriffs in evacuating prisoners from the storm's path, Gusman refused the help, stating, "We're going to keep our prisoners where they belong."[69] More than six thousand prisoners were locked in OPP when Gusman and Nagin decided not to evacuate the jail.[70] As usual, Black people made up 90 percent of the people caged in OPP, with another 200 jail beds filled with ICE detainees. Not only were none of these prisoners evacuated but Gusman also brought in hundreds more adult prisoners evacuating from St. Bernard Parish (over 270 people) and youth prisoners from the juvenile jail, the Youth Study Center (354 youth). Even after it was announced that the jail would not be evacuated, NOPD continued to arrest and book 300 New Orleanians on "crimes" such as failing to pay court fines and fees.[71] In these critical hours and days, sheriff deputies were tasked with quadruple bunking cells and turning a first-floor gymnasium into a jail dormitory *instead* of amassing vital supplies.[72] According to a former employee, Gusman seemed unfazed when informed that the jail was woefully unprepared and there was a scarcity of water, food, flashlights, and batteries. He simply responded, "Those are incidentals, and we'll deal with them later."[73]

Jail officials kept prisoners in the dark about the predicted devastation of Hurricane Katrina, prohibiting phone calls beginning August 26.[74] By the time the storm hit New Orleans three days later, all prisoners were on lockdown. Soon after the hurricane made landfall, OPP lost power. By the time the levees broke, the jail was overfilled with nearly eight thousand people who had been abandoned to the flood. They had to cope with the rising waters in the dark. One OPP survivor recalled, "Time continue to pass by, water still rising. No food for us to eat. Finally, a female deputy came by; we shouted to her about our conditions. She then replied there's nothing we can do because there's water everywhere and she left. At this point water had risen to at least 4 ft deep. I thought for sure I would never see freedom again."[75] Floodwaters that were so toxic that they stripped cars of their paint filled the OPP complex from six to ten feet.[76] To avoid dehydration in the late summer heat, prisoners drank the contaminated water that trapped them.[77]

Not only did the toxic waters threaten OPP prisoners' lives but the denial of medical care also had disastrous impacts on their health. More than half the people locked up at the time of the storm required regular medication. The lack of medication was especially severe for the many HIV-positive prisoners in the jail who relied on a highly regimented and time-sensitive drug regimen. Going without their antiviral medication for even a day or two had the potential to render their drug treatment irreversibly ineffective. One HIV-positive prisoner's T-cells dropped to their lowest-ever levels. Two of the ten pregnant women in OPP suffered miscarriages during the storm.[78] Children became sick from the contaminated water, with one boy reporting that his feet "turned all white, with mildew and sores on them. I was throwing up blood."[79]

Prisoners rapidly realized that no one was going to save them except themselves. Numerous deputies abandoned their posts in the flooded jail. The job walk-offs became so widespread that the associate warden turned the jail's carceral capacities on its staff: he began locking deputies on the floors they were working to keep them from quitting.[80] To stay above the water, prisoners scrambled onto top bunks when they could, scaled walls to the jail's roof, and swam through the waters to higher floors. One wheelchair-bound prisoner remembers being abandoned by deputies to the point that he "actually drowned" until "a guy on the tier knew CPR and brought me back to life."[81] Prisoners broke windows to let in more air and attempted to signal to helicopters for help by setting fires and waving signs outside OPP's windows that read, "Help, no food dying."[82]

Other prisoners sought to escape this nightmare. In the Templeton III building, people worked together for twelve hours with a basketball hoop "to try to make a hole out of the building. Eventually the detainees managed to create a hole that was barely large enough for some of the smaller prisoners to wiggle through."[83] Although it is not known how many prisoners escaped for their lives, there are multiple corroborated reports that sniper shots were fired at escapees. It was later reported that the bullets were rubber, but they still had the power to knock people down into the floodwaters.[84]

Escapees were not the only prisoners targeted with violence. At one point, the decision was made to move prisoners from one section of the jail to another. The sheriff's antiriot Special Investigation Division (SID) was called on for this task. Its members arrived with mace, riot batons, and beanbag-loaded shotguns. In response to prisoners' requests for food and water and information about evacuating, SID deputies answered them by "spraying mace and shooting beanbag guns demanding silence." One deputy described this action this way: "In a normal circumstance, I would have said it was excessive, but under the circumstances we were in, I would say it was appropriate."[85] Deputies similarly hit youth and threatened them with guns to their heads in the name of keeping order.[86]

Relief did not come even after the state finally evacuated OPP. After days of tortuous conditions, DPSC personnel arrived in riot gear and commanded prisoners' evacuation using pepper spray, tasers, and rubber-bullet guns. Prisoners recount that they were instructed to leave behind all their belongings, including medications and legal paperwork. It took at least three days for all the prisoners to be evacuated from the jail. As the prisoners waited for rescue boats in floodwaters for up to twelve hours, DPSC guards threatened those who had difficulty keeping their heads above the water—stating that if the prisoners did not learn to swim, "they had a body bag with [their] name on it."[87] As people were evacuated, they were brought to the Broad Street overpass, which the state had essentially turned into an open-air prison. While OPP survivors waited for transportation out of the city to another jail or state prison, the DPSC guards and remaining OPP deputies forced them into a slave ship configuration. One survivor related that as soon as they arrived at the overpass, "The guards were then placing us in rows. Each row were back to back and the next row were the same. This was going on all through the night. We had to sleep sitting up."[88] When incarcerated survivors attempted to stretch or stand up, corrections officers pepper sprayed, tasered, or sicced police dogs on them. Prisoners repeatedly collapsed from sunstroke and dehydration.[89] The metalanguage of incarceration, race, and class ensured that imprisoned women were not offered even the slightest forms of paternalistic gendered protection from guards.[90] A female prisoner attested that the deputies "made us urinate and make bowel movements in our clothes where we sat. It was inhumane, humiliating, and also degrading. I and other females we on our ministration [sic] and had no sanitary napkins to change our old ones. We wore what we had on for 3 days. Some of us had ministral [sic] blood all over us. The SID and SWAT team called us 'crackheads,' 'whore,' 'bitches' and all sorts of other names."[91]

The abuse and violence leveled against OPP survivors within the jail and on the overpass were legitimized by elected officials and popular media alike. Their status as already imprisoned individuals often served as evidence of their innate criminality and thus savagery. Whereas initial reports framed the state's management and evacuation of the flooded jail as an "unbelievably orderly" process, OPP survivors were depicted as chaotic and violent.[92] New Orleans city councilman Oliver Thomas told media that prisoners were rioting and had taken hostages.[93] In contrast, DPSC staff were lauded as heroic "cavalry."[94] Together such baseless reports reified the longstanding narrative that the violence of OPP was rooted in the violent nature of prisoners rather than the disposability characterizing the New Orleans punishment regime.

When OPP survivors were bused out of New Orleans, they left public view but continued to be trapped in deplorable penal conditions. The DPSC sent women prisoners to Angola, whereas youth were reimprisoned at the Jetson Center for Youth.[95] At first the state sent men to the Elayn Hunt Correctional Center. At Hunt, thousands of OPP survivors were confined in a muddy field. One prisoner described the conditions at Hunt as "like a concentration camp."[96] On the rare occasion when guards delivered food to the field, "they took bags with one or two sandwiches and threw them over a barbed wire fence, and you had to fight for it like dogs."[97] The lack of food was matched by the lack of medical care. Prisoners continued to go without crucial medications, and no one at Hunt assessed OPP survivors' medical needs, even though they had spent days in toxic water, and many had visible sores, rashes, peeling skin, and other abrasions.[98]

Prison staff coupled their violent negligence with physical and verbal aggression. It is unsurprising that when they had little food, nothing to do, and had suffered through a week of traumatic events and uncertainty about their future, OPP survivors began fighting. Fights over food and turf occurred alongside sexual assaults. As one OPP survivor remembers, guards watching the fights commented, "They are a bunch of animals; let them kill themselves. They are from New Orleans."[99] In one widely recalled incident, a man who had been stabbed in the face went to the guards standing outside the fenced-in field for help. Instead of taking him to medical care, the guards shot rubber bullets at his abdomen.[100]

Violence against OPP survivors was not unique to Hunt. Parish officials in northwest Louisiana opened Bossier Parish Maximum Security Jail ahead of schedule to imprison OPP evacuees. At Bossier, OPP survivors were barely fed and routinely beaten. One man recalls that after he informed prison guards that his release date had passed, a guard "pepper sprayed me through the food slot in his cell." Later a group of guards returned to his cell to beat and taser him—peppering the beatings with racist slurs.[101] Similarly sadistic guard behavior was documented at the Jena Correctional Facility. The state reopened Jena, the youth jail at Tallulah that had been shut down by the Juvenile Justice Project of Louisiana (JJPL) a few years prior, to incarcerate evacuated prisoners. Jena was staffed by DPSC correctional officers and by guards from New York City's Rikers Island. At one point, white guards forced Black prisoners to engage in an act reminiscent of the sexual-racial torture inflicted on prisoners at Abu Ghraib.[102] Prisoners recounted to legal advocates that guards instructed them to line up in parallel lines, place their hands on their head, and "press their groin against the buttocks of the detainee in front of them," while a guard taunted them by saying, "Hard dicks to soft ass! I know y'all are getting hard because I am."[103]

OPP survivors were left locked up, forgotten in jails and prisons scattered across Louisiana and beyond, with the state showing little to no regard for their release. Everywhere OPP survivors found that their time served grew from one month to three months to six months and longer—with some people locked up for more than a year after OPP flooded. Thousands of individuals served these extended sentences, which were termed "Katrina Time." Some people were locked up well beyond their release dates, whereas others spent much, much longer behind bars than the maximum sentence limit for crimes for which they had not even been formally charged.[104] At least one woman died while still imprisoned after her release date.[105]

A confluence of long-standing problems embedded within the criminal legal system, along with Louisiana officials' indifference to OPP survivors' cases, produced a de facto suspension of habeas corpus.[106] The state's shuffling of prisoners here and there made it extraordinarily difficult for family and friends to track them down. Given people's mass displacement from New Orleans, OPP survivors had few avenues for finding their loved ones and letting them know where they were incarcerated. Moreover, the already inadequate Orleans Parish public defender's office was shattered, leaving six lawyers responsible for more than five thousand cases.[107]

In keeping with the federal government's neoliberal abdication of the responsibility for rebuilding homes to young, unskilled volunteers, the bulk of the critical work of tracking down OPP survivors and determining the status of their cases was done by nonprofit organizations such as the Louisiana Capital Assistance Center and law school volunteers. Rather than the state guaranteeing OPP survivors' right to counsel and a fair and speedy trial, the Louisiana legislature passed a bill during a Katrina special session that barred "lawsuits by people kept in prison past their release dates."[108] Not until January 2006 did Judge Calvin Johnson finally give DAs a deadline for charging OPP survivors and order that people who had already served their full sentences be released.[109] In October 2006, some prisoners were still languishing in Louisiana's extensive network of jails and prisons who had yet to see counsel and were only released on a judge's order.

Emergent Organizing for a Just Reconstruction

Within days of the levee breaks, racial justice activists started strategizing about what could be done. Looking back, it may seem that what happened in those first days and in the coming weeks and months was straightforward, even predictable. But at the time hardly anything was clear. The death toll first predicted for the city was in the thousands. Evelyn Lynn, who had recently moved to New Orleans to work with the JJPL, recalls, "The experts were saying that New Orleans was going to be flooded for years to come. People were saying that folks could never move back to the city, and none of us really knew what to make of what."[110] For those who managed to get back in the city by faking press passes or sneaking past the National Guard, it was crystal clear that the state's disaster governance strategy pivoted on racist criminalization. The National Guard patrolled the streets as an occupying army, a citywide curfew was instituted, and military-style helicopters were ever present in the sky. The NOPD arrested people for committing offenses such as littering even as the city was covered in debris.[111]

With New Orleans's future in grave doubt, people shared a sense of urgency that something needed to be done. In the words of Xochitl Bervera, "The criminalization of particularly Black poor people in New Orleans . . . was such a big part of what created the need for a response."[112] Relationships built over the preceding years between local and national activists proved vital for the development of an organizing response to Hurricane Katrina. When New Orleans CR organizer Tamika Middleton was waylaid by the storm, a New York-based CR organizer, kai lumumba barrow, sprang into action. A Black feminist veteran of antiprison and antipolicing organizing, barrow saw responding to Katrina as a principled political obligation "because this was, in my estimation, the worst disaster Black folks have experienced since slavery."[113] She coordinated a conference call for New Orleans and national CR activists to strategize an abolitionist response to the storm.[114] During this call, CR "decided we wanted to intervene, and we started building up organizing nationally around the three R's: relief, recovery, rebuilding."[115]

Local and national Black Leftist organizers began framing post-Katrina struggles within an expansive internationalist framework of Reconstruction and radical human rights.[116] This move was both pragmatic and visionary. On one hand, organizers were looking for legal and political structures for redress that went beyond the Bush administration, which had already proven its disregard for Black suffering. On the other hand, grassroots activists sought not to solely respond to the storm from a place of defense but rather from a place of movement-building that took aim at transforming the root causes that produced the disaster of Katrina.

In doing so, activists unequivocally placed the Hurricane Katrina social movement response in the lineage of the internationalist Black radical tradition. Social movement leaders began naming the post-Katrina period as the "Third Reconstruction for the Gulf South," a period in which the US nation-state should be pressured to finally fulfill the promises and obligations to Black southerners that were never fully realized during Black Reconstruction or the mid-twentieth-century Black freedom movement.[117] In racial justice organizations and spaces, the terminology of reconstruction effortlessly replaced the more sanitized state discourse of "recovery" and "rebuilding." By framing Hurricane Katrina in terms of human rights rather than civil rights, organizers intentionally hearkened back to the Black human rights tradition embodied by figures such as W. E. B. Du Bois, William Patterson, and Paul Robeson who through the Civil Rights Congress famously turned to the United Nations for redress against the US government's anti-Black racism in their petition, *We Charge Genocide*.[118]

Over the next several years, visits to and from the UN to testify on the post-Katrina injustices of housing, labor, education, reproductive justice, and policing would become commonplace among local activists seeking global solidarity.[119] The right of return became grassroots activists' rallying cry—explicitly linking the displacement of Black New Orleanians and Gulf Coast residents to the struggles of displaced Palestinians by highlighting how Katrina survivors, like Palestinians, were thrown off their land by militarized forces to ethnically cleanse a geographic area for new settlers: this cast the plight of the Black South with those of the Global South. The human rights categorization of internally displaced persons became one of the primary tools that organizers used to agitate for people's right to come and stay home.[120]

Although Black Marxists primarily affiliated with Community Labor United and the People's Hurricane Relief Fund were the initial champions of the reconstruction framework, New Orleans activists had also articulated racial justice activism through human rights prior to Katrina.[121] The New Orleans environmental justice organization Advocates for Environmental Human Rights positioned their work in a human rights paradigm, while previous campaigns around immigrant detainees in OPP were led by Amnesty International and Human Rights Watch. Moreover, the work of the New Orleans chapter of INCITE! resonated with an internationalist human rights framework, making connections between gender-based interpersonal violence and state violence at home and abroad. The Southern Center for Human Rights and the US Human Rights Network, both antiracist organizations based in Atlanta, offered regional support to local organizers. Even when not explicitly named as such, human rights in the Black radical tradition permeated post-Katrina struggles.

Initially it was the brutal neglect at OPP and the extended incarceration of people doing Katrina Time that opened new avenues for political engagement. After antideath penalty advocates with the Louisiana Crisis Assistance Center (LCAC)[122] won a moratorium on the death penalty, they redirected their staff capacity to tracking down OPP survivors lost in Louisiana's prisons and jails. Ursula Price, who was working as an investigator for LCAC at the time, remembers that this decision was made after the organization realized that if "we had a few clients in OPP and it took us weeks to locate them," how long was it taking for "those thousands of other people?"[123] LCAC investigators interviewed more than two thousand survivors about their experiences and to collect information for their habeas petitions.[124] Thousands of other OPP survivors were interviewed by people doing similar projects with the Southern Center for Human Rights, the Louisiana Association of Criminal Defense Lawyers, and the ACLU National Prison Project.

Advocates with JJPL similarly focused their work on those imprisoned in the penal system doing Katrina Time. To support families in reconnecting with their incarcerated children, Friends and Families of Louisiana's Incarcerated Children and JJPL staff went to evacuation shelters and offered their help to parents trying to track down their kids. In shelter after shelter, when JJPL staff would ask over the loudspeaker whether anyone was a parent or a loved one of someone in a juvenile prison, dozens of people would come up to them looking for both children and adults who had been in OPP. As the stories of people being left to drown in OPP snowballed, several JJPL staff felt called to confront the adult penal system and began internally discussing how to best move that work forward.[125]

CR activists became alerted to what was happening at OPP through their relationships and conversations with JJPL staff.[126] These organizers decided that their Katrina campaign would focus on gaining amnesty, release, and the complete expungement of people's records for "Prisoners of Katrina"—the people abandoned in OPP and those arrested for "trying to take care of themselves and their loved ones," what the state defined as "looting."[127] As CR organizer Middleton put it, "When you got into it, it was the only logical step. . . . What would be the thing you would ask for that's less than this when you consider all the things that [jailed and criminalized people] experienced?"[128] The amnesty campaign would "push, push, push this conversation around what happened to folks in OPP."[129] For barrow, the call for amnesty would "raise questions around the PIC [prison industrial complex] as a whole and the ways it impacts Black bodies specifically and also to raise it to a human rights issue."[130] CR organizers demanded that everyone doing Katrina Time deserved unconditional freedom. This campaign would both push an abolitionist edge in local criminal justice organizing and be an anchor for the rebuilding the New Orleans's CR chapter.

As local activists sorted out the contours of post-Katrina organizing around the criminal legal system, Community Labor United and the People's Hurricane Relief Fund organized a strategy meeting at the historic Black freedom Penn Center in South Carolina to develop a people's reconstruction program. An outcome of this meeting was the creation of working groups ranging from one on labor that focused on building Black–Brown worker unity to a criminal justice working group for which the problem of the jail took center stage. Staff from CR and JJPL talked about the information they had gathered about the jail and OPP survivors. In this meeting Lynn first connected with veteran New Orleans organizer Althea Francois who was working with the Southern Center for Human Rights in Atlanta and was trying to get her own daughter, an OPP survivor, out of jail. Although the criminal justice working group fizzled out, the development of such relationships would prove vital for future organizing.[131]

In October 2005, New Orleans activists and advocates held a press conference outside the still-empty jail to publicly testify about the racial violence enacted against criminalized survivors during the storm. The press conference was the first in a long line of events using truth-telling to disrupt the dominant law-and-order state narrative and make demands for systemic change. Together CR, JPPL, ACLU, the People's Hurricane Relief Fund, Friends and Families of Louisiana's Incarcerated Children, the NAACP Legal Defense Fund, and Human Rights Watch publicly recounted for the first time the dangers the state had exposed incarcerated individuals to at OPP: the abandonment by guards, the lack of food and water, the contaminated floodwaters. In contrast to the official narrative, which maintained that the flooding of the jail was unavoidable, organizers asserted that Gusman was squarely to blame in his failure to make an evacuation plan.[132] Joe Cook of the ACLU disputed Gusman's narrative that no one had died as he had been told that a deputy "found three dead bodies in the jail," and there were still 327 people missing from the official list of evacuated prisoners.[133]

Organizers foregrounded the stories of mothers of OPP survivors. One woman shared that she had no knowledge of her son's whereabouts until three weeks after the storm, and it was still unclear when he would be released and they would be reunited. Althea Francois recounted that her daughter was arrested immediately before the storm, but because the bail bond companies were already shuttered, she could not be bailed out before the hurricane (figure 4.1). In a firm and quiet outrage, Francois shared the thoughts running through her head during and after the storm:

FIGURE 4.1 Althea Francois speaking at Katrina OPP Press Conference holding a photo of her daughter trapped in the system doing "Katrina Time," October 12, 2005. Still from *I Won't Drown on That Levee and You Ain't Gonna Break My Back*, directed by Ashley Hunt. Courtesy of Ashley Hunt.

Is she safe? Is she even alive? Do they have food or water? Is she dry? Was she evacuated? How? Where to? . . . Two weeks pass. I am frantic. I am becoming ill. I continue to tell her eight-year-old daughter and her four-year-old son that their mother is safe and we will find her. I finally learned by constantly asking anybody and anyone until someone's aunt who was employed at OPP [told me] that the women were moved to Angola. My heart sinks. I was allowed to pay her bond two weeks ago, maybe three weeks ago. And she's still in Camp F. It's been over a month and a half, and she is very ill, sleeping on the floor. There's so many, there are thousands of other people being held, I know illegally, who have no one out here, whose family member may not even know where they are right now, let alone to pull through trying to traverse this system.[134]

Francois refused to exceptionalize her family's trials and tribulations. Rather she shared her story to illuminate the vicious harm that the state was afflicting on thousands of incarcerated people and families. If Francois, a savvy organizer with access to legal resources, had this much difficulty getting her child out of jail, how difficult must it be for the families scattered across the nation with little to no resources?

Although organizers focused the October 2005 press conference on the atrocities directly tied to the federal flood, they refused to single out these catastrophes as due solely to Hurricane Katrina. As Tamika Middleton proclaimed, "Katrina's aftermath reflects the way we as a nation increasingly deal with social ills. Police and imprison primarily poor Black communities for crimes that are reflections of poverty and desperation." According to Middleton, that the first new construction after Katrina was a jail made clear that the roots of the problem were in the state's carceral logic of "law-and-order first. Meeting needs and saving lives last."[135] Xochitl Bervera explained, "We've heard it said if we just keep Black folks out, if we keep poor folks out of this city, somehow public safety will increase. We want to say very publicly that is not what public safety is about."[136] Just as public safety did not improve with the growth of OPP, nor would it improve with the displacement of Black working-class and poor New Orleanians. As Bervera declared, what was needed now was "full community involvement and total reconstruction of what we know as a public safety system."[137]

Although the media barely registered that this press conference, it rattled Sheriff Gusman.[138] According to Lynn, "he came out and started screaming at us . . . he kept calling us liars because we said that people were missing."[139] But when organizers tried to confront him, he tried to run away. As Middleton recounts, "Here is this ten-foot-high watermark and there's the sheriff running away. Refusing to face accountability."[140] It was only the beginning of New Orleans organizers taking on the power of the sheriff in their fight to undo the city's punishment regime.

After the press conference, CR organizers focused their efforts on making the amnesty campaign a reality. With Middleton stretched in her responsibilities as the CR southern regional coordinator, kai barrow came to New Orleans to get the amnesty campaign and chapter rebuilding off the ground. With a big-tent approach to organizing, barrow brought together both local New Orleanians and the influx of activist volunteers looking to contribute to the just reconstruction of New Orleans. CR members and legal volunteers helped build case studies of people doing Katrina Time, while barrow worked with a ragtag group of activists to mobilize faith communities to call on the city and state for amnesty.[141] To heighten public demands for amnesty, CR held a weekend of events called "Amnesty for Prisoners of

Katrina: A Weekend of Reconciliation and Respect for Human Rights" in December 2006. The weekend included workshops, a public lecture in support of amnesty by abolitionist-scholar Angela Davis, and an interfaith pray-in on Sunday.[142]

Even though the weekend of events had strong turnout and widespread media coverage and it drew more people to the local CR chapter, it did not move state and city officials as organizers hoped it would. But that does not mean it did not have lasting impacts. Through this organizing, Critical Resistance developed abolitionist organizing infrastructures that challenged disaster racism. It helped popularize an antiracist critique of the state's response to criminalized people. By refusing to leave anyone behind in the narrow demarcations of "guilty" and "innocent," CR demonstrated the hollowness of rendering some people and not others as deserving of freedom. Moreover, grassroots activists critically connected the dots between the extraordinary racial state violence enacted in the wake of Hurricane Katrina and the everyday crisis of criminalization confronting Black New Orleanians. This political analysis and sensibility would critically infuse the pivotal struggle to shrink OPP when FEMA granted millions to renovate and rebuild the jail over the next few years.

· · · · · ·

The hurricane was never the primary disaster that hit New Orleans. Instead, the neoliberal state's turn to organized abandonment and racial criminalization was the disaster. The fortification of punitive infrastructures over preceding decades in tandem with disinvestments in socialized caring infrastructures ensured that, rather than being saved, the people of New Orleans were sacrificed in the name of law-and-order. Yet amid these carceral crises, grassroots organizers forged other visions.

They imagined what a reconstructed New Orleans could be—a city that did not revolve around the jailing and policing of its residents but a place where no one was made disposable. Over the next several years, community organizers would take these lessons developed in the storm's immediate aftermath and push to transform the city's criminal legal system, including by taking on one of the linchpins of the Louisiana punishment regime, the OPP.

5 Reconstructing the New Orleans Criminal Legal System in the Wake of Hurricane Katrina

In the post-Katrina world in this city, everything that could go wrong was going wrong and it wasn't hard to find people who had been impacted one way or the other, either by the police department or either by the jail. Our job [at Safe Streets/Strong Communities] was to reach out to those families, collectivize their stories, and train them to take on these leadership roles to start being advocates for themselves.

—Norris Henderson

Crises can give you opportunities that you wouldn't normally have, but you have to be ready for them.

—Ursula Price

On the afternoon of February 3, 2011, more than one hundred Orleans Parish Prison Reform Coalition (OPPRC) members and supporters filled New Orleans City Council chambers to demand that the city council impose a cap on OPP's size. A buzz was in the air as activists holding signs that read "1438 CAP" and "DECOMISSION NOW" opposed Sheriff Gusman's proposal to leverage millions in FEMA funds to expand the jail closer to its pre-Katrina size. During the public comment period, speakers implored the council to back the proposed jail cap of 1,438 beds instead, arguing that reinvesting in jail expansion would repeat the racist punitive practices that had created everyday crises for New Orleanians long before the levees broke. The city council aligned with OPPRC over Gusman and voted in favor of the bed cap, which meant that by 2012, OPP would have less than half the beds it did in 2010: this would represent an 80 percent cut to the jail's total size since Hurricane Katrina. It was a victory that was the result of years of organizing to undo the carceral logics that had dominated decades of New Orleans governance.

How antiracist community organizers achieved this feat is the question at the heart of this chapter. This examination of how the severe crises affecting the criminal legal system was leveraged to scale back carceral power shows how acute crises can be turned into political opportunities for undoing the carceral state. Community activists started new grassroots organizations, reanimated coalitions, and won victories in campaigns that seemed impossible to even dream about before the storm. Guiding this grassroots activism was the theory of change that meaningful transformation of the New Orleans punishment regime required the people directly harmed by the criminal legal system to be at the forefront of organizing.

This period of anticarceral community organizing can be demarcated into two interconnected phases of post-Katrina activism.[1] The first phase (2005–2008) was centered on pushing for immediate reforms to the public defender office and the NOPD in tandem with long-haul organizing against the violence of OPP. Although many local and national groups were involved in this activism, Safe Streets/Strong Communities, colloquially referred to as "Safe Streets," facilitated much of the organizing. Through grassroots research, base-building, campaign organizing, and media work, Safe Streets organized, in the words of Evelyn Lynn, "to change conditions and to create a better future and world for people's families and communities."[2] Out of this organizing came the overhaul of the New Orleans indigent defense system, the creation of the Office of the Independent Police Monitor, and a new popular narrative about the harms of the New Orleans criminal legal system.

The second phase of this activism (2008–2013) coalesced around the rebuilding of Orleans Parish Prison. Although Gusman was able to reopen OPP less than two months after the storm, the damages it incurred from the federal flood meant that it lost thousands of beds of jailing capacity. With premature deaths continuing to occur within the jail and FEMA poised to grant millions of dollars to rebuild OPP, community activists reanimated the Orleans Parish Prison Reform Coalition (OPPRC) to end routinized jail violence and to contest Gusman's proposal to expand the jail. OPPRC built a citywide campaign for a smaller jail that highlighted the inhumanity of the jail and the perverse financial incentives of the per diem system first crafted under the Hayes Williams federal court order. In early 2011, the city council placed a cap of 1,438 jail beds on the rebuilt OPP—almost six thousand fewer beds than OPP's pre-storm capacity. Although Sheriff Gusman never stopped agitating to expand the jail, OPPRC shifted the conversation in ways that continue to reverberate to this day.

Transforming the System: Safe Streets/Strong Communities

Founding Safe Streets/Strong Communities

In the first months after Hurricane Katrina, right at the beginning of New Orleans's rebuilding process, the sentiment that the criminal justice system was in crisis was shared across the political spectrum. However, there was no agreement on how the system should be reformed: three trajectories were advocated. City government officials such as Mayor Nagin, the NOPD leadership, and Sheriff Gusman urged the expansion of carceral infrastructures through deploying the Louisiana State Police and National Guard indefinitely, intensifying crackdowns on migrant workers, and rebuilding OPP as quickly and as largely as possible. They claimed not only that law-and-order was necessary for recovery but also that this crisis was an opportunity to banish the so-called criminal element from New Orleans for good. The second path forward advocated by many city council members, good government groups, and other liberal elites was that the New Orleans criminal justice system was broken, and now was the time to modernize the system to bring it more in line with other cities. Those holding this position advocated for moderate reforms such as creating a day reporting center—a non-residential "supervision and treatment program" as an alternative to incarceration centers—as well as adequately funding indigent defense and improving conditions in adult and youth jails.[3] Grassroots organizations such as the Juvenile Justice Project of Louisiana (JJPL), Critical Resistance, and the nascent Safe Streets/Strong Communities adopted a third position. This was a critical moment to push for transformative reforms to the criminal legal system as a strategy of dismantling the systemic racism and classism that produced the Katrina crisis. This approach involved not only fighting back against law-and-order interventions but also being proactive in organizing for the creation of new policies and institutions.

A cluster of JJPL staff members—Evelyn Lynn, Jack Cassidy,[4] Barry Gerharz, and Norris Henderson (who had started working at JJPL not long after his release from Angola in 2003)—received the blessing of JJPL's executive director to spin off a new organization to focus on the adult system.[5] Thus was born Safe Streets/Strong Communities in late 2005 to leverage the crisis of Hurricane Katrina as an opportunity to "reconstruct a public safety system that creates safe streets and strong communities for everyone, regardless of race or economic status."[6] Through foregrounding the role of anti-Black racism and economic precarity in producing the injustices of the criminal legal system, Safe Streets organized to undo the violence and corruption of the New Orleans punishment regime. Wearing bright-orange shirts and known for their fearless truth-telling, Safe Streets' staff and members were a force to be reckoned with.

Safe Streets was based on the JJPL model of combining policy, legal, media, and grassroots organizing to induce change at the roots of overincarceration and policing.[7] Safe Streets organizers, in the words of Xochitl Bervera, realized that "because everything's shut down there's an opportunity to overhaul it all. If Katrina wiped it out, then we could step in, and, in a different way, shift the rebuilding."[8] Although at times the campaigns of Safe Streets dove-tailed with more liberal positions, the organization was clear that their ultimate goal was total transformation of the New Orleans criminal legal system and a radical redefinition of what constituted public safety achieved through a grassroots people-powered movement. Safe Streets built the organization around three campaigns: completely overhauling the indigent defense system, attaining greater police accountability around abuse and corruption, and downsizing the jail.[9] These three priorities were identified because of their potential power to address Katrina-related punitive state racial violence *and* to reform the root problems in the criminal legal system that created a lack of safety for Black and working-class New Orleans communities. In the words of Evelyn Lynn, "We saw campaigns as a way to organize and mobilize people in order to do that leadership development work and in order to provide an opportunity to confront targets and change the system."[10]

Shepherding these campaigns required staffing and financial resources. Some individuals easily made the transition from JJPL to Safe Streets, assuming similar roles. But as Norris Henderson remembers, "The question remained, 'Who's gonna run it?' I was drafted to be the director, and I was like, I don't know. I hadn't been home that long, and even though I had leadership skills and management skills from inside, this was something different. It had a real budget, a real staff. So, we went with a codirector model with me and Xochitl Bervera [of FFLIC] becoming co-directors."[11] Xochitl Bervera had gained valuable experience in the campaign to shut down the Tallulah youth prison. Henderson had just received a Soros Justice Fellowship to launch the organization, Voice of the Ex-Offender (VOTE), to continue the aims of the Angola Special Civics Project by organizing formerly incarcerated people. The Soros Foundation agreed to move the fellowship funding to Safe Streets to help it get off the ground.[12] Ursula Price had also recently received a Soros Fellowship to organize around OPP, which was also brought under the Safe Streets banner.[13] Althea Francois became involved with Safe Streets while still a staff member of the Southern Center for Human Rights (SCHR) but was soon hired as a Safe Streets organizer. In 2006, Bervera left New Orleans, and Cielo Cruz, who had been organizing against the criminalization of immigrant reconstruction workers, replaced her as associate director. Member-leader Robert Goodman would join the team as another community organizer. Taking over a small nook of four offices and a couch in the same building that housed JJPL and Friends and Families of Louisiana's Incarcerated Children in the hyper-policed Central City neighborhood, Safe Streets got to work.

Overhauling Indigent Defense

Safe Streets began by rolling out an indigent defense campaign. Though the jail initially captured the organizers' attention, they knew that squaring off against the sheriff would be challenging. Focusing on indigent defense targeted the problem of inadequate counsel that contributed to Katrina Time. For years, legal advocates had identified the need to reform indigent defense. Through their relationships with criminal defense attorneys, Safe Streets organizers realized that there were lawyers primed and ready to overhaul the indigent defense board structure and staff. As Xochitl Bervera recalls, "The idea of flipping the [indigent defense] board, of getting folks out who had been negligent in their duties and getting our folks to take it over became clear as a good possibility of what was winnable at the time."[14]

Like many US cities, indigent defense in Orleans Parish was severely underfunded. Although district attorneys received significant state and parish funding, indigent defense received only $7.5 million a year of state funds to be split equally among each of the state's forty-one indigent defense offices. Traffic tickets and fines and fees for municipal offenses primarily funded public defense. This paltry funding strategy ensured that indigent defense in Orleans Parish, where extensive policing and prosecution were the norm, was underfunded and that the dollars funding indigent defense disproportionally came from the pockets of Black New Orleanians targeted by racial profiling in traffic stops and everyday arrests.[15]

Through conversations with people doing Katrina Time, organizers learned that problems with indigent defense went beyond a lack of funding. To build support for indigent defense reform, Safe Streets and SCHR partnered to release joint reports that centered incarcerated people's stories, differing from previous efforts that primarily viewed the issue as a legal problem. Interviews with 102 people confined in OPP during Katrina revealed that on average people were incarcerated pretrial for "385 days, with the longest wait being 1,289 days and the shortest being 179."[16] Not only had none of the indigent defendants seen their Orleans Indigent Defense (OID) attorney in the six months since the storm, almost none of them had seen their attorney outside the courtroom in the six months *prior* to Hurricane Katrina.[17] While attorneys, investigators, and law students worked for months pro bono to track down indigent OPP survivors, not one OID attorney had sought out a single client after the storm.[18]

Not only underfunding but also OID policies undermined meaningful defense. On paper OID attorneys worked full time, but because they could take on an unlimited number of private cases, in essence the OID program was "getting part-time attorneys at full-time pay."[19] This system subsidized private-practice defenders with public dollars, and then they showed little obligation to indigent clients beyond trying to convince them to hire them as private attorneys.[20] Evelyn Lynn described the scenario as OID attorneys telling clients, "'I have so many cases as a public defender, I can represent you, but if you want good representation, you should contract with me and my private firm.' . . . So, folks would dole out however many thousands of dollars that they could pull together and still get crap defense. There really wasn't a public defender system."[21]

Moreover, the Louisiana Indigent Defense Assistance Board had little oversight of local indigent defense boards.[22] Local district judges appointed OID board members based on campaign contributions.[23] Lacking any enforceable criteria, the OID Board in turn appointed attorneys to the OID primarily on the basis of personal relationships. As the SCHR report outlined, under this system, "when a judge disliked a particularly active public defender, OID Board members would have the public defender re-assigned or terminated."[24] Furthermore, the head of the OID Board was Frank DeSalvo, the lead attorney for the local police union. Safe Streets argued it was a conflict of interest for the police officers' attorney to hold this role.[25] As Lynn explained, this arrangement encouraged corruption in that DeSalvo "was paid to defend abusive and corrupt cops in court and in the media and also got to select the lawyers representing clients in the criminal legal system. . . . Usually he chose his friends to serve as indigent defenders. Even when they weren't his friends, they knew if they provided a rigorous defense for their clients, they would be in DeSalvo's crosshairs.'"[26]

Safe Streets and SCHR sought to use their reports as one of many means of increasing pressure for reform. A few weeks before their release, legal advocates successfully petitioned Criminal District Judge Arthur Hunter to order an investigation of the indigent defense system's operations. At the press conference on the release of their reports, Safe Streets built on this win by calling for the resignation of the entire OID board.[27] Their reports garnered such media attention that three members of the OID Board resigned in disgrace within a few days—leaving DeSalvo as the sole remaining board member.[28] Media and judges condemned the interrelationship among elements of the indigent defense system, DeSalvo's conflict of interest, and Katrina Time. *Times-Picayune* columnist James Gill penned an editorial that read, "Louisiana has never met its constitutional obligation to provide effective counsel for defendants who can't afford to pay for it. But post-Katrina the poor might as well be living in a police state."[29] Following these pressures, DeSalvo resigned from the OID Board.

The resignations of members of the OID Board that Safe Streets had advocated for had now materialized. Reformist judges appointed a completely new indigent defense board while the state allocated $2.8 million for Orleans Parish to rebuild the office.[30] Safe Streets activists helped attract renowned civil rights attorneys Jon Rapping and Charles Ogletree to help rebuild the public defender office. They recruited committed defense attorneys and trained them in best practices.[31] One of the first policies put in place was a prohibition against attorneys taking private clients.[32] The New Orleans changes provided momentum for reforms at the state level. A coalition of criminal defense reformers facilitated the passage of legislation that ensured greater oversight of indigent defense boards and workload limits for public defenders.[33] Although public defense remained woefully underfunded at the state and local level, Safe Streets saw this legislation as a step in the right direction for countless poor defendants.

Building their Power: Base Building and Collectivizing Stories

Although the indigent defense campaign was built on policy and media strategies, Safe Streets organizers knew that winning meaningful reforms to the NOPD and OPP would require building a base. As Cielo Cruz relates, "Our theory of change was that the most impacted people are the people who need to be in the decision-making seat of transforming systems that are oppressing them. A big part of what we were trying to do was work with the membership. The other thing we were trying to do was to try and create strategies that toggled between immediate, urgent crises and building long-term policy changes and structural change."[34] Building a base—of actively involved people who had been personally targeted and harmed by the criminal legal system or were the loved one of someone who had—was no easy task. Rather than using an Alinsky style of community organizing that eschewed questions of ideology in favor of building power through transactional tactics, Safe Streets operated from a style of transformative organizing.[35] They developed their members' collective analyses of the systemic conditions that overdetermined Black poor and working-class New Orleanians as targets of the criminal legal system; the organization then trained them in nuts-and-bolts organizing skills to build the people power required to wage campaigns that focused on root problems and made material improvements in people's lives. At the same time, members and staff developed relationships that deepened their understanding of the systems they were up against and their commitments to one another.

Safe Streets approached outreach, the initial work of base-building, from multiple angles. In the words of Norris Henderson, their outreach efforts were guided by the concept, "We're looking for people who are looking for us."[36] At first, this was a challenge. Evelyn Lynn recalls, "We had a couple of trial and errors in doing outreach. We started with handing out fliers. But then we had no way to get in contact with folks afterwards. So that was a miss. Then we started gathering petitions and postcards so we could both engage folks and get their contact information to follow up. But the most effective way we were able to engage and recruit folks was through knocking doors and our community survey process."[37] Safe Streets surveyed people as they were released from OPP about their experiences with the NOPD and OPP. Waiting outside the jail, Safe Streets activists would offer cigarettes and their cellphones to people who had just been released while explaining that they were collecting information about people's interactions with the police and experiences in OPP. Through this process, Safe Streets connected with more than five hundred people during 2006. Many of them ended up coming out to a Safe Streets meeting and joining the organization.

Safe Streets conducted even more targeted outreach by identifying people who had experienced police or jailing violence. As Henderson recounts, "The newspaper would report something, and we would go and find the family and invite them to come to a meeting."[38] Safe Streets' approach of organizing families became a defining characteristic of their base-building efforts. As Henderson explains, people got involved as "whole families. However big these families were, it was kind of like an expansion."[39] Not just nuclear families but also extended families made up much of Safe Streets' membership. As is often the case in community organizing, "mothers were galvanizing forces," often taking the lead in bringing new people in and speaking out against the state violence their loved ones had experienced.[40]

Before long, word about Safe Streets spread. At one of their first mass meetings, Xochitl Bervera remembers. "Evelyn called me being like, 'I don't know what to do. There are already seventy people here! It's fifteen minutes before the meeting starts' . . . The race became how to meet the organizing energy."[41] Local police misconduct attorney Mary Howells, who was working with the Madison family around the Danziger Bridge shootings, brought the Madisons to a Safe Streets meeting, and they became member-leaders.[42] In addition, word about the organization spread through the informal channels of the Louisiana penal system. With Henderson's reputation from Angola buoying people's trust in the organization, letters poured in from imprisoned people asking Safe Streets to track down their families.[43]

Sometimes the outreach strategies overlapped. One of the people Safe Streets connected with through the jail surveys was William Tanner, the man who had tried to help Henry Glover and had his car torched by the NOPD.[44] Not long after Tanner connected with Safe Streets, he showed up at the office to see what could be done about the NOPD's brutality against Henry Glover and those who tried to help. Although Tanner's story seemed inconceivable, Henderson assigned Althea Francois "to see if there was something we could do. . . . Althea took this to heart. And as this thing started manifesting itself we realized that we really have a real problem."[45] Safe Streets brought Tanner and the Glover family into the fold by supporting their individual efforts for legal redress and bringing them into the collective work of pushing for NOPD oversight.

Safe Streets' primary membership came from what Ursula Price described as their "natural base," the two Black neighborhoods in which the city and capital had historically disinvested from schools, housing, and jobs and invested instead in policing and incarceration: Central City, the neighborhood with the highest per capita incarceration rate in the city, and River Gardens, the HOPE VI redevelopment that replaced the St. Thomas housing projects.[46] These neighborhoods proved vital for organizing not only because of their targeting by law enforcement but also because of their history of community organizing against police brutality and the neoliberal razing of public housing in the 1990s. Cielo Cruz recounts, "One of the things that we were blessed with was that we worked really closely with former St. Thomas resident leadership," many of whom lived in the few public housing units still in River Gardens.[47] As Price notes, working with the St. Thomas leadership set the tone as "they were already familiar with the ability of organizing to make change."[48]

Through monthly meetings, Safe Streets staff and member-leaders facilitated members coming together as a collective organization. In addition to providing political education and information about current campaigns, Safe Streets organizers strove to have members see themselves as one unified body. One of the challenges was that members fit generally into two camps: those who themselves or their family had experienced police violence and those who themselves or their family had experienced OPP violence. As Henderson recounts, "In the early stages, it was convincing people that they are all in this fight together. Your son could not have ended up in jail if he had not had contact with the police. And then the lights start coming on. This is something systemic. This is not just an isolated incident. So your struggle is their struggle and vice versa. . . . Initially people would say, 'I thought this meeting was about—' and then somebody would speak up and draw those intersecting lines, and then they started seeing it."[49] As people came to see how their fights, and thus their fates, were intricately linked, storytelling became a key strategy for members to build relationships, develop collective analyses of power, and begin to heal from the trauma of punitive state violence and death.

A feminist ethos of emotional care also shaped the development of their membership structure. According to Cruz, an important and painful "part of our membership strategy was" recognizing that "the police are creating this larger and larger net of people who need to be connected to other people who have gone through what they have gone through."[50] Henderson describes that engaging people emotionally helped them see how their struggles were interlinked: "It was easy to organize that core group of people because that mother over here who's crying about losing her son or her son being abused. There was another mother, another family member over here, feeling the same way. . . . They became each others' shoulder and ear because they wanted the same thing for each other. They were in struggle . . .

their coming together gave them a space to heal."[51] In valuing people's emotional vulnerability and courage in sharing their stories of punitive state violence, Safe Streets created a space for previously disparate people to forge powerful bonds and see themselves as part of something larger.

Even though Safe Streets staff appreciated that people felt comfortable sharing their stories at member meetings, Henderson notes that they were never "collecting stories for the sake of stories but taking those stories and empowering people" to use their experiences to push forward systemic changes.[52] Organizers would ask, "What do you want to do about this? Do you want to file a complaint? Do you just want to do a press conference? Or do you just want to do nothing you just need to show up at a meeting?"[53] People had a newfound sense of activism after Hurricane Katrina. Lynn recalls the sense that people "had just had enough" and that "we deserve better here and we're going to fight for it."[54]

Safe Streets also organized members to see themselves as part of a national movement for racial and economic justice. They brought dozens of members to the historic 2007 US Social Forum in Atlanta, where the just reconstruction of the Gulf Coast took center stage as a pivotal national struggle for Black liberation and against neoliberalism. There they built alliances with the national Right to the City alliance and other grassroots organizations. Henderson recalls one powerful moment when members met "Amadou Diallo's mom and they saw that strength and power in her and that energized them. . . . People were able to connect with other people, not just nationally, but internationally who were in different struggles."[55] Although Safe Streets activists always focused on local conditions, they never saw their struggles as provincial but as part of a broader movement that traversed local and regional scales.

Safe Streets' campaign work harnessed people's concerns and complaints in a unified direction. Henderson remembers, "Once they were given a target and realized who could give them what they needed, then [organizing] became easy."[56] Bervera relates that after the storm people were also "a little less afraid" of coming together and speaking out. Or they "were [more] angrier than afraid" and were "more like 'What the hell do we have to do?'"[57] People's stories of the injustices of the criminal legal system became powerful tools in their grassroots campaign work. Henderson explains, "People really needed to galvanize the limited resources they had to fight back," and what "they had to fight back was them telling these stories."[58] Speaking out and naming the reality of police and jail violence before, during, and after the storm became one of Safe Streets' core tactics.

Campaigning for NOPD Oversight: The Independent Police Monitor

The next campaign that Safe Streets focused on was the creation of an independent police monitor (IPM). Even though the atrocities of the Danziger Bridge shooting and Henry Glover murder heightened the urgency of the campaign, Safe Streets also saw the need for a structure that could rein in quotidian forms of police violence. The idea for an IPM initially developed out of a Pennington-era Police-Civilian Task force formed in 2001 after an NOPD officer shot an unarmed teen in the Algiers neighborhood. Given ongoing police misconduct and the limits of existing police reforms, the Task Force proposed the creation of the position of an independent police monitor, but it did not gain traction.[59] The institutions that were supposed to provide police oversight were woefully inadequate. The Office of Municipal Investigations (OMI), created following the NOPD's 1980 killing of Black residents in Algiers, was limited to officer-involved shootings and was located under the mayor's purview. The Public Integrity Bureau (PIB), founded under Pennington after NOPD officer Len Davis put a hit on Kim Groves after she reported him to Internal Affairs, had a broader mandate, but it was under the command of the deputy police chief.

Safe Streets contended that the city needed something new. They advocated for the creation of a body with broad authority to investigate NOPD complaints and oversee the PIB while being politically independent from the NOPD *and* the mayor. As Jack Cassidy explained, having the IPM be politically independent was critical because the NOPD is always the "mayor's police department" and the mayor could not be expected to remain impartial.[60] Although Safe Streets considered advocating for an NOPD community oversight committee, their research suggested that such bodies tended to have little power and were prone to internalizing police narratives over time. For Safe Streets, an IPM with subpoena power and dedicated revenue could be a powerful site of redress for New Orleanians who had experienced police abuse. It could also be a tool for racial justice organizing. For instance, at the same time as the IPM campaign, Safe Streets activists generated a "dirty cops database." Between this research and the people power of their membership, the organization believed that an IPM would open the door for them to campaign for the firing of particularly abusive and corrupt NOPD officers.

The need for an IPM was reinforced by staff's discussions with members. Henderson recalls his experience taking a Safe Streets' member to the PIB to file a brutality complaint: "When we pulled up, she wouldn't get out of the car. I was like, we'd come too far now for you to be quivering. But she said the most profound thing . . . She said, 'Man we going to the police on the police.' And it made me realize, really, how systemic this problem was. We were going to complain to somebody who was a part of this problem."[61] Through this exchange, Henderson more fully recognized the chilling effect that the NOPD's killing of Kim Groves still had on people and the importance of an independent body that residents could trust.

The IPM campaign's first hurdle was the widespread perception in the initial months after the storm that, even though NOPD officers fled their posts and Superintendent Eddie Compass resigned under the pressure of Katrina, overall local law enforcement were heroes. After NOPD officers beat a Black sixty-four-year-old retired schoolteacher on Bourbon Street for public drunkenness in October 2005, reporters took pains to assert that the NOPD could not be held accountable for their actions because of poststorm stress.[62] At the time, if you criticized the cops, "people assumed you were fringe."[63] Even at a mayoral task force meeting on police accountability, religious leaders were enraged when Cassidy outlined the historical abuses of the NOPD.[64] Taking on the unquestioned pro-police ideology by revealing the NOPD's ongoing and everyday violence became a key pillar of Safe Streets' campaign.

Safe Streets saw the national spotlight on New Orleans as the fulcrum for shifting public perception about the NOPD. They figured if they could get national media to pay attention, local media would follow and pressure city officials to take Katrina police violence seriously. Jack Cassidy pitched the real story behind the Danziger shootings to CNN and introduced their reporters to the Madison family.[65] In May 2006, CNN released the first piece of journalism on the Danziger shooting that took the words of Lance Madison seriously.[66] By the time the Danziger families filed federal lawsuits against the NOPD, CNN and NPR had released sympathetic reports, and even the *Times-Picayune* had called into question the NOPD's credibility.[67] In addition, Safe Streets connected with A. C. Thompson and ProPublica about the NOPD's assassination of Henry Glover and the Danziger shootings.[68] Thompson's reporting bolstered the IPM campaign and revived the Danziger campaign after the legal case was dismissed by state courts.

While Hurricane Katrina gave people a national platform on which to testify about the spectacular violence committed by the NOPD, Safe Streets organizers were clear that the IPM campaign also needed to highlight the police's everyday abuses. As discussed earlier, during 2006 Safe Streets collected more than five hundred surveys about people's experiences with the

NOPD. In capturing stories about the day-to-day harassment and abuses of the NOPD, these surveys sought to dislodge the notion that the police were a source of safety and to codify what was well known within Black working-class and poor communities throughout the city but was disavowed by political elites. The categories and checklists of Safe Streets' surveys pointed to the multitude of law enforcement harms, such as racial slurs, public strip searches, theft, car damage, and evidence falsification. The survey's section on people's experiences of physical harm provided *seventeen* options from broken bones to sexual assault and from dog bites to gunshot wounds.

Safe Streets' surveys operated not only to document state cruelty but also to redefine public safety outside punitive logics. They asked the critical question of where people wanted the state to direct the $500,000 being spent weekly on maintaining National Guard patrols in New Orleans. People were asked to indicate which services should be invested in to improve public safety: job development, a living wage, rent control, education, public transportation, affordable healthcare, mental health services, playgrounds, or more police.[69] Safe Streets' survey refused the logics of positivist research that reify dominant ideologies and instead wielded the survey as a political tool for intervening in the notion that equated public safety with policing.

On October 22, 2006, Safe Streets released their survey findings in the report *Crisis of Confidence* with a march protesting police brutality through the River Gardens housing complex. The march location called attention to the heightened policing that public housing residents experienced in River Gardens where the private management company and market-rate residents routinely called the police on them for not following white middle-class norms.[70] *Crisis of Confidence* asserted that policing was a "crisis that has roots long before Hurricane Katrina"[71] and focused on the everyday forms of police misconduct that rarely elicited public attention. Two-thirds of respondents were afraid that they or their loved ones would be harmed by the police and feared being harassed for legally gathering in public spaces; more than half respondents reported NOPD harassment. The report documented that, although people did not trust the NOPD across racial lines, 71 percent of Black men reported being harassed by the police, with 31 percent experiencing police harassment daily.[72] Overwhelmingly, respondents described the NOPD as "racist," "dirty," and "dangerous."[73]

Because the NOPD's problems could neither be explained away as the fault of a few rotten apples nor simply as a product of Katrina, the Safe Streets report demanded systemic reforms to the NOPD. Their primary recommendation was the establishment of a fully funded IPM by March 2007. Safe Streets also called for the collection of demographic data on stops and arrests to document and eradicate racial profiling and an end to broken window policing practices.[74] The third recommendation was that the NOPD cite rather than arrest people for traffic violations and misdemeanors. Moreover, *Crisis of Confidence* documented that residents believed that investments in education and youth opportunities would improve community safety. Against Mayor Nagin's claim that it was imperative to keep the National Guard in the city, the report found that most people did not support the militarization of the city and would rather state resources be spent on reconstruction projects: "housing," "levees," and "bringing my people home."[75] *Crisis in Confidence* disrupted the normalization of punitive logics while offering an alternative political imagination of how to instill security in post-Katrina New Orleans.

Local media described *Crisis of Confidence* as a wake-up call—a feat for any grassroots organization.[76] A *Times-Picayune* editorial asserted that the NOPD needed to take seriously "how tainted the department's image remains among some residents."[77] This positive publicity bolstered Safe Streets' IPM campaign. Yet this reception was not without contradictions. Unsurprisingly, media coverage foregrounded the report's finding that people's distrust of the police made them unwilling to report crime.[78] It is not unexpected that media would latch onto this piece of the report. The script that policing reforms were necessary to ensure more effective policing had been a dominant narrative since Pennington served as chief. At times, even Safe Streets' activism aligned with this position: *Crisis of Confidence* hailed Pennington's reforms and gestured toward the need for a New Orleans police force that was "professional, fair, and that the community can trust."[79] It is not entirely surprising that such ideas infused aspects of the work of Safe Streets, which was not impervious to hegemonic thinking. Yet, liberal reformism did not dominate *Crisis of Confidence* nor IPM organizing. Negotiating this tension—wanting to gain mainstream support while not limiting their political vision—continued throughout the IPM campaign.

Safe Streets also drew attention to the crisis of law enforcement violence through grassroots human rights convenings. On the second anniversary of Hurricane Katrina, the People's Hurricane Relief Fund (PHRF) held an international tribunal on US human rights violations at which Katrina survivors provided five days of testimony. Safe Streets members testified about the abandonment of prisoners in the flooded OPP, the police shootings on the Danziger Bridge, and the racial criminalization of New Orleanians.[80] A few months later, Safe Streets held their own hearing, "The Role of Law Enforcement in the Reconstruction," to demonstrate that "there is a public safety crisis in New Orleans—but it's not, as many people argue, because there aren't enough cops on our streets, in our neighborhoods, and in our schools. It's actually the opposite. In New Orleans post-Katrina, poor and low-income communities encounter police in ways that don't increase public safety and in ways that actually make peoples' efforts at rebuilding their lives more difficult, if not impossible."[81] The hearing underlined how criminalization intersected with gentrification, the privatization of public housing, school closures, and the exploitation of immigrant labor.[82]

While helping change public narratives about the NOPD, Safe Streets exerted direct pressure on the city council to create an Office of the Independent Police Monitor (OIPM). In March 2006, Safe Streets organizers and allies testified at city council hearings about instances of police brutality ranging from direct physical violence and false arrests, to police officers stating that they joined the force "to put Black people away," and to immigrant workers being forced at gunpoint to rebuild an NOPD officer's house without pay. They argued that this pattern of abuse required that city hall create an OIPM and conduct a nationwide search for a new police chief.[83] In response, the City Council Budget Committee urged Mayor Nagin to apply for a grant or earmark funds in the next year's budget for an OIPM.[84]

Yet rather than pushing this proposal forward, Mayor Nagin collaborated with Governor Blanco and Senator Mary Landrieu to keep the National Guard in the city and to lobby for federal policing funds to, in the words of Senator Landrieu, "put the fear of justice back into the gangs and drug-distribution network now reemerging in New Orleans."[85] Although Nagin gave lip service to the OIPM proposal, he did not include funding for it in his 2007 budget. However, the city council added $200,000 to the budget for an OIPM because of the positive reception of Safe Streets' campaign.[86] Yet, without an ordinance creating the OIPM, this allocation was meaningless.

Realizing that they needed a greater understanding of the technicalities of municipal governance, the Safe Streets staff researched where the OIPM should be housed within city government. This work was aided by Jack Cassidy, who left Safe Streets to work for a city council member; in this position he could support the OIPM ordinance from the inside. At the same time, good governance groups were pushing for the creation of an Office of the Inspector General (OIG) to provide greater transparency. Although these groups easily secured support for creating an OIG, they were still advocating for it to be written into the city charter with dedicated funding.[87] Because the inspector general oversaw other city departments *and* had subpoena power, Safe Streets staff approached the recently hired inspector general, Bob Cerasoli, to see whether he would be amenable to housing the IPM in his office. After learning he was sympathetic to their goals, the organization decided that "we would house the IPM under the Inspector General for the time being. Once we gained enough power, we would separate it out into its own independent office—it was a tactical coalition-building move."[88]

As Safe Streets worked with City Councilman James Carter on crafting an OIPM ordinance, the NOPD's inability to function without scandal strengthened public support for the independent monitor. On October 1, 2007, brass band musicians held an impromptu memorial procession through the Treme neighborhood for tuba player Kerwin James.[89] Ethnomusicologist Matt Sakakeeny described what happened next: "At 8 P.M. in response to a noise complaint, multiple police cars—lights ablaze, sirens drowning out the music—descended on the procession of about a hundred people, and officers arrested Derrick Tabb and trombonist Glen David Andrews as they were playing the traditional spiritual 'I'll Fly Away.' The charges were Disturbing the Police and Parading without a Permit."[90] Amid public debate about gentrification and the policing of Black New Orleans cultural traditions, *Times-Picayune* columnist Lolis Eric Elie asserted that the city needed to create an OIPM.[91] Then days before the city council vote, an off-duty NOPD officer erratically drove across the Crescent City Connection Bridge, grazed a bridge police officer with his truck, and smacked another officer.[92] As Ursula Price recounts, the tide had shifted: "Even people who had never had a police encounter were very well aware of police corruption. It wasn't just a myth anymore. . . . We shifted from Warren Riley saying, 'Those people,' meaning Safe Streets, 'are just thugs and of course they don't like the police,' to the whole world acknowledging that there's something wrong with NOPD."[93]

Safe Streets' goal was for the city council to vote unanimously in favor of the OIPM ordinance. A unanimous vote would demonstrate a mandate for NOPD oversight and provide backing for the incorporation of the OIG and OIPM into the city charter. On the morning of the vote, however, Councilman James Carter took Norris Henderson aside to tell him that they had a problem: council members Cynthia Hedge-Morrell and Cynthia Willard-Lewis were not supportive of the OIPM ordinance. Henderson was flabbergasted. How could it be that the only two Black women council members were against their proposal? Carter explained that Willard-Lewis did not want to appear soft on crime, and because two of Hedge-Morrell's sons were police officers, Hedge-Morrell had adopted a defensive posture on the NOPD.[94]

It was ultimately the personal connections tying the New Orleans Black middle class together that caused these councilwomen to change their stances. Unlike most public comment periods that operate primarily as a performance, the OIPM comment period actually influenced the vote. Part of Safe Streets' strategy was to have its members testify about NOPD violence. Included in this group was Dr. Romell Madison, the brother of Danziger shooting victim Ronald Madison. Henderson recalled, "Unbeknownst to us was that Dr. Madison, who was a dentist, was Willard-Lewis's dentist. Hedge-Morrell is their cousin. [When] Dr. Madison got up to go speak . . . their position changed."[95] Hedge-Morell and Willard-Lewis could not so easily dismiss the testimony of Dr. Madison, in their eyes a trusted member of the Black middle class, as they could the routinely derided Black working-class membership of Safe Streets. Although we cannot know what went through their minds as he spoke about the tragedy of his brother's murder, I think it is not unreasonable to believe that they imagined it could have just as easily been one of their family members gunned down by the NOPD on the bridge between the largely Black middle-class neighborhoods of New Orleans East and Gentilly. The city council voted 7–0 for the OIPM ordinance.[96] In October 2008, the New Orleans's electorate voted 3 to 1 to incorporate the OIG into the city charter and to fund the office in perpetuity.[97]

After the OIPM ordinance passed unanimously, the police attempted to hollow out the victory. The Louisiana Fraternal Order of Police lobbied for a state bill that would block the IPM's access to police personnel files. Safe Streets turned to the state legislature, which defeated the bill. The resignation of IG Bob Cerasoli for health reasons also hampered Safe Streets's efforts. The shortcomings of hitching the IPM to the IG office were exposed when the interim IG began making backroom deals. He told the police union and city officials that, in exchange for the permanent IG position, he would not appoint someone to be the independent police monitor who would be too hard on the NOPD.[98] A hastily conducted IPM search followed, leading to the appointment of an inside candidate without racial justice or police oversight credentials. Safe Streets called foul.[99] They raised enough public outcry that within a month the IPM resigned, and a hiring search began anew with significant input from Safe Streets and other community stakeholders.[100] Although the search committee still included NOPD leadership, the selection of Susan Hutson in spring 2010 was seen by Safe Streets as a victory.[101]

Targeting the Jail's Power

Organizing around OPP proved to be the most difficult of Safe Streets' campaigns. Sheriff Gusman had reopened OPP's Central Lockup without making meaningful repairs on October 17, 2005. OPP had lost thousands of beds due to flooding, and so Gusman borrowed Sheriff Foti's idea and erected "temporary" tents to increase the jail's capacity by 700 beds.[102] Despite the widespread stories of neglect at OPP during the storm, there were no local, state, or federal investigations of Gusman's actions and inactions. Even academic scholarship regurgitated the language of Gusman's public relations office.[103] With sectors of the New Orleans Black middle class forming a protective shield around Gusman as the city's first Black sheriff, organizers who criticized Gusman ran the risk of being labeled racist.[104] When Gusman easily won reelection in 2006, his continued oversight of the rebuilding of OPP dismayed activists who worried that he would use his power to expand the jail.

Given the structural autonomy of the sheriff's office, Safe Streets grappled with how to target Gusman. Ursula Price began "just posting up outside of the jail and talking to people about how delayed their release had been."[105] Safe Streets organizers learned that people could only be released from OPP if they could provide an address where they would be living—something that was nearly impossible in post-Katrina New Orleans because people were constantly moving from one temporary home to the next. These conversations provided a fuller picture of the still toxic conditions at OPP. Price realized they needed to "not just hold [the Sheriff's office] accountable for their failure to protect these people during the evacuation, but prevention."[106] Although at first Safe Streets thought this might take the form of a class action suit, they soon learned that the state barred such a legal challenge under the Prison Litigation Reform Act.

Building on the success of their press conference held outside the jail in the weeks after the flood, Safe Streets pushed for a public reckoning with the malignant neglect of OPP prisoners and the long-standing crisis of the jail. They worked with the ACLU National Prison Project to research what had happened at the jail before, during, and after the hurricane. Their research was initially published in *Dollars & Sense*. "Down by Law: Orleans

Parish Prison before and after Katrina" argued that to understand the roots of the problem one had to go back to Foti's massive jail expansions and everyday cruelties that marked OPP.[107]

The article tied the growth of the jail to the financial incentives of the per diem system, which fueled the sheriff's political patronage system and contributed to the imprisonment of people whose main offense was their inability to make bail. Not only did the per diem system foster a lack of financial accountability for the sheriff's office, as Jack Cassidy explained, because the municipal per diem was only the paltry amount of $22.39, "it creates this totally perverse incentive to have as many inmates as possible."[108] Moreover, although FEMA denied funds to reopen the public schools, it reimbursed the Louisiana DPSC at a per diem rate of $32.49 to imprison OPP survivors. "The projected reimbursement for just *one day*, December 19, 2005, was $146,495.42. At that daily rate, DOC was expecting to be reimbursed roughly $13 million dollars for holding 4,215 prisoners from September 1 until December 1, 2005. . . . There is a serious financial disincentive for the DOC to move quickly on releasing prisoners."[109] The logic of the per diem system was leading to the slow release of people doing Katrina Time.

"Down by Law" concluded with an outline of Safe Streets' goals for reforming OPP:

- Close Orleans Parish Prison and replace it with a physical structure and living conditions that are safe and humane for everyone.
- Ensure that detention is only used to protect public safety or ensure court appearances.
- Build, expand, and support alternatives to incarceration.
- Ensure that the operation, control, and budgeting of the jail system is transparent and accountable to the community it serves and is not used as a mechanism for political power and patronage.[110]

While still predicated on the notion that some people required jailing, Safe Streets' demands signaled the coming of a new era of jail organizing by foregrounding the argument that the best way to ensure people's safety was by subjecting fewer people to the horrors of OPP at all.

Many of the ideas in "Down by Law" shaped the ACLU National Prison Project's *Abandoned and Abused: Orleans Parish Prisoners in the Wake of Hurricane Katrina*, written in collaboration with Safe Streets and other local organizations. Based on the stories of more than one thousand OPP survivors, *Abandoned and Abused* remains the most comprehensive documentation of the state's treatment of OPP prisoners during and after Hurricane Katrina. The report repudiates the official narrative that no harm was done and illuminates how the state's barbarity was entirely avoidable.[111] *Abandoned and Abused* highlights Gusman's lack of evacuation plans, in contrast to the extensive plan of the Louisiana SPCA.[112] It zeroes in on how the size of OPP's population was predicated on the imprisonment of thousands of predominantly Black and poor people on municipal and misdemeanor charges, and questions why state, federal, immigrant, and juvenile prisoners were being held at OPP.[113] The sheriff's per diem invoices labeling "prisoners as units" spoke volumes about the dehumanization of this budgetary arrangement.[114] The report concludes that since reopening the jail after Katrina, Gusman was doubling down on the practices that left people vulnerable to premature death.[115]

Abandoned and Abused made explicit to a national and local audience that reforming OPP was pivotal to a just reconstruction of New Orleans. Although Gusman denied any wrongdoing, Safe Streets kept public attention focused on the continuing deaths at the OPP.[116] As Cielo Cruz recalls, death overdetermined OPP activism: "The jail piece [of the organizing] was the most painful and visceral. And the deaths. People dying in the jail."[117] Premature death at OPP was so normalized that it was next to impossible to garner any government or media attention to this crisis. Evelyn Lynn recounts that at one of Safe Streets' first vigils, "We had a pretty good turnout of over one hundred people supporting the family of a man who had died. We contacted reporters to get them to cover the story, and they just weren't interested. One reporter, who refused to cover the story, told us, 'It wasn't newsworthy because people die in OPP every day.'"[118]

Given Gusman's intractability, Safe Streets joined forces with Critical Resistance (CR), to lessen the power of the penal system through another strategy: expunging people's arrest records. This dovetailed with CR's amnesty work. New Orleans CR organizer Mayaba Liebenthal conducted "research with law student volunteers to figure out what the actual legal recourse for amnesty would be."[119] They identified two options. The first was a blanket executive pardon in which the governor could issue clemency for every person caught in the Hurricane Katrina law-and-order hysteria. CR organizers considered this option to be "appropriate and overdue" because the use of clemency would signal that the state had failed to enact justice and that the public could be better served "outside the bounds of the traditional criminal justice system."[120] However, the politicization of clemency over the preceding decades and the election of neoconservative Bobby Jindal as governor in fall 2007 doomed the use of this tactic.

CR then turned to the second, more limited option: the expungement of people's criminal records. Under Louisiana law, misdemeanor arrest records could be destroyed, but felony arrest records could only be expunged—meaning that they could be removed from public access but not totally erased. However, the records of those who had served jail time, which included most of those who were unable to afford bail, were ineligible for expungement. Despite the narrow scope of expungement, CR decided to move ahead with this option because it had the power to mitigate the state restrictions placed on criminalized people.[121] Moreover, expunging people's arrest records could help bring people home after the storm because "the frequent use of background checks, particularly for housing and employment, greatly jeopardizes displaced residents' rights to return home."[122]

Safe Streets and CR held a free "Expungement Day" in spring 2008 to which they widened the scope to everyone and anyone looking to expunge their records. Altering their definition of success in response to shifting conditions, CR decided to "define [the amnesty campaign] as a win" if even "ten people's records were wiped clean."[123] For Safe Streets, an Expungement Day would lead to a material improvement in the lives of criminalized people. As Henderson noted, it would demonstrate, contrary to the idea that Black working-class New Orleanians were under- and unemployed by choice, that "our folks want to work. It's these [legal] impediments that prohibit them from working."[124]

Months of work went into planning Expungement Day. CR and Safe Streets conducted outreach with members and through canvassing; Safe Streets got local judges to waive court fees; prison abolitionists in Chicago held fundraisers for the event; and volunteers were trained in the necessary paperwork. More than a nonprofit version of the disciplinary state bureaucratic processes New Orleanians were habituated to, Expungement Day would be a community event with food and drink and social justice organizations tabling. When the day finally arrived, more than four hundred people lined up around the block of the Treme Community Center in hopes of getting their criminal records erased. Hundreds of people made connections that day that they otherwise might not have had with attorneys and organizations, and media coverage brought heightened visibility to the many ways that high arrest rates negatively affected New Orleanians.[125]

Although successful in many ways, Expungement Day also highlighted the capacious discretionary power of the criminal legal system. Of the 400-plus people in attendance, only about 50 people were eligible to have their records fully expunged. Most people either had served jail time and so were ineligible or had more arrests on their record than the state allowed them to expunge.[126] Moreover, when expungement paperwork was sent to the state police to clear people's records, they were arbitrarily not expunging people's records. Price explains that they had the power to "decide if this conviction is too important to expunge, I'm not going to do it. I'm not refunding your money, and I'm not communicating this back to the judge."[127] Yet because the day highlighted the palpable need for record expungement, CR decided to hold ongoing legal clinics and trainings on expungement to more widely disseminate this technical legal knowledge.[128] Expungement Day not only showed that countless people were in need of the material relief that expungement offered but also served as a point of entry to make broader political connections about the inherent injustice of the criminal legal system. Through Expungement Day, activists deepened relationships, brought in new people to organizations, and pointed to the necessity for further organizing to chip away at New Orleans carceral infrastructure.

Orleans Parish Prison Reform Coalition: Downsizing OPP

On the third anniversary of Hurricane Katrina, New Orleans was on edge. A hurricane named Gustav was barreling through the Gulf, and with the levees still not fortified to the levels necessary to fully protect the city, Mayor Nagin declared that Hurricane Gustav was "the mother of all storms" and ordered a mandatory evacuation of Orleans Parish.[129] Anxiety was palpable as people boarded up their windows, ate up the food in their freezers, and made plans of when and where to go. Although many people were leery about the city's new program to evacuate carless residents to militarized shelters, thousands of people without better options lined up to be taken to undisclosed shelters for an unknown length of time.

Amid fears of another hurricane, Safe Streets was busy organizing a third anniversary commemorative march. Crisscrossing the city from OPP to the shuttered Charity Hospital, and then to the sites of bulldozed public housing, Safe Streets' march on that third anniversary highlighted the ongoing struggles against disaster racism and neoliberal recovery. After walking miles in the late August heat and humidity, marchers discussed their evacuation plans over food and drink at the Treme Community Center. At this moment, Safe Streets received the news that Sheriff Gusman was evacuating the jail.[130] Overextended and overwhelmed, Safe Streets realized they did not have the organizational capacity to respond.

While Hurricane Gustav largely spared New Orleans, it took a few weeks for people to return.[131] As Cielo Cruz recounts, "In the midst of all this chaos, we find out—there's this sixty million dollar bond that the sheriff has put on the ballot for October and wait that's in two weeks. . . . The bond passed and we got our asses handed to us. We're like we can't take a hit like this. . . . The sheriff had flown this under the radar. We were caught unaware, and so we weren't able to defeat it. We just didn't have time."[132] This vote reauthorized the municipal bond that Sheriff Foti had aggressively campaigned for to expand OPP in 1989 and 1990.[133] Gusman asserted that this jail tax was critical for getting OPP closer to its pre-Katrina size and that the city was in a "unique window of opportunity" because property taxes would be stretched by the FEMA money coming to the city.[134]

Following the reauthorization of the jail millage, activists realized the need for more concerted organizing around the rebuilding of OPP. The main vehicle for this activism was the reenergized Orleans Parish Prison Reform Coalition (OPPRC). Originally a coalition made up of progressive Christians, criminal defense attorneys, advocacy nonprofits such as the ACLU, and others involved in rehabilitative jail programs, OPPRC was founded to pressure candidates to make commitments on reforming conditions of confinement and ensuring that legal and constitutional standards were followed during the 2004 sheriffs' race.[135] OPPRC held candidate forums and succeeded in getting every candidate, including Gusman, to sign onto their platform on improving jail conditions.

But after Hurricane Katrina, OPPRC underwent a renewal. While OPPRC started meeting again not long after the storm, a burst of energy followed the jail millage vote. Safe Streets' jail campaign work was channeled into the coalition.[136] Soon advocacy mainstays like the ACLU, the Vera Institute, and faith-based organizations were joined by multiracial grassroots organizations such as Safe Streets, VOTE, Critical Resistance, and the Congreso de Jornaleros—widening the coalition's perspectives and reach. OPPRC's political orientation and priorities also shifted post-Katrina. According to founding member Don Everard,

> The original group . . . really did not address the size of the jail. We were more concerned about specific things that maybe you could tinker with to make it more humane and to make it more effective,

but it wasn't really challenging the size of it. But then, that became the issue. I mean, once the jail had shrunk a small amount, and the city didn't fall apart, I think it was pretty damn clear that we didn't need a jail that big anymore.[137]

As OPPRC took a more hard-hitting stance through actions that called out the violence of mass incarceration, some of its members representing mainstream organizations took a step back. For many, this move was preferable to them reining in OPPRC's politics. In the words of Henderson, "Just get out of the way because we're going to continue to throw bricks."[138] Those who remained in this growing and broad coalition strategized how to materialize a "safer, smaller, more humane" jail.

Changes were also occurring at Safe Streets. After years of nonstop organizing many staff members were ready for a change. Evelyn Lynn decided that her time in New Orleans had come to an end, and she moved to Atlanta. Norris Henderson retuned to VOTE where Cielo Cruz joined him, and Ursula Price ended up (for a time) in the Office of the Independent Police Monitor. Robert Goodman was forced out when he was rearrested on a decades-old charge and was locked up for months. These departures illuminate the toll that ceaseless organizing had not only on individual organizers in the first years after the storm but also on organizations' capacities to meet the pace of the post-hurricane state.

Yet, as the years passed, organizers, although still tired, were on firmer ground. Cruz recalls that by 2010, activists in New Orleans were "in slightly better shape. We've been working together for almost five years. We learned a lot of hard lessons. We've been through a lot of post-Katrina heartbreak."[139] Furthermore, in the words of kai barrow, "There was growing demand among people who did not fear public struggle. Who were relentless about showing up."[140] The pace of the city was also starting to slow as many of the major state rebuilding decisions had been made and the rotation of national activists coming in and out of town had mostly stopped. People's personal lives were also, by and large, stabilizing. The political landscape was not defined by acute crisis as it had been in those first years after the storm.

But building a coalition is never easy work.[141] While everyone involved in OPPRC believed that the jail's problems were structural and required systemic transformation, the widening of the coalition necessitated that people adapt to different strategies and ideologies. For the more policy-oriented organizations accustomed to winning reforms based on their status as experts with hard facts and figures, it could be a stretch to foreground the testimonial forms of evidence that community activists centered. Furthermore, OPPRC included a mix of prison abolitionists who were primarily associated with Critical Resistance and of members who identified as jail reformers who sought to lessen New Orleans's reliance on incarceration but not abolish OPP altogether. Despite these growing edges and, at times, disagreements, much of OPPRC's power came from its breadth.

Moreover, the reach of OPP's harms produced the reality that an evergrowing number of people had a stake in dismantling the jail's power. Although the dominant paradigm for approaching racial justice in New Orleans, especially related to the injustices of the criminal legal system, pivoted on anti-Black racism, the Congreso de Jornaleros brought political visibility to the relationship between xenophobia, the jail, and ICE. Even though OPP had incarcerated immigrant detainees since the 1980s, first through contracts with INS and then with ICE, historically most immigrants locked up at OPP were not arrested in Orleans Parish. However, after Hurricane Katrina a growing number of immigrant workers, mostly Latinx, came to rebuild the city. At the same time, following federal and local directives, the NOPD and National Guard started harassing people at day laborer corners. As former Congreso organizer Jacinta Gonzalez put it, "People would be picked up for looking for work and we would go find them in the jail."[142] Yet Gonzalez and other organizers quickly learned that some Congreso members were not being released because Sheriff Gusman was submitting to ICE hold requests—holding people beyond their release date so that ICE had time to determine whether they wanted to detain the individual for deportation. In many cases, OPP was keeping people jailed on ICE holds for weeks and months past the forty-eight hours the law authorized. As Gonzalez explained, Congreso came to identify OPP as a key target of immigrant justice organizing in that "schools, hospitals, city hall, everywhere you went it was a battle to even create some space [for immigrants] to be able to be there. . . . But the one place where it was arms wide open was the jail. NOPD had no problem arresting people, bringing people into OPP where the sheriff was working with ICE."[143] Congreso joined OPPRC because they saw the coalition's work as being in alignment with their campaigns. Gonzalez remembers that members like Norris Henderson and Ted Quant exemplified a spirit of "political generosity" in sharing with Congreso members "the history of [criminal justice] institutions, racial dynamics in the South, opening up space to have conversations about racial tensions."[144] OPPRC deepened multiracial organizing from a politics of solidarity against the multifaceted racism of jailing.

Pivotal to the functioning and effectiveness of OPPRC was its codified coalition structure. Initially the coalition operated relatively informally: people could drop in and out of coalition meetings, and the presumption of unanimity structured discussions. When kai barrow moved back to New Orleans in 2010, she not only facilitated the CR New Orleans chapter to join OPPRC but she also contributed her years of experience in horizontal organizing to the coalition. Barrow worked with Dana Kaplan of the Juvenile Justice Project of Louisiana (JJPL) to shepherd OPPRC in adopting a more formal structure: developing points of unity on their politics and principles, outlining rights and responsibilities of different tiers of coalition members, and putting in place consensus as the decision-making structure.[145] These systems created containers of accountability and guidelines for working through sticky political questions, ensuring that OPPRC was governed by greater democratic participation and a smoother process.[146]

For barrow and some other abolitionists in the mix, implementing this structure for OPPRC was also politically strategic. Barrow knew coming into OPPRC that CR as a small ragtag group of abolitionists might be sidelined by the legal nonprofits in the room.[147] She recalls thinking, "We're going to be the odd people out if we just agree [to majority voting] because we're not part of this network. . . . We are not going to be valid and legitimate in this coalition and therefore our voices will be silenced."[148] To ensure that CR's abolitionist position was not marginalized, barrow advocated for a consensus decision-making structure. Although a consensus structure would not transform OPPRC into an abolitionist project, it kept an abolitionist edge alive within the coalition and pushed public conversations on the jail further to the Left.

Indeed, OPPRC's very first political point of unity guiding the coalition was not about conditions of confinement, but rather, "We recognize that New Orleans has the most number of prisoners, per capita, nationwide and are working to minimize the jail population."[149] By bringing to the forefront the need to shrink the jail population, OPPRC suggested that meaningful reform could not be achieved without scaling back mass incarceration. Furthermore, OPPRC expressed a different vision of how to produce safe communities:

- We support the reallocation of funds from incarceration and detention to building the infrastructure of a caring community.

Recreational, educational, mental and physical healthcare, affordable housing and transportation, accessible information, and jobs and job training will make our communities safe, sustainable and thriving places to live.

- We support the adoption and implementation of alternative policies and practices to permanently decrease the number of people arrested and imprisoned. Community-based restorative and transformative programs, comprehensive reentry services, and an investment in meeting people's basic needs, such as food, housing, healthcare, and meaningful work, are steps towards realizing genuine public safety.[150]

For OPPRC, public investment in policies rooted in care, along with disinvestment from carceral infrastructures, would provide greater security than locking up large swaths of New Orleanians.

This is not to say that conditions of confinement were not of concern. OPPRC deeply cared about the medical neglect, sexual violence, and other abuses inflicted on prisoners. Cruz recalls, "We connected with a lot of people who were experiencing abuse and violence in the jail . . . being able to lift up their stories and have events and vigils and raising awareness around how bloody things had become."[151] But how to press for greater accountability remained elusive. While the Hayes Williams federal court mandates over OPP had been lifted, the preceding federal case over OPP, *Hamilton v. Morial*, was still in place. Yet the only real power the case continued to wield was that the municipal per diem system was tied to it. The city could not end this budgetary arrangement so long as Hamilton was in place.[152] Confronting the limits of federal interventions, however, did not cause OPPRC to abandon efforts to improve conditions. Leveraging the findings of *Abandoned and Abused*, they pushed the DOJ to investigate conditions in hopes that it would provoke a federal consent decree.[153] To the dismay of Gusman, the DOJ investigated the jail and reported conditions as unconstitutional in the fall of 2009.[154]

OPPRC's campaign heated up when FEMA announced it was allocating nearly $100 million to rebuilding OPP, and Gusman declared his plans to expand the jail to 5,862 beds.[155] Although this represented a decrease from OPP's pre-Katrina capacity of almost 7,200 beds, Gusman's proposal would add more than 2,000 new beds to OPP's 2010 capacity, and he saw this expansion as the first step to increasing OPP to 8,000 beds.[156] Gusman contended that the city needed an enlarged jail complex to "protect the lives and property of our city residents."[157] However, Gusman's proposal had to be approved by the city's zoning process. The mundane processes of land use presented a political opportunity for OPPRC. Cielo Cruz explains, "We felt like we could control the number of beds" because "when it came to zoning and things that city council had control over, we felt like we had a much better chance" than if Gusman had final say.[158]

Around the same time, elections shifted the New Orleans political landscape. In early 2010, New Orleans elected a majority white city council *and* mayor for the first time in decades. Following newly elected mayor Mitch Landrieu's appointment of a white police chief, many residents expressed their unease that New Orleans as a majority Black city had an overwhelmingly white political power structure so soon after Hurricane Katrina.[159] For OPPRC, these racial dynamics opened new pressure points. Barrow recounts, "All of the power forces that used to be Black and could relate to a Black community, even if it's just through an imagination of what an identity meant, were now vacant. I mean very obviously missing so that was one factor that we exploited. . . . Race in terms of leadership. Race is terms of populace was something that was shifting, and we were able to draw links between the expansion of beds and the current moment."[160] The lack of Black elected officials heightened Black communities' disidentification with city governance; the current city leadership could not make spurious appeals for punitive infrastructure as being in the interest of Black communities as had previous Black tough-on-crime administrations. Moreover, sectors of the white liberal elite were relatively self-conscious about the overrepresentation of white elected leadership. When and where they could, the OPPRC named OPP's everyday violence as anchored in state racism.

It first appeared that the city council might acquiesce to Gusman's jail proposal. During the summer of 2010, when council members voted on Gusman's plan, OPPRC activists showed up to contest the expansion—asking why the city was quick to reinvest in jailing when affordable housing, public education, and mental health care were all but forgotten. Although the council then voted 7–0 to approve Gusman's plan, they *also* added twenty-four provisions qualifying its approval. One provision held that before the council would vote to give the jail's zoning full legal force, they were to hear recommendations on the jail's ideal size from a mayoral Criminal Justice Working Group.[161] This announcement gave OPPRC organizers grounds for both trepidation and hope. Although it was promising that city leaders were not simply going along with Sheriff Gusman's proposal, the composition of the Criminal Justice Working Group was skewed toward carceral state-makers: it included Sheriff Gusman, NOPD superintendent Ronal Serpas, and Orleans Parish DA Leon Cannizzaro. Overall, OPPRC saw the creation of the Criminal Justice Working Group as a positive development in that it would give them more time to organize.[162]

Even though the jail's bed space had already been cut in half since Hurricane Katrina, OPPRC aimed not only to keep Gusman from expanding OPP but also to downsize the jail even more. OPPRC's members routinely pointed out that at 3,500 beds OPP was *already* the largest per capita jail in the nation. Yet how large the jail should be was never a clear-cut issue within the coalition. Most members of OPPRC believed they should push for a *cap* on the number of beds, whereas CR wanted to press for *zero* beds. While CR always knew they would have to compromise on this vision within OPPRC, consensus decision-making structure steered OPPRC to engage in dialogue about zero beds versus a cap.[163] After much discussion OPPRC decided to demand a hard cap on OPP's size—not only for this construction project but also going forward. But what should the cap be? Researching the size of jails in other southern cities as well as neighboring Jefferson Parish, OPPRC landed on 850 beds as a more appropriate size jail for a city of New Orleans's size.

OPPRC's strategy to determine the "right size" of OPP illuminated the extent to which the normalization of mass incarceration shaped even activist frameworks. While researching the per capita jailing rate of other locales made sense insofar as OPPRC organizers aimed to bring New Orleans within national norms, it failed to account for how the rise of mass incarceration fabricated the national average because every major city in the United States had expanded their jails over the preceding forty years. Pegging a "right size" for OPP to other cities' jail sizes implicitly condoned the growth of incarceration elsewhere as a "reasonable" rate of imprisonment—rather than acknowledging how other cities jailing rates were also produced through the racist neoliberal logics of urban law-and-order.

This begs this question: What would it have looked like to push for a smaller jail not based on the national averages of mass incarceration but on New Orleans's jailing capacity before the city's explosion of its carceral infrastructure in 1970? In 1960 when New Orleans had the largest population in its history—627,525 residents, almost double the 2010 population—OPP had a bed capacity of only 450 beds; then, New Orleans had one-thirteenth of the jailing capacity the city had in 2010 and just over one-half the capacity of an 850-bed OPP. Although it is unlikely that OPPRC could have convinced the public to reduce OPP's size to such a degree—calling for 850 beds was itself radical—it is worth asking what would have happened if they made the bed cap demand outside the liberal concept that averages are the most equitable formulations.

OPPRC's campaign highlighted both the social and economic costs of mass imprisonment, foregrounding the recklessness of giving Gusman free rein to expand OPP. Cielo Cruz emphasized, "Here are all of these people dying in the jail and here is the sheriff getting more money."[164] Although OPPRC clearly pointed to Gusman's accountability, they underlined the structural factors at play, rather than alleging that a different sheriff could have rectified OPP's ills. OPPRC argued that the jail harmed not only individuals behind bars but also families whose already limited money and time were redirected to negotiating with attorneys, bail bondsmen, and the sheriff's office. Having an oversized jail did not produce greater public safety but "makes police more disposed to arrest people for low-level offenses."[165] OPPRC also refuted Gusman's argument that incarcerating state prisoners in OPP benefited imprisoned New Orleanians by making them physically closer to their loved ones. Henderson explained that state prisoners at OPP had fewer programs available to them and that jail visitation consisted of only fifteen minutes through plated glass compared to the one- to two-hour visits at Angola where "you can hug your mama and hold your kids."[166]

Financially OPPRC focused on two issues. Refuting Gusman's claim that the city should take full advantage of FEMA funds, OPPRC pointed out that, even though the federal government would finance the building of the new jail, New Orleans taxpayers would be responsible for maintaining the increased operating costs for generations. The second issue to become a centerpiece of their campaign was that the per diem budgetary system incentivized mass incarceration through the imperative of constant carceral growth. A smaller jail with a static operating budget that the sheriff was directly accountable for would mean that more city funds would be available to meet healthcare, educational, and social service needs.

OPPRC organized to build broad public support for a smaller jail. Their members canvassed neighborhoods and events to educate people and collected close to 1,500 signatures in support of a smaller OPP. They played on the NIMBY tendencies of homeowners by conducting a teach-in with the Mid-City Neighborhood Association, whose district encompassed the jail, leading to the neighborhood association coming out against jail expansion. In addition to writing letters to the editor, they cultivated relationships with the publication *The Lens* to get meaningful coverage on the jail's redevelopment. OPPRC took out a full-page ad in the *Times-Picayune*, to which people contributed $22.39 to the ad's cost, the municipal per diem rate, to sign on to the demand that city reject Gusman's proposal for an expanded jail (figure 5.1). Among the people who signed onto the ad were high-profile New Orleanians: actor Wendell Piece, Judge Calvin Johnson, trumpet player Kermit Ruffins, and civil rights veteran Lolis Edward Elie.

OPPRC's organizing powered a shift in public discourse. For the first time in decades, newspapers published articles sympathetic to OPPRC's arguments against a larger jail.[167] The *Times-Picayune* published an op-ed refuting Gusman's claims and asserted that the bloated OPP "is not a result of the crime rate. It's the result of bad policy" and the per diem system.[168] Unlike previous debates, not a single letter to the editor was published in favor of an enlarged jail. One resident unaffiliated with OPPRC wrote to the *Times-Picayune* to share his view that "we incarcerate way too many people for our **size** city. We need to solve the core problems, or at least begin addressing them, rather than simply locking more and more people up."[169]

The OPP size debates occurred as liberal prison reform gained mainstream traction. After decades of grassroots antiprison activism, mass incarceration began capturing liberal attention in the 2000s. Although President Obama failed to deliver meaningful reforms—his most noteworthy action being reducing the sentencing disparity between crack and powder cocaine—his presence in the White House as someone at least willing to allude to the role of racism in the penal system influenced political debate.[170] Furthermore the activist discourse on "mass incarceration" was brought into the mainstream with the publication of Michelle Alexander's *The New Jim Crow* in early 2010, which popularized a narrative linking anti-Black racism to the prison boom.[171] The national resurgence of race-conscious reform produced the contradiction of legitimizing OPPRC's jail cap demand while the mainstreaming of reform sidelined more expansive visions that called for "investment in meeting people's basic needs" as the cornerstone of true public safety.[172]

Meanwhile Sheriff Gusman butted heads with other city officials. Although he tried to model himself on Sheriff Foti, he had almost none of Foti's savviness, especially when it came to his budget. Gusman refused to supply a detailed accounting of OPP's spending but routinely demanded funding increases. When the city council and Mayor Landrieu refused to increase his budget, he threatened to go to a federal judge to force the city to increase the per diem rate *and* to pull his sheriff's deputies from working at the Criminal District Court—further straining Gusman's political relationships.[173] A growing feud emerged between Gusman and Landrieu

FIGURE 5.1 Orleans Parish Prison Reform Coalition smaller jail ad, September 8, 2010.

over the jail, a dynamic that spilled over into Landrieu's allies on the city council.

OPPRC managed to push the Criminal Justice Working Group to hold two public meetings on the rebuilding of the jail in the fall of 2010, but they proved fraught. The working group balked at challenges to their technocratic approach to determining the ideal size for OPP. Deputy mayor Andy Kopplin, the working group's chair, was visibly disdainful of grassroots activists, going so far as to state at one meeting, "We are not required to have this meeting. You should be glad we're even here." Kopplin announced at the beginning of each meeting that the group's final recommendations would be primarily based on a quantitative study by the JFA Institute research team that the Criminal Justice Working Group believed would focus on current and projected arrest rates.

Even so, OPPRC activists committed to putting a more critical analysis of jailing on the record. When one person challenged arrest rates as a valid unit of measurement, asking whether the Criminal Justice Working Group had considered how racial profiling affected arrests, she was told race was not a relevant factor or up for discussion. Community activists repeatedly repudiated this logic by pointing to the structural connections between racial profiling, state disinvestments in healthcare and education, the impoverishment of Black communities, and the city's high jailing rate. Several mothers made affective appeals by sharing their stories of the emotional and financial toll of having their loved ones locked up. Implicit in these testimonies was that experiential knowledge should be as valuable as the "expert knowledge" of the sheriff, DA, judges, and other city officials. Rather than excluding such information as "irrelevant" or "biased," such subjective knowledge should be integrated into the Criminal Justice Working Group's recommendations. Even when OPPRC members spoke the quantitative language of the working group by explaining that, if OPP had the same number of beds as the national average of one bed for every 388 residents, the jail's capacity would shrink to 850 beds, they were told that data was not pertinent. Although no one spoke in favor of a larger jail, the meetings were demoralizing.[174]

In a surprise turn of events, the JFA Institute's study on the ideal size of OPP was more aligned with OPPRC's position than with Gusman. The study, which became known as the "Austin Report," took a firm stance against using numbers to justify carceral futures: "Inmate and correctional population projections should not be seen as magic boxes used to predict the future, but instead as tools for understanding the origin and direction of prisoner population changes based on current and alternative criminal justice policies."[175] In contrast to most carceral consultants, lead author James Austin had a track record of publishing work critical of mass incarceration.[176] The report showed that OPP's population was already declining because of diminishing crime rates, a smaller city population, and recent criminal justice reforms.[177] The report concluded that the largest jail "needed" over the next decade was 3,121 beds and stated, "There is no basis to project increases in the OPP population."[178]

In fact, the Austin Report projected how OPP could shrink even more. It asserted that the jail's existing population was inflated due to incarcerating state and federal prisoners and the racial and gender disparities of Black men being incarcerated for above-average stretches of time.[179] It named New Orleans as a site of hyper-incarceration *not* because its crime rate was higher but because of draconian city policies, including the per diem system. The Austin Report contended that if Orleans Parish policies were brought in line with those of other Louisiana cities, OPP would be between 722 and 1,426 beds.[180] It went on to show that OPP's capacity could be reduced by another 1,300 beds if some further moderate reforms were put in place.[181]

Following the public hearings and the Austin Report, the Criminal Justice Working Group recommended that OPP be rebuilt with "a maximum capacity of 1,438 inmates . . . capable of accommodating any type of prisoner under any jurisdiction" and that the five other remaining jail structures "be decommissioned or demolished."[182] It also recommended that there be an examination of whether state and federal prisoners should be imprisoned at OPP, of the appropriateness of the per diem system, and of racial disparities in the length of incarceration of African Americans. Unsurprisingly, Sheriff Gusman, DA Cannizzaro, and conservative Judge Paul Sens (whose brother was the head of purchasing at OPP), voted against the clause that existing jail buildings be demolished, arguing they may be needed for future expansions.[183] Mayor Landrieu gave his "blessing" to the proposed 1,438 bed cap.[184]

Even as OPPRC recognized that having 1,438 beds meant that OPP would still be 1.7 times larger than the national average, they decided to support this cap.[185] At the final city council vote, with which this chapter opened, OPPRC activists speculated whether the council would abide by the Criminal Justice Working Group's recommendations or capitulate to Gusman. After an hour of public comment overwhelmingly in favor of the 1,438-bed cap, the council unanimously voted in favor.[186] For the first time in history, it became city policy to scale back, not scale up, New Orleans's jailing capacity.

Along with the bed cap victory, OPPRC and member organizations focused on leveraging federal legal systems to lessen the jail's violence. The day before the city council vote, Congreso filed a federal lawsuit against the sheriff's office on behalf of two immigrant reconstruction workers who had been held for 91 and 164 days, respectively, on ICE holds.[187] The lawsuit argued that ICE holds were predicated on racial profiling of who was a noncitizen. But the suit went beyond these two individual cases. As Gonzalez explained, "They were suing for damages, but the real purpose was to try to get [Gusman] to stop submitting to ICE holds."[188] Congreso directly connected the lawsuit to the OPPRC demand for a smaller jail. They held a twenty-four-hour prayer vigil outside Gusman's office between the filing of the lawsuit and the city council vote, and activists spoke at the council vote about how Gusman's voluntary participation in ICE holds added to the bloated size of OPP. Bolstered by the bed cap, Congreso leveraged the pressure of the lawsuit to push Gusman to stop submitting ICE hold over the next two years. Congreso members held a women's action outside the jail and shamed Gusman at a fundraiser for domestic violence—linking his jail policies to exacerbating partner violence.[189] Congreso also pushed the city council to pass a resolution prohibiting Gusman from keeping people on ICE holds.[190] Although the resolution did not have much teeth, it would pressure Gusman to start negotiating with Congreso members on ICE holds as part of the settlement of the lawsuit. In the summer of 2013, Congreso succeeded in getting Gusman to agree to no longer allow ICE agents into his jail without a warrant or to submit to ICE holds, with carve-outs for people convicted of homicides, aggravated rape, or robbery with a firearm.[191] Although there were limits to this policy, Congreso recognized this was the first such policy in the South and one of the few in the United States.[192]

Simultaneously OPPRC focused on securing a consent decree to circumscribe, if not end, violence within OPP. In addition to using billboard ads to focus the public's attention on how the per diem system undermined decarceration, OPPRC petitioned the Department of Justice to investigate jail conditions. OPPRC held public DOJ hearings where middle-aged Black men, Latinx immigrant workers, and queer and trans Black youth testified about endemic violence at OPP.[193] Around this time the Southern Policy Law Center filed a federal lawsuit on behalf of OPP prisoners charging unconstitutional conditions in regard to medical care and violence.[194] As the abuses at OPP became officially known, the US marshals and then ICE pulled their prisoners from OPP.[195] Gusman—losing standing day by day in the courts and the press—closed down the House of Detention ahead of schedule and transferred five hundred state prisoners out of the jail.[196] After the DOJ issued a scathing report and the courts found for the SPLC plaintiffs, the city and federal judge Lance Africk negotiated a consent decree in 2013.[197] With this federal ruling asserting that the per diem system directly contributed to OPP's problems, the city replaced the municipal per diem system with a static, detailed operating budget for fiscal year 2015.[198]

Still, Gusman did not give up his vision of a larger jail. As soon as the city council passed the ordinance on the maximum size of OPP, Gusman embarked on a new set of strategies to subvert the bed cap. Gusman intentionally designed the new two-building jail complex with a large space between the buildings—a move OPPRC initially questioned as a space seemingly designed for future expansion. Although at first Gusman denied such allegations, within a year he proposed to the Criminal Justice Working Group and city council that the open space be turned into a "Phase III" for OPP.[199] Soon after, the *Times-Picayune* began to backpedal from its support for the bed cap, publishing an editorial that perhaps Gusman was right that more beds were needed to classify and separate prisoners.[200] Sheriff Gusman attempted to leverage the consent decree to his own ends by asserting that he could not meet the court's guidelines without adding on Phase III for prisoner medical and mental health care.[201] Between 2011 and as of this writing in 2023, federal judges have aligned with Gusman and pushed for the city to build Phase III in the name of constitutionality, while city leaders have gone back and forth on supporting or challenging this proposal in the face of OPPRC's organizing amid the ups and downs of city revenues in the face of the COVID-19 pandemic.[202]

・・・・・・

The day before the 2013 hurricane season began, OPPRC was prepared. Word had gotten out that the city had a new disaster policy for OPP. If a Category 3 hurricane or higher was in the Gulf of Mexico, the sheriff was to release the majority of prisoners on their own recognizance until the storm had passed or, in the event of a mandatory evacuation, until ten days after the city repopulated. OPPRC held an action to publicly pose the question, Why didn't the city extend the same protections of release year-round, given that, in the words of Cielo Cruz, "it's a Category 5 inside the jail."[203] While Mayor Landrieu held his annual hurricane preparedness press conference at the Mississippi River, OPPRC activists and their allies quietly assembled a few yards away. Wearing bright red t-shifts emblazoned with "EVACUATE O.P.P. NOW," fifty people silently formed a circle around an altar built of fabric on which were placed candles and paper silhouettes covered in red handprints, each with a name of one of the forty-one people whose lives had been lost in OPP since Hurricane Katrina. Don Everard led the group in a prayer. A prayer that the summer's hurricane season would be mild. A prayer for the people locked away in OPP. A prayer that, in the event of a major hurricane, Mayor Landrieu would use his powers to declare the jail in a state of emergency and order its evacuation. Gradually reporters left the mayor's press conference to observe the prayer circle and interview OPPRC leaders. Although OPPRC knew it was unlikely Landrieu would agree to their call, the protest raised the question of why so many people remained caged in a fundamentally violent institution.

After years of confronting an intractable city government driven by the goal of building up carceral capabilities, Hurricane Katrina provided an unexpected opening. Yet this political opportunity was not sufficient on its own. It took the strategic efforts of a broad range of activists to build grassroots power and shift some of the guiding approaches and practices surrounding public safety. Reflecting on that time, Mayaba Liebenthal describes how organizers' energy mimicked the post-Katrina environment: "After the storm, the ground was very fertile. The trees were growing extra shit, the caterpillars were everywhere, there were watermelons this big. This sort of freak-out moment that nature was having, we were having ourselves. . . . All sorts of new things grew."[204] The activism to shrink New Orleans' carceral infrastructure in the first five years after the floods occurred not despite the crisis of Hurricane Katrina but because of how grassroots organizers leveraged the crisis for movement building.

Safe Streets/Strong Communities, Critical Resistance, and the broader Orleans Parish Prison Reform Coalition leveraged the national spotlight on the city after Hurricane Katrina to call attention to the systemic racial violence of the courts, the police, and the jail. Through their tireless campaigning, Safe Streets initiated an overhaul of the public defender system so that fewer people would end up in prison; pressed for the creation of the Office of the Independent Police Monitor so that fewer people would be brutalized, harassed, and arrested by the NOPD; and held Expungement Day in collaboration with Critical Resistance so that fewer people's lives would be curtailed by their arrest records. OPPRC managed to win the unthinkable victory of shrinking the jail by thousands of beds and pressuring the city and the courts to end the per diem system so that fewer people were imprisoned and would die in OPP. Although often unrecognized, post-Katrina organizing built on previous generations of movement work—from the Angola Special Civics Project to CR South—while activism within the post-Katrina period also built on other efforts.

For grassroots organizers, one of the biggest successes of this period was that these wins were accomplished by the people power of working-class Black and Brown people trying to remake home in New Orleans. Cielo Cruz shares,

> People who are most impacted and have the most experience with the system were in the forefront of the push to make change. That that model won and we were able to show that is the way it should be done everywhere. If you're just trying to have some reports and some policy experts go to your elected officials and deal directly, that is not a meaningful and good process. People have to be involved. That leadership has to be there.[205]

The power of this organizing went beyond building up and cutting back institutions to transforming people's understanding of how change could be made in New Orleans. This base-building and leadership development work was critically accompanied by, in the words of Jacinta Gonzalez, "political clarity in terms of the longer-term vision around abolition . . . where they were trying to build power, what could be won and how to maneuver and deliver material wins."[206]

6 To Walk down the Street without Fear

Curbing Criminalization and Demanding Life in the New Orleans Tourism Economy

• •

> When it comes to LGBTQ youth, the issues get real, especially with trans women. As a youth-led organization, we focus our energy on trans women of color, because we think that wins for trans women of color will lead to wins for all of us. If trans women are able to get jobs and walk down the street without harassment or discrimination, we know the doors will open for others.
> —BreakOUT!

> This French Quarter, this piece of ground that we are on, is one of the most important economic engines for the city, for the region, and for the state of Louisiana.
> —Mayor Mitch Landrieu, French Quarter crime press conference, 2015

> We didn't start this patrol because cops are corrupt but because there are not enough of them.
> —Bob Simms, French Quarter Management District Security Task Force

After years of grassroots organizing for redress for the NOPD's killing of Black storm survivors, the Department of Justice (DOJ) formally opened an investigation into the NOPD in 2010. In the face of this limited, yet real, political opening, New Orleanians mobilized to push for policing reforms that would curtail extraordinary and everyday police violence. Locally, a group of predominantly Black LGBTQ youth coalesced around the DOJ's presence to organize against racialized and sexualized gender policing. They formed BreakOUT! to fight against the racial criminalization of LGBTQ youth in New Orleans.

At the same time, newly elected Mayor Mitch Landrieu promoted the aggressive revitalization of the tourist economy to prove New Orleans could be a thriving city once again. The city remained a highly contested space, even as the crisis of the immediate post-Katrina years had abated. Drawing on federal antisex trafficking initiatives, multiagency law enforcement efforts cracked down on an array of offenses deemed a risk to tourism. Although the French Quarter only covers a square mile, its political significance in city governance and its importance in the public imagination vastly exceed its size. At a time when Black working-class and poor residents were being pushed to the city's margins through skyrocketing housing costs and a dearth of living-wage work, municipal investments were earmarked for tourism and law enforcement initiatives in the French Quarter. These dynamics typify the punitive neoliberal logics governing contemporary New Orleans and the ones BreakOUT! organizes against.

BreakOUT!'s grassroots activism against the crisis of criminalization was in dialectical relation to the strategizing of the French Quarter Management District's (FQMD) Security Task Force whose policing initiatives were then implemented across the city. In tracking these two linked stories, this chapter uncovers how the policing of racialized gender and sexuality has become central to urban capital accumulation schemes such that struggles over everyday criminalization serve as a pivot point for the future of New Orleans.

In the name of protecting the tourist economy, the FQMD, with Mayor Landrieu's backing, organized to expand public and privatized forms of law enforcement and surveillance in the French Quarter that would regulate public spaces along race, class, and gender lines, with an emphasis on policing trans and queer people and places. In direct contrast, the organizing of BreakOUT! is animated by a Black trans feminist politics committed to making New Orleans a place where LGBTQ youth of color can "walk down the street without fear." Founded and led by primarily Black trans girls who had been entrapped in the penal system, BreakOUT! offers an urgent critique of workings of the carceral state under gendered racial capitalism.[1] BreakOUT!'s "We Deserve Better" campaign highlights how direct engagement with the state's contradictory nature can be vital ground for an abolitionist politics that extends collective life. In doing so, they contest capital's rendering of LGBTQ youth of color as deviant surplus populations and the notion that Black trans and queer people are, to borrow from Katherine McKittrick, "ungeographic," always already out of place.[2] Against a world where acute and structural violence cut short their lives, BreakOUT!'s politics of life not only declares that #BlackTransLivesMatter but also invests, in the words of Jose Esteban Muñoz, in a "queer futurity"[3] that stretches our understanding of Henri Lefebvre's statement that the right to the city is "a transformed and renewed right to urban life."[4] Or, to follow the activism of BreakOUT! making New Orleans a place where notions of safety are transformed from being defined by police and prisons to being defined as collective investments and unmitigated access to housing, healthcare, education, and jobs.

We Deserve Better: Contesting Racialized Sexual and Gender Police Violence

BreakOUT! was founded in the shadows of the NOPD's post-Katrina crisis of legitimacy. When the Civil Rights Division of the DOJ announced that they would investigate the NOPD, grassroots organizers pushed for the DOJ to place the NOPD under a consent decree. During most of 2010, several organizations coordinated DOJ listening sessions on people's experiences with the NOPD.[5] Through one listening session, an informal group of Black queer and trans youth coalesced into the organization BreakOUT!

The DOJ's investigation of the NOPD coincided with the 2010 release of the report, *Locked Up and Out*, which charted the experiences of LGBTQ youth in the Louisiana juvenile justice system. *Locked Up and Out* was spearheaded by Juvenile Justice Project of Louisiana (JJPL) youth advocate Wes Ware, who had previously engaged in organizing with Xochitl Bervera and Althea Francois. He had moved to New Orleans a few years after Katrina to work for JJPL.[6] Written in collaboration with youth behind bars, *Locked Up and Out* documents how LGBTQ youth, primarily of color, are funneled through the penal system, the siloing of juvenile justice work from queer activism, and how queer and trans youth are routinely stopped and harassed by the NOPD while walking down the street.[7]

By the time the report was distributed in the summer of 2010, many of the young people Ware worked with on it had been released. Yet once these queer and trans youth were back home in New Orleans, there was no real political organization to harness their energy. At the same time, Ware was building a relationship with Milan Nicole Sherry—a young Black trans women interning at JJPL who was deeply embedded in the world of Black trans New Orleans. When they heard that Women with a Vision, a longstanding Black feminist organization, was coordinating a DOJ listening session on LGBTQ people's experiences with the NOPD, Sherry and Ware recruited several of the young Black LGBTQ folks they knew to participate.[8] Although such listening sessions typically serve as a performance of concern by the liberal state, the young people in attendance flipped the script—moving beyond the notion that the DOJ could save them and remaking the space to their own ends. They seamlessly transitioned from testifying about the NOPD's everyday violence to imagining solutions. Ware recalls,

> They quickly started talking about what they would like to see—what the possibilities were, and what the DOJ should [do]. . . . I remember scrambling for chart paper and putting it up on the wall and just writing down all the things young folks were saying about we should do this or that. The city should be spending money this way and not that way. The DOJ representative just had to sit there while people just started running with these ideas . . . *that* was the first BreakOUT! meeting.[9]

Their visioning did not end with that single DOJ meeting. An initial group of six youth—Milan Nicole Sherry, Kenisha Harris, Lhundyn Palmer, Amhari Alexander, Dee Dee Jackson, and Jonathan Willis—began meeting together weekly, with staffing support from Ware, as the founding members of BreakOUT![10] Soon the nascent organization drew others who were directly affected by policing or imprisonment. While BreakOUT!'s members mainly comprised LGBTQ youth of color, the organization initially included a few white LGBTQ members.

BreakOUT! collectively developed a shared political analysis of criminalization while sharpening activist skills through Building Our Power (BOP), an organizing and leadership development program. BOP participants gained a political education, learning about the history of policing and different resistance struggles from the Stonewall riots to the New Orleans Black Panther Party. With many of them searching for work, they also attended workshops on skills such as resume writing. As founding member Lhundyn Palmer relates, their coming together was exciting because they had been alienated from mainstream LGBTQ organizations, which

> don't focus on the things that impact me and my type of girl that walks that street. They focus on more of, [it's] cliché to say gay marriage back then, but it was. . . . You're not focused on the things that are really impacting the girls that y'all don't see in the clubs or that you don't see having a nine to five. Let's talk about the things those girls go through. Let's talk about the girls who are living at the bottom.[11]

Instead of being sidelined from what constituted proper gay activism, BreakOUT! created space for predominantly LGBTQ youth of color to direct activism based on their lived experiences.

One of the most meaningful activities they did in those early months was charting out a "problem tree" on the issues facing members. Through this activity, participants conceptualized the problems confronting their lives as rooted in the intertwined systemic oppressions of racism, heterosexism and transphobia. At the center of their problems was the everyday criminalization of their existence. As Sherry explains,

> For a lot of us, our experience was that police were profiling us to be sex workers. . . . When you encountered the officers, it was a very traumatizing experience. When you're young . . . you don't know when the police is taking advantage of you or when they're not. And as far as the power that officers hold could be very intimidating for a person that has no power at all. So the fact that you will be misgendered and [will] not really push back against the police, because then that can lead to arrest. As far as police call you out of your name, and you correct them, that can lead you to arrest. So, it was a lot of misgendering. Profiling. Officers were abusing their authority. There were a lot of times where I myself had to perform sexual favors to officers just to avoid arrest.[12]

BreakOUT! identified the NOPD's power to stop, frisk, and sexually assault trans and queer people of color, particularly Black trans girls, with impunity under the umbrella of policing sex work as activating the cycle of criminalization that ensnared them.

Their analysis of the NOPD's gendered and sexual policing practices was anchored in an understanding, to borrow from Emily Hobson, that "all policing of sexuality, queer or straight, is racialized."[13] As primarily Black LGBTQ young people, the centrality of racism in their police encounters was never in question. Many of BreakOUT!'s members had family—almost always cis and straight Black men—who were caught up in the criminal legal system. Yet they recognized that the way *they* were targeted by law enforcement as young Black trans women and queer people was qualitatively different. They also knew that white LGBTQ youth generally did not experience the types of policing that shaped their everyday lives due to the generalized protections of whiteness afforded to individuals and their different geographic locations in the city. White LGBTQ youth who were part of BreakOUT! were less likely to have encountered the criminal legal system while just walking down the street. Instead, they usually had been in and out of the child welfare system; incarcerated in a juvenile prison from a very young age, frequently for offenses categorized as "serious" by the state; and often had cognitive disabilities. This suggested that a confluence of factors usually had to be at play to erode the protection of whiteness typically granted to white LGBTQ youth by the criminal legal system.

The NOPD's policing of Black LGBTQ youth, while resonating with aspects of police abuse based on race, class, and cis-masculinity, took a distinct form at the nexus of anti-Black racism and gender nonconformity. Cops routinely stopped them for being young trans women of color walking down the street, called them homophobic and transphobic slurs, groped them under the guise of determining their "real" gender, and charged them with falsely identifying themselves when their gender presentation or chosen names did not match the official sex and name on their IDs. For Black LGBTQ youth, it was important to expand the notion of stop and frisk to include the sexual assault they experienced at the hands of the police. The NOPD's rampant coercion of Black trans girls into sexual activity under the explicit or implicit threat of arrest simultaneously illustrated how sexual violence could be used to enforce gender norms *and* fit into the centuries-old pattern of the state's systematic disregard of Black women's sexual autonomy.[14] The NOPD's policing of gender and sexuality served as another state racial project directed at disciplining and controlling Black New Orleanians.

In addition, BreakOUT!'s critique of the police's profiling of Black trans girls as sex workers raised attention to how racism and transmisogyny produced their structural class position. As BreakOUT! explained, "LGBTQ youth, particularly young Black transgender women, are disproportionately experiencing the harmful effects of the criminal justice system due to disparities in housing, employment, education, and social service providers."[15] BreakOUT! members and other young LGBTQ people of color often were pushed out of their homes due to familial homophobia and transphobia and out of the school system because of their intersecting experiences of transphobic and heterosexist bullying and racist disciplinary targeting. With the already meager Louisiana social safety net further shredded after Hurricane Katrina, almost all resources for homeless youth were provided through overextended nonprofit agencies that had, at best, mixed politics on LGBTQ issues. With housing costs skyrocketing, finding a safe place to stay was more challenging than ever. Moreover, jobs were hard to come by for those without a high school diploma. For those who did graduate high school, the few jobs available provided minimum-wage work that was almost impossible to survive on—and often even those jobs were out of reach due to discriminatory hiring practices. Black trans girls were systematically excluded from the legitimate workforce, which is to say rendered as surplus labor, under gendered racial capitalism.

Thus, it should come as no surprise that many, but by no means all, young Black trans women turned to street-based sex work and other criminalized economic survival strategies to make ends meet. Although Black trans girls were overrepresented in sex work—particularly in the historically disinvested Tulane Avenue area and the heavily invested tourism epicenter of the French Quarter—their overdetermination as criminalized subjects meant that law enforcement presumed that any and all Black trans girls were sex working. Most, if not all, young Black trans women spent a fair amount of time in the public sphere because of their lack of access to private spaces, which led to more everyday contact with the NOPD. Hence the political question was not delineating whether a given girl was "innocent" or "guilty" but how racial state violence was wielded in the twinned projects of sex work and gender policing. BreakOUT!'s aim to curtail the discretionary power of the NOPD to profile Black trans women as soliciting sex work challenged the logic of criminalizing an entire group of people based on their race and gender for their own systematic exclusion from the post-Katrina political economy. From this political framework developed the We Deserve Better campaign, aimed at eradicating the NOPD's gender policing and state-sanctioned sexual violence in the spring of 2011.[16]

Along with identifying the roots of its members' criminalization, early BreakOUT! meetings were devoted to grassroots organizing training. Members learned how to map the political landscape, pinpoint who held the power to make change, identify their allies and their opponents, delineate the difference between a strategy and a tactic, and build power to escalate a campaign. Although they were skeptical that the DOJ's investigation would lead to meaningful reforms on its own, they also knew that building a strong campaign depended on the federal investigation's verification of the NOPD profiling and sexual harassment of Black trans girls and other queer youth of color. They charted out how not only to provide useful information to the investigation but, in the words of Ware, also how to begin "organizing the DOJ" to take a stance against the NOPD's racialized, gendered, and sexualized policing.[17] They coordinated DOJ forums for young queer and trans people of color at which they could share their experiences *and* convey to the DOJ investigators their understanding of the systematic violence of the NOPD. In using these strategies, BreakOUT! implicitly identified one of the central contradictions of the carceral state: the state is not a singular entity but a multiscalar institution of institutions, and organizers can leverage one sector of the state against another to scale back carceral power—even as activists identified the state as the primary arbiter of violence in their lives.

During this time, BreakOUT! collaborated with several racial justice groups to craft a People's Consent Decree that activists hoped the DOJ would adopt. BreakOUT! saw participating in crafting this decree as an opportunity to articulate their own visions for LGBTQ policing reforms. Although at first some activists balked at the inclusion of such reforms in the decree, claiming that they watered down attention to anti-Black racism, ultimately the People's Consent Decree included reforms aimed at curbing the NOPD's misconduct against LGBT people.[18]

When the DOJ released its report, it was clear that the listening sessions had an impact. Although the DOJ did not adopt the People's Consent Decree, its report drew on community activists' stories and insights. It indicted the NOPD for its systematic disregard for civil rights and widespread legal violations: the NOPD "frequently uses excessive force and conducts illegal stops, searches, and arrests with impunity."[19] The DOJ noted the NOPD's pervasive patterns of "bias"—that is, police profiling—against African Americans, Latinx, youth, and LGBT people.[20] The report documented how the NOPD's statistic-oriented policing practices, which measure success based on the number of arrests, underpinned and colluded with discriminatory policing.[21] Moreover, the report discussed how the NOPD targeted LGBTQ people of color and how Black trans women were routinely profiled as sex workers, often leading them to be charged with the notorious "crimes against nature" law, which restricted their abilities to find employment and housing.[22] Although the DOJ had not yet issued a consent decree, for BreakOUT! the inclusion of their stories within the official DOJ report was a victory. Not only did it validate what they had long known but in its validation it also shifted the ideological terrain to be more fertile for future policing campaigns.

Although reining in NOPD violence was important, BreakOUT!'s overarching goal was never simply to seek better policing procedures but to "starve the beast" of the penal system by preventing arrests and thus incarceration.[23] Thus, they pushed for a policy clearly delineating that gender identity, expression, and sexual orientation did not constitute reasonable, suspicious, or probable cause for a police stop, in concert with new regulations to restrict cops' harassment of queer and trans people. Focusing on changing policy was key. Founding member Lhundyn Palmer explains, "We have to start with the law. We can't start fight[ing] for our rights if our rights are not even written down."[24] BreakOUT! understood that racial and gender violence was baked into the NOPD, but they also realized it was unrealistic to ignore current state policy and hope that the carceral state would wither away. BreakOUT! researched and brainstormed the contours of an ideal policy that would reduce the harms inflicted by the NOPD.

BreakOUT!'s We Deserve Better campaign was accompanied by the distribution of a manual created by the organization, "Your Guide to Street Safety & Preserving Your Rights with the Police" (figure 6.1). While recognizing the state as a primary propeller of violence in their lives and focused on chipping away at the NOPD's power, they recognized that policy change meant little if people did not know their legal rights or how to advocate for themselves. Sherry relates that before BreakOUT! was formed, "It was very easy for police to take advantage of me, as far as just misgendering me. Illegal profiling me. . . . It kind of became a norm to me."[25] Being harassed repeatedly by the NOPD and not knowing their rights, Sherry and countless others normalized their everyday police shakedowns. As Andrea Ritchie describes, gendered and racialized law enforcement violence is rendered as "simultaneously ordinary and out of the ordinary."[26] The BreakOUT! guide spelled out what the police could and could not legally do, what questions to ask and statements to make during a police stop, and how to report police problems to BreakOUT! Along with distributing the guide, the organization gave out compact mirrors stamped with the BreakOUT! logo and with important phrases such as "Am I under arrest?" and "I do not consent to this search" printed on the inside. Even if it was merely a harm-reduction strategy, learning about one's rights and standing against punitive state violence still had the power to interrupt the systematic devaluing of their lives.

Around this time, BreakOUT! approached the NOPD with initial recommendations for a LGBTQ policy. Although organizers did not expect the NOPD to accept their recommendations, they believed that directly asking them to do so was the first step in escalating their campaign. As expected, the NOPD officials rejected their recommended policy but made an unexpected offer. They invited BreakOUT! to train the NOPD on LGBTQ issues (likely as a preventive measure against the forthcoming DOJ consent decree). Hesitant, BreakOUT! staff decided they needed more information: they contacted trusted allies about the pros and cons of training the police. Under BreakOUT!'s decision-making structure, such decisions were never

FIGURE 6.1 BreakOUT! "Your Guide to Street Safety & Preserving Your Rights with the Police." Art by Tommy LeBlanc. Courtesy of the artist.

staff's alone to make but needed consent from the membership. According to Ware,

> We came back to membership and said the NOPD want us to train them and asked members how they felt about that. At first, I think some members were excited to tell a police officer what they should and shouldn't be doing. But it wasn't long before in that same meeting, we asked members if training the police would put us in a position of power? And we were able to go back to the foundation we already laid around our vision and looking strategically at our campaign goals and what we wanted. Pretty quickly young people articulated that it would not put us in a position of power and, in fact, could really hurt the organization and our campaign. Not to mention we also had young people in the room who were like hell no, we're not going to go in front of the same people that are bribing and brutalizing us, physically and sexually, and train them to do it better . . . no.[27]

In working through this tricky political question, BreakOUT! reached a consensus that training the NOPD would legitimize their abusive practices and undermine more meaningful policy change.

However, members did express that they wanted their voices to be heard. They wanted the public, including the NOPD, to hear about their negative experiences with law enforcement and their recommendations for reform. To do this, they made a short video titled *We Deserve Better* in collaboration with FosterBear Films. The video highlighted BreakOUT! members' experiences with the NOPD and emphasized that the police were a "hindrance to our safety."[28] In the film, one young person states, "I don't trust the police at all. I don't believe the police can do anything to save us because if that was the case, they wouldn't hurt us by locking us up and putting us in jail or in prison just for the fact of what a person looks like, or a person's gender, or what they want to be or how they dress or how they act or the way they talk. If a man sounds like a sissy, or a female sounds like a man."[29] Real safety would mean the ability to "go down the street without being harassed" and to have access to jobs.[30] Though widely shared on social media and shown to some officers, the NOPD soon deemed the film "too controversial."[31]

The We Deserve Better campaign received a boost after the DOJ reached a consent decree agreement with the city in July 2012. At the time, it was one of the most extensive consent decrees ever placed on a municipal police department, and the most explicit DOJ decree regarding discriminatory LGBTQ policing practices.[32] Along with mandating that the NOPD be "specifically prohibited from using harassing, intimidating, or derogatory language regarding or toward LGBT individuals," the consent decree stated, "Officers shall not construe sexual orientation, gender identity, or gender expression as reasonable suspicion or probable cause."[33] Moreover, it included this guidance: "Officers will not subject transgender individuals to more invasive or more frequent frisk procedures due to transgender status. Officers shall not frisk any person for the purpose of determining that person's gender or to view or touch the person's genitals."[34] The decree directed the city to undo punitive practices that led to disproportionate numbers of LGBTQ people of color being locked up.

Yet the work was not done. The New Orleans city government was required to pass a series of new policing reforms before the DOJ consent decree monitors would release the NOPD from their oversight. BreakOUT! accelerated its process of finalizing their own proposed policy, which they presented to city council in the fall of 2012. Along with BreakOUT! testifying about NOPD violence against queer and trans youth of color and presenting their policy proposal, representatives from OPPRC, JJPL, Congreso, Safe Streets/Strong Communities, the Office of the Independent Police Monitor, VOTE, and the New Orleans LGBTQ Community Center came out to support BreakOUT's proposal.[35] Presenting this policy on record at City Hall, rather than in private meetings, was strategic not only for disseminating their ideas but also because one of BreakOUT!'s goals was for the NOPD to go on the record that they would meet with BreakOUT! before adopting any policy. With the NOPD promising that BreakOUT! would have the power to comment on any proposed police policies, BreakOUT! felt confident about their ability to influence the city's LGBTQ policy.

Shortly thereafter, however, the city began backtracking on its commitments. Mayor Landrieu at first lauded the NOPD consent decree, but when he realized that it would cost millions of dollars to implement it, on top of the millions required for the OPP consent decree, he implored the federal judge "to hold off" on its execution.[36] When that request was struck down, the NOPD wrote watered-down reform policies that many local activists surmised were aimed at maintaining discretionary power and keeping costs down.

BreakOUT! organized their members and allies to demand that the NOPD stay true to its word on adopting a meaningful LGBTQ policy. When they heard that the NOPD had sent a proposed policy to the city attorney's office, BreakOUT! wrote a letter to NOPD Superintendent Serpas reminding him of his commitment and asking why they had yet to see this policy. BreakOUT! then drafted a petition urging Serpas to release the draft NOPD LGBTQ policy; it quickly garnered 300 signatures.[37] BreakOUT! organizers also wrote a letter to the editor to the French Quarter-based LGBT+ magazine *Ambush* to mobilize the broader queer community. The letter tied the profiling of Black trans women walking down the street to the policing of Black men riding their bikes and to "Latino workers driving home," which "does nothing to make us safer." It stated that now is the time for the NOPD to increase accountability in its reform process.[38]

The NOPD finally agreed to a meeting with BreakOUT! at which NOPD presented the department's proposed LGBTQ policy. BreakOUT! organizer Derwin Wilright Jr. described it as "rubbish" in that "it didn't explain a lot of things correctly [and was] really vague and just brief."[39] Yet BreakOUT! staff brought the draft policy to their membership to read, discuss, and provide feedback. After this collective meeting, they sent the NOPD (along with the DOJ) five pages of line edits detailing everyone's concerns. BreakOUT! asserted the proposal was unacceptable for the following reasons: its contradictory and clinical language around gender identity and sexuality, the weakness of the provisions about prohibiting discriminatory policing, and the lack of stipulations about stop and frisk data collection. Given that the NOPD had stopped three of their members without cause in the past week alone, it was clear that a strong policy was needed. Moving ahead with weak policies without real community input undermined the DOJ's investigation and consent decree. BreakOUT! informed the NOPD that they would be demanding that the department hold public hearings on any proposals.[40] In the words of Milan Sherry, "You can't make policies about us, without us."[41]

BreakOUT! kept their word, holding "Stop the Frisk: Rally against Racial and Gender Profiling" on May 9, 2013, in front of NOPD headquarters. Speakers demanded transparency and public hearings on proposed NOPD policies. Interspersed with the chants "NOPD keep your hands off of me" and "We deserve better," youth organizers gave speeches about how the city was not taking the problems of policing seriously enough. Milan Sherry explained that Mayor Landrieu's recent statement on policing reforms encapsulated the problem when "he said that he thought racial profiling was wrong. We should be aggressively pursuing people not because of race but because of behavior. But we all know that being Black is the behavior. We know that being transgender is the behavior." Breaking down the false dichotomy between police profiling based on identity and the "unbiased" policing of criminal activity, BreakOUT! pointed to how Landrieu's and, by extension, the NOPD's heralding of colorblind and genderblind logics papered over the centrality of racism and transphobia to everyday policing. When BreakOUT! approached the NOPD headquarters to deliver their demands, NOPD officers locked the front door. Although the NOPD did not open the door despite the crowd's loud chants of "let us in, let us in," BreakOUT! felt fortified by the widespread support for their demands.

A few days after the rally, the NOPD invited BreakOUT! leaders to a closed-door meeting about proposed reforms. Refusing to be the only ones at the table, BreakOUT! brought along representatives from other organizations including Congreso and the Office of the Independent Police Monitor. At this meeting they obtained enough of their objectives—including that one's perceived or actual gender identity and sexual orientation did not constitute reasonable suspicion or probable cause—that they decided the NOPD policy was good enough to claim as a success.

After two years of organizing, the city formally enacted Policy 402, which governs the NOPD's treatment of LGBTQ individuals in June 2013.[42] BreakOUT! celebrated the announcement as a victory that could be leveraged for future struggles. Yet, as Derwin Wilright Jr, said, "We recognize that much more must be done to ensure the safety of queer and trans youth of color on the streets of New Orleans."[43] To get the word out about Policy 402, BreakOUT! updated their Guide to Street Safety to include the new restrictions on LGBTQ policing. Members coordinated a photo shoot to publicize Policy 402 and other legal information through a social media campaign (figure 6.2).

A year after achieving the win of Policy 402, BreakOUT! released *We Deserve Better: A Report on Policing in New Orleans by and for Queer and Trans Youth of Color*. Along with sharing the survey data and testimonials that BreakOUT! collected on law enforcement's sexual harassment and arrests of LGBTQ youth of color, the report also pointedly rejected the narrative that the oppression these youth experienced reduced their existence, as one supposed supporter had described them, to "living in the streets like rats."[44] They stated, "We are not your rats. We're doing the best we can in a city that has provided us with very few resources. We are surviving. We are resilient. We are creative and resourceful. . . . We can tell you exactly what

FIGURE 6.2 BreakOUT! #KnowYourRights social media campaign, 2013. Photograph by Rush Jagoe. Courtesy of the photographer.

is wrong in this city and exactly what needs to change."[45] Toward that end, the report outlined a series of recommendations for reducing the power of punitive urban governance and expanding the city's capacity to meet LGBTQ youth of color's material needs.

We Deserve Better noted that, even as "Policy 402 is a great start," there was still work to be done to fully implement the consent decree: crafting more detailed policies for the use of police cameras, ending the NOPD's collusion with ICE, and having the NOPD acknowledge the harm it had done to New Orleanians. The report described how the consent decree was already being undercut by Landrieu's request for 100 state troopers to supplement the police force in the French Quarter after a high-profile shooting. The report demanded that the state police be removed from the French Quarter not only because more law enforcement generally increased people's vulnerability to arrest but also because the state troopers were outside the bounds of the DOJ consent decree. They argued for the repeal of a new state criminal law, which they believed to have been written at least partially in response to Policy 402, that further criminalized solicitation and was explicitly targeted at sex workers and homeless people.[46] Furthermore, "money should be shifted from more police to providing more housing opportunities for youth in our city."[47] The report proposed that the city should not only develop a job training program but also actively help youth to obtain living-wage work.[48] The final recommendation was to end the school-to-prison pipeline for LGBTQ youth by creating safer and affirming educational environments.

Through the We Deserve Better campaign, BreakOUT! activists organized to disrupt the normalization of the NOPD's racialized and gendered profiling and state-sanctioned sexual violence and to lessen the scope and power of the NOPD. In doing so, they disavowed the notion that their safety was located in heightened policing and contended that true security would only come from meaningful investments in the social infrastructures from which they had been structurally excluded. As Derwin Wilright explained, the purpose of We Deserve Better was to work toward a society that did not equate police with safety: "I want a world with community accountability where we aren't relying on the police. . . . As Black and Brown people and LGBTQ people, the police has never really done anything for us except stop our youth and tear apart our families. I would like to see a day when the NOPD is not who we rely on but instead ensure we can hold each other accountable in communities without using violence or guns."[49]

Securing the New Orleans Tourism Economy

In the fall of 2015, BreakOUT! asked whether I could track down the ordinances that authorized the presence of state troopers in New Orleans and to determine which entity was behind the uptick in private patrols in the French Quarter. Wes Ware shared that the deployments of state troopers appeared to be a workaround of the consent decree. This saturation policing was also reminiscent of a recent crackdown on housing-insecure LGBTQ youth around Tulane Avenue as the area underwent redevelopment following the opening of a new medical complex to replace the public Charity Hospital. The expansion of policing in the city's tourism epicenter seemed to be pushing out queer and trans youth of color in a similar way, serving racial capital's vision of a new New Orleans.

One of the long-standing contradictions of the New Orleans tourism economy has been the racial policing of sex, even as debauchery has been a significant tourist draw. Historian Alecia P. Long demonstrates that New Orleans's appeal as a "tourist destination that encouraged and facilitated indulgence, especially in prostitution and sex across the color line" can be traced back to the city's remaking of itself after the Civil War.[50] In the late nineteenth century, city leaders grappled both with the allure of the relatively tolerant culture of sexual and racial transgressions and their desire to promote New Orleans as governed by reform-minded Jim Crow respectability and capital. To resolve this contradiction, city officials sought to contain racialized commercial sex by partitioning the neighborhood of Storyville into an official vice district while ramping up the policing of sex work outside the neighborhood bounds, which included enacting residential segregation laws limiting where sex workers could live.[51]

To appease complaints from the US Navy during World War I, the city shut down Storyville, and commercial sex across the legal spectrum returned to the French Quarter.[52] Reformers turned again to law enforcement to shore up their desires for a chaste tourism economy. After World War II, Bourbon Street became a battleground between historic preservationists who believed sex shows sullied property values and strippers and nightclub owners who earned their living on the tourist sex dollar.[53] After the city banned "lewd entertainment" and instituted raids on nightclubs, many bars closed.[54] In advance of the 1984 World's Fair, Connick orchestrated a war on vice in the French Quarter by authorizing raids on sex work establishments and gay bathhouses.[55] Gay residents picketed the First

District NOPD Station to protest the raids and everyday police harassment, which they experienced when waiting to take the bus to the World's Fair.[56]

As mayor, Mitch Landrieu strengthened the neoliberal tourist economy and swelled the ranks of law enforcement in the name of post-Katrina revitalization. His aggressive promotion of tourism led the industry to dominate the New Orleans political economy on an unmatched scale. During his tenure, his administration lobbied for a new billion dollar airport, recruited major conventions and sporting events to the city, and pushed through one of the most lax short-term vacation rental regulations in the nation over widespread opposition.[57] In just over ten years after Hurricane Katrina, New Orleans broke a new record for the number of visitors annually at 10.5 million people in 2016.[58] It was not a coincidence that 2016 marked the first year since the storm that more people migrated out of the city than moved in, as working-class communities—predominantly Black and Latinx—were pushed out to the suburbs or left the greater metropolitan area because of rising housing costs and the lack of living-wage work.[59]

The criminalization of deviant sex and gender together with the remaking of racialized urban space to meet neoliberal imperatives—particularly in tourism economies—is not unique to New Orleans.[60] As Christina Hanhardt documents, NYPD chief William Bratton "first tested [broken windows policing] in Greenwich Village, home to the famed Stonewall riots and one of the world's best-known gay enclaves."[61] This displacement strategy was then exported to other areas of New York City marked for speculative development, under which other populations (the homeless, young Black and Latino men, and sex workers) came under siege.[62] Police crackdowns on sex work have been critical in securing tourism gentrification across the globe.[63] As Erica L. Williams recounts in her work on Salvador, Brazil, the tourist economy marks different racial-gender-sexual relations to space through the figure of the racialized sex worker. Black women, perceived to be sex workers, "have a queer relationship to the touristic landscape due to the fact that they are always already seen as sexually deviant or somewhere out of place."[64] The criminalization and displacement of sex workers (real and perceived) of color are critical to enhancing the spatialized capital accumulation of tourist economies.

Federal antisex trafficking initiatives bolstered tourism policing in the first decades of the twenty-first century. An unlikely alliance between antiprostitution and antipornography feminists and the Christian Right developed when it appeared the Right had lost the culture war on sex work.[65] Repackaging antisex work politics under the banner of sex trafficking—a criminalizing frame that sought to undercut sex work activists' claims to bodily autonomy by reframing most (if not all) sex work as coerced through a punitive victim's rights narrative—antisex trafficking advocates found a champion in President George W. Bush. Although the federal Victims of Trafficking and Violence Protection Act was passed in 2000 under President Clinton, the Bush administration increased criminal sanctions and federal and local law enforcement funding through the DOJ and the newly created Department of Homeland Security (DHS).[66] During his tenure, President Obama expanded the scope of the domestic war on trafficking. In the fall of 2012, Obama announced the relaunch of DHS's "Blue Campaign" to train local law enforcement in antitrafficking tactics.[67]

Amid this renewed moral panic, state actors, antitrafficking advocates, and media spread the rumor that the 2013 Super Bowl, held amid the Mardi Gras season in New Orleans, would be a magnet for sex trafficking—thereby legitimizing heightened law enforcement cooperation. The FBI and ICE, in collaboration with ten state and local policing agencies, coordinated "Operation Innocence Lost" to crack down on perceived sex trafficking. Social service nonprofits and businesses disseminated flyers urging the public to be on the lookout for sex trafficking victims—in other words, to profile people as sex workers—under the War on Terror mantra of "if you see something, say something."[68] French Quarter hotels even branded their soaps with antitrafficking messages.

Although the imagined figure of the sex trafficking victim that animated federal law enforcement initiatives is a white, cisgender, young woman or girl, it was clear to BreakOUT! and their coconspirators at Women with a Vision that it would most likely be trans women of color who would be profiled by the public and police as sex workers. BreakOUT! activists considered publicly challenging Operation Innocence Lost but instead directed their energy at a harm-reduction approach of keeping people safe, given their limited capacity and the real concern that as a youth organization their opponents could weaponize their critiques into criminalizing the organization for supporting minors in sex work. Leading up to the Super Bowl, they handed out know your rights pamphlets and encouraged members to take cars, rather than walking, when going out. In the ensuing days, emboldened police stopped trans women on the street to demand that they share their Social Security numbers and taunted them on their megaphones. Operation Innocence Lost choreographed a mass arrest of eighty-five people—fifty-three in New Orleans and thirty-two in Baton Rouge. Only two of these people were booked on trafficking charges, with most arrested on low-level prostitution, narcotics, and weapons charges and several children taken ("rescued" in the language of law enforcement) by Family Services when the sting arrested their mothers for sex work.[69]

Mayor Landrieu transformed the heightened policing surrounding such mega-events from extraordinary to everyday urban governance. Although in his first term, Landrieu instituted a hiring freeze on NOPD officers due to revenue shortages, his second term was marked by heavy investments in policing and surveillance. Over the summer of 2014, Landrieu's office capitalized on a high-profile shooting on Bourbon Street to bring one hundred state troopers to New Orleans to temporarily reinforce the NOPD. Even though the state police were concentrated in the French Quarter, Landrieu also directed them to neighborhoods throughout the city. The mayor also convinced the city council to direct $3 million from the New Orleans Convention Visitor's Bureau to create "NOLA Patrol," a civilian patrol to focus on "quality of life" issues, and to fund an NOPD detail for Bourbon Street.[70] Moreover, Landrieu began petitioning Governor Bobby Jindal for the *indefinite* assignment of state troopers to New Orleans. Obfuscating the data that street crime was at some of its lowest-ever levels, Landrieu contended that deployment of the state troopers was a necessary stopgap measure for what he claimed was a shortage of officers confront rising crime.[71]

Calls for more policing also came from French Quarter residents and business owners. After a burglary at a local bar and the attempted mugging of a server, a group of primarily white middle- and upper-class New Orleanians, including at least one self-identified white supremacist, held a pro-police protest in January 2015.[72] The "Citizens Rally to End Crime in the Quarter" held at Jackson Square on Twelfth Night (January 6) called on Landrieu to get tougher on crime. Protesters chanted, "What do we want? Troopers! When do we want them? Now!" while holding signs that read "What's the PLAN? Where are our COPS? Where is the MONEY? When will ATTRITION STOP?" and "Welcome to Landrieuville! Home of Robbers, Stabbers & Rapists."[73] Controversial millionaire and French Quarter resident Sidney Torres IV ran TV ads attacking Landrieu after his home was broken into.[74]

A few days after the French Quarter protest, Landrieu redoubled his plea to Governor Jindal for state troopers, claiming that state augmentation of the NOPD was essential for state revenue generation.[75] Jindal partially relented by upping the number of state troopers stationed in New Orleans during the 2015 Mardi Gras season. The hotel industry, which had a vested interest in keeping tourists happy, committed the necessary funds for keeping the state troopers in the French Quarter throughout 2015.[76] Still this was not enough. For more than a year, French Quarter homes and businesses were covered with signs that read "Caution: Walk in Groups. We ♥ the NOPD. We just need more."

During 2015, policing tactics old and new were instituted in the French Quarter. Sidney Torres provided more than $300,000 of seed money for the creation of a new private patrol, its structure modeled on his French Quarter garbage collection company that operated in a public–private partnership with the city.[77] The regular three-person patrol made up of off-duty NOPD officers who had arresting power, drove up and down the Quarter streets in GPS-tracked black Polarises with blue lights flashing. These private patrol officers were to break up undesirable behavior and respond to calls through an app that Torres made for people to report "suspicious activity."[78] In other words, the app conscripted everyday people into broken windows policing. The appeal of the app in the midst of the French Quarter anticrime frenzy, which was marketed just as much, if not more so, to tourists as residents, could not be denied. Within its first few months 9,800 people (double the population of the French Quarter) downloaded the app, and more than 3,000 reports were made, leading to 123 arrests.[79]

Yet against the notion that Torres was conducting a one-man crime-fighting crusade, popularized by the likes of the *New York Times*, was the reality that these policing developments happened under the umbrella of the French Quarter Management District (FQMD).[80] The Louisiana state legislature created the French Quarter Management District in 2007 to revitalize the French Quarter and address the post-Katrina and systemic issues confronting the neighborhood."[81] Tourism capitalists lobbied for the French Quarter Management District's creation to counter depictions of the French Quarter "as a place of lawlessness and despair." The area's tarnished, post-Katrina image was negatively affecting the number of tourists, conventioneers, and locals visiting the area, causing some restaurants and shops to permanently close their doors.

A political subdivision of the state of Louisiana, the FQMD is a business improvement district: a public–private partnership with the purpose of revalorizing a specific geographic area through a special taxing district.[82] The FQMD siphons off public tax dollars that their board—made up of French Quarter business owners and upscale neighborhood residents, with a few token appointments from the mayor's office and city council—then can spend with relatively little oversight.[83] For issues beyond the jurisdiction of the FQMD, the Board has the ear of elected officials, who are committed to keeping them content. The FQMD is an example of how contemporary neoliberal urban governance carves up political space to meet capital interests with minimal public accountability.

After a shooting on Bourbon Street in 2011, the FQMD formed a Security Task Force committee[84] to increase policing and surveillance in the name of protecting the tourism economy.[85] In their first years of operation, they successfully advocated for the passage of two criminal municipal ordinances. One to renew a youth curfew in the French Quarter, and the second to prohibit "aggressive solicitation" within the neighborhood. Although the antisolicitation ordinance was targeted at panhandling, its imprecise wording allowed it to also be directed against people whom police viewed as soliciting sex work.[86] Moreover the FQMD launched "SafeCam" in October 2012 for residents and businesses to register surveillance cameras with the NOPD. Between 2012 and 2015, SafeCam registered nearly 1,400 cameras, and the FQMD worked with the NOPD to expand it to a citywide program.[87]

The FQMD organized to expand police power amid the French Quarter crime panic. They quickly brought Torres's private security detail under their purview, using public funds funneled through the New Orleans Convention and Visitors' Bureau and the hotel self-assessment tax. The private patrol reported to the Security Task Force leadership in alignment with the Eighth District NOPD. However, the FQMD was not content to add a private security detail of three officers. They wanted the ongoing presence of state troopers in the French Quarter to supplement the NOPD. With the hotels' funding for state troopers ending at the new year, another financing plan was needed. The FQMD strategized with city leadership to put on the October 2015 ballot a proposal for the formation of an Economic Development District (EDD), with the exact boundaries of the FQMD and with the sole purpose of issuing a sales tax to fund public safety (map 6.1). This quarter-cent sales tax would finance thirty state troopers (with, at a minimum, seven patrolling at any time) and the operations of the French Quarter Security Task Force for five years. Proponents of the EDD predicted that the sales tax would generate $2 million a year. If passed, this revenue would be matched by annual allocations of $1 million from the Convention Center, $1 million from the New Orleans Convention and Visitors Bureau, and $500,000 from the city's portion of the hotel tax assessment revenue. Thus, if voters approved the EDD, $4.5 million would be pumped each year into intensifying French Quarter policing through 2020.[88]

Although only residents of the French Quarter could vote on the EDD, the outsized significance of the proposal meant that serious political capi-

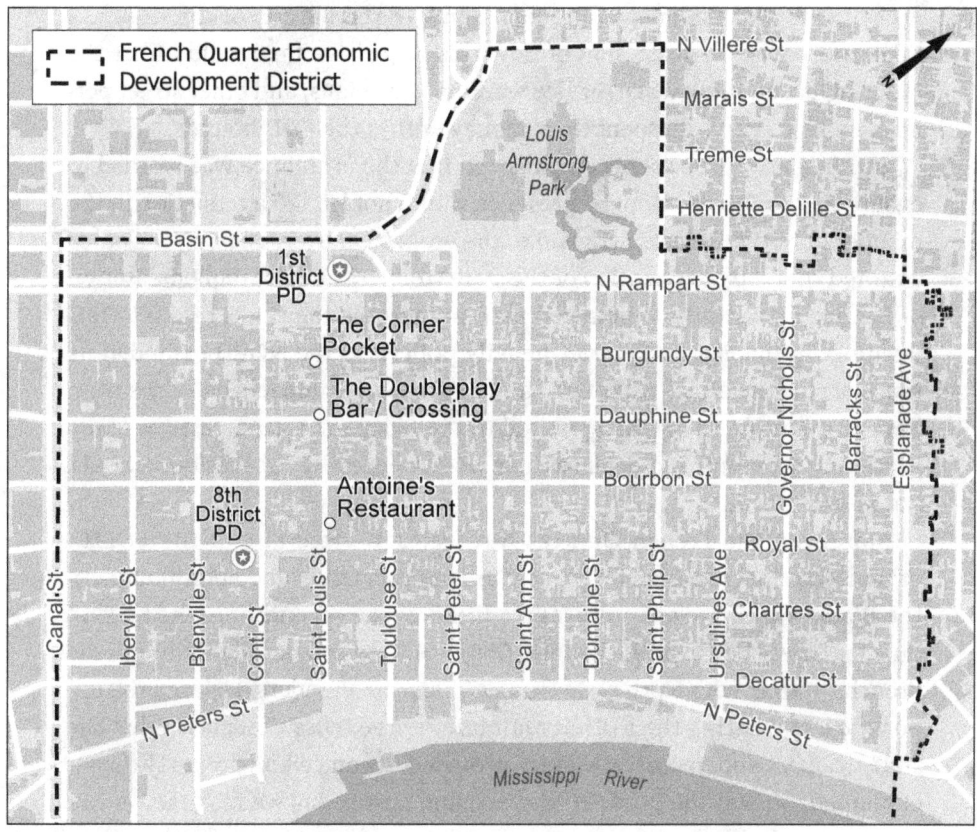

MAP 6.1 2016 French Quarter Economic Development District map. Prepared by Jeff Levy from the University of Kentucky Pauer Center for Cartography and GIS.

tal went into winning those residents' votes. It was endorsed by organizations representing tourism and other capital interests, including the French Quarter Business League, the New Orleans Business Council, the New Orleans Convention and Visitors Bureau, and the Louisiana Restaurant Association and by the daily newspaper, the *Advocate*.[89] The "nonpartisan" Bureau for Governmental Research praised the innovation of funding a public safety measure with sales tax, rather than a property millage, given that the primary beneficiaries of state troopers were out-of-town visitors, not residents.[90] The argument that the financial burden of the proposal primarily lay with tourists figured heavily in promotions of the tax. In the informational meeting held by the mayor's office and the FQMD to sway voters in favor of the EDD, it was repeatedly asserted that the primary targets of this quarter-cent sales tax would be visitors. Although it was acknowledged that

French Quarter residents would bear some of the burden of the sales tax hike, there was no discussion of how this regressive tax would affect the French Quarter's low-wage service workers, musicians, and other street performers who regularly spent their money within the EDD bounds.

Significantly, proponents emphasized that the ordinance was worded to ensure that the state troopers' presence would not lead to a reduction in the number of NOPD officers assigned to the French Quarter. The mayor's office asserted that the combination of the state troopers and the implementation of Landrieu's recently announced plan to increase the ranks of the NOPD would keep the French Quarter heavily policed as the NOPD extended its reach across the city.[91] Although the state troopers' impacts on crime were hard to quantify, the FQMD pointed to the troopers' 1,174 arrests over the preceding six months to declare their work a necessity that residents could not afford to end.[92]

Moreover, the French Quarter Advocates, a close ally of the FQMD, organized a "Second Line for Safety." An appropriation and abomination of the Black working-class cultural tradition of the second line, the Second Line for Safety began at the historic Congo Square and paraded through the French Quarter with a pro-state trooper message. Paraders declared the importance of creating the EDD in maintaining the *sense* of security that the state troopers and the private patrol provided. As one white property owner explained, "It was the Wild, Wild West, and now today we feel like we can go outside with the comfort knowing we have police security for the neighborhood."[93] Although the EDD proposal easily passed with 78 percent in favor, the low turnout for the election and the limited number of city residents eligible to vote on the EDD meant that fewer than one thousand people voted on an issue that would have citywide ramifications on policing.[94]

While the meetings of the Security Task Force are officially public, they are not held in a government building but in a backroom of Antoine's Restaurant—a site where the city's official and unofficial power brokers have made backroom deals since 1840. While tourists are served in the front dining room, the white elite of the city dine in the privacy of the various backrooms (some named for the city's exclusive and secretive Mardi Gras krewes). The Security Task Force holds most of its meetings during the break between lunch and dinner service in the Mystery Room, with its red walls covered in framed and yellowing twentieth-century news clippings. A projector is set up for presentations of maps and surveillance footage of crime "hot spots." At the center of the room is a long table where the ten or so active members of the Security Task Force discuss the security needs of the French

Quarter. On occasion an outsider like me can find a seat at the far end of the table, but typically the only space available is a chair in the corner.

During the period I actively attended their meetings, the Security Task Force members were all white French Quarter business or property owners in their forties to sixties.[95] Usually the only visible person of color in the room was a Black NOPD officer serving as a liaison for the Eight District. The typical patriarchal divisions of labor structured the meetings: men talked and suggested big ideas, while women took notes and spoke occasionally. Most meetings were run by Security Task Force chairman Bob Simms, a mild-mannered British man who since retirement had volunteered his time to coordinate the private detail. Most meetings were easygoing, moving between details of how many miles the Polarises were driven and how many arrests were made to visioning how to instill greater security in the Quarter.

The first time I attended one of the Security Task Force meetings I was well prepared to explain who I was and why I was there. But to my surprise no one seemed to notice me, even as I conspicuously scribbled field notes. It was not until the second meeting I attended that I was asked to sign in. The most attention I ever received was when one of the older white women smiled at me when I entered the room, a gesture that I imagined was based on our common identity markers and presumed shared politics. It seemed to be inconceivable to Security Task Force members that someone in attendance would be critical of their plans, but given the power and authority the FQMD wielded, that would not matter. On occasion, when French Quarter crime was in the news, the local TV news crews would film the Security Task Force meetings, but to my knowledge the only segment that ever aired was a very public clash between Bob Simms and Sidney Torres about the direction of the private patrol.[96]

Despite the easygoing camaraderie of the participants, enveloping these meetings was an affect of fear. Before attending their meetings, I thought that their gestures to public safety were a form of capitalist posturing. But once I was in the room with them, I realized that, more than their monthly statistics, it was their *feelings* that the French Quarter was dangerously out of control that shaped their initiatives.[97] Individuals frequently related that they would not take their trash out or walk their dogs after dark without being armed with a gun or mace. I was shocked hearing the type of street crime that they believed was likely to occur without their intervention: gun battles in Jackson Square, drive-by shootings between rival drug dealers, and terrorist attacks on Bourbon Street. These discussions would be humorous if not for the fact that their underlying fears and delusions were channeled into policing projects. Listening to them revealed the power that elite people's individualized feelings have over the direction of urban governance regimes, in contrast to the routine dismissal of survivors of police violence as "too emotional" in their demands for accountability and justice.

Security Task Force members unequivocally asserted that tighter security was needed to protect property values and the tourism economy. As the very business and property owners who stood to directly benefit from increased valorization of the French Quarter, I argue we can see the Security Task Force as an example of everyday racial capital organizing that, unlike community activist groups like BreakOUT!, had managed to obtain a piece of the state's monopoly on legitimate violence within a particular territory.[98] As Simms once stated, "We're all competing for customers but competition should stop in terms of security." This logic was condensed in a story, which I took to be an urban legend, that was related at multiple meetings. The story went that a family from Mississippi visiting New Orleans for the first time decided to take a walk on the Moonwalk, a broad walking path bordering the Mississippi River, when, in broad daylight, they were accosted by a shoeshine hustler.[99] After refusing to pay the hustler the few dollars he demanded, he threatened the family with a knife. While the family was lucky to be saved by a local passerby, they immediately got in their car and drove back home. Regardless of who recounted this story, the person always ended by noting that the family was likely to never come back to New Orleans. Such occurrences were "terrible for business."[100] Security Task Force members would then take pains to explain, to no one in particular, that protecting the French Quarter was not only critical to the city but also to the state because French Quarter tourist dollars were the engine of Louisiana's economy.

At the core of the FQMD's security strategies was a broken windows geographic imagination of disorder and crime. Admiration for Giuliani's neoliberal remaking of Times Square was regularly expressed by Security Task Force members. Former FQMD president Robert Watters would routinely assert that lawlessness had overtaken the French Quarter and trumpeted the need to "eradicate the systematic environment that creates crime in the French Quarter." The "criminogenic environmental factors" that the task force members believed produced lawlessness in the French Quarter were the keywords of broken windows policing: noise, loitering, lack of streetlights, graffiti, drug use, and the visibility of homelessness and sex work. Security Task Force members fancied themselves experts in French Quarter street crime and discussed the need to teach out-of-town state troopers about quality-of-life issues—from street artists selling their work outside designated locations or homeless people sleeping in doorways that were the first signs of a "broken window." Their sense of the power of small-scale rule enforcement went as far as them suggesting that if they could get bars to instill dress codes, social order would follow. Security Task Force members were clear that stopping people for such small infractions was also a strategy for identifying people with outstanding warrants and sending them to jail.[101]

Key to their policing tactics was tackling "problem blocks." Parroting CompStat policing logic, Bob Simms began almost all meetings by outlining the previous month's problem blocks, using maps and surveillance footage to highlight which areas were cause for concern. Over the months I attended the meetings, the location of the problem blocks hardly ever changed: the 800–1000 blocks of Bourbon Street, the 100 and 200 blocks of Royal Street, the 800–1000 blocks of St. Louis Street, and the area around Jackson Square. Security Task Force members contended that "all crime starts on Bourbon Street," and hence it was a crucial location for "proactive policing." Attendees often chimed in to list other areas where they had witnessed unwanted behavior—usually around their residences and businesses. The solutions rarely varied: have the private patrol visibly stationed on key corners with their blue lights flashing to deter crime and have the NOPD representative relay the issues to the Eighth District. The NOPD took the Security Task Force's desires seriously; often within the span of a single meeting, the NOPD officer would report that she had acquired a commitment from her commanding officers that an NOPD patrol would be assigned to the problem areas.[102] Law enforcement saturation demonstrated to visitors the city's investment in public safety.

Unlike Torres's initial conception of the private security detail as an alternative to the NOPD, the FQMD understood their private patrol to be at its best when flanking the NOPD. A slide often included in Simms's PowerPoint presentations read, "ONE TEAM: NOPD/LSP/FQSTF." As Simms explained, "We didn't start this patrol because cops are corrupt but because there are not enough of them." The Security Task Force maintained that the private security detail was most effective when it deferred to the NOPD leadership. Sharing information between the private detail reduced the NOPD and state troopers' response times, and armed robbery rates went down. At several meetings, people brainstormed ways to work more closely with

Homeland Security and the ATC to strengthen surveillance and boost raids on targeted strip clubs in the name of combating sex trafficking.

At the same time, the Security Task Force was frustrated about how policing and jailing reforms limited the scope of their security measures. They acknowledged that they had attached the EDD public safety tax to the state troopers, rather than the NOPD, to remove French Quarter policing from the limitations of the NOPD consent decree; yet other reforms were harder to subvert. They bemoaned that the NOPD was still subject to a rule put in place during Chief Pennington's tenure that prohibited NOPD officers from working off-duty security at bars. Their biggest frustration was that since OPP had downsized, police officers and state troopers were more hesitant to arrest people for quality-of-life offenses. They met with Sheriff Gusman to see what could be done to make more space for the people arrested in the French Quarter.

This is not to say that the Security Task Force members did not have their own visions for enhancing policing in the French Quarter. Extending surveillance and other big data policing technologies was central to their work of investigating and preventing crime. As noted earlier, coordinating private surveillance camera registrations with the NOPD was one of the Security Task Force's first projects. Over the course of 2015 and 2016, the Security Task Force advocated for the implementation of a more extensive surveillance camera system to make sure the French Quarter was "blocked in effectively." It would integrate people's personal surveillance cameras feeds, including those located inside people's homes, into the NOPD's system.

Yet the major surveillance plan the Security Task Force advocated was the installation of license-plate reader cameras along the perimeter of the French Quarter. The license-plate readers would tie into a statewide system used to track cars identified as being connected to criminal activity. Although such an idea had long been discussed, it was only with the updating of the streetcar line on Canal Street and construction of the new streetcar line on N. Rampart Street that there was the necessary fiber-optic infrastructure. By capturing the license plates of cars driving in and out of the French Quarter, the police would be able to tell whether a car was stolen or otherwise on record as being involved in another crime. The cameras could potentially capture footage of people leaving the French Quarter who were "fleeing the scene of a crime." The city easily approved the perimeter camera program, given the neighborhood's status as "critical city infrastructure." Before long, Security Task Members were working with the NOPD, state troopers, and Homeland Security to identify camera placements.[103] Although Security Task Force members recognized that some people might be worried about the privacy impacts of these surveillance system, they dismissed that potential unease as secondary to security needs. And when the Security Task Force member spearheading the expansion of the camera program stated that, even if it was Big Brother-esque, "safety is safety," the whole room nodded in agreement.

The where and the how of the Security Task Force's policing program were relatively straightforward: the question of *who* they were policing was more fraught. The task force was clear that although tourists partook in many of the behaviors—loitering, drug use, hiring sex workers—that they believed served as the nefarious "broken window," it was not tourists' behavior that was alarming. Rather it was the presence of the people the Security Task Force members named as "undesirables"—homeless people, gutter punks, street-based sex workers, "transgenders," and, to some extent, street musicians and performers—that the task force worked to criminalize. Central to their understanding of social order was the displacement of certain types of people (Black, poor, deviant, local, criminal) so that other people (tourists, white, middle class, law-abiding) people could arrive. The FQMD's commitment to pushing out those engaged in criminalized economic activity (hustling, panhandling, drug dealing, escort work) or legal economic activity outside the vision of the FQMD (dive bar stripping, busking musicians) through policing can be understood as yet another post-Katrina round of accumulation by dispossession.[104]

The Security Task Force was most explicit about wanting to remove homeless people from the French Quarter. This emphasis was not surprising, given the history of tourism gentrification projects seeking to decontaminate urban space from the specter of poverty.[105] When describing problem blocks, task force members commonly described them as a "bumfest," and the lion's share of app reports were regarding homeless people. In addition to directing the private detail and other police to arrest homeless people, the task force worked to make the neighborhood inhospitable to them. They convinced the city to remove newspaper stands because of homeless people's tendency to lean and congregate around them. The Security Task Force also replaced the trashcans that were fairly easy to retrieve food scraps from with "green" and "animal proof" trashcans from which it was next to impossible to extract anything without a key. Even though public drinking is legal throughout the city, the FQMD sought to restrict homeless people's ability to buy "to go" drinks within the Quarter. Having identified that most homeless people bought their alcohol from the only major grocery store in the French Quarter, the task force unsuccessfully attempted to persuade the store managers to make it a store policy to prohibit the selling of alcohol to homeless people.

Still, Security Task Force members did not want to appear too harsh against "deserving" homeless people. In conversations about policing homelessness, they would often clarify that "we should have our sympathies for real homeless people" and that public safety issues were primarily caused by those they deemed undeserving: panhandlers "whose job it is to come down to the quarter to do this" and then "they go back to a home to a house paid for by taxpayers," and "true vagrants" or gutter punks whose housing insecurity was a "lifestyle choice." Although their vitriol against unworthy homeless people materialized in criminalization, their sympathies for the deserving homeless also resulted in displacement. Over several meetings, they strategized how to convince the city to open a low-barrier homeless shelter. For them, such an institution could handle the needs of homeless people, particularly those suffering from mental illness, in a contained environment away from tourists. This solution was not only limited insofar as it did not address any of the underlying issues that produce homelessness, such as the lack of affordable housing, living-wage work, and mental health care in New Orleans, but it also neatly aligned with the carceral logic of jailing. The fix to complex social and economic problems was the creation of more institutionalized spaces to warehouse surplus populations.[106] One of the officials they primarily partnered with on this shelter was Sheriff Gusman.

Although less overt, the Security Task Force also focused on policing deviant gender and sexuality that they believed tarnished the reputation of the French Quarter. Getting rid of sex work in the French Quarter was one of their specific objectives. When task force members anecdotally recounted the issues they confronted around their homes and businesses, they often pointed to the prevalence of "hookers and pimps" on the street. At one meeting, Simms ran through a series of surveillance photos to demonstrate the success of the private detail officers in preventing someone perceived to be a sex worker from soliciting on a street corner. And when a local restaurant owner came to a task force meeting to report stories of sex workers "preying on tourists" around her restaurant, the task force and the NOPD coordinated a sting operation on sex workers in the area.[107] Furthermore, task force members, including former FQMD president Robert Watters, the owner of several French Quarter strip clubs, were encouraged when they heard the ATC was planning to raid unwanted strip clubs to root out sex trafficking.

Closely connected to the policing of sex work was the task force's targeting of queer people and places. On multiple occasions, members alluded to the late-night problems caused by "transgenders," whom they often figured as being of color and housing-insecure. The members presumed that trans people's assumed engagement with sex work and drugs scared away tourist dollars while lowering their own property values. The task force was also fixated on policing known queer areas of the French Quarter. Although never explicitly identified as such, the majority of the "problem blocks" that the task force discussed were those home to gay bars. These areas included both the greatest concentration of gay bars in the French Quarter, colloquially known as "gay Bourbon," and blocks of working-class dive bars. Two queer dive bars, located down the street from one another, were deemed as bookending the worst area within the French Quarter: the Corner Pocket, known for its male strip shows, and the Double Play, which catered to a customer base of people of color, trans women, and drag queens. Task force members routinely complained that these bars were an "incubator for prostitution and drugs" and spent considerable time brainstorming how to shutter them while stationing security details on these corners. Their inability to force the bars to close, at least at the time of this writing, is suggestive of the FQMD's limits despite their power.

Yet race and racism remained the most coded elements of the task force's policing efforts. One of the few times racism was directly referenced was by Bob Simms and others, when they expressed dismay that their app seemed to be used as a tool for racial profiling in that Black people congregating was repeatedly reported as "suspicious activity." Yet this app usage was not only unsurprising but also predictable. Simone Browne reminds us that "enactments of surveillance reify boundaries, borders, and bodies along racial lines . . . where the outcome is often discriminatory treatment of those who are negatively racialized by such surveillance."[108] Not only the app and the surveillance cameras but also all the work of the FQMD was shaped by an anti-Black imaginary of who was in and out of place in the French Quarter. It takes no stretch of the imagination to recognize that the criminalized figures the FQMD sought to displace—the street hustler, the homeless person, the sex worker, and the trans woman—were coded as Black in the minds of task force members. Even if they were not, it is impossible to imagine that they were not so coded in the minds of the NOPD and the state troopers on whom the task force relied. As BreakOUT! showed, it was often through supposedly race-neutral policing practices such as the targeting of sex workers that New Orleans law enforcement engaged in anti-Black racist profiling.

The only time I witnessed task force members unambiguously turn to racism in their explanation of disorder and crime in the French Quarter was through xenophobic discourse during a brainstorming session about how to rein in the sex work happening around the Corner Pocket and Double Play bars. After someone suggested asking taxi drivers to keep watch on the area, the idea was quickly shot down: they were "untrustworthy" because they are the ones "who pick up the prostitutes from the bar all the time." In addition, given that taxi drivers were mostly "aliens," they should be deported for engaging in such criminal activity. The ease with which the task force members rendered taxi drivers as deceitful immigrants who had no right to stay in the United States, regardless of their actual citizenship status, pointed to the underlying ideology of the FQMD that people of color were not to be trusted in the French Quarter and that the Security Task Force had the right to criminalize and banish them to secure the sanctity of the tourist economy.

It was only a matter of time until the FQMD had to grapple with statistics showing that the correlation between the security detail and the state troopers' presence and the crime rate was not as linear as they had assumed it would be.[109] Bob Simms conceded that even when the French Quarter was officially getting safer, "crime was actually just being pushed around" to the adjoining neighborhoods. Yet this did not change the FQMD's position on policing. For the task force, the answer was increasing policing saturation throughout the city. They backed a proposed property tax that Mayor Landrieu put on the ballot to fund the expansion of the NOPD in the spring of 2016. Given that the state trooper plan had always been viewed as a temporary solution, it is not surprising that the FQMD backed Landrieu's vision of police expansion.

Mayor Landrieu proposed a "public safety" millage to fund his police expansion program, "Operation Relentless Pursuit." Even though Landrieu had already allocated the city's first surplus funds in years to increasing the NOPD's 2016 budget by $10.5 million and relaxed the recruitment standards for NOPD officers, it was still not enough. Landrieu argued that beefing up the NOPD from 1,100 to 1,600 officers, a 40 percent increase, by 2020 would require a new dedicated funding source. If passed, the millage would direct $17.7 million a year into the NOPD's coffers.[110] Landrieu and the NOPD framed the public safety millage as about "rebuilding" the NOPD to where it was pre-Katrina. However, they elided that with New Orleans' 2016 population being 100,000 people lower than before the storm, the addition of 500 police officers would bring the NOPD to its highest-ever rate of officer to resident *and* almost double the national officer-to-resident rate.[111] Landrieu deliberately tied the policing millage to a millage to pay for the firefighters' pension fund after decades of the city underfunding it—a popular local issue.[112] With support from mainstream news and research centers, the public safety millage appeared to be an easy sell.[113]

On learning about the proposed new policing millage, BreakOUT! staff and I discussed potential opportunities for intervention. Although we assumed it would pass, we also knew that letting that happen without pushing against the narrative that more police equaled more safety would be a missed opportunity. However, BreakOUT! was busy with internal organizational work and could not do much more than talk about voting against it at various LGBTQ events and fundraisers. In conversation with BreakOUT! I decided to plan, in coordination with other groups, a political education event designed not only to encourage people to vote against the millage (most people did not even know there was an election scheduled) but also to provide a broader political education about the relationship between city taxes and racial justice and to deepen conversations about police abolition. Although the event had a low turnout, BreakOUT! staff and members and abolitionist organizer kai barrow held space to talk about policing innovations in the French Quarter, the impacts of hyper-policing on trans women of color, and how liberalism undermines liberatory movements.[114] Convinced that the event was a failure, I was surprised when a FAQ sheet I made on the policing tax went viral on social media—partially due to BreakOUT! including it in an email blast—and was referenced in an alternative paper's voter guide.

Another surprise followed when the policing millage was handily defeated. Although 62 percent of white New Orleanians voted in favor of the policing tax, only 38 percent of Black New Orleanians did.[115] I do not wish to suggest that our small efforts flipped the election—people's general aversion to property taxes likely influenced voters more than antipolice politics—yet it was reassuring that even with all the carceral strategizing of the mayor and groups like the FQMD, residents still were not convinced to invest their resources in expanding the NOPD.[116]

FIGURE 6.3 #BlackTransLivesMatter billboard above BreakOUT! office, 2015. Photograph by Wesley Ware. Courtesy of the photographer.

Demanding Life: From #BlackTransLivesMatter to Vice to ICE

On a chilly February day in 2015, I was driving to the BreakOUT! office to conduct an interview when I received the text message, "We need to reschedule the interview. Death in community in NOLA." Less than two hours later, I received in my email a press release about how another young Black trans woman, Penny Proud, was found dead and that we must remember #BlackTransLivesMatter. Before long, BreakOUT! erected a billboard on top of their office building, facing a heavily trafficked thoroughfare (figure 6.3). Along with an image of Penny Proud, the billboard read, "10 Transgender Women have been murdered so far in 2015. Invest in jobs, housing, and education to keep us safe." BreakOUT! soon organized the NOLA Trans March not only to call attention to the epidemic of murders committed against trans women but also to ask the question, What were the conditions of possibility for Black trans life?

While tourism capitalists organized to enhance policing in the French Quarter, BreakOUT! entered a new phase of activism that illuminated how the net of criminalization cut short the lives of Black trans girls. Black trans girls had always been one of its principal constituencies, but at this time BreakOUT! unapologetically foregrounded their experiences. With its activism focusing on police violence, BreakOUT! also broadly worked to end the criminalization of LGBTQ youth. This meant not only confronting the state violence of the criminal legal system but also responding to how gendered and sexualized racial criminalization limited people's access to material resources of housing, healthcare, education, and employment and undermined people's emotional well-being. BreakOUT! asserted that Black trans liberation necessitated not only the denaturalization of Black trans death but also an investment in Black trans social reproduction through the construction of more livable worlds.[117] Through this program building, they called attention to the fact that ending the state violence of criminalization fundamentally necessitated "far more than the individual liberty to access urban resources" but also "the exercise of a collective power to reshape the processes of urbanization."[118] Their lives depended on a right to a dignified place in New Orleans—not as how it was but how it could be.

BreakOUT!'s insistence that Black trans life could not and would not be reduced to the tragedy of premature death was situated within two national political developments: the rising political visibility of Black trans women and the emergence of the Black Lives Matter movement. The case of CeCe McDonald, a young Black trans woman who was imprisoned for defending herself from a racist and transphobic attack, gained national attention through grassroots organizing.[119] Concurrently, Black trans women Janet Mock and Laverne Cox were afforded celebrity status and used their platforms to speak out against transphobia, racism, and violence targeted at trans women of color.[120] Simultaneously an affirmation and a political demand, Black Lives Matter—developed by Black feminists in response to George Zimmerman being found not guilty for the murder of Trayvon Martin—was catapulted into a national movement after the uprising of the people of Ferguson, Missouri, against the police murder of Mike Brown.[121] Over 2014 and 2015, protests erupted throughout the nation as the death toll of Black people killed at the hands of law enforcement continued and the Black Left built out the movement infrastructure.[122] Embedded in national movement currents, BreakOUT! was shaped by and extended such political analyses and organizing strategies.

Out of this political moment and their previous organizing, BreakOUT! developed activism around #BlackTransLivesMatter. Whereas the Movement for Black Lives foregrounded feminist and queer politics, BreakOUT! felt more attention needed to be given to the plight of Black trans women both locally and nationally. As Milan Sherry recounts, although she identified with Black Lives Matter, she wondered where was the place for Black trans women:

> When we talk about Black Lives Matter, do we mean Black lives, Black trans lives? . . . Trans women are being murdered at a terrible rate. Each and every year it seems like the number goes up. And we're already at 22 trans women of color being murdered this year, and one even being from New Orleans who went by the name of Penny Proud. So I lift her up and I bring her into this room, along with London Chanel and Kristina Grant and Papi Edwards and Tiffany Edwards and Ty Underwood. I bring all those women into this room because those women were silenced by violence. At the end of the day when we talk about as far as Black Trans Lives Matter, we just don't really just talk about those women or individuals who have been murdered. We talk about those individuals who committed suicide. We talk about ourselves, those that are still living that are still fighting. That are still out surviving.[123]

For Sherry, the different degrees of outrage elicited by the extralegal and state killings of Black men versus the murders of Black trans women spoke volumes about the valuation of Black trans women's lives even within antiracist movements. Fully accounting for the epidemic of Black trans premature death necessitated a reckoning with the matrix of systems that devalued Black trans life—from carceral violence to the lack of gender-affirming healthcare, housing security, and employment. Too often anti-Black and antitrans violence overshadowed the multifaceted and resourceful strategies that Black trans women employed to survive and thrive. In the words of C. Riley Snorton, the power of Black Trans Lives activism emerged from its "invest[ment] in securing the existence of black and trans people in the present and the future . . . a demand for new structures for naming that evince and eviscerate the conditions that continually produce black and trans death."[124]

BreakOUT! channeled these frustrations into a Trans March of Resilience (TMOR). As Sherry explained to me, the march was planned to move beyond the long-standing Trans Day of Remembrance, which was typically characterized by "folks holding vigils, and reading names off of the list of the trans women that were murdered that year. But there was no change really being created. If anything, it was very depressing, it was very traumatizing, so this year we wanted to . . . take it to the streets to do the Trans

March of Resilience to let the world know, to let New Orleans know, what this day is for us—a recognition of our resistance and resilience."[125] In addition to a march, there was a week of activities including a panel discussion, a graduation for the Building Our Power cohort, and a healing justice drum circle at Congo Square. This week of action did not dwell in the space of spectacularized violence and death but highlighted that if "antitrans violence is also and always already an articulation of antiblackness," trans liberation and Black liberation were intrinsically interdependent.[126]

The panel discussion, "My Existence Is Political: Talking Trans," kicked off the week of activities. A collaboration between BreakOUT! and Women with a Vision, the panel discussed the limits of representational politics. BreakOUT! member Lhundyn Palmer brought up the conundrum that "trans is trending." On one hand, trans people were gaining greater visibility and thus more attention to their experiences of violence. On the other hand, organizations without any previous commitments to fighting transphobia were incorporating a token trans person into their organization just to gain access to new foundation funding. In Sherry's words, "We're either a token or a trophy." Visibility did not ensure valuation. Woven into this panel discussion was BreakOUT!'s contention that racial and economic justice needed to be at the center of movements for trans liberation. At some point, Sherry remarked whether one could consider Caitlyn Jenner a role model as one might count Laverne Cox, given that Jenner's life trajectory as a rich white person did not reflect their life experiences. Unlike them, Jenner never had to engage in sex work or pick pockets to survive, and she had access to healthcare that allowed her to transition at home, while girls on the street were pumping black-market silicone and dying in motel rooms.[127] Jenner's recognition as a trans celebrity did not translate into advancement for the greater collective.

At the TMOR rally and march, BreakOUT! highlighted the conditions that undermined the lives of Black trans people while also affirming trans resilience. Close to 150 people gathered at Congo Square to join BreakOUT!'s call on the city to make Black Trans Lives Matter.[128] Sherry asked the crowd, "What's the problem? Are we the problem?" To which people shouted back, "Racism, patriarchy, transphobia, police violence." Sherry stated that the purpose of the march and rally was to change the narrative that trans people were problems to be fixed to highlighting the root problems that needed to be transformed. Sherry invited participants to second line to City Hall and rejoice in Black trans resistance. BreakOUT! led the march with a banner that read, "How can I walk down the aisle when I can't walk down the street?" and "Give us our roses while we are still here." BreakOUT! incorporated immigration justice into TMOR, and their comrades at Congreso served as protest marshals. As the day of the march was also a day for national antideportation actions, Congreso and BreakOUT! distributed "Not1More" signs—equally fitting calls against the Obama deportation regime and against Black trans premature death.

At City Hall, BreakOUT! presented their "Platform for a Safer City" that outlined what was needed for trans and gender-nonconforming youth of color to walk down the street without fear: employment and housing programs, an end to discriminatory policing by all law enforcement, a smaller and safer jail, an end to immigrant detention and deportations, the repeal of laws criminalizing HIV, and the promotion of safe and affirming schools.[129] In other words, it called for a fundamental restructuring of city priorities and investments. While BreakOUT! organizers took the platform to the offices of the mayor and city councilors to ask them to sign on, other BreakOUT! leaders asked marchers to participate in a die-in for the twenty-two trans people who had been killed during the past year. As people lay down on the sidewalk, BreakOUT! staff outlined people's bodies in chalk for City Hall officials to see that day. When BreakOUT! organizers returned, it was announced that the city council had proclaimed today would be recognized as the Trans March of Resilience, which was celebrated even though it was not matched by a commitment to any of their demands in their platform.

The ethos of investing in life over death went beyond this week of activities to infuse BreakOUT!'s programs. As organizer Jai Shavers explained, BreakOUT!'s work became focused on "not only what criminalization and what policing issues folks were facing, but also what folks needed, what folks wanted as the alternative to that, and what would actually make folks feel safe. . . . Out of that we got jobs, education, and housing. Following up on that is us wanting to go deeper into each of those, figuring out what is wrong with jobs, education. and housing for LGBTQ youth of color specifically. Why aren't those resources available?"[130] Part of BreakOUT!'s strategy was a harm-reduction approach of working with institutions to be more inclusive of LGBTQ youth. Staff facilitated workshops with local schools to stem school pushouts and the school-to-prison pipeline and met with homeless shelters to offer advice on how to be more welcoming for LGBTQ youth of color.

In addition to these external interventions, BreakOUT!'s created programs to meet its members' material and emotional needs, which echoed the Black Panther Party's survival pending revolution work. In creating spaces for members' social reproduction in tandem with contesting criminalization and other forms of state violence, BreakOUT! sought to engender a collective future for trans and queer youth of color. At the same time, that BreakOUT! felt the need to fill such gaps in the social infrastructure indexed the racialized and gendered impacts of neoliberal restructuring in New Orleans. It is not hard to draw a straight line between the lack of state investment in relevant public education, living-wage work, gender-affirming mental and physical healthcare, public transportation, and affordable housing and BreakOUT!'s development of a high school equivalency program, or their policy of paying members for their labor on behalf of the group, or its coordination of volunteer-provided transportation to meetings and events. BreakOUT! even discussed buying property that could serve as housing for members, going so far as looking into buying a motel on Tulane Avenue.

BreakOUT!'s POSH Academy exemplified their approach to meeting LGBTQ youth of color's needs in the face of a woefully inadequate school system. Almost the entire public school system in New Orleans was unilaterally converted into an atomized charter school network with no public accountability in the aftermath of Hurricane Katrina. In that system Black youth were subjected to overly harsh and punitive discipline processes that reentrenched and extended preexisting racist practices of school-based criminalization.[131] Such discipline policies also harshly punished LGBTQ youth for transgressing gender norms and other infractions; this was often the beginning of their members' experiences of criminalization.[132] Although many members wanted to attain their high school diploma through the High School Equivalency Exam (HiSET), the prohibitive costs, combined with the transphobia and homophobia pervading most HiSET classes, proved a barrier to LGBTQ youth of color. For these reasons, BreakOUT! decided to start POSH Academy, a free HiSET program to provide small classes and individual support to BreakOUT!'s members.

Along with starting POSH Academy, BreakOUT! created temporary and part-time work opportunities for members, many of whom were short on cash. Having paid work provided financial support in addition to serving as a form of job training and a way to flesh out their resumes. Moreover, paying people for their labor was politically important as a model of refuting the normalization of economic exploitation and dispossession that members experienced as LGBTQ people of color.[133] Some of these opportunities were short term, such as paying members to collect surveys for national research projects, whereas other work assignments lasted several months. For example, by 2015 the Building Our Power (BOP) program had grown into a robust multi-month political education and development program with defined cohorts. Everyone in BOP received a stipend for participation, and in turn each cohort collectively fundraised for the next cohort's stipends. BOP graduates could also apply to help coordinate future BOP cycles as paid interns. These forms of paid work were also a pathway for some members to be hired as full-time staff.

This materialist analysis also informed BreakOUT!'s healing justice work. Given members' experiences confronting racism, homophobia, and transphobia; being profiled and abused by the NOPD; serving time in jail and prison; and living housing- and job-insecure lives, BreakOUT! knew that emotional healing and care were vital. As BreakOUT!'s first healing justice coordinator Nia Faulk describes it, healing justice

> is the cycle that there is trauma you've been through, you've identified the trauma. You've figured out what the needs [are] from that. You've found multiple pathways to healing and then you shared back to the community. So, no one's pain and trauma is alone or solo. Healing justice is a set of practices, ideas, and values that centers the wholeness of ourselves, our communities, and the earth. Healing justice organizing is the strategic use of these practices . . . to bring it back into the community so we all have pathways to be whole.[134]

Building on the more informal knitting circles and the somatics work of BreakOUT!'s early days, Faulk created the Healing as Resistance Together program for members to build relationships and affirm their worth. After members shared that it was important that their healing organizing had a paid component, Faulk set up a system of fundraisers with highly resourced organizations and used those funds to pay members to organize monthly healing justice nights on topics such as self-defense or crystals. For Faulk what was most important was not the specific topics but "about us coming together, having fun, telling our stories, and healing from the shit that has happened in the past but also getting paid and being able to see ourselves of worthy of that pay. Inherently valuable."[135] Part of healing justice's appeal was its resonance with witchy queer culture. This appeal to magic was more than an escapist fantasy: it was about BreakOUT! adopting a politic that encompassed both the necessity of dismantling systems of state violence *and* the importance of building up other forms of collective power.

As Faulk shared, it was "about building power internally and once that power is so strong no one can deny it . . . The bigger magic that is who we are."[136]

BreakOUT!'s insistence on life was never solely limited to contesting the criminalization of Black LGBTQ youth but also encompassed coalition-building with other communities targeted by state violence. Within BreakOUT!'s first year, they developed an alliance with the Congreso de Jornaleros, which initially comprised mostly straight and cisgender Central American men, many were undocumented and working in the reconstruction.[137] BreakOUT! and Congreso organizers brought their members together to learn about their distinct yet overlapping experiences of racist criminalization under the banner of "Vice to ICE." Although at first it might appear surprising that undocumented cisgender and straight adults would be those with whom BreakOUT! most closely aligned, I argue that it makes sense from the vantage point of radically expansive queer politics. BreakOUT! and Congreso's movement-building was rooted in a joint recognition of their "shared marginal relationship to dominant power" as criminalized populations in the post-Katrina political economy.[138]

Through story circles and other sharing exercises, BreakOUT! and Congreso members identified similarities among themselves and deepened their collective understanding of criminalization as a strategy of social control. Often, there was a language barrier between the two groups, and so organizers served as interpreters and developed strategies for nonverbal communication. Whereas many BreakOUT! members' ancestors built the city of New Orleans while enslaved centuries ago, many Congreso members rebuilt the city after the storm. But as soon as their labor was no longer needed, they were pushed out of the city through criminalization, arrest, incarceration, and deportation. Latinx people were always presumed to be undocumented; Black trans girls were always presumed to be sex workers. Moreover, because often the primary forms of labor available to them were criminalized, both groups were vulnerable to wage theft. And they both struggled to acquire proper identification that reflected who they were, which made it more difficult to find safe and secure housing. Importantly both groups drew on long histories of their people's resistance to fuel and shape their contemporary activism.

Through this recognition of their linked struggles, BreakOUT! and Congreso collaborated in public organizing. Sometimes this took the form of just speaking up for each other. For instance, at a city council hearing on whether OPP's bed cap should be lifted, BreakOUT! spoke out against the sheriff detaining immigrants while Congreso contended that city funds could be better spent on jobs, housing, and education for LGBTQ youth. Congreso also helped make the protest art for the Trans March of Resilience, while BreakOUT! coordinated a wellness team for Congreso members who blockaded the streets outside the regional ICE office to protest raids and deportations during the summer of 2015. They also prioritized joyful relationship-building such as through dance-offs.

As BreakOUT!'s relationship with Congreso deepened, they started to build relationships with the local queer and trans Latinx community. At one point, one of the Congreso members reached out to BreakOUT! for help when her trans daughter—Arely Westley—ended up getting locked up. BreakOUT! supported the family in navigating the case while BreakOUT! members started writing letters to Westley.[139] On her release, Westley got involved with BreakOUT! Through participating in general meetings and BOP, Westley "started to learn and see everyday issues with both of my communities, Latinx and LGBT." She soon got "involved with issues dealing with criminalization and discrimination because I didn't want youth of my age [to] have to face what I was facing."[140]

Before long, Westley was hired as the Vice to ICE organizer to develop and deepen the work between BreakOUT! and Congreso. Westly not only served as a liaison between the two organizations but also deepened BreakOUT!'s political education around immigration and deportations. She connected non-Latinx staff and members to the vibrant and growing local LGBTQ Latinx community by bringing them to events such as the Latinx drag performance contest, Miss Primavera, and she encouraged her friends from the Latinx LGBTQ community to take part in BreakOUT!'s programs. While BreakOUT! had long talked about their work through the language of "youth of color," like most racial justice organizations in New Orleans, they had practiced their activism principally through the lens of anti-Black racism. Even as many people involved in BreakOUT! were open to it becoming a more explicitly multiracial organization, for others it was a stretch to reimagine the organization as both a Black and Brown space. Staff realized that more political education was needed on the distinctions between "immigrant," "Latinx," and "Spanish-speaking" while also being careful not to erase Black Latinx people. Westly began coordinating ESL classes for some of the new members, and monthly member meetings started to include simultaneous interpretation.

BreakOUT!'s move to turn the crisis of gendered and sexualized racist criminalization into an opening for multiracial organizing provides a glimpse into how new political solidarities can enliven our work of collective life-making and devise more free worlds.

・・・・・・

The election of Donald Trump to the US presidency in November 2016 promised a ramping up of state violence against communities of color, immigrants, poor and working-class people, and LGBTQ people in the name of securing the future of white supremacy, heteropatriarchy, and neoliberal class war. Like many grassroots organizations throughout the country, BreakOUT! triaged to face this emergency. They created a Trans Defense Fund and held free legal clinics for people to legally change their names and gender markers, move forward with immigration proceedings, and expunge arrest records. A few days after the election, BreakOUT! announced their refusal to stop fighting for a more free world:

> This is the time that we have all been building for. Whether we have been developing young leaders ready for a revolution, educating youth on skills to sustain themselves outside of the system, or creating avenues for people to own their power, this is what we have been building for. **We have been waiting for that moment, when the forces are all the way against us, when our backs are against the wall, when we are left with no other choice but to harness the strength of our ancestors and the knowledge from our work**. This is the time we activate those "superpowers." While no one, not even Trump, can predict the precise consequences of him being in office, we do know that it is time to exercise our **duty to fight for our freedom**, as all the reforms and changes we have so passionately worked for are in jeopardy of being destroyed.[141]

In direct contrast, Mayor Landrieu and the New Orleans city government responded to Trump's election by expanding the FQMD's initiatives and desires into a citywide program. During the week of Trump's inauguration, Landrieu and Governor John Bel Edwards announced a new $40 million security plan for New Orleans. Taking a cue from the ideas and practices of the FQMD's Security Task Force, the plan pledged to intensify surveillance and policing throughout the city. It included the installation of 240 surveillance cameras and 160 license-plate readers in twenty designated crime hot spots (including the French Quarter); the integration of private security cameras in the French Quarter and Central Business District into the NOPD's surveillance system; the development of a centralized NOPD command center to monitor the surveillance camera feeds 24/7; the enhancement of police patrols in the French Quarter; the construction of new street infrastructure on Bourbon Street to prevent terrorist attacks; restrictions on permitted activities at Jackson Square; and the requirement that all bars close their doors at 3 A.M. and install security cameras to feed into the NOPD Command Center.[142] Key to this plan was carceral cooperation between the FQMD, the NOPD, the Louisiana State Troopers, and DHS.

Public outcry in response to this plan called attention to the fact that, although such interagency policing programs and surveillance systems were already draconian under the Obama administration, such a program with Trump in the White House and Jeff Sessions as attorney general had the potential to be catastrophic to Black and immigrant communities in New Orleans. While organizing forced the city council to scrap portions of the plan (notably the requirement that bars install surveillance cameras), most of it has since been implemented, with blinking surveillance cameras located almost everywhere, reminding us that the neoliberal Democrats will never support oppositional movements for collective freedom.

BreakOUT!'s organizing points us to the liberatory possibilities of queer politics as called for by Cathy Cohen, "organized not merely by reductive categories of straight and queer, but organized instead around a more intersectional analysis of who and what the enemy is and where our potential allies can be found."[143] During their first five years, BreakOUT! built an organization grounded in the transformative politics of an intersectional and materialist Black trans feminism to contest the criminalization of LGBTQ youth of color, racial and gender police profiling, and state-sanctioned sexual violence. BreakOUT! not only achieved concrete wins that lessened the grip of the carceral state but also has asserted and affirmed the value of Black trans life in a city that renders such life disposable to the imperatives of gendered racial capitalism. Yet, although their victories point to the capacity of small grassroots organizations to curb police violence, the reality that these gains in dismantling the carceral state have not been matched by meaningful reinvestments in the social wage has meant that Black and Brown LGBTQ communities (among others) continue to be produced as surplus at alarming rates under the neoliberal tourist economy. The transformative politics of abolition urgently requires us to change that dynamic—to scale up our commitments both to dismantling state violence and to investing in collective public care as we seek to end premature death and celebrate the possibilities of life.

Conclusion
Making Freedom

....

History is made by a series of collective battles, now defeats, now victories.
—Peter Linebaugh

In April 2020, activists in dozens of cars with "Free Them All" signs taped to their windows circled the Orleans Justice Center, the Juvenile Justice Center, the New Orleans ICE Field Office, and City Hall.[1] Across the nation and world, organizers in similar protests were demanding the release of incarcerated people in the wake of the coronavirus pandemic. With prisons, jails, and detention centers poised to become epicenters of disease and premature death, New Orleans activists and advocates called on officials to release people from the jail and to curtail arrests. In a letter to elected officials, the Orleans Parish Prison Reform Coalition (OPPRC) and allies stated, "During hurricane Katrina, inmates were left for dead as water rose within the OPP. We fear that the coronavirus will make these groups' detention into a death sentence similar to the time when inmates were abandoned in OPP. You have the power to prevent this."[2] In linking the state's disregard for incarcerated life in the face of COVID-19 to the disposability of jailed people during Hurricane Katrina, organizers highlighted how the crisis at hand was part of a longer pattern of racist organized abandonment.[3] Calling on this knowledge, organizers pushed state officials to act differently this time: to put life over death.

To an extent, this organizing expanded freedom. While the number of releases granted and the restrictions put on arrests by state officials were more limited than organizers demanded, the New Orleans jail population soon hovered between 800 and 900—lower than it had been in decades.[4] This decline in incarceration combined with the dramatic municipal revenue shortages accompanying the pandemic shifted the political terrain around the addition of "Phase III" to OPP. In 2019, federal judge Lance Africk had aligned with Sheriff Gusman and ordered the city to build an eighty-nine-bed Phase III facility to incarcerate people with acute mental illness. City leaders initially agreed to this plan of increasing bed space while capping the number of people incarcerated in the jail to 1,250. However, after COVID-19's onset, city leaders argued that Phase III was a "waste of taxpayer dollars" and that Judge Africk did not have the authority to mandate a new jail facility.[5] The Phase III debate was central to the 2021 Orleans Parish sheriff's election. Gusman squared off against Susan Hutson, New Orleans's Independent Police Monitor, whose platform included opposition to Phase III. Hutson's defeat of Gusman was seen by many as a final defeat of the proposed facility. Yet despite the new sheriff being opposed to its construction, the federal judge continues to override her position and push for a new medical jail facility.[6]

This snapshot of struggles around the New Orleans jail amid the COVID-19 crisis exemplifies this book's recurring theme: what is deemed a crisis is a site of political struggle. For criminalized people and their loved ones, the onset of the pandemic was a crisis because they were rightfully concerned about prisons, jails, and detention centers turning into death camps. For many state officials, their understanding of the crisis was shaped both by narrow conceptions of public safety primarily defined through street violence and by concerns about the costs of incarceration following plummeting tourism sales taxes and state oil revenues in the spring of 2020.[7]

Differing conceptualizations of the crisis informed the solutions put forth. Antijail activists seized on this moment to advance decarceration. The national calls to "free them all" in the spring of 2020 did not appear out of thin air but emerged from the local and national political infrastructures that had been steadily built in the preceding years. Organizers mobilized for immediate releases while also leveraging the crises of the pandemic to push elected officials to roll back jail-building plans.

Turning such crises into opportunities for abolitionist organizing required activists to be prepared. They needed preexisting organizations to maneuver through, a solid analysis of likely state responses, and clear demands at the ready. A few months later, "free them all" organizing fed into the eruption of protests against police violence. Amid the uprisings against the police murders of George Floyd and Breonna Taylor, the long-standing abolitionist sensibility coalesced into the demand to defund the police. Like abolitionist organizing to free them all, activism to defund the police had roots in the articulation of groups such as Safe Streets/Strong Communities and BreakOUT! that increased safety would not come from more police but from increased investments in social institutions. Abolitionist organizers intervened in the crises of 2020 to undo long-standing carceral state violence and push for a reorganization of the political economy from profits and austerity to one invested in public care and collective life.

Yet, state responses to carceral crises continued to be informed by racist and neoliberal understandings of violence and safety. Since Arthur Mitchell, Hayes Williams, Lee Stevenson, and Lazarus Joseph filed their federal lawsuit to rein in the dehumanizing violence of Angola, state responses to conditions of confinement complaints have been uneven at best. On the one hand, liberal reformers pushed to increase funding and the capacity of jails and prisons in the name of restoring incarcerated people's constitutional rights. On the other hand, sheriffs and tough-on-crime policy makers learned to seize on federal lawsuits and consent decrees to justify their expansion of carceral facilities. Both camps justified incarceration over release, disavowing the possibility that the best condition for people was not to be confined at all. Moreover, federal judges' decisions in such cases were focused on bringing prisons and jails within constitutional standards rather than undoing the structural violence of incarceration. Assessing carceral harm and violence through the constitutional framework of "cruel and unusual" punishment is inherently limited: all punishment is, by definition, cruel, and what is considered unusual is not static but situated in time and space. What was once unusual—the prevalence of double bunking or life sentences or solitary confinement—can easily become commonplace and thereby fair and just under constitutional standards.

Yet at the same time, judges' decisions are based not only on their own reading of constitutional law but also on the maneuvers of other state and nonstate actors. Judicial mandates and allowances have been shaped by mobilizations from the Black freedom movement shifting the ideological terrain for judges to find for incarcerated plaintiffs in the 1950s and 1960s, the Louisiana Sheriffs' Association's lobbying to incarcerate immigrant detainees in parish jails in the 1980s, and the Congreso de Jornaleros's issuance of lawsuits in pursuit of ending ICE holds in the years after Katrina. Federal courts are a contradictory site of struggle. Indeed it was under the watchful eye of the federal courts that Louisiana was directed to modernize and increasingly expand prisons and jails—further ensconcing carceral infrastructures in the Louisiana landscape. The courts have been neither a savior nor a site to be abandoned but a locus of power to approach in tandem with targeting the different arenas of the state likely to be tasked with responding to their orders.

The Louisiana penal system has been and continues to be developed through various alignments and contestations among state sectors. Decisions regarding building a new prison or reforming the scope of law enforcement are routinely the domain of intersecting political bodies and individuals. This means, as I demonstrate over the course of this book, that multiscalar cooperation among municipal, parish, state, and federal agencies has been key in making Louisiana into a carceral state. And as the case of Phase III has highlighted, state officials are rarely in neat alignment. Sheriff Gusman's lobbying for Phase III to subvert the OPPRC bed-cap win was oriented toward the federal courts, because he argued this expansion was necessary to meet consent decree standards for prisoner medical care. Yet with funding and land use in the domain of city government, the mayor and city council also had a say, but their positions have not been fixed. A changing suite of politicians were elected during the years of the Phase III debate, while political alliances were made and broken. In these fissures, activists organized to defend previous material wins and to shift the terms of debate against jailing. This activism included the tactic of electoral organizing to replace Gusman with Hutson, based on the reasonable belief that without the Orleans Parish sheriff gunning for new jail construction, Phase III would be dead in the water. However, the fact this has not been the case brings into stark relief the limitations of electing so-called progressive carceral officials in halting the extension of punitive state violence.

Louisiana's carceral developments have many points of origin and regularly travel beyond the state's boundaries. Mayor Marc Morial and NOPD Superintendent Pennington adopted broken windows policing from New York City's Mayor Giuliani and Bill Bratton in the 1990s under the banner of the "Pennington Plan," which has since been exported to and applied in Puerto Rico.[8] Louisiana was an early innovator when it turned the temporary spatial fix of incarcerating state prisoners in parish jails to meet federal court mandates into a long-term geographic solution for prison overcrowding in the 1980s and 1990s. More and more states subsequently followed Louisiana's lead in relying on jailing infrastructure to manage their penal populations, shoring up a new norm in the US's carceral geography.

Grassroots organizers have leveraged various facets of the state against itself to rein in carceral state power and extend collective freedom. From BreakOUT!'s strategy of leveraging the DOJ's presence to reduce the NOPD's discretionary power to the Angola Special Civics Project's development of state legislation to chip away at life without parole sentencing, antiracist activists have been adept at instigating grassroots policy struggles that take advantage of the multifaceted nature of the state. At the same time, carceral states are agile and capacious. When a particular arena of punitive state capacity is limited by external or internal limits or pressures, policy makers have turned to other arenas and, at times, created new infrastructures—from the Department of Corrections and the state legislature turning to the parish jail system to maintain the incarceration of state prisoners amid overcrowding crises, to Sheriff Gusman turning to the federal courts when OPPRC's organizing pushed the city council to limit the capacity of OPP, to Mayor Landrieu bringing in the state troopers to police New Orleans following the DOJ consent decree. This dialectic of carceral state adaption and anticarceral contestations has required organizers to nimbly engage in multiscalar political struggles. For instance, after Safe Streets' organizing resulted in the creation of the Office of Independent Police Monitor, the police union lobbied the state legislature to undo it, compelling Safe Streets to pivot to state-level organizing to maintain its victory.

Moreover, whether a campaign is won or lost, the struggles surrounding it materially and ideologically shape the ground for future organizing. The various struggles to chip away at the criminal legal system—changing state and municipal sentencing laws, reorganizing the public defender's office, and decreasing the jail's size—have ensured that less people have spent time behind bars. This liberatory organizing has also shifted public discourse on the criminal legal system, sowing fertile terrain for heightened demands such as "free them all." Although such a demand has yet to be met, its wide circulation indexes an abolitionist shift in antiprison organizing and its growing presence in broader debates. Even though abolition remains marginal to formal power structures, the fight against mass incarceration has been pushed into the mainstream by various antiprison organizers over the last several decades. In 2017, Louisiana Governor John Bel Edwards championed a series of moderate criminal justice reform bills aimed at reducing Louisiana's state prison population and saving the state millions of dollars. Although the frequent overstating of the Edwards reforms and the widespread erasure of grassroots campaigns in propelling prison population drops may suggest a clear example of reformist co-optation, the passage of these laws also serves as a reminder of how oppositional activists have and can alter the grounds of political legitimacy and state power.[9] Navigating this contradiction of struggle is essential for assessing achievements and charting paths forward.

Acute crises in the carceral state are built on the long-standing crises of state racism and neoliberal restructuring that render certain segments of the population disposable to floods, pandemics, and more. The political project of criminalization dialectically justifies and intensifies racism. Black people (in particular, but not only) are marked as imprisonable, while caging is legitimized through characterizing the people behind prison walls as inherently inferior to those on the outside. The crises that facilitate and normalize premature death from jail medical neglect to police shootings are fundamentally tied to neoliberal policies and ideologies that fetishize individual responsibility and private gains at the expense of commitments to the public good. The ramping up of state spending on prisons and policing to secure "public safety" is sutured to disinvestment and rejection of the kinds of institutions and policies that are essential for collective security: hospitals and healthcare, flood infrastructures and climate change mitigations, affordable and safe housing, living-wage and dignified work, public education and childcare, among others.

The disparate investments that characterize law-and-order austerity in Louisiana illuminate the centrality of racial criminalization and carceral power to neoliberal restructuring. Punitive power has been and continues to be pivotal to the management of Louisiana's economy in periods of both prosperity and precarity. Through global, national, and local political economic contradictions and realignments, policy makers have tied Louisiana to the volatile industries of petrochemicals in tourism. In doing so, they have cut taxes on the wealthy while asserting that revenue needs will be primarily met by "outsiders": relatively low mineral revenues on petrochemical companies and high sales taxes on tourists. In reality, these policies have intensified regressive taxation overall while creating unnecessary fluctuations in state, parish, and municipal budgets. Moreover, the volatility of these economies, attacks on unionization, increased mechanization, cuts to welfare and other social programs, the expansion of low-wage tourism jobs, and more have made large sectors of Louisiana structurally under- and unemployed. Such economic policies intensify precarity, while prisons, jails, and policing become understood as the only legitimate sector to fund. Carceral institutions are positioned as critical to the regulation of racialized and gendered populations excluded from the formal labor market and displaced for speculative urban developments. This is why crises such as Hurricane Katrina and COVID-19 turned into disasters for Louisiana broadly and New Orleans more specifically. It is also why seemingly mundane questions of fiscal policy and economic development are key arenas for abolitionist politics. For example, the intertwining of bond markets, water infrastructure, and criminalizing regimes made headlines in 2022. After the overturning of

Roe v. Wade, which triggered the state's total abortion ban, the New Orleans city government announced it would not enforce the criminalization of abortion. In response, Louisiana's right-wing attorney general Jeff Landry led the Louisiana Bond Commission in blocking the financing of upgrades to the New Orleans water, drainage, and sewage systems as punishment.[10] Although this decision was rescinded after widespread outcry against the "politicization" of bonds, it serves as a reminder that what a state decides to finance and how—whether hospitals or jails, schools or prisons—is always a political decision.[11]

Even as Louisiana activists have won significant reforms to decrease the number of people targeted for policing and imprisonment, the fact that neoliberal governance continues to reign supreme means that large swaths of Louisiana residents remain vulnerable to death-dealing crises of all kinds. So long as state governance is oriented toward facilitating capital accumulation predicated on the deepening of racialized and gendered economic inequality, rather than ensuring people's stability, health, and well-being, countless Louisianans will be produced as surplus criminalized populations.

In other words, the racial logics of disposability, extraction, and dispossession are at the core of the twinned projects of neoliberal economics and mass incarceration. This fact entails two further truths: one, dismantling mass criminalization is vital to any social movement committed to the end of neoliberalism and, more broadly, capitalism; and two, although ending racial capitalism does not necessitate the abolition of prisons and police, prisons and police cannot be abolished without the end of racial capitalism.

Abolitionist Infrastructures

Abolition is a world-making project. Striving to unmake carceral geographies requires a reconstruction of political, economic, and social structures toward collective freedom. If racism is the production of premature death, then the antiracist project of abolition is fundamentally a project of fostering collective life. Through engagement in place-making practices, abolitionists strive to build a world where they and others, known and unknown, are free to live longer and fuller lives.[12] Yet like all antiracist world-making projects, from the underground railroad and Black Reconstruction to the decolonization of the Global South, abolition is made through the development of political infrastructures to counter and replace the prevailing systems of racial capitalism and state violence.[13]

The realization of abolition geographies is, by definition, long-haul work. Building abolitionist infrastructures is not quick and tidy but an iterative process that is adaptive to shifting political conditions and local contexts. With those facts in mind, I offer that abolitionist infrastructures entail the creation of clear organizing structures that enable veteran and new activists to build people power; political education and research into the different logics, sites, and levers of carceral power; clear demands focused on the root of the problem; respect for a multiplicity of tactics and strategies depending on the political context; nonsectarian approaches to coalition work in tandem with clear political principles; and the humility to honestly assess the effectiveness of previous organizing and adapt as needed.

As traced across the pages of this book, creating a different kind of world begins with the humble activity of organization building to harness people's political power. There are multitudes of people eager to be brought into the liberation of work of abolition, but first we need to have the structures to bring them in. While this might appear simple, organizational development requires a host of political decisions and actions such as identifying the focus of your activism and your theory of change to steer your direction, determining how to bring people into your organization from broad-based door knocking to small study groups, choosing decision-making structures, delineating roles or work groups to carry out organizational goals, and engaging participants in continual leadership development ranging from media training to how to coordinate a direct action to the political histories of past struggles. At times building such a formation will develop out of preexisting organizations; at other times it will form in response to a crisis; and in other instances, it will emerge from the identification of a new problem or political opening. In any regard, it is essential that there are clear ways to bring people into an organization—such as through general meetings or orientations—and to engage them in various actions that draw on and build their skills. For example, in the Angola Special Civics Project, its members did legal research, corresponded with legislators, did outreach in the prison, and more. Through such activities, people build relationships and develop trust, as well as shape the organization and expand its capacity to make change.

Relationships suture organizations. Relationship building is not tangential to organizing work—it is the heart of organizing. Through prioritizing getting to know each other and sharing what brings people into the room, people can recognize how their struggles are inherently interlinked, rather than an atomized experience. Creating space for people to share their stories can be healing and deepen a collective sense of belonging with one another. Through the everyday care work of showing up during hardships, navigating interpersonal challenges, and celebrating together, people deepen trust in one another. Prefiguring the world we seek to create demands that we build relationships rooted in solidarity, mutuality, democracy, and collectivity.

Central to the building of anticarceral organizations is learning from the experiences and wisdom of criminalized people and their loved ones. Insofar as carceral power has been predicated on the widespread and routine disavowal of policing and imprisonment as a form of racial state violence, integrating the experiential knowledge of people directly harmed by punitive governance clarifies the various effects of the criminal legal system while also refuting the carceral logic that criminalized people are not to be trusted. At the same time, it is important to attend to differential experiences of people's criminalization and incarceration along lines of race, gender, sexuality, class, citizenship, ability, and age to understand the various ways the carceral state maintains and reifies hierarches.

This is not to advocate for the romanticization of incarcerated and criminalized people and their political positions. One of the dangers in any social movement is to expect that oppressed people have one unified political perspective. Liberal reformist, tough-on-crime, and abolitionist political positions can be held by all types of people.[14] In other words, political ideology still matters alongside experience. To paraphrase kai lumumba barrow, although the old organizing adage of meeting people where they're at is a fine first step, it is not an endpoint. Instead, people should work together to collectively share and sharpen their analyses of the problems at hand and to hone strategies for making a more free world.[15]

For such reasons political education and research are indispensable components of abolitionist infrastructures. Every single organization documented in this book conducted some form of political education, whether in the form of researching state and municipal laws, or facilitating story circles for people to share their experiences of racial and gender criminalization, or studying how activists attempted to rein in police power in other cities. Often this process of research is embedded in the work of a campaign— such as when Safe Streets identified that they needed to understand the structures and processes of the New Orleans city charter and budget in their advocacy for an independent police monitor, when Critical Resistance investigated mechanisms for amnesty, or when BreakOUT! asked me to figure out who the power players were in French Quarter policing. Mapping out the different spaces and levers of mass criminalization, policing, and imprisonment reveals a host of potentially strategic points to intervene and dismantle punitive state power: land use decisions made by municipalities and school boards; state legislative decisions on criminal laws, sentencing, and parole; support of prisoners' lawsuits, campaigns, and strikes; federal, state, and municipal budget hearings; banks that invest in prison and jail construction bonds; elections of state and city officials; and city and parish contracts with ICE. Abolition in practice means attending to the intricacies and contradictions of carceral state-making.

Alongside research into the various material dynamics of carceral statecraft is political education about the beliefs, narratives, and logics that prop up carceral geographies. Approaching political education from a standpoint of "political generosity," to borrow from Jacinta Gonzalez, serves as a reminder that we all have things to learn and share, especially as carceral state justifications are updated in response to shifting political conditions. Political education can take many forms, such as examining the different ways anti-Black racism and xenophobia justify criminalization, unpacking how ideas of "deserving" versus "undeserving" prisoners (innocent versus guilty, nonviolent versus violent, children versus adult, etc.) reinforce the legitimacy of caging, or clarifying the relationship of neoliberalism to conceptions of public safety. Developing a collective analysis is important for figuring out how to identify and maneuver around narrow "solutions" to punitive state violence—such as gender-responsive prisons or community oversight of police—that further entrench punishment regimes, as well as to craft counternarratives to shift public commonsense.

Building on such political study, abolitionist demands are a mix of visionary and pragmatic. At their best, they toggle between meeting people's needs in the here and now and stretching us toward an abolitionist horizon. For instance, campaigns to end cash bail seek to provide people an immediate respite from the ransom of the jail system while delegitimizing pretrial detention as a step toward a jail-less future. Developing such grassroots policy demands necessitates a clear-eyed delineation between reformist reforms and nonreformist, or abolitionist, reforms.[16] It means always keeping at the forefront the question of whether a particular reform will chip away at the scope and power of the criminal legal system or whether it will reinforce or expand the resources and validity of the carceral state. For example, fighting to reduce police budgets versus allocating more money for "anti-bias" training. Even campaigns organized around maintaining the status quo, such as preventing a new jail from being built or expanded, can be organized to push the edge of abolition. As Ruth Wilson Gilmore reminds us, "Policies are a script for the future."[17] OPPRC did not only demand that Gusman not expand the jail with FEMA funds but also that the OPP shrink in size. Critical Resistance not only worked to find people lost in the system doing Katrina Time but also called for amnesty for all. In both scenarios, organizers made demands that they understood as reasonable for getting at the root problems. Although neither group obtained their exact demands, they still gained more ground than previously imagined. If city and state officials are already going to push for compromises, abolitionists do not need to cede ground to appear more reasonable in anticipation.

Turning demands into reality necessitates an understanding of the repertoire of strategies and tactics available and which are the right fit for a given situation. Advocating for grassroots abolitionist policy—whether against building a new jail or prison, reducing law enforcement power and funding, getting officials to cut ties with ICE, agitating for the end of solitary confinement, or pushing for decriminalization of various offenses—generally requires a mix of approaches. Internal research—is often the foundation for broad-based and targeted political education—such as writing reports, teach-ins, meetings with key stakeholder groups, letters to the editor—aimed at swaying the public on a given issue. Translating a demand into a policy often requires working with sympathetic elected officials to champion an issue. Sometimes it makes sense to engage in electoral campaigns for particular candidates with abolitionist commitments or around public votes. At other times, protests and rallies might be strategic to demonstrate public support for a given issue. And at other points, heightened confrontations with state power, such as protesting officials' positions at high-profile events or direct actions blockading streets or shutting down carceral construction, can buoy a campaign. Even with the limits of lawsuits discussed earlier, legal interventions can be useful in halting a particular policy or program or slowing down a process to create more space for organizing. Not all these strategies may fit within a particular organization or political landscape, but it is critical to understand their role and how they can work together to turn a demand into a victory.

Yet if we recognize that abolition is not only about dismantling carceral systems but also about building up institutions and practices that extend collective life, we must also see abolitionist infrastructures as encompassing new kinds of caring structures.[18] They can be fashioned through work both outside and within the state: the development of community-based transformative justice work around sexual and nonsexual harms, the expansion of the social wage (universal healthcare, free public higher education, full employment, guaranteed paid family leave), the advancement of solidarity economics (community land trusts, permanently affordable housing co-ops, and worker co-ops), and just transitions from destructive industries from prisons to petrochemicals.

Perhaps the trickiest infrastructure to develop for the growth of abolitionist politics is the creation of coalitions. Because mass incarceration is so capacious, criminalized people and their loved ones are not the only ones who have a stake in undoing carceral power. Many different people have an interest in abolishing law-and-order austerity and punitive governance: teachers' unions, environmental justice activists, public librarians, residents of areas proposed for jails and prisons, healthcare workers, reproductive justice organizers, and more. Building people power to take on mass criminalization requires bringing together as many people as possible.

Yet, most people's initial approach to questions of policing and prisons is still through the prism of reform rather than abolition. This does not mean, however, that people on the reformist end of the spectrum cannot work in coalition with abolitionists. Coalitions are, as Bernice Johnson Reagon reminds us, not spaces to "look for comfort."[19] Unlike organizations that form around more unified political positions and shared identities, coalitions are, by definition, a more expansive grouping of organizations that work toward a particular goal or demand. Although coalition members will not agree on everything, that does not mean they cannot move in alignment around goals such as releasing political prisoners or stopping a new jail from being constructed or decriminalizing certain offenses. Indeed, it is often through participation in such struggles that people move toward abolition.

Coalitions are at their sturdiest when united around clearly articulated shared principles. Developing political points of unity can help organizations coalesce their vision and theory of change through discussion and debate. For example, clarifying that the goal is for fewer people to be locked up and for the criminal legal system to have less power can help people assess that their demand is to push for an end to ICE holds in a jail rather than simply more translation services. Outlining such principles is particularly important for helping steer a coalition when officials offer compromises. Should you support the decriminalization of some offenses if officials will also ratchet up other penalties? Should you back a jail cap of 1,438 beds over the 850-bed cap you were aiming for? In other words, having clear political lines is essential to keep from slipping into a reformist mode but also our coalitions should be broad enough that abolitionists do not miss out on the opportunity to build bridges, to expand the base of antiprison and antipolicing activists, and to win material victories that lessen carceral violence.

Organizing is always a gamble. But even when a campaign is lost or an organization disbands, previous struggles do not evaporate into thin air. The stakes of abolitionist movement building can make it tempting to maintain a nonstop pace of organizing, but taking the time to reflect and adjust is vital for the long-haul work of abolition world-making. This can mean reflecting on how certain tactics worked or not; mapping out how political conditions such as national or local elections, economic shifts, or global pandemics created opportunities or unforeseen challenges; or considering what needs to be done to defend a victory or what new avenue needs to be taken to push forward a demand yet again. Such adjustments can also be focused on internal dynamics such as working through conflicts that emerged in coalitions or, like the Angola Special Civics Project, restructuring an organization to deepen democracy and participation. Reflective processes can also extend beyond a single organization or coalition through the documentation of lessons learned to share with other activists near and far. Moreover, abolitionist organizing is an iterative process of organizing at the edge of abolition over and over again. As carceral state-makers update punitive technologies, rhetoric, and strategies, organizers must reckon with the reality that a campaign that was once seen as the horizon of abolition might over time be seen as short-sighted. Hence, part of the arsenal of abolitionist infrastructures is the humility to learn from such carceral state adaptions and to be as nimble as one can while moving forward with the knowledge and experience of a given time and space.

Animating these abolitionist infrastructures are an overarching belief and commitment to transformation. The political sensibility that guides abolitionists holds not only that things must change but also that we can make them change. Organizers may not have all the answers right now, but they do share a common understanding that in ways big and small we will remake our society, economies, political structures, social relations, and ourselves so that no one and no place are rendered disposable. We will make a world together where everyone can be free.

Notes

Archival Abbreviations for Notes

ALR	ACLU of Louisiana Records 1970–1985, Amistad Research Center, Tulane University, New Orleans, LA
CCDDR	City Council District D Records, Special Collections and City Archives, New Orleans, Public Library, New Orleans, LA
CJG	Councilman-at-Large Joseph I Giarrusso, Special Collections and City Archives, New Orleans, Public Library, New Orleans, LA
CJC	Councilman James Carter—District C Records (2006–2010), Special Collections and City Archives, New Orleans, Public Library, New Orleans, LA
CROP	Critical Resistance Organizational Papers, Oakland, CA
CSM	Councilmember Shelly S. Midura—District A Records, 2006–2010, Special Collections and City Archives, New Orleans, Public Library, New Orleans, LA
DCBR	Department of Corrections Board Records 1977–1979, Louisiana State Archives, Baton Rouge, LA
DCNC	Department of Corrections News Clippings 1972–1984, Louisiana State Archives, Baton Rouge, LA
DTP	David Treen Papers, Louisiana Research Collection, Howard-Tilton Memorial Library, Tulane University, New Orleans, LA
EDMP	Ernest "Dutch" Morial Papers 1929–1995, Amistad Research Center, Tulane University, New Orleans, LA
EDP	Economic Development Publications 1962–1976, Louisiana State Archives, Baton Rouge, LA
GLRPS	Governor's Office Long Range Prison Study Files, 1972–1980, Louisiana State Archives, Baton Rouge, LA
HWVJM	*Hayes Williams et al. v. John McKeithan et al.*, No. Civil Action 71–98 (M.D.La 1975), National Archives and Records Southwest Region, Fort Worth, TX
JSP	James L. Stovall Papers 1943–1997, Hill Memorial Library, Louisiana State University, Baton Rouge, LA
KNPP	Keith Nordyke Personal Papers, Baton Rouge, LA
LRL	Legislative Research Library 1982–1998, Louisiana State Archives, Baton Rouge, LA

LRLP   Legislative Research Library Publications 1992–2004, Louisiana State Archives, Baton Rouge, LA
LSPC   Louisiana State Penitentiary Correspondence 1952–1964, Louisiana State Archives, Baton Rouge, LA
LSPR   Louisiana State Penitentiary Records 1952–1962, Louisiana State Archives, Baton Rouge, LA
MBPP   Melissa Burch Personal Papers, Ann Arbor, MI
MCRN   Mayor C. Ray Nagin—Mayor's Office Administration Subject/Correspondence Files, Special Collections and City Archives, New Orleans, Public Library, New Orleans, LA
MEMR   Mayor Ernest N. Morial Records 1977–1986, Special Collections and City Archives, New Orleans, Public Library, New Orleans, LA
MMP   Marc H. Morial Papers 1994–2002, Amistad Research Center, Tulane University, New Orleans, LA
OTR   Oliver Thomas Records, Special Collections and City Archives, New Orleans, Public Library, New Orleans, LA
SBR   State Budget Reports 1970–1989, Louisiana State Archives, Baton Rouge, LA
SCJPR Southern Coalition on Jails and Prisons Records, 1974–1980, Southern Historical Collection, Louis Round Wilson Special Collections Library, University of North Carolina, Chapel Hill, NC
SGPP   Shana M. griffin Personal Papers, New Orleans, LA

Introduction

1. Carleton, *Politics and Punishment.*

2. US Department of Justice, *Prison and Jail Inmates at Midyear 1998*, 8; US Department of Justice, *Prisoners in 2021*, 15. In 2020 Mississippi's incarceration rate of 586 people imprisoned per 100,000 residents surpassed Louisiana's incarceration rate of 581 people imprisoned per 100,000 residents. This marks a decline in both Louisiana and Mississippi's incarceration rate over the preceding years.

3. Gramsci, *Selections from the Prison Notebooks*; Weber, "Politics as a Vocation"; Hall, "The State in Question"; Mann, *States, War, and Capitalism.*

4. Gilmore and Gilmore, "Restating the Obvious"; Canaday, *The Straight State.*

5. Gilmore, *Golden Gulag*, 26.

6. Hall et al., *Policing the Crisis*, 217.

7. Louisiana Budget Project, "Poverty in Louisiana: Census 2019."

8. Robinson, *Forgeries of Memory and Meaning*; Camp, *Incarcerating the Crisis.* The intertwining of criminalization and capitalist restructuring is not unique to neoliberalism: scholars have documented increasing criminalization alongside European enclosures and the development of the Jim Crow order and convict leasing as discussed in detail later. However, what marks neoliberalism's punitive turn is the scale of policing and imprisonment. Foucault, *Discipline and Punish*; Linebaugh, *The London Hanged.*

9. Gilmore, *Golden Gulag*, 28.

10. Following David Harvey and Ruth Wilson Gilmore, organized abandonment can be understood as systematic capital and state disinvestment of particular areas. This is in dialectical relation of places, and the people living there, being rendered as devalued and often disposable. This disinvetment and devaluation is part of broader geographic economic restructuring toward increased capital accumulation such as through the production of certain places as sacrifice zones or as part of the cycle of disinvestment and speculative development in the built environment. While organized abandonment pre-dates neoliberalism (Harvey indeed first discussed this term in relation to redlining policies), the enactment and normalization of organized abandonment from disinvestments in public transportation to the Flint water crisis to the rollback of US public health mitigations for COVID-19 is a hallmark of neoliberal governance. Harvey, *The Limits to Capital*; Gilmore, "Forgotten Places and the Seeds of Grassroots Planning."

11. Watts, "Resource Curse?"; Mitchell, *Carbon Democracy*; Riofrancos, *Resource Radicals*.

12. Sindler, *Huey Long's Louisiana*; Sanson, "What He Did and What He Promised to Do . . ."

13. Mitchell, *Carbon Democracy*; Colten, "An Incomplete Solution."

14. Woods, *Development Drowned and Reborn*.

15. Theriot, *American Energy, Imperiled Coast*.

16. Riofrancos, *Resource Radicals*, 172.

17. Gotham, "Tourism Gentrification"; Hackworth, *The Neoliberal City*; Parker, *Masculinities and Markets*; Stein, *Capital City*.

18. Sakakeeny, *Roll with It*.

19. As Foucault articulated, "Prison 'reform' is virtually contemporary with the prison itself: it constitutes, as it were, its programme. From the outset the prison was caught up in a series of accompanying mechanisms, whose purpose was apparently to correct it, but which seem to form part of its very functioning, so closely have they been bound up with its existence throughout its long history." Foucault, *Discipline and Punishment*, 234.

20. Omi and Winant, *Racial Formation in the United States*; Goldberg, *The Racial State*.

21. Goldberg, *The Racial State*, 16.

22. On this point, it is important to note that the capacious power of race is due to its not simply being equivalent to "heritage" or phenotype. Thus, although Blackness and criminality have been knitted together since Jim Crow other populations—Muslims, Central American migrants, not-quite white Appalachians, among others—have also been racialized as criminal at different historical conjunctures. Gilmore, *Golden Gulag*; Cacho, *Social Death*; Schept, *Coal, Cages, Crisis*.

23. Robinson, *Black Marxism*, 26. Emphasis in original.

24. Gilmore, "Abolition Geography and the Problem of Innocence"; Pulido, "Flint, Environmental Racism, and Racial Capitalism."

25. Oshinsky, *Worse than Slavery*; Mancini, *One Dies, Get Another*; Lichtenstein, *Twice the Work*; Smith, "Giuliani Time"; Wilson, *America's Johannesburg*; Goldberg, *The Racial State*; Ngai, *Impossible Subjects*; Glenn, *Unequal Freedom*; Gilmore, *Golden Gulag*; Parenti, *Lockdown America*; Hanhardt, *Safe Space*; Berger, *Captive Nation*; LeFlouria, *Chained in Silence*; Haley, *No Mercy Here*; Bhandar, *Colonial Lives of Property*; LeBrón, *Policing Life and Death*; Schept, *Coal, Cages, Crisis*.

26. For a groundbreaking articulation of these interwoven formations see Haley, *No Mercy Here*.

27. Kohler-Hausman, *Getting Tough*, 5.

28. Cedric Robinson outlines the Black radical tradition as "the continuing development of a collective consciousness informed by the historical struggles for liberation and motivated by the shared sense of obligation to preserve the collective being." Robinson, *Black Marxism*, 171. The Black radical tradition does not simply pass down from generation to generation but is continually made and remade as people confront the racial capitalist state and struggle for what Robin D. G. Kelley aptly names "freedom dreams." Kelley, *Freedom Dreams*.

29. Charles Payne's writing on the Mississippi organizing of the Student Non-Violent Coordinating Committee is perhaps that best example of capturing the nuanced processes of organizing. Payne, *I've Got the Light of Freedom*.

30. Ransby, *Ella Baker*, 118.

31. On this point I am indebted to the thinking and organizing of the Black radical tradition and autonomist Marxism, particularly James, *The Black Jacobins*; Kelley, "'We Are Not What We Seem'"; Robinson, *Black Movements in America*; Cleaver, *Reading Capital Politically*; Federici, *Caliban and the Witch*; James, *Sex, Race, Class*; Linebaugh and Rediker, *The Many-Headed Hydra*.

32. My thinking on political openings draws on Doug McAdam's work on political process theory in relation to the development of the civil rights movement. In *Political Process and the Development of Black Insurgency, 1930–1970*, Doug McAdam argues that widespread protests and social movements develop from the combination of existing grassroots organizations and expanding political opportunities. For McAdam, "any event or broad social process that serves to undermine the calculations and assumptions on which the political establishment is structured occasions a shift in political opportunities." McAdam, *Political Process*, 41.

33. Du Bois, *Black Reconstruction*; Davis, *Are Prisons Obsolete?*

34. Gilmore, *Golden Gulag*; CR 10 Publications Collective, *Abolition Now!*

35. Césaire, *Discourse on Colonialism*.

36. Robinson, *Forgeries of Memory and Meaning*, 198. Moreover, what is often viewed as "backwardness" is more accurately understood as evidence of the structural underdevelopment of the region. Woodward, *Origins of the New South*; Fields, "The Nineteenth-Century American South"; Cobb, *The Most Southern Place on Earth*; Woods, *Development Arrested*; Wilson, *America's Johannesburg*; Marable, *How Capitalism Underdeveloped Black America*; Woods, *Development Drowned and Reborn*; Smith, *Uneven Development*.

37. Ayers, *Vengeance and Justice*; Thompson, "Blinded by a 'Barbaric' South."

38. On work debunking the private prison and prison labor narratives, see Gilmore, *Golden Gulag*, 19–22; Kilgore, "The Myth of Prison Slave Labor Camps in the U.S."; Gilmore, "The Worrying State"; Stein, "Still Bringing the State Back In."

39. Hamilton and Henderson, *Angola*; Bergner, *God of the Rodeo*; Adams, "The Wildest Show in the South"; Browne, "Rooted in Slavery"; Schrift, "The Wildest Show in the South"; Martin et al., "Racism, Rodeos"; Childs, *Slaves of the State*; Benns, "American Slavery, Reinvented"; Kennedy, "Today They Kill with the Chair"; Krissah Thompson, "From a Slave House to a Prison Cell: The History of Angola Plantation," *Washington Post*, September 21, 2016; Gillespie, "Placing Angola."

40. Fierce, *Slavery Revisited*; Oshinsky, *Worse than Slavery*; Mancini, *One Dies, Get Another*; Lichtenstein, *Twice the Work of Free Labor*; Davis, "From the Prison of Slavery to the Slavery of Prison"; Curtin, *Black Prisoners and their World*; Blackmon, *Slavery by Another Name*; LeFlouria, *Chained in Silence*; Haley, *No Mercy Here*.

41. For scholarship on contemporary mass criminalization and resistance in the US South, see Perkinson, *Texas Tough*; McTighe and Haywood, "There Is NO Justice in Louisiana"; Schoenfeld, *Building the Prison State*; Chase, *We Are Not Slaves*; Brown, "ICE Comes to Tennessee"; Schept, *Coal, Cages, Crisis*. For critical carceral studies work on other regions, see Gilmore, *Golden Gulag*; Bonds, "Discipline and Devolution"; Lynch, *Sunbelt Justice*; Bonds, "Economic Development"; Schept, *Progressive Punishment*; Burton, "Organized Disorder"; Felker-Kantor, *Policing Los Angeles*; Norton, "Little Siberia"; LeBrón, *Policing Life and Death*; Balto, *Occupied Territory*. For work that tells a national story, see Beckett, *Making Crime Pay*; Mauer, *Race to Incarcerate*; Gottschalk, *The Prison and the Gallows*; Parenti, *Lockdown America*; Wacquant, *Punishing the Poor*; Alexander, *The New Jim Crow*; Richie, *Arrested Justice*; Murakawa, *The First Civil Right*; Berger, *Captive Nation*; Gottschalk, *Caught*; Hinton, *From the War on Poverty*; Ritchie, *Invisible No More*; Kohler-Hausman, *Getting Tough*; Story, *Prison Land*; Thuma, *All Our Trials*; Felber, *Those Who Know Don't Say*.

42. Although Naomi Murakawa clearly tracks the centrality of Dixiecrats in the development of the LEAA, this attention to regional political blocs in national punitive politics generally has been ignored in studies of US mass incarceration. Murakawa, *The First Civil Right*.

43. On this point I depart from scholars who have implied that the South offers an origin story of mass incarceration, an argument I see as reinforcing southern exceptionalism. Perkinson, *Texas Tough* and, to a lesser extent, Robert Chase, *We Are Not Slaves*.

44. In the words of H. L. T. Quan, "Social inquiries that seek to be emancipatory necessarily require us to take life seriously . . . peopling theories with histories so that the stakes of livable life cannot be exchanged for something lesser." Quan, "Emancipatory Social Inquiry," 119.

45. Smith, "Contours of a Spatialized Politics."

46. I was surprised to find that the last academic monograph on the Louisiana penal system, Mark T. Carleton's *Politics and Punishment*, was published in 1971— the year my research pointed to as the turning point of the Louisiana penal system.

47. *Angolite* staff sent an issue to each member of the state legislature, the governor, and the head of the DOC.

48. For more on the history of the *Angolite* see former editor Wilbert Rideau's memoir *In the Place of Justice*.

49. Hall et al., *Policing the Crisis*.

50. I was able to conduct most of my oral history interviews and engage in ethnographic research with BreakOUT! because of previous personal relationships. As a city inundated with parachute researchers following Hurricane Katrina, it was not uncommon to be told during interviews that people were talking to me because they knew of my investment in ending punitive state violence in Louisiana or had been vouched for by a trusted comrade or colleague.

Chapter 1

1. Ehrenkrantz Group, *Louisiana Prison System Study*, 8, Box 1, GLRPS; US Department of Justice, *Prisoners in 1980*, 2.

2. Carleton, *Politics and Punishment*, 8; Wurtzburg and Hahn, *Hard Labor*, 1–4; Shugg, *Origins of Class Struggle in Louisiana*, 60–61. While some European immigrant men and later most of their descendants would be brought into the category of whiteness, at this point they were outside the bounds of the legal, political, and social protections of whiteness.

3. Adamson, "Punishment after Slavery," 557; Fierce, *Slavery Revisited*, 72; Lichtenstein, *Twice the Work of Free Labor*, 23; Oshinsky, *Worse than Slavery*, 32; Davis, "Racialized Punishment," 97.

4. Hall, *Africans in Colonial Louisiana*, 145. This is not to say that all Black people or other people of color were slaves in Louisiana. New Orleans, in particular, was home to a sizable population of free people of color—primarily Creoles of color but also non-Creole Black people. However, I have found little documentation of the policing of free people of color in New Orleans until after Louisiana was incorporated into the United States. Bell, *Revolution, Romanticism*, 75.

5. Wurtzburg and Hahn, *Hard Labor*, 3.

6. Carleton, *Politics and Punishment*, 8–9; Wurtzburg and Hahn, *Hard Labor*, 4–5.

7. As early as 1805, New Orleans prisoners were forced to work on chain gangs in public building demolition and construction, street cleaning, and levee work. Rothman, *Slave Country*, 99.

8. Wurzburg and Hahn, *Hard Labor*, 5.

9. Wurtzberg and Hahn, *Hard Labor*, 6.

10. Wurtzberg and Hahn, *Hard Labor*, 8.

11. Du Bois, *Black Reconstruction*, 166–80; Houzeau, *My Passage*, 44; Davis, "From the Prison of Slavery," 76.

12. Du Bois, *Black Reconstruction*, 178–79.

13. Carleton, *Politics and Punishment*, 15.

14. As quoted in Carleton, *Politics and Punishment*, 16.

15. Carleton, *Politics and Punishment*, 17.

16. Woods, *Development Arrested*, 79.

17. Davis, "From the Prison of Slavery," 80; Curtin, *Black Prisoners*, 41.

18. Woods, *Development Arrested*, 5.

19. Davis, "Racialized Punishment," 100–101; Heather Ann Thompson reminds us that convict leasing also has roots in the North. Yet, the extent to which convict leasing was employed in the South was markedly different than the scale it reached in the North. Thompson, "Blinded by a 'Barbaric' South."

20. Carleton, *Politics and Punishment*, 17–19.

21. A smaller segment of prisoners worked at the Baton Rouge penitentiary alongside a night shift of coolie laborers. After coolies staged an uprising for better working conditions, James discontinued the practice of hiring them. Carleton, *Politics and Punishment*, 19–20; Woodward, *Origins of the New South*; Jung, *Coolies and Cane*, 199.

22. Hair, *Bourbonism and Agrarian Protest*; Carleton, *Politics and Punishment*, 23–35.

23. Carleton, *Politics and Punishment*, 32–45; Fierce, *Black Prisoners*, 7–8.

24. Carleton, *Politics and Punishment*, 45, footnote 32.

25. It widely circulates that the plantation Angola was named for the country of origin of many of the enslaved people who were forced to labor there. However, there is no evidence to this assertion. On the contrary, until the early 1800s, most enslaved people in Louisiana were from the Senegambia region of Africa. Moreover, historian Joshua Rothman demonstrates that when Tennessee planter Isaac Franklin named the plantation "Angola" in the 1830s, "none of the people Franklin enslaved [there] had African names, and most were too young to have been born in Africa." In the regurgitation of this "fact," we are unwittingly repeating an anti-Black planter mythology that collapsed all of Africa into a singular region in pursuit of raising their status as planter elite. Hall, *Africans in Colonial Louisiana*; Rothman, *The Ledger and the Chain*.

26. Carleton, *Politics and Punishment*, 29–30.

27. Robinson, *Black Marxism*, 113; Smallwood, *Saltwater Slavery*.

28. Carleton, *Politics and Punishment*, 45–46. Louisiana's death rate was four times the national average.

29. Carleton, *Politics and Punishment*, 38, 50–51, 72. The Prison Reform Association was not opposed to prisoners working but believed that a system under state control could be reformed into a kinder and expanded system of punishment. The abolition of the Louisiana lease was also packaged within a broader political program aimed at the disenfranchisement of Black voters and the breaking of biracial populism. Mancini, *One Dies, Get Another*, 149–50.

30. Carleton, *Politics and Punishment*, 79–92.

31. "Board of Control Buys Two Places," *Times-Picayune*, December 5, 1900; "Changes in the Convict System," *Times-Picayune*, January 9, 1901; "Sims Wisely Wonders, after Seeing the First Convict Farm at Angola, Why the Great State Did Not Adopt the Splendid System Long Ago,'" *Times-Picayune*, April 16, 1901.

32. "Changes in the Convict System"; "Another Plantation Wanted by the Board of Control," *Times-Picayune*, June 24, 1905.

33. "The New Century in the State's Convict System," *Times-Picayune*, July 14, 1901.

34. "Sims Wisely Wonders"; "The ratio of black males to white males in the levee camps was 99 to 1, on the sugar plantations, 55 to 1." Carleton, *Politics and Punishment*, 100–101.

35. C. Harrison Parker, "State Penitentiary System a Success," *Times-Picayune*, September 1, 1905; "Prison Reform Ideas Voices," *Times-Picayune*, February 15, 1910; Carleton, *Politics and Punishment*, 139.

36. "Penitentiary System a Credit to the State," *Times-Picayune*, January 21, 1906; "Penitentiary Cost to State under Long Set at $1,000,000," *Times-Picayune*, June 2, 1930.

37. Memo from R. M. Cherp to Department of Institutions, Folder: La. St. Penitentiary & L. C. & I. School 1961 Feed Grain Program, Box 1, LSPR.

38. Ehrenkrantz Group, *Louisiana Prison System Study*, 25, Box 1, GLRPS.

39. E. R. Anderson to Senator J. C. Gilbert, February 22, 1961, Folder: The Governor's Committee on Angola, Box 1, LSPR. There is a slight discrepancy in the letter between the number of prisoners that the Director of Industries states were working at Angola (1,178) and the total from adding up the numbers from the various divisions (1,105). Either way the proportion of prisoners working at Angola at this time was around 34–35 percent. The breakdown of labor divisions were as follows: sugar mill: 66 prisoners; canning: 40 prisoners; printing plant: 10 prisoners; license tags: 55 prisoners; soap factory: 33 prisoners; abattoir: 22 prisoners; dairy: 12 prisoners; swinery: 18 prisoners; and farming: 849 prisoners.

40. "Mutiny of Prisoners at Angola Farm," *Times-Picayune*, June 21, 1906; "Another Escaped Convict," *Times-Picayune*, November 10, 1907; Herbert B. Mayer, "Escapes and Near Escapes at Louisiana's Penitentiary," *Times-Picayune*, September 7, 1913; "Whipping of Men at Convict Farms Result of Strike," *Times-Picayune*, November 4, 1915.

41. Carleton, *Politics and Punishment*, 138; "Prison Officials Defend Angola Honor System," *Times-Picayune*, December 17, 1928. There were more trusties employed at Angola then there were free people employed in the entire penal system.

42. Carleton, *Politics and Punishment*, 136; "Penitentiary Cost to State under Long Set at $1,000,000"; "Blood Took Penitentiary out of Red Records Show," *Times-Picayune*, May 11, 1941.

43. "Trusties and Free Personnel Deny Brutality Reports," *Times-Picayune*, March 22, 1951; Carleton, *Politics and Punishment*, 121, 150.

44. Ehrenkrantz Group, *Louisiana Prison System Study*, 2–3, Box 1, GLRPS.

45. Ehrenkrantz Group, *Louisiana Prison System Study*, 2–3, Box 1, GLRPS; Carleton, *Politics and Punishment*, 161–63; "Changes Urged in Penal System," *Times-Picayune*, May 7, 1946. David Theo Goldberg reminds us that classificatory schemas have long been central to liberal administrative racial state rule, because such systems serve to create order through hierarchal modes of inclusion and exclusion. Thus, we can see the fetishization of classification as "the answer" to the Louisiana prison crisis as part and parcel on a much longer strategy of control for the liberal racial capitalist state. Goldberg, *The Racial State*, 94.

46. "Building Program Nears Completion at State Prison," *Times-Picayune*, April 25, 1955; Ehrenkrantz Group, *Louisiana Prison System Study*, 2–3, Box 1, GL-RPS; Carleton, *Politics and Punishment*, 160.

47. "Two Convicts Escape from the Angola Prison Farm," *Times-Picayune*, October 25, 1901; "Another Escaped Convict," Mayer, "Escapes and Near Escapes at Louisiana's Penitentiary"; "Mutiny at Angola," *Times-Picayune*, June 21, 1921; "Two Die, Six Shots as Gunfire Halts Break at Angola," *Times-Picayune*, August 12, 1934; "Blood Took Penitentiary out of Red Records Show"; "Angola Convict Sought in Area," *Times-Picayune*; "Angola Probe Welcomes," *States-Item*, August 1, 1974, Folder: July–September 1974, Box 2, DCNC.

48. Kenneth "Biggy" Johnston, interview by author, March 25, 2016.

49. Michael Glover, "A Man and a Prison," *Angolite*, July/August 1991.

50. Glover, "A Man and a Prison."

51. Berger, *Captive Nation*, 58; Felber, *Those Who Know Don't Say*.

52. Johnston, interview, March 25, 2016.

53. Glover, "A Man and a Prison."

54. "Edwards Appointees," *States Times*, April 24, 1972, Folder: March–August 1972, Box 1, DCNC; "Is It True What They Say about Elayn Hunt?" *Unitarian Fellowship of Baton Rouge newsletter*, March 26, 1972, Folder: March–August 1972, Box 1, DCNC.

55. Bissonette, *When the Prisoners Ran Walpole*, 41–66; "Louisiana Prisons: Crime Reducer or Crime Producer?" *States-Item*, April 23, 1972, Folder: Special Series 1972–1974, Box 2, DCNC.

56. "Lt. Governor Fitzmorris Says, 'No Attica at Angola,'" *States Times*, October 13, 1972, Folder: September–December 1972, Box 1, DCNC. For years and years, Attica served as the object lesson that Louisiana politicians and prison officials sought to learn from and avoid.

57. "Editorial: The Penal System: A Tough Task Ahead," *States Times*, May 20, 1972, Folder: March–August 1972, Box 1, DCNC; "Prison Reform Bills Win Approval," *Morning Advocate*, June 8, 1972, Folder: March–August 1972, Box 1, DCNC; "Inmate Guards to Be Replaced at State Prison," *State Times*, July 11, 1972, Folder: March–August 1972, Box 1, DCNC. There was a simultaneous suit on the issue of prison security filed in response to the killing of a guard that prison officials pinned on prisoners affiliated with the Black Panther Party, the Angola 3. Richard Munson, "Kilbourne, West Feliciana Jury Agree on Pen Security Probe," *Morning Advocate*, June 3, 1972, Folder: March–August 1972, Box 1, DCNC.

58. "Reform at Angola" *States-Item*, December 17, 1973, Folder: September–December 1973, Box 1, DCNC; "State Said Moving toward a Unified Corrections System," *Daily Reveille*, January 23, 1974, Folder: January–March 1974, Box 2, DCNC.

59. "Editorial: The Penal System: A Tough Task Ahead," Folder: March–August 1972, Box 1, DCNC; "Government Revamp Shelved, Roemer Says," *States-Item*, October 25, 1972; "Reform at Angola."

60. "Prisoner Legal and Communications Group Activities," *Angolite*, February 1975.

61. Allen Katz, "Break up Angola—Penologists," *States-Item*, August 20, 1974, Folder: July–September 1974, Box 2, DCNC.

62. *State of Louisiana Budget, Fiscal Year 1972–1973*, 2, Box 3, SBR; *State of Louisiana Budget, Fiscal Year 1974–1975*, 2, Box 3, SBR.

63. Arrighi, *The Long Twentieth Century*, 309–355; Gilmore, "Globalisation and US Prison Growth"; Cleaver, *Reading Capital Politically*, 24–28; Harvey, *A Brief History of Neoliberalism*, 9–19; Prashad, *The Darker Nations*; Stein, *Pivotal Decade*, 101–129; Gindin and Panitch, *The Making of Global Capitalism*, 122–159.

64. Mitchell, *Carbon Democracy*, 174–185; Nore, "Oil and the State"; Prashad, *The Darker Nations*, 188; Stein, *The Pivotal Decade*, 74–83.

65. Arrighi, *The Long Twentieth Century*, 322; Stein, *The Pivotal Decade*, 102–3.

66. Louisiana Department of Natural Resources, *First Oil Well in Louisiana*; Colten, "An Incomplete Solution," 92–93.

67. Colten, "An Incomplete Solution," 93.

68. Colten, "An Incomplete Solution," 93.

69. Scott, "The Structure of the Louisiana Economy," 11.

70. Painter, "Oil and the American Century," 24.

71. Richardson and Scott, "Mineral Resources"; Louisiana Legislative Auditor, *State Mineral and Energy Board Mineral Lease Royalty Rates*; Louisiana Department of Natural Resources, *Louisiana Severance Tax*.

72. Weber, "Historical Development of the Louisiana State Tax Structure," 44–49.

73. Richardson and Scott, "Mineral Resources," 118.

74. Weber, "Historical Development of the Louisiana State Tax Structure," 50.

75. Weber, "Historical Development of the Louisiana State Tax Structure," 50–51.

76. Weber, "Historical Development of the Louisiana State Tax Structure," 50.

77. Woods, *Development Drowned and Reborn*, 223.

78. *State of Louisiana Budget, Fiscal Year 1972–1973*, 1–2, Box 3, SBR; *State of Louisiana Budget, Fiscal Year 1973–1974*, 1–2, Box 3, SBR; *State of Louisiana Budget, Fiscal Year 1974–1975*, 1–2, Box 3, SBR; *State of Louisiana Budget, Fiscal Year 1975–1976*, 1–2, Box 3, SBR; *State of Louisiana Budget, Fiscal Year 1976–1977*, 1–2, Box 3, SBR; *State of Louisiana Budget, Fiscal Year 1977–1978*, 1–2, Box 3, SBR; *State of Louisiana Budget, Fiscal Year 1978–1979*, 1–2, Box 4, SBR; *State of Louisiana Budget, Fiscal Year 1979–1980*, 1–2, Box 4, SBR. A new severance tax passed in 1972 allowed for additional petrochemical revenue even before the OPEC price hike.

79. *Executive Budget 1972–1973*, vol. 1, Box 5, SBR; *Executive Budget 1973–1974*, vol. 1, Box 1, SBR; *Executive Budget 1974–1975*, vol. 1, Box 1, SBR; *Executive Budget 1975–1976*, vol. 1, Box 1, SBR.

80. *Executive Budget 1972–1973*, vol. 1, Box 5, SBR.

81. "After Candidates for Angola," *Times-Picayune*, March 26, 1967.

82. Murakawa, *The First Civil Right*, 85–90.

83. Parenti, *Lockdown America*, 8; Murakawa, *The First Civil Right*, 86.

84. Parenti, *Lockdown America*.

85. Arend, *Showdown in Desire*, 101–11; Murakawa, *The First Civil Right*, 73.

86. Criminal Justice Coordinating Council Status Report FY 72 Funds, March 12, 1974, Folder 9, Box 68, EDMP; New Orleans Police Department Crime Prevention Unit Grant Proposal, 1974, Folder 22, Box 67, EDMP.

87. Paul Atkinson, "Connick Defeats Garrison in Photo-Finish D.A. Election," *Times-Picayune*, December 16, 1973. In 1973 New Orleans voters also elected Criminal Sheriff Charles Foti and Coroner Frank Minyard for the first time. They would, respectively, serve thirty and forty years. Together Foti and Connick would have significant impacts on the Louisiana punishment regime in the coming decades.

88. "Connick Seeks Election as DA," *Times-Picayune*, July 1, 1973; Don Gross, "Connick Wants Anti-Crime Unit," *Times-Picayune*, August 30, 1973.

89. Dwight Ott, "Connick Hits Penal Code," *Times-Picayune*, April 9, 1975, Folder: April–May 1975, Box 3, DCNC.

90. "Career Criminal Bureau for N.O.," *Times-Picayune*, March 19, 1975, Folder: January–March 1975, Box 3, DCNC.

91. Criminal Justice Coordinating Council Grant Application, January 24, 1975, Folder 16, Box 67, EDMP.

92. Criminal Justice Coordinating Council Grant Application, 19, January 24, 1975, Folder 16, Box 67, EDMP.

93. Special Meeting CJCC Executive Committee, January 28, 1975, Folder 12, Box 68, EDMP; "Career Criminal Bureau for N.O."

94. "A Review of the Criminal Justice Coordinating Council," 97, 1978, Folder 2, Box 49, EDMP.

95. "A Review of the Criminal Justice Coordinating Council," 97, 1978, Folder 2, Box 49, EDMP.

96. J. Douglass Murphy, "Two Inmates Question DA Connick's Sanity," *Times-Picayune*, November 22, 1975, Folder: November–December 1975, Box 3, DCNC.

97. "Criminal Justice Coordinating Council Criminal Justice Plan 1975," 1, Folder 13, Box 38, EDMP; Summary of the Proposals for the Allocation of Part C Funds to Louisiana's Planning Regions, 1976, Folder 20, Box 67, EDMP.

98. "A Review of the Criminal Justice Coordinating Council," 34, 1978, Folder 2, Box 49, EDMP.

99. "Criminal Justice Coordinating Council Criminal Justice Plan 1975," 3, Folder 13, Box 38, EDMP.

100. CJCC Executive Meeting Minutes, February 20, 1974, Folder 9, Box 68, EDMP; Special Meeting CJCC Executive Committee, January 28, 1975, Folder 12, Box 68, EDMP.

101. *Williams v. McKeithan* C.A 71-98 (M.D.La, 1975), *US Magistrate Special Report*, 449–85, KNPP.

102. *Williams v. McKeithan* C.A 71-98 (M.D.La, 1975), *US Magistrate Special Report*, 451, KNPP.

103. *Williams v. McKeithan* C.A 71-98 (M.D.La, 1975), *US Magistrate Special Report*, 452, KNPP.

104. *Williams v. McKeithan* C.A 71-98 (M.D.La, 1975), *US Magistrate Special Report*, 456, KNPP.

105. *Williams v. McKeithan* C.A 71–98 (M.D.La, 1975), *US Magistrate Special Report*, 449–85, KNPP.

106. *Williams v. McKeithan* C.A 71–98 (M.D.La, 1975), *US Magistrate Special Report*, 450, KNPP.

107. *Williams v. McKeithan* C.A 71–98 (M.D.La, 1975), *US Magistrate Special Report*, 466, KNPP.

108. *Williams v. McKeithan* C.A 71–98 (M.D.La, 1975), *US Magistrate Special Report*, 466, KNPP.

109. *Williams v. McKeithan* C.A 71–98 (M.D.La, 1975), *US Magistrate Special Report*, 478, KNPP.

110. *Williams v. McKeithan* C.A 71–98 (M.D.La, 1975), Judgment and Order, 2, KNPP.

111. *Williams v. McKeithan* C.A 71–98 (M.D.La, 1975), Judgment and Order, 2–12, KNPP.

112. *Williams v. McKeithan* C.A 71–98 (M.D.La, 1975), Judgment and Order, 5, KNPP.

113. *Williams v. McKeithan* C.A 71–98 (M.D.La, 1975), Judgment and Order, 17, KNPP.

114. This is not to ignore the fact that violence among prisoners was a real concern and one explicitly named by Mitchell, Hayes, Stevenson, and Joseph.

115. Singh, *Black Is a Country*, 1–14; Melamed, *Represent and Destroy*, 18–26; Murakawa, *The First Civil Right*, 151–52; Woodward, *The Strange Career of Jim Crow*; Woods, *Development Arrested*; Wilson, *America's Johannesburg*.

116. Kunzel, *Criminal Intimacy*, 150–51.

117. Kunzel, *Criminal Intimacy*, 169.

118. Lawrence R. Anderson, Jr., letter to Shawn Moore, April 5, 1977, Folder: Flowers v. Phelps, Box 1, ALR. Emphasis added.

119. "Federal Judge Orders Reforms at Angola," *States-Item*, June 11, 1975, Folder: June 1975, Box 3, DCNC; J. Douglass Murphy, "Officials Have No Idea What to Do about Order on Angola," *Times-Picayune*, June 12, 1975, Folder: June 1975, Box 3, DCNC.

120. Murphy, "Officials Have No Idea What to Do about Order on Angola"; "Two-Year Time Limit Termed Impossible for Angola Changes," *States-Item*, June 17, 1975, Folder: June 1975, Box 3, DCNC; *Williams v. McKeithan* C.A 71–98 (M.D.La, 1975), Judgment and Order, 19, KNPP.

121. J. Douglas Murphy, "Fearing the Worst: 'Hot Summer' Seen for Angola," *Times-Picayune*, June 19, 1975, Folder: June 1975, Box 3, DCNC.

122. Murphy, "Fearing the Worst."

123. Wilbert Rideau, "Angola—Louisiana's Sore That Won't Heal," *Shreveport Journal*, July 2, 1975, Folder: June 1975, Box 3, DCNC.

124. Rideau, "Angola."

125. "Editorial: Quit Procrastinating on Angola Emergency," *Advocate*, June 17, 1975, Folder: June 1975, Box 3, DCNC; Pierre V. Degruy, "Connick's Endeavors in Legislature Pay Off: Entire Package Is Passed," *Times-Picayune*, July 31, 1975, Folder: June 1975, Box 3, DCNC.

126. Pierre V. Degruy, "Connick Fights Good Time," *Times-Picayune*, June 11, 1975, Folder: 1975, Box 3, DCNC.

127. Degruy, "Connick Fights Good Time;" "Multiple Offender Measure Being Sent to House Today," *States-Item*, June 26, 1975, Folder: June 1975, Box 3, DCNC; "Appeal Is Expected on Crediting Inmates Pre-Trial Jail Time," *State Times*, July 30, 1975, Folder July–August 1975, Box 3, DCNC.

128. Murphy, "Officials Have No Idea What to Do about Order on Angola."

129. "7.5 Million Funds Sought for Angola Improvements," *State Times*, July 10, 1975, Folder: June 1975, Box 3, DCNC.

130. "Stadiums Win, Angola Loses, Judge Laments," *States-Item*, July 17, 1975, Folder: July–August 1975, Box 3, DCNC; C. M. Hargroder, "Angola Order Stands," *Times-Picayune*, July 17, 1975, Folder: July–August 1975, Box 3, DCNC.

131. *State of Louisiana Budget, 1975–1976*, 1, Box 3, SBR.

132. "Stadiums Win, Angola Loses, Judge Laments."

133. Hargroder, "Angola Order Stands."

134. Hargroder, "Angola Order Stands"; "Cost to Renovate Angola Could Be $100 Million," *Morning Advocate*, July 18, 1975, Folder: July–August 1975, Box 3, DCNC.

135. "Edwards Orders Angola Reform Efforts Beefed Up," *Shreveport Journal*, July 18, 1975, Folder: July–August 1975, Box 3, DCNC.

136. Similar cases occurred in Bossier City, LaSalle Parish, and Jefferson Parish and for expanding work-release centers in Greater New Orleans.

137. In Louisiana, most parishes are governed by a police jury, which is an elected body that serves both legislative and executive functions. The name originates from the fact that when they were first created in the 1800s maintaining law-and-order was one of their primary purposes. Alison Watson, "Several Jurors Oppose Transfer of CCI to State," *Shreveport Journal* (Shreveport, LA), July 18, 1975, Department of Corrections Newsclippings 1972–1984, Box 3, Folder: July–August 1975, LSA. Less than a year later, the police jury did an about-face and proposed to the state that it could have CCI for $4.3 million. However, the state turned down the proposal given the high price, and it then determined that a 500-bed facility was needed.

138. Bonnie Davis, "Residents Will Protest Use of Carver School as Prison," *Shreveport Times*, July 24, 1975, Folder: July–August 1975, Box 3, DCNC.

139. Lynn Stewart, "State May Seize Site in Caddo for Prison," *Shreveport Times*, August 19, 1975, Folder: July–August 1975, Box 3, DCNC.

140. "Old Inmate Move May Be Contested in N.O.," *State Times*, April 22, 1976, Folder: April–May 1976, Box 4, DCNC.

141. Representative Ron Faucheux raised the question whether an entire parish was specific enough for the legislature to authorize general obligation bonds.

142. Richard Boyd, "Council Vows to Fight East N.O. Prison Facility," *States-Item*, April 23, 1976, Box 4, Folder: April–May 1976, DCNC; Clancy DuBos, "Suit Filed to Stop Proposed Housing of Angola Inmates," *Times-Picayune*, April 28, 1976, Box 4, Folder: April–May 1976, DCNC; "Prison Plan Attack Outlined," *Times-Picayune*, April 29, 1976, Box 4, Folder: April–May 1976, DCNC.

143. Patricia Gormin, "Homes Closed to Inmates," *States-Item*, April 30, 1976, Box 4, Folder: April–May 1976, DCNC.

144. "Prisoner Move Is Suspended," *Shreveport Journal*, May 13, 1976, Box 4, Folder: April–May 1976, DCNC.

145. Deidre Cruse, "Moving Some Inmates from Angola Discussed," *Morning Advocate*, July 25, 1975, Folder: July–August 1975, Box 3, DCNC; "663 Inmates Will Be Moved from Angola," *State Times*, August 1, 1975, Folder: July–August 1975, Box 3, DCNC.

146. Frances Seghers, "Central Residents Protest Transfer of Prisoners," *Morning Advocate*, August 7, 1975, Folder: July–August 1975, Box 3, DCNC.

147. Gibbs Adams, "Inmate Transfer Plans Grind to a Halt Once Again," *Morning Advocate*, August 15, 1975, Folder: July–August 1975, Box 3, DCNC.

148. Gerald Moses and Linda Lightfoot, "Edwards Agrees to Prison Plan," *State Times*, August 21, 1975, Folder: July–August 1975, Box 3, DCNC.

149. "Facilities for Prisoners," *State Times*, July 22, 1975, Folder: July–August 1975, Box 3, DCNC.

150. "Five Sites Found Excellent for Housing Angola Inmates," *Morning Advocate*, September 16, 1975, Folder: September–October 1975, Box 3, DCNC.

151. Lois White, "Council Resolution Opposes Prison Plan," *Lake Charles American Press*, October 10, 1975, Folder: September–October 1975, Box 3, DCNC.

152. "World War II Troopship May Be Used as Floating Louisiana Prison," *Monroe Morning World*, October 26, 1975, Folder: September–October 1975, Box 3, DCNC.

153. "Gov't Reported against Floating Prison for La." *State Times*, December 10, 1975, Folder: November–December 1975, Box 3, DCNC.

154. "Prison Decentralization—Tough Decisions," *Shreveport Times*, August 17, 1975, Folder: July–August 1975, Box 3, DCNC.

155. Seghers, "Central Residents Protest Transfer of Prisoners"; "A Petition: Keep the Convicts in Angola," *Red River Journal*, September 17, 1975, Folder: July–August 1975, Box 3, DCNC; "Residents Question Angola Transfer," *American Press*, October 10, 1975, Folder: September–October 1975, Box 3, DCNC; "Sound Off," *Shreveport Journal*, March 8, 1976, Folder: January–March 1976, Box 4, DCNC.

156. Davis, "Residents Will Protest Use of Carver School as Prison."

157. Ralph Vinson, "Jungle Justice," *States-Item*, August 22, 1975, Folder: July–August 1975, Box 3, DCNC.

158. Thomas E. Morgan, "React to Prison Transfer Proposals," *Morning Advocate*, August 28, 1975, Folder: July–August 1975, Box 3, DCNC.

159. Murphy, "Two Inmates Question DA Connick's Sanity."

160. Woods, "Sittin' on Top of the World," 47–48; McKittrick, "On Plantations, Prisons, and a Black Sense of Place," 951.

161. "'Urban Site' Asked for Local Prison," *Shreveport Times*, July 25, 1975, Folder: July–August 1975, Box 3, DCNC.

162. Bill Day, "Keep Convicts Out," *Red River Journal*, October 8, 1975, Folder: September–October 1975, Box 3, DCNC.

163. Davis, "Residents Will Protest Use of Carver School as Prison."

164. Davis, "Residents Will Protest Use of Carver School as Prison"; Richard Munson, "Petition Backing Move of Inmates Signed by 1,000 Jackson Residents," *State Times*, August 17, 1975, Folder: July–August 1975, Box 3, DCNC; Boyd, "Council Vows to Fight East N.O. Prison Facility."

165. White, "Council Resolution Opposes Prison Plan."

166. "The Candidate Who Means Business: Jimmy Faircloth," *Alexandria Daily Town Talk*, September 24, 1975, Folder: September–October 1975, Box 3, DCNC; Day, "Keep Convicts Out."

167. "Angola Has Ample Space for Expansion," *Red River Journal*, September 24, 1975, Folder: September–October 1975, Box 3, DCNC; "Opposition to Prison Expansion Is Voiced," *Morning Advocate*, January 15, 1976, Folder: January–March 1976, Box 4, DCNC; Dale Curry, "Jurors Tell Corrections Head to Spell out Angola Troubles," *Morning Advocate*, March 31, 1976, Folder: January–March 1976, Box 4, DCNC.

168. "Angola Has Ample Space for Expansion."

169. "Angola Decentralization Urged," *Morning Advocate*, September 5, 1975, Folder: September–October 1975, Box 3, DCNC.

170. "Prison Decentralization—Tough Decisions"; "'Urban Site' Asked for Local Prison," *Shreveport Times*, July 25, 1975, Folder: July–August 1975, Box 3, DCNC.

171. "Urban Site Asked for Local Prison."

172. Milford Fryer, "Residents Opposing Plans to Construct Prison in St. Gabriel," *Morning Advocate*, May 21, 1976, Folder: April–May 1976, Box 4, DCNC; Richard Munson, "Court Order Restrains Plan to Transfer Inmates," *Morning Advocate*, August 9, 1975, Folder: July–August 1975, Box 3, DCNC. Critical geographers have debunked this prison booster economic development argument. See Gilmore, *Golden Gulag*; Bonds, "Discipline and Devolution"; Bonds, "Economic Development, Racialization, and Privilege."

173. A prime example is "A Festering Sore," *Shreveport Journal*, September 11, 1975, Folder: September–October 1975, Box 3, DCNC.

174. "Another View on Inmate Transfer," *Morning Advocate*, August 29, 1975, Folder: July–August 1975, Box 3, DCNC.

175. "Street Forum: New Jail Here," *Daily Advertiser*, August 3, 1975, Folder: July–August 1975, Box 3, DCNC; "A Positive Approach to Penal Reform," *Morning Advocate*, August 15, 1975, Folder: July–August 1975, Box 3, DCNC; "Bossier Prison Site Reported Ruled Out," *Morning Advocate*, March 19, 1976, Folder: January–March 1976, Box 4, DCNC.

176. "Big Prisons Not Answer," *Times-Picayune*, October 2, 1975, Folder: September–October 1975, Box 3, DCNC.

177. "When Readers Speak: The Problems of Angola from the Other Side of the Fence," *Morning Advocate*, September 18, 1975, Folder: September–October 1975, Box 3, DCNC.

178. Tommy R. Mason, "Lifer's," *Angolite*, August 1975, 23.

179. Wilbert Rideau, "The Population Explosion," *Angolite*, May/June 1976, 6.

180. "State Preparing to Move Some Angola Inmates Out," *State Times*, July 24, 1975, Folder: July–August 1975, Box 3, DCNC.

181. Marilyn Goff, "Red Beans & Rice," *St. Francisville Democrat*, July 24, 1975, Folder: July–August 1975, Box 3, DCNC; Munson, "Court Order Restrains Plan to Transfer Inmates."

182. Munson, "Court Order Restrains Plan to Transfer Inmates"; Adams, "Inmate Transfer Plans Grind to a Halt Once Again"; "Court Blocks Angola Move of Prisoners to Hospital," *Daily Reveille*, September 4, 1975, Folder: September–October 1975, Box 3, DCNC.

183. Roy Miller, "Talks on Angola Transfers Set in E. Feliciana," *Morning Advocate*, August 14, 1975, Folder: July–August 1975, Box 3, DCNC.

184. Munson, "Petition Backing Move of Inmates Signed by 1,000 Jackson Residents."

185. "Police Jury to Stay out of Inmate Transfer Suit," *Morning Advocate*, August 19, 1975, Folder: July–August 1975, Box 3, DCNC.

186. "Court Blocks Angola Move of Prisoners to Hospital."

187. "Supreme Court to Decide Fate of State's Angola Reform Plan," *States-Item*, October 3, 1975, Folder: September–October 1975, Box 3, DCNC.

188. Roy Miller, "State Plans Appeal of Ruling Blocking Prisoner Transfer," *Morning Advocate*, September 4, 1975, Folder: September–October 1975, Box 3, DCNC.

189. Rafael Bermudez, "State Is Appealing Angola Inmate Transfer Ban Ruling," *State Times*, September 4, 1975, Folder: September–October 1975, Box 3, DCNC.

190. Bill Lynch, "Angola Session May Be Forced," *States-Item*, September 30, 1975, Folder: September–October 1975, Box 3, DCNC.

191. Deidre Cruse, "500 Inmates to Be Moved from Angola to Jackson," *Morning Advocate*, October 28, 1975, Folder: September–October 1975, Box 3, DCNC.

192. Bill McMahon, "La. Approves Pen Projects Bonds Issue," *State Times*, November 25, 1975, Folder: November–December 1975, Box 3, DCNC.

193. "State to Begin Taking Inmates to Dixon Unit," *State Times*, April 1, 1976, Folder: April–May 1975, Box 3, DCNC.

194. Ed Anderson, "Connick Attacks Parole Board Plan," *Times-Picayune*, October 28, 1975, Folder: September–October 1975, Box 3, DCNC.

195. "Records Eyed," *Morning Advocate*, November 15, 1975, Folder: November–December 1975, Box 3, DCNC. In a more bombastic moment, Harry Connick said that he would personally stand at the prison gates with a shotgun to keep people from getting out if the state implemented mass early release. In turn, jail house lawyers Biggy Johnston and John McCormick filed a lawsuit questioning Connick's sanity. "Connick Says He'll Be at Angola Gates to Stop Releases," *State Times*, November 8, 1975, Folder: November–December 1975, Box 3, DCNC; Murphy, "Two Inmates Question DA Connick's Sanity."

196. "Criminals Face Harsher Penalties as New Law Takes Effect," *States-Item*, September 17, 1975, Folder: September–October 1975, Box 3, DCNC.

197. Walt Philbin, "Judge Scores DA's Use of Multiple Offender Law," *States-Item*, September 11, 1975, Folder: September–October 1975, Box 3, DCNC.

198. "Early Release Possible for Some in N.O. Jail," *Morning Advocate*, July 20, 1975, Folder: July–August 1975, Box 3, DCNC.

199. "Edwards Jail Order Killed by Fitzmorris," *States-Item*, July 22, 1975, Folder: July–August 1975, Box 3, DCNC.

200. *Williams v. McKeithan* C.A 71-98 (M.D.La, 1975), Civil Docket, n.p., HWVJM; C.M. Hargroder, "Judge Limits Angola's Inmate Admittance," *Times-Picayune*, September 6, 1975, Folder: September–October 1975, Box 3, DCNC.

201. Pierre V. DeGruy, "Packed Prison Feared," *Times-Picayune*, September 12, 1975, Folder: September–October 1975, Box 3, DCNC.

202. Paul Atkinson, "Giarrusso Suggests Tents to House Angola Prisoners," *Times-Picayune*, November 6, 1975, Folder: November–December 1975, Box 3, DCNC. NOPD Superintendent Giarrusso was angry that the state's financial responsibilities were displaced onto the city and proposed that a long-term solution might be to expand OPP.

203. Roy Reed, "Louisiana's Jails Are Being Packed," *New York Times*, September 18, 1975, Folder: September–October 1975, Box 3, DCNC; "Caddo Jails Are Nearing Peak Capacity," *Morning Advocate*, October 20, 1975, Folder: September–October 1975, Box 3, DCNC; "Sheriff Says Lafayette Needs More Jail Space," *Morning Advocate*, November 10, 1975, Folder: November–December 1975, Box 3, DCNC.

204. Deirdre Cruse, "Prisoner Swap Is Agreed to by U.S. Court," *State Times*, November 20, 1975, Folder: November–December 1975, Box 3, DCNC.

205. "La. Prison Situation Reported 'Shell Game,'" *Morning Advocate*, April 21, 1976, Folder: April–May 1976, Box 4, DCNC.

206. Curry, "Jurors Tell Corrections Head to Spell out Angola Troubles."

207. C. Paul Phelps, who had been second in command under Elayn Hunt, was appointed to head the DOC in early 1976 after Hunt's diagnosis and sudden death from breast cancer.

208. Curry, "Jurors Tell Corrections Head to Spell out Angola Troubles."

209. "Angola to Reopen for New Inmates," *States-Item*, April 22, 1976, Folder: April–May 1976, Box 4, DCNC.

210. Paul Bartels, "Prison Sites Bill Back on Calendar," *Morning Advocate*, June 8, 1976, Folder: June–September 1976, Box 4, DCNC; "House Panel OKs Local Gov't Votes on Prison Sites," *State Times*, July 27, 1976, Folder: June–September 1976, Box 4, DCNC.

211. "Barracks Prison Money Put back in Capital Bill," *Times-Picayune*, October 13, 1976.

212. Act 528 §1, *Official Journal of the House of Representatives of the State of Louisiana*.

213. *Executive Budget 1976–1977*, vol. 1, 9, Box 1, SBR; "Edwards Outlines 10-Year $82-Million Prisons Plan," *Times Picayune*, July 8, 1976, Folder: June–September 1976, Box 4, DCNC.

214. *Executive Budget 1976–1977*, vol. 1, Box 1, SBR.

215. "Edwards Says Prison Plans Are Opposed," *State Times*, May 26, 1976, Folder: April–May 1976, Box 4, DCNC.

215. Wilbert Rideau, "Angola Here to Stay," *Angolite*, March/April 1976, 33–34.

217. "Edwards Outlines 10-Year $82-Million Prisons Plan"; J. Douglass Murphy, "A Huge Place for Us Really Bad Guys," *Times-Picayune*, July 30, 1976,

Folder: June–September 1976, Box 4, DCNC; Deidre Cruse, "House Reduces Use of Jackson Barracks as Prison Facility," *State Times*, June 30, 1976, Folder: June–September 1976, Box 4, DCNC; Charles M. Hargroder, "Senate Sends Prison Bonds OK to Edwards, Adjournment Early," *Times-Picayune*, August 20, 1976; *Capital Outlay Budget. Fiscal Year 1976–1977*, 58, Box 5, SBR.

218. J. Douglass Murphy, "State's Prison Plans Surpass U.S. Order," *Times-Picayune*, August 8, 1976, Folder: June–September 1976, Box 4, DCNC.

219. Ehrenkrantz Group, *Louisiana Prison System Study*, 73–74, Box 1, GLRPS.

220. Ehrenkrantz Group, *Louisiana Prison System Study*, 8, 75, Box 1, GLRPS.

221. Commission Membership List, Folder 1, Box 3, JSP; "Senate Concurrent Resolution No. 3," First Extraordinary Session of Louisiana Legislature 1976, Folder 2, Box 3, JSP.

222. Rev. James Stovall, "Talk to the Louisiana District Attorneys' Association," March 10, 1978, Folder 2, Box 3, JSP.

223. Governor's Pardon, Parole, and Rehabilitation Commission Minutes of Meeting, January 14, 1977, Folder 1, Box 3, JSP; Charles M. Hargroder, "Barracks Prisoners Few," *Morning Advocate*, January 15, 1977.

224. Ehrenkrantz Group, *Louisiana Prison System Study*, 56, Box 1, GLRPS.

225. A presentation by Jack Foster of the national bipartisan Council of State Governments significantly influenced their work. Jack D. Foster, Remarks before the Governor's Pardon, Parole, and Rehabilitation Commission, May 9, 1977, 2, Folder 2, Box 3, JSP.

226. Memo to Members of the Governor's Pardon, Parole, and Rehabilitation Commission from James L. Stovall, January 31, 1978, Folder 3, Box 3, JSP.

227. Comprehensive System for Prison Release and Rehabilitation, 1978, Folder 4, Box 3, JSP.

228. Senator Fritz Wihdhorst, Proposed Parole Legislation, Folder 2, Box 3, JSP; Rev. James Stovall, "Prisons and Prisoners in Louisiana," April 5, 1978, Folder 8, Box 3, JSP.

229. Comprehensive System for Prison Release and Rehabilitation, 1978, Folder 4, Box 3, JSP.

230. LDAA Position Statement on the Recommendations of the Governor's Commission on Pardon, Parole, and Rehabilitation, 2, Folder 2, Box 3, JSP.

231. LDAA Position Statement on the Recommendations of the Governor's Commission on Pardon, Parole, and Rehabilitation, 2, Folder 2, Box 3, JSP.

232. LDAA Position Statement on the Recommendations of the Governor's Commission on Pardon, Parole, and Rehabilitation, 3, Folder 2, Box 3, JSP.

233. Rev. James Stovall, Letter to Mr. Camille F. Gravel, Jr., April 10, 1979, Folder 4, Box 3, JSP.

234. *State of Louisiana Budget, Fiscal Year 1979–1980*, xvii, Box 4, SBR; Rev. James Stovall, Letter to Governor Edwin Edwards, July 19, 1979, Folder 4, Box 3, JSP.

235. There is inconsistency in the name of this commission in the archive. At times it is referred to as the Prison System Study Commission, at others as the Governor's Office Long Range Study Commission, and at other times simply as the

"Master Plan." I choose to refer to it as the Prison System Study Commission because this was what they called themselves in their major reports.

236. Ehrenkrantz Group, *Louisiana Prison System Study*, Box 1, GLRPS.

237. Louisiana Commission on Law Enforcement and Administration of Criminal Justice Grant Application, 6, April 1, 1978, Box 1, GLRPS; Ehrenkrantz Group, *Louisiana Prison System Study*, 181, Box 1, GLRPS.

238. Ehrenkrantz Group, *Louisiana Prison System Study*, 3, 66, Box 1, GLRPS.

239. Ehrenkrantz Group, *Louisiana Prison System Study*, 4, Box 1, GLRPS.

240. Schept, *Progressive Punishment*, 121.

241. Ehrenkrantz Group, *Louisiana Prison System Study*, 12, Box 1, GLRPS.

242. Ehrenkrantz Group, *Louisiana Prison System Study*, 120, Box 1, GLRPS.

243. Ehrenkrantz Group, *Louisiana Prison System Study*, 11, 123–24, Box 1, GLRPS.

244. Ehrenkrantz Group, *Louisiana Prison System Study*, 126–27, Box 1, GLRPS.

245. Ehrenkrantz Group, *Louisiana Prison System Study*, 130–31, Box 1, GLRPS.

246. Ehrenkrantz Group, *Louisiana Prison System Study*,133–34, Box 1, GLRPS. Although this proposal was popular at the time with decarceration activists involved with the Louisiana Coalition on Jails and Prisons and the national prison moratorium movement, this political debate was nowhere to be found in the final report or the accompanying archival materials. This is somewhat surprising given that John Vodicka of LCJP was a member of the commission.

247. Ehrenkrantz Group, *Louisiana Prison System Study*, 12, Box 1, GLRPS.

248. For more on the capaciousness of "alternatives to incarceration," see Schept, *Progressive Punishment* and Story, *Prison Land*.

249. Prison System Study Commission, *Solving the Prison Problem*, Folder: Community Corrections Act, Box 3, GLRPS.

250. Internal Community Corrections Act notes, Box 3, Folder: Community Corrections Act, GLRPS; Peter Tattersall, Letter to Mr. A Breed, April 20, 1979, Folder: Technical Proposal, Box 2, GLRPS.

251. C. Paul Phelps, Letter to Robin C. Ford, July 11, 1979, Folder: NIC Correspondence General, Box 2, GLRPS.

252. Ehrenkrantz Group, *Louisiana Prison System Study*, 35, 62, Box 1, GLRPS.

253. Ehrenkrantz Group, *Louisiana Prison System Study*, 6, 63, Box 1, GLRPS.

254. Ehrenkrantz Group, *Louisiana Prison System Study*, 195–204, Box 1, GLRPS.

255. Woods, *Development Arrested*, 256.

256. Ehrenkrantz Group, *Louisiana Prison System Study*, 62, Box 1, GLRPS.

257. "Editorial," *Angolite*, March/April 1977, 9.

258. *Executive Budget 1979–1980*, vol. 1, Box 2, SBR; *Executive Budget 1980–1981*, vol. 1, Box 2, SBR.

259. Johnston, interview, March 25, 2016; "Brief Shots," *Angolite*, November/December 1976, 8.

260. Alan Citron, "More Maximum Security Inmates at Angola?" *Times-Picayune*, March 24, 1978; "Homosexuality Is a Problem at CCI," *Shreveport Times*, April 10, 1980.

261. "Board of Corrections Minutes," June 16, 1977, Folder 1, DCBR; "Busting Open," *Angolite*, May/June 1977, 9–12; "Editorial," *Angolite*, May/June 1977, 20–22.

262. "Angola Accusations Should Be Investigated," *State Times*, August 10, 1978.

Chapter 2

1. Michael Glover, "A Man and a Prison," *Angolite*, July/August 1991, 30–31.

2. Ehrenkrantz Group, *Louisiana Prison System Study*, 33–34, Box 1, GLRPS.

3. "Projection of Males in DOC Jurisdiction (Excluding Those on Appeal in Local Jails)," Folder 9, Box 3, JSP; Louisiana Division of Administration, *The Governor's Corrections Plan*, April 1990, 7.

4. Louisiana Division of Administration, *The Governor's Corrections Plan*, April 1990, 7.

5. "The Longtermers: A Study," *Angolite*, March/April 1977, 28–36.

6. Louisiana Division of Administration, *The Governor's Corrections Plan*, April 1990, 7.

7. "Edwards Outlines 10-Year, $82-Million Prisons Plan," *Times-Picayune*, July 8, 1976; Marsha Shuler, "Treen Plans on Earmarking Oil Bonus Funds to Aid Jails," *State Times*, April 10, 1981; "Anti-Crime Money Won't Be Cut, Treen Says," *Times-Picayune*, February 17, 1982.

8. Here I am following Ruth Wilson Gilmore and Craig Gilmore, who define "anti-state state" building as occurring when state actors justify their decimation of social services using the rhetoric of needing to shrink the state, all the while growing state capacities, in the aggregate, through new institutional arrangements that expand the state's capacity for coercion in the form of police, jails, and prisons. Gilmore and Gilmore, "Restating the Obvious," 141–162.

9. Although the goal of this election strategy—codified in the 1974 Louisiana constitution—was to further squeeze out Republicans from state politics, over time the open primary format would prove to do the exact opposite.

10. For more on the disputed 1872 Louisiana governor's race see Du Bois, *Black Reconstruction in America*, 482–484. "GOP Backs Only Viable Candidates," *Times-Picayune*, January 3, 1979.

11. There is still much to be researched about Metairie and Jefferson Parish as key bases for the Right not only in Louisiana but also for the nation writ large as gestured to by McGirr in *Suburban Warriors*, 13.

12. James H. Gill, "Track Record of Candidates," *Times-Picayune*, January 13, 1979; Iris Kelso, "Not Easy to Beat Treen," *Times-Picayune*, September 23, 1979.

13. Bill Lynch, "Treen Says He'll Operate Objectively," *Times-Picayune*, May 22, 1979; Bill Lynch, "Bi-Partisan Office Pledged by Treen," *Times-Picayune*, June, 25, 1979.

14. Kelso, "Not Easy to Beat Treen"; "Treen for Governor—An Editorial," *Times-Picayune*, September 30, 1979; Joe Massa, "Councilman Giarrusso to Endorse Treen Today," *Times-Picayune*, October 10, 1979; Charles M. Hargroder, "Change Moral Tone—Treen," *Times-Picayune*, October 17, 1979.

15. "30 Local Black Political Groups Back Lambert," *Times-Picayune*, September 28, 1979; Charles M. Hargroder, "Fitz Admits Stationing Guards in Parishes," *Times-Picayune*, October 31, 1979.

16. Iris Kelso, "Home Won for Treen," *Times-Picayune*, December 10, 1979; Clancy DuBos, "Walker: An Oracle and a Mentor in Louisiana Politics," *Times-Picayune*, December 10, 1979.

17. "That Stinking Prison," *Times-Picayune*, December 7, 1979.

18. Alan Citron, "Prison Funds Rising, but Crime Is Too," *Times-Picayune*, September 30, 1979; Fitzmorris Campaign Committee, "Fitzmorris . . . Leader for the '80s," *Times-Picayune*, October 27, 1979. Heightened public attention on the previously little remarked-on practice of clemency followed the controversial revelation that a law firm that represented recent successful clemency petitioners also served as counsel to Governor Edwards. Pierre V. DeGruy and J. Douglass Murphy, "Gravel's Firm Plays Top State Clemency Role," *Times-Picayune*, March 18, 1979.

19. Pierre V. DeGruy and J. Douglass Murphy, "Candidate Express Views on Clemency Controversy," *Times-Picayune*, April 1, 1979.

20. "It's Going to Be Tough," *Angolite*, May/June 1980, 11.

21. As Sarah Haley documents, Georgia officials passed similar legislation that allowed their Prison Commission to grant parole to anyone serving a life sentence after ten years. Haley, *No Mercy Here*, 174.

22. Burk Foster, "What Is the Meaning of Life," *Academy of Criminal Justice Sciences*, May 9, 1995, www.burkfoster.com/MeaningofLife.htm.

23. Rideau and Wikberg, *Life Sentences*, 225.

24. Biggy Johnston, "Rope without a Noose: Legal Spectrum," *Angolite*, September/October 1982, 62–67.

25. "The Forgotten Men," *Angolite*, May/June 1980, 23–56.

26. Kenneth "Biggy" Johnston, interview by author, January 15, 2011.

27. Rideau, *In the Place of Justice*, 75.

28. "On the 10–6 Front," *Angolite*, March/April 1983, 55–60. The terminology of "natural life" is an obfuscation and an affront. First, there is nothing natural about a life spent in a cage. Second, given the extensive evidence that time spent behind bars shortens people's lives, the life of one who is locked up is a life marked by premature death, not a healthy "natural" life.

29. "Connick Takes Issue with Penal Study," *Angolite*, January/February 1978, 27.

30. "Treen Speaks out on Pardons," *Angolite*, November/December 1981, 6.

31. Rideau, *In the Place of Justice*, 170.

32. "Life: No Rhyme, No Reason," *Angolite*, September/October 1982, 32.

33. Norris Henderson, interview by author, December 14, 2010.

34. Governor's Commission on Criminal Justice Interim Report, March 12, 1981, Folder 12, Box 769, DTP; "Governor Announces Program on Law Enforcement and Criminal Justice," *Eunice Gazette*, May 3, 1981, Folder: Treen, David, Box 10, DCNC; "Crime & Politics," *Angolite*, May/June 1981, 10.

35. Donald Bollinger address to Louisiana law enforcement, 1980, Folder 2, Box 703, DTP; "38 Arrested in French Quarter on Vice Charges," *Times-Picayune*, September 13, 1980.

36. Hinton, *From the War on Poverty*, 279.

37. Litchfield letter to Nungesser, "Criminal Justice Coordinating Council," May 12, 1980, Folder 3, Box 687, DTP; Duncan S. Kemp, III letter to Governor Dave Treen, May 29, 1980, Folder 2, Box 687, DTP; Litchfield to Brinkman, "Accomplishments of the Administration in the Criminal Justice Area," September 15, 1981, Folder 4, Box 796, DTP.

38. Louisiana Coalition on Jails and Prisons, "Women in Prison Neglected, Abused," *Inside*, November–December 1979, Folder: Louisiana Coalition, Box 2, SCJPR; Southern Prisoners' Defense Committee letter to Richard Crane, RE: Camp J, Louisiana State Penitentiary, January 3, 1980, Folder: Head v. Phelps, Box 2, ALR. "Camp J Sued," *Angolite*, November/December 1980, 17.

39. Phelps, letter to Nungesser, Cade, Mouton, and Beoubay, June 5, 1980, Folder 1, Box 667, DTP.

40. "The Changing of the Guard," *Angolite*, November/December 1981, 10.

41. National Moratorium on Prison Construction, *Jericho*, Winter 1981/1982, Folder: 9/19/81–10/21/82, Box 8, DCNC.

42. Rideau, *In the Place of Justice*, 166–167.

43. Rideau, *In the Place of Justice*, 166.

44. "Ban on LCJP Literature Upheld," *Angolite*, September/October 1980, 15.

45. Joe Massa, "City Intensifies War on Criminals," *Times-Picayune*, May 4, 1980; Molly Moore, "Crime Tops Poll of N.O. Problems," *Times-Picayune*, June 22, 1980.

46. Housing Authority New Orleans Security Program proposal, 1980, Folder 2, Box 687, DTP; Joe Massa, "City Intensifies War on Criminals," *Times-Picayune*, May 4, 1980; Greater New Orleans State Representatives letter to Governor Treen, April 14, 1980, Folder 5, Box 703, DTP.

47. Joe Massa, "Council to Decide on Use of Money for Youth Study Center," *Times-Picayune*, November 27, 1980; Charles M. Hargroder, "N.O. Request for Grant 'too Big' for Aid on Jobs," *Times-Picayune*, December 23, 1980.

48. Hirsch, "New Orleans: Sunbelt in the Swamp," 100–137; Souther, *New Orleans on Parade*, 2.

49. Gotham, "Tourism Gentrification," 1103–05; Sakakeeny, *Roll with It*, 96–97.

50. Souther, *New Orleans on Parade*, 78–184. Mayor Dutch Morial was hesitant to adopt this tourism economic development strategy, preferring to invest in manufacturing jobs in New Orleans East. However, the Reagan administration's cutting of economic development funds left Morial without the resources to implement this plan.

51. Robert A. Roland to Mayor Ernest 'Dutch' Morial, April 18, 1980, Folder 2, Box 687, DTP.

52. Background document, n.d., Folder 17, Box 56, EDMP.

53. Carroll and Marye, *The New Orleans Criminal Justice System 1983*, 6.

54. Gary Hines, "Parish Prison Meets Federal Judge's Deadline," *Shreveport Journal*, November 5, 1982, Folder: 10/2/81–12/31/82, Box 8, DCNC.

55. "A Noble Effort," *Angolite*, July/Aug 1982, 24.

56. "A Noble Effort," *Angolite*, July/Aug 1982, 24; "The Reality of Crime," *Angolite*, September/October 1982, 18–22; "The Moment of Truth," *Angolite*, May/June 1982, 12.

57. "Jail Overcrowding" Memo to Nungesser from Phelps, October 3, 1980, Folder 8, Box 666, DTP.

58. ACLU of Louisiana Legal Docket, September 29, 1979, Folder: Legal Docket Louisiana 1970s, Box 7, ALR; "Suits Filed against the Department for January," Memo to Phelps from Crane, February 13, 1980, Folder 8, Box 666, DTP; Louisiana Coalition on Jails and Prisons, *Inside*, October 1980, Folder: Louisiana Coalition, Box 2, SCJPR.

59. Walt Philbin, "Deputies Cheer Sheriff's Prison Caper," *State Times*, April 15, 1980, Folder: 1980, Box 7, DCNC.

60. *Williams v. McKeithan* C.A 71–98 (M.D.La, 1975), Civil Docket List, 5, HWVJM.

61. "State Prisoners Removed from Parish Jails," *Gazette*, n.d., Folder: Parish Inmate Transfers, Box 10, DCNC.

62. "Status of the Louisiana Commission on Law Enforcement," Litchfield to Governor Treen, October 8, 1980, Folder 3, Box 656, DTP; Mouton, letter to Litchfield, October 10, 1980, Folder 7, Box 666, DTP; Mouton, letter to Litchfield, December 16, 1980, Folder 7, Box 666, DTP; "Parish Prisons' Improvement Program," Mouton memo to Governor Treen, December 17, 1980, Folder 7, Box 666, DTP.

63. Roussel to Bollinger, Memo: Activities for the Period March 9–13, 1981, Folder 1, Box 815, DTP.

64. Litchfield to Brinkman, "Accomplishments of the Administration," September 15, 1981, Folder 4, Box 796, DTP.

65. *Executive Budget 1980–1981*, vol. 1, A-11, Box 2, SBR.

66. Shuler, "Treen Plans on Earmarking Oil Bonus Funds to Aid Jails."

67. Excerpt of Minutes of State Bond Commission Meeting, October 13, 1981, Folder 1, Box 740, DTP.

68. "Comments on Governor David C. Treen's Criminal Justice Package," Folder 4, Box 796, DTP.

69. Richardson and Scott, "Mineral Taxes and Revenues," 127.

70. *Executive Budget 1980–1981*, vol. 1, A-11, Box 2, SBR; Louisiana Division Mid-Continent Oil and Gas Association, *Louisiana Oil & Gas Facts*, 5, Box 1, EDP; Stein, *Pivotal Decade*, 266.

71. Nore and Turner, *Oil and Class Struggle*; Silverstein, *The Secret World of Oil*, 200–212.

72. *Executive Budget 1984–1985*, vol. 1, A-5-A-6, A-13, Box 2, SBR; Louisiana Legislative Fiscal Office, *Direct Mineral Revenue, 1969–2014*; Richardson and Scott, "Mineral Taxes and Revenues," 128–129.

73. Treen letter to Dufrene, November 6, 1980, Folder 7, Box 796, DTP; Black, "Louisiana State Expenditures," 34; Prasad, "The Popular Origins of Neoliberalism."

74. *Executive Budget 1981–1982*, vol. 1, A-3-A-4, Box 2, SBR; *Executive Budget 1982–1983*, vol. 1, A-3-A,4, Box 2, SBR; Prasad, "The Popular Origins of Neoliberalism," 351–353; Stein, *Pivotal Decade*, 263–264.

75. *Executive Budget 1982–1983*, vol. 1, A-4, Box 2, SBR.

76. "State Budgets to Be Cut within a Week," *Daily News*, October 28, 1982, Folder: 1/6/82–12/31/82, Box 8, DCNC; Charles Hargroder, "Treen Calls Special Session to Act on Fiscal, Other Issues," *Times-Picayune*, December 31, 1982, Folder: 1/6/82–12/31/82, Box 8, DCNC; *Executive Budget 1983–1984*, vol. 1, A-4, Box 2, SBR.

77. "The Fiscal Crunch," *Angolite*, March/April 1983, 18.

78. *Executive Budget 1983–1984*, vol. 1, A-11, Box 2, SBR.

79. *Executive Budget 1983–1984*, vol. 1, A-11, Box 2, SBR. Louisiana officials also believed that a service-oriented economy was the only economic recovery solution possible for New Orleans in their decision to host the 1984 Louisiana World's Fair. They hoped it would not only be a "needed boost for the city's tourist industry" but also would have positive effects for the state as a whole, even as they admitted it would only create temporary jobs.

80. *Executive Budget 1983–1984*, vol. 1, A-4, Box 2, SBR.

81. *Executive Budget 1982–1983*, vol. 1, A-3, Box 2, SBR; *Executive Budget 1983–1984*, vol. 1, A-4, Box 2, SBR.

82. Ronni Patriquin, "Treen: La. Won't Pay for Local Jails, Projects," *Shreveport Journal*, March 3, 1982, Folder: Treen, David, Box 10, DCNC; State Bond Commission Minutes, April 13, 1982, Folder 3, Box 853, DTP.

83. Cyrus J. Greco letter to Governor Treen, RE: State Prison Problems, October 21, 1982, Folder 3, Box 956, DTP.

84. "Editorial: The Double-Bunking Issue," *Angolite*, September/October 1982, 16.

85. "Treen's Prison Policy Challenged," *The Angolite*, September/October 1982.

86. "Editorial: The Double-Bunking Issue."

87. "Treen's Prison Policy Challenged."

88. "Editorial: The Double-Bunking Issue." For more on imprisoned intellectuals' writings on prisons and fascism see Rodriguez, *Forced Passages*, 127–140.

89. *Williams v. McKeithan* C.A 71–98 (M.D.La, 1975), "Questions and Answers," Folder 4, Box 956, DTP.

90. Hargroder, "Treen Calls Special Session to Act on Fiscal, Other Issues"; State Bond Commission Meeting Minutes, September 14, 1982, Folder 5, Box 852, DTP; State Bond Commission Meeting Minutes, August 24, 1982, Folder 3, Box 853, DTP; *Williams v. McKeithan* C.A 71–98 (M.D.La, 1975), Civil Docket List, 12, HWVJM; "The Overcrowding Crisis"; Dan Even, "Prison Funds Approved," *Daily News*, December 9, 1982, Folder: 1/6/82–12/31/82, Box 8, DCNC.

91. Governor Treen to Mouton and Greco, May 14, 1982, Folder 2, Box 956, DTP.

92. "The Fiscal Crunch," *Angolite* March/April 1983, 28.

93. "Budget Cut Priorities Need to Be Examined," *Winn Parish Enterprise*, December 1, 1982, Folder: 1/6/82–12/31/82, Box 8, DCNC.

94. "Life: No Rhyme, No Reason," *The Angolite*, September/October 1982, 41.

95. Bill McMahon, "Corrections Increase Raises Legislators' Ire," *Morning Advocate*, April 27, 1983, Folder: Miscellaneous 1/11/83–4/19/83, Box 9, DCNC.

96. "The Overcrowding Crisis," *The Angolite*, January/February 1983, 49.

97. Greco memo to Governor Treen, December 13, 1982, Folder 4, Box 956, DTP.

98. Poston, letter to Governor Treen, April 8, 1981, Folder 3, Box 750, DTP.

99. Governor Treen, letter to Poston, April 15, 1981, Folder 3, Box 750, DTP.

100. "Governor Signs into Law Anti-Crime Legislation," August 5, 1982, Folder 2, Box 956, DTP.

101. Gottschalk, *The Prison and the Gallows*, 86.

102. Gottschalk, *The Prison and the Gallows*, 87–89.

103. Gottschalk, *The Prison and the Gallows*, 126. The entire Baton Rouge rape crisis center staff resigned in protest and were replaced by criminal justice employees.

104. The term "carceral feminism" works to both define and critique the political framework that gender justice is best achieved through increasing surveillance, policing, and incarceration. Although first coined by Bernstein in her article "Militarized Humanitarianism Meets Carceral Feminism," the underlying thinking has been articulated by a number of women of color and antiracist feminists in texts such as Sudbury, "Introduction: Feminist Critiques"; Critical Resistance and INCITE! Women of Color against Violence, "Gender Violence and the Prison-Industrial Complex"; Braz, "Kinder, Gentler, Gender Responsive Cages"; Thuma, *All Our Trials*.

105. Richie, *Arrested Justice*. For more on the alternatives offered to such narrowing of the antiviolence movement see Thuma, *All Our Trials*; Ruttenberg, "A Feminist Critique of Mandatory Arrest."

106. "Push for Crime Victims' Rights Timed for Legislature by Treen," *Associated Press*, April 12, 1982, Folder: Treen, David, Box 10, DCNC.

107. "Treen Names 6-Point Rape Control Plan," *Comet*, March 11, 1982, Folder: Treen, David, Box 10, DCNC.

108. Wells, "Southern Horrors," 57–82; Carby, "On the Threshold of Woman's Era"; Hodes, "The Sexualization of Reconstruction Politics," 402–17; Wiegman, "The Anatomy of Lynching," 445–67; Sommerville, "The Rape Myth," 481–518; Haley, *No Mercy Here*, 109.

109. Davis, *Women, Race & Class*, 172–201.

110. Scott, "The Structure of the Louisiana Economy," 16.

111. Scott, "The Structure of the Louisiana Economy," 14.

112. Scott, "The Structure of the Louisiana Economy," 16.

113. Louisiana Legislative Fiscal Office, *Louisiana Relative Unemployment Rates*.

114. This racial disparity in unemployment is not unique to Louisiana. Shulman, "Why Is the Black Unemployment Rate?"; US Department of Labor, Bureau of Labor Statistics, *The Economics Daily*, 2017.

115. Felicity Barringer, "White-Black Disparity in Income Narrowed in 80's, Census Shows," *New York Times*, July 24, 1992.

116. Black, "Louisiana State Expenditures," 34.

117. One of the few investments the state bond commission made in jobs was it provided financing to shopping malls and Wendy's hamburger chains in the name of economic development—a tacit support of low-wage job development. State Bond Commission Meeting Minutes, November 30, 1982, Folder 4, Box 852, DTP.

118. Marx, *Capital*, vol. 1; Marx and Engels, *The Communist Manifesto*, 12; Smith, *Uneven Development*, 120–23.

119. The creation of an unemployed segment of the population serves two primary purposes. One, it creates a reserve labor force that can be called on to fill labor shortages at key moments. Two, it serves as an implicit threat to the employed that if they make too many demands on capital, such as for better wages and benefits or shorter workdays, there is a pool of workers available to replace them.

120. Woods, *Development Arrested*; Wilson, *America's Johannesburg*; Glenn, *Unequal Freedom*.

121. Parenti, *Lockdown America*, 238–239.

122. For more on this see Foucault, *Discipline and Punish*; Linebaugh, *The London Hanged*; Linebaugh and Rediker, *The Many-Headed Hydra*.

123. US Department of Justice, *Correctional Populations in the United States, 1985*, 57.

124. "The Fiscal Crunch"; C. M. Hargroder, "Senate OK Goes to Airport Unit," *Times-Picayune*, June 12, 1970.

125. "Treen's Prison Labor Plan," *Times-Picayune*, April 14, 1982.

126. E. J. Rousselle, "Prison Labor," *Times-Picayune*, July 24, 1982, Folder: 6/17/81–12/31/82, Box 8, DCNC.

127. John Vodicka, "Prisoner Abuse," *Times-Picayune*, April 21, 1982, Folder: 6/17/81–12/31/82, Box 8, DCNC.

128. "Labor Blocks Inmate Labor," *Angolite* July/August 1981, 9; "Inmate Labor: The Second Time Around," *Angolite* July/August 1982, 21; Mike Thomas, "Exploiting Convict Labor," *Angolite* July/August 1982, 22; "Editorial: Inmate Labor," *Angolite* July/August 1983, 11–12.

129. Thomas, "Exploiting Convict Labor," 22.

130. "Inmate Labor Bill Fails in Final Hours," *Daily Courier*, July 14, 1982, Folder: 6/17/81–12/31/82, Box 8, DCNC; "Inmate Labor Bill Put to Rest," *American Press*, January 18, 1983, Folder: Inmate Labor Bill, Box 9, DCNC; Marsha Schuler, "Panel Kills Inmate Labor Bill," *Morning Advocate*, April 29, 1983, Folder: Inmate Labor 1983, Box 9, DCNC. The only measure the legislature could get passed was a law that parishes could use prisoners in jails to work on local road projects, echoing the earlier "good roads program." Lichtenstein, "Good Roads and Chain Gangs."

131. "Utilizing Prison Labor; Good Idea, Bad Time?" *Daily Enterprise*, October 18, 1982, Folder: 6/17/82–12/31/82, Box 8, DCNC.

132. Gilmore, "An Interview with James Kilgore," 6–7.

133. Even these forms of prison labor blurred the line between productive and reproductive labor. Such commodities (including agricultural crops) continued to be sold only within Louisiana through the state use system whereby other state agencies and departments were encouraged to buy prisoner-made goods. So even within this system, the state was not making a profit as much as saving the state money through one state department generating revenue from selling to another state department; most often the various prisons sold commodities to each other.

134. Tommy Mason, "Moving Out," *Angolite* March/April 1976, 30.

135. Only 293 of more than 8,000 prisoners were involved in such work. Pesek, Ross, and White, "Present Operations: Office of Agri-Business," December 16, 1982,

I-2, Folder 5, Box 869, DTP; Governor's Commission on Criminal Justice, "Proposed Legislation for the 1982 Regular Session," Folder 1, Box 956, DTP.

136. "Oops . . . It Didn't Work Out," *Angolite*, January/February 1982, 6.

137. "Agri-Business Operations Trimmed," *Angolite*, March/April 1982, 6.

138. *Executive Budget 1983–1984*, vol. 1, A-4, Box 2, SBR; "Sheriff Layrisson Angry over Jail Fund Postponement," *Vindicator*, May 25, 1983, Folder: May-June 1983, Box 7, DCNC.

139. Maginnis, *The Last Hayride*, 28.

140. Maginnis, *The Last Hayride*, 208.

141. "An Angry Client in Louisiana Kills His Lawyer and Himself," *Associated Press*, August 19, 1983; Maginnis, *The Last Hayride*, 212–17.

142. Maginnis, *The Last Hayride*, 314–15.

143. In 1984, the Department of Public Safety and the Department of Corrections were combined into the Department of Public Safety and Corrections because there is a state constitutional limit on the number of state departments, and Governor Treen, as one of his last acts in office, founded the Louisiana Department of Environmental Quality.

144. "A New Beginning," *Angolite* March/April 1984, 23–36.

145. "Short Term Jail Relief," *Shreveport Times*, May 8, 1983, Folder: May-June 1983, Box 7, DCNC; Mary Durusau, "Bond Issue Dead, Crowded Jails Issue Still Alive," *Shreveport Journal*, May 12, 1983, Folder: May-June 1983, Box 7, DCNC; "In Their Infinite Wisdom," *Angolite*, November/December 1985, 11.

146. Chevalier, letter to Governor Treen, Re: Financing Technique for State and Local Correctional Facilities, February 16, 1983, Folder 2, Box 974, DTP.

147. Although he noted that LRBs would allow for the state and municipalities to exceed debt beyond current limitations, he failed to mention the higher interest rates of LRBs and the additional fees attached to them in contrast to GOBs.

148. Chevalier reassured Treen that it was extremely unlikely that the state would actually terminate a lease on a state project such as a jail, because the state saw such projects as vital public infrastructure.

149. Chevalier, letter to Governor Treen, Re: Financing Technique for State and Local Correctional Facilities, February 16, 1983, Folder 2, Box 974, DTP.

150. Governor Treen, letter to Chevalier, March 17, 1983, Folder 2, Box 974, DTP.

151. "Louisiana State Prisoners Held in Local Jails, 1979–1988," Folder 9, Box 3, JSP.

152. Act 893, *Official Journal of the House of Representatives of the State of Louisiana, Regular Session*, July 11, 1985.

153. The cosponsors of the bill were Rep. Raymond Laborde of Avoyelles Parish; Rep. Edward D'Gerolamo of Jefferson Parish; Rep. John Alario of Jefferson Parish; Rep. James David Cain (brother of DOC warden Burl Cain) of Allen, Beauregard, and Calcasieu Parishes; Rep. Eddie Doucet of Jefferson Parish; Rep. Hunt Downer of Terrebonne and Lafourche Parishes; Rep. Buddy Leach of Allen, Beauregard, and Vernon Parishes; Rep. Kevin Reilly of East Baton Rouge Parish; Rep. Joe Delpit of East Baton Rouge Parish; Rep. Francis Coleman of East Carroll, Madison,

Morehouse, Ouachita, Richland, and West Carroll Parishes; Rep. Clyde Kimball of West Baton Rouge and Pointe Coupe Parishes; Rep. Diana Bajoie of Orleans Parish; Rep. J. Thibodeaux of Acadia and Lafayette Parishes; Senator Nat Kiefer of Orleans Parish; Senator Donald Kelly of Winn, Grant, Natchitoches, Rapides, Red River, and Sabine Parishes; Senator Armand Brinkhaus of Avoyelles Parish; Senator Nunez of Jefferson Parish; Senator Hank Lauricella of Jefferson Parish; Senator Leonard Chabet of Terrebonne and LaFouche Parishes; Senator BB. "Sixty" Rayburn of Washington, St. Helena, St. Tammany; and Tangipahoa Parishes, and Senator Bryan Poston of Beauregard, Calcasieu, and Vernon Parishes.

154. Executive Order EWE 85–85 of December 3, 1985. In author's personal possession.

155. Foley, Judell, Beck, Bewly, Martin, & Hicks letter to Louisiana Correctional Facilities Corporation, December 30, 1985. Closing Documents, $155,775,000 Louisiana Correctional Facilities Corporation Lease Revenue Bonds, Series 1985. In author's personal possession.

156. Certificate as to Arbitrage, Closing Documents, $155,775,000 Louisiana Correctional Facilities Corporation Lease Revenue Bonds, Series 1985, In author's personal possession.

157. "In Their Infinite Wisdom," 11–12.

158. Bankston to Governor Edwards, November 27, 1985, Folder 15, Box 3, JSP.

159. James L. Stovall, Speech Notes, Folder 15, Box 3, JSP; James L. Stovall, Untitled Writing, Folder 15, Box 3, JSP. Allen Parish, one of the other sites selected for a prison, had already turned to carceral state-building in response to having the highest unemployment rate in the state—30.2 percent. In 1983, the parish successfully petitioned for a new federal detention center—Oakdale Detention Center. Edgar Poe, "Boost for Allen Parish," *Times-Picayune*, February 23, 1983, Folder: Miscellaneous 1/11/83–4/19/83, Box 9, DCNC.

160. Stovall, "Basic Information," 4, Folder 9, Box 3, JSP.

161. Rev. James L. Stovall to Stephanie L. Alexander, May 23, 1986, Folder 15, Box 3, JSP; Repeals Correctional Facilities Corporation and Provides for Defeasance of the Bonds, H.R. 973 (1986).

162. "More of the Same," *Angolite*, January/February 1987, 9–10.

163. Goodwin and Jasper, "Caught in a Winding, Snarling Vine," 38.

164. Rideau and Wilkberg, *Life Sentence*, 233.

165. Henderson, interview, December 14, 2010.

166. Foster, "What Is the Meaning of Life." By 1994, there were more than 2,500 people serving life without parole sentences in the Louisiana prison system. "Lifers," *Angolite*, November/December 1984, 4.

167. Jasper, "Social Movement Theory Today," 967.

168. "A New Beginning"; Norris Henderson, interview by author, October 7, 2010.

169. Johnston, interview, March 25, 2016.

170. Johnston, interview, March 25, 2016.

171. Johnston, interview, January 15, 2011.

172. Johnston, interview, January 15, 2011.

173. "The Forgotten Men," *Angolite*.

174. "The Effects of Dunn," *Angolite*, March/April 1982; Johnston, "A Rope without a Noose" *Angolite*; "On the 10–6 Front," *Angolite*.

175. "The Turner Death Knell," *Angolite*, March/April 1985.

176. Tommy Mason, "The Lifers Association," *Angolite*, September/October 1982, 50.

177. Mason, "The Lifers Association," 51.

178. Mason, "The Lifers Association," 61.

179. "Life: No Rhyme, No Reason," 32, 39.

180. "Life: No Rhyme, No Reason," 40–41.

181. "Life: No Rhyme, No Reason."

182. The first legal spectrum column was published in 1977. Biggy Johnston, "Legal Spectrum," *Angolite* July/August 1977, 21–22; "Legal Spectrum," *Angolite*, September/October 1978, 13–16; Johnston, "A Rope Without a Noose: Legal Spectrum," *Angolite*; Biggy Johnston, "Legal Spectrum," *Angolite*, November/December 1987, 52–61. Johnston also wrote columns for the Louisiana Coalition on Jails and Prisons newsletter. Kenneth Johnston, "The Burger Court: Closing the Doors," *Inside*, March 1977, Folder: Louisiana Coalition, Box 2, SCJPR.

183. "Conversations with the Dead," *Angolite*, September/October 1978, 31–49; "The Forgotten Men," 57–64.

184. "The Crisis Reports," *Angolite* March/April 1985, 22–27.

185. Frank Blackburn letter to John King, September 28, 1981, Folder 1, Box 864, DTP.

186. Henderson, interview, December 14, 2010.

187. Henderson, interview, December 14, 2010.

188. Wilbert Rideau, "Special Civics Project," *Angolite*, November/December 1987.

189. Johnston, interview, January 15, 2011; Henderson, interview, December 14, 2010; "The New Jailhouse Lawyer," *Angolite*, March/April 1979.

190. Wilbert Rideau describes Henderson as "the most popular of Angola's prisoners" in his memoir. Rideau, *In the Place of Justice*, 228.

191. Eugene Dean, interview by author, December 31, 2010.

192. Henderson, interview, December 14, 2010.

193. Checo Yancy, interview by author, January 7, 2011.

194. Henderson, interview, December 14, 2010.

195. "Change in Prison Population and Incarceration Rates, 1979–1987, The Nation and Louisiana," Folder 9, Box 3, JSP; "The Crowded Cage," *Shreveport Journal*, August 9, 1988. Of the 15,000 state prisoners, 3,500 were held in parish jails at this time. "DOC Inmates in Parish Prisons, 1982–1988," Folder 9, Box 3, JSP.

196. "A Public Service Announcement," *Angolite*, July/August 1987.

197. Katy Reckdahl, "Not Barred," *Gambit Weekly*, March 30, 2004.

198. Ted Quant, interview by author, February 9, 2011.

199. Quant, interview; Henderson, interview, December 14, 2010; Johnston, interview, January 15, 2011; Rideau, "Special Civics Project."

200. Rideau, "Special Civics Project."

201. Quant, interview; Rideau, "Special Civics Project."

202. Quant, interview.
203. Henderson, interview, December 14, 2010; Quant, interview.
204. Rideau, "Special Civics Project."
205. Floyd Webb, "Special Civics Project," *Angolite*, January/February 1990.
206. Rideau, "Special Civics Project."
207. Rideau, "Special Civics Project."
208. Jack Wardlaw, "Frankly We Need More Frankness," *Times-Picyaune*, September 27, 1987; "Office to Cut Fraud, Waste Is Promised by Roemer," *Times-Picayune*, October 8, 1987; "2 More Papers Endorse Roemer," *Times-Picayune*, October 4, 1987; "An Editorial: Roemer for Governor," *Times-Picayune*, September 27, 1987.
209. "Edge of Madness," *Angolite*, July/August 1986, 20.
210. David Maraniss, "Edwards Cuts His Losses," *New York Times*, October 26, 1987.
211. Henderson, interview, December 14, 2010; Quant, interview; Rideau, "Special Civics Project."
212. Henderson, interview, December 14, 2010.
213. Floyd Webb and Ron Wikberg, "The Price is Right," *Angolite* September/October 1989, 20.
214. Wilbert Rideau and Ron Wikberg, "The Omen II," *Angolite*, July/August 1989, 10–21; Linda Ashton, "Louisiana Inmates Blame Unrest on Governor: Roemer's Stinginess with Clemency Has Created 'Time Bomb,' Lifers Claim," *Associated Press*, July 23, 1989; Rideau, *In the Place of Justice*, 194–202.
215. *Williams v. McKeithan* C.A 71-98 (M.D.La, 1975), Civil Docket List, n.p. HWVJM.
216. Judge Polozola as quoted in Rideau and Wikberg, "The Omen II," 14–15.
217. Rideau and Wikberg, "The Omen II."
218. Rideau and Wikberg, "The Omen II," 15.
219. Rideau and Wikberg, "The Omen II," 17.
220. Rideau and Wikberg, *Life Sentences*, 255.
221. Henderson, interview, December 14, 2010.
222. Henderson, interview, December 14, 2010.
223. Webb, "Special Civics Project"; Johnston, interview, January 15, 2011.
224. Yancy, interview. This sentiment speaks to what Dan Berger notes in *Captive Nation*: the "collectivizing of life" among male incarcerated activists is illustrative of a political commitment to care that belies some of the patriarchal norms produced through sex-segregated prisons. Berger, *Captive Nation*, 175.
225. Yancy, interview.
226. Johnston, interview, January 15, 2011; Henderson, interview, December 14, 2010; Webb, "Special Civics Project."
227. Henderson, interview, December 14, 2010.
228. Henderson, interview.
229. Yancy, interview.
230. Flo Clarence Goodlow and Ron Wikberg, "A Noble Effort," *Angolite*, May/June 1990; Johnston, interview, January 15, 2011; Henderson, interview, December 14, 2010; Yancy, interview.

231. *Associated Press*, "Louisiana Inmates Offer Reform Package," *Dallas Morning News*, March 26, 1990.

232. Naomi Farve, interview by author, March 21, 2011; Goodlow and Wikberg, "A Noble Effort." Farve was also previously known as Naomi White-Warren Farve.

233. Henderson, interview, December 14, 2010.

234. Dean, interview; Henderson, interview, December 14, 2010; Yancy, interview.

235. Yancy, interview.

236. Dean, interview; Henderson, interview, December 14, 2010; Yancy, interview.

237. Dean, interview; Henderson, interview, December 14, 2010; Yancy, interview; Michael Glover, "Call for Unity," *Angolite*, January/February 1991.

238. Dean, interview.

239. Farve, interview; Johnston, interview, January 15, 2011.

240. Yancy, interview.

241. Yancy, interview.

242. Henderson, interview, December 14, 2010.

243. Johnston, interview, January 15, 2011.

244. Rideau, *In the Place of Justice*, 241.

245. Henderson, interview, December 14, 2010; Rideau, *In the Place of Justice*, 242–246.

246. Johnston, interview, January 15, 2011.

247. Rideau and Wikberg, *Life Sentences*, 256.

248. Louisiana Division of Administration, *The Governor's Corrections Plan*, 41; *Louisiana Prison System Study*, Box 1, GLRPS. Since the 1980s, the number of prisoners pardoned by governors has steadily dropped. Governor Mike Foster pardoned 460 people over his two terms. Kathleen Blanco pardoned 285 people, only 87 of whom were still behind bars during her single term. Bobby Jindal pardoned only 83 people between 2009–2016, whereas Governor John Bel Edwards issued 213 pardons between 2016–2021. All pale in comparison to the thousands pardoned by Edwards and his predecessor Governor McKeithan. Jan Moller, "Hundreds of Louisiana Prisoners Wait for Governor to Decide on Pardons," *Times-Picayune*, May 17, 2012; Kevin Litten, "Bobby Jindal Grants Pardon to 21 Offenders," *Advocate*, January 7, 2016; Louisiana Board of Pardons & Committee on Parole, *2021 Annual Report*.

249. "Privatized Prison—Louisiana," *Angolite*, January/February 1990, 9; "Allen Correctional Center: Open for Business," *Angolite*, January/February 1991, 5; J. Robert Lilly and Paul Knepper, "Prisonomics: A Global Cash In," *Angolite*, May/June 1992, 35–54.

Chapter 3

1. Christopher Cooper, "Foti's Wish Comes True: Prisoner Space for 7,140," *Times-Picayune*, October 20, 1993.

2. Louisiana Jails and Prisons, "Jail Project Update," Folder: Louisiana Coalition, Box 2, SCJPR.

3. Here I am working with and stretching David Harvey's conceptualization of a spatial fix as a "spatial resolution to capitalism's contradictions." While I argue

throughout this book that the endemic crises of the Louisiana penal system are intimately tied to the endemic crises of racial capitalism (for instance, surpluses of finance capital being put to use in the building of new prisons and jails), in my framing of jailing as a temporary spatial fix and long-term geographic "solution" to prison overcrowding I am also calling attention to how state officials similarly seek to resolve one of the central contradictions of mass imprisonment, overcrowding, through geographic restructuring—from turning to jails or double bunking—which merely displaces the problem, rather than getting to the true root of the crisis. Harvey, "The Spatial Fix," 6.

4. Criminal Sheriff Highest Daily Population Comparative, Fourth Quarter and Year to Date, January 16, 1996, Folder 12, Box 2, OTR.

5. *Williams v. McKeithan* C.A 71–98 (M.D.La, 1975), Civil Docket List, n.p., HWVJM.

6. Louisiana Coalition on Jails and Prisons, "Mini-Issue," *Inside*, October 1980, Folder: Louisiana Coalition, Box 2, SCJPR; John Vodicka, "Louisiana's Jails: House of Horrors," *Inside*, Summer 1981, Folder: Louisiana Coalition, Box 2, SCJPR; Louisiana Coalition on Jails and Prisons, "Orleans Jail Beatings," 1–5, Folder: Louisiana Coalition, Box 2, SCJPR.

7. Amended Consent Decree, December 7, 1983, *Williams v. McKeithan* C.A 71–98 (M.D.La, 1975), KNPP.

8. Henry C. Remm, Jr. letter to R. James Kellogg, March 8, 1982, Folder: Consolidated Jail Cases, Box 3, ALR.

9. Henry C. Remm, Jr. letter to R. James Kellogg, March 8, 1982, Folder: Consolidated Jail Cases, Box 3, ALR. Additional evidence of this practice can be found in the archive of the Hayes Williams court documents: "MOTION to amend consent order for Jefferson Parish Counsel and Sheriff," November 1, 1982, *Williams v. McKeithan* C.A 71–98 (M.D.La, 1975), Document 492, Box 2, HWVJM.

10. Tyler Bridges, "Costs Bars Solution to La. Jail Crowding," *Times-Picayune*, July 24, 1989; City of New Orleans, Office of Criminal Justice Coordination, *Grants in the War on Crime*, 120; Bares and Nunez, *Highlight Legislation of the 1989 Regular Legislative Session*, 12–14, Box 2, LRL; "New Drug Court—New Orleans," *Angolite*, May/June 1989, 12; "Rivers Appointed Drug Czar," *Angolite*, May/June 1989, 14.

11. *Williams v. McKeithan* C.A 71–98 (M.D.La, 1975), Civil Docket List, n.p., HWVJM; Coleman Warner, "Overflowing Jail Swamped by Wave of Drug Busts; Council Pays for 500 More Beds," *Times-Picayune*, July 7, 1989.

12. Louisiana Coalition on Jails and Prisons, "Jail Deaths: An Epidemic," *Inside*, April/May 1982, 4, Folder: Louisiana Coalition, Box 2, SCJPR.

13. *Williams v. McKeithan* C.A 71–98 (M.D.La, 1975), Civil Docket List, n.p., HWVJM; Mark M. Gonzales letter to Martha Kegel, March 16, 1986, Folder: Gay Prison, Box 11, ALR.

14. Louisiana Coalition on Jails and Prisons, "Jail Litigation: An Assessment," *Inside*, April/May 1982, 10, Folder: Louisiana Coalition, Box 2, SCJPR.

15. Floyd Webb and Ron Wikberg, "The Price Is Right," *Angolite*, September/October 1989, 13; "City Sides with Foti in Jail Overcrowding," *Times-Picayune*, July 19, 1989; Bridges, "Costs Bars Solution to La. Jail Crowding."

16. Bridges, "Costs Bars Solution to La. Jail Crowding."

17. *Williams v. McKeithan* C.A 71–98 (M.D.La, 1975), Civil Docket List, n.p., HWVJM; "Plan Would Open 1,000 Extra State Prison Beds," *Times-Picayune*, August 2, 1989; "600 Prisoners to Be Moved to State Jails," *Times-Picayune*, August 3, 1989.

18. Ed Anderson and Susan Finch, "Roemer Oks Action to Cut Jail Crowding," *Times-Picayune*, August 17, 1989.

19. Bureau of Governmental Research, *Financing City Government in New Orleans: Outlook '90*, April 1990, 44, Folder 4, Box 27, MMP.

20. Ed Anderson, "N.O. Area Jails Tight Despite State's Help," *Times-Picayune*, September 16, 1989.

21. Louisiana Division of Administration, *The Governor's Corrections Plans*, 17.

22. Louisiana Division of Administration, *The Governor's Corrections Plans*, 7–9.

23. Louisiana Division of Administration, *The Governor's Corrections Plans*, 19–27.

24. Louisiana Division of Administration, *The Governor's Corrections Plans*, 5–6.

25. Louisiana Division of Administration, *The Governor's Corrections Plans*, 67.

26. Louisiana Division of Administration, *The Governor's Corrections Plans*, 60.

27. Louisiana Division of Administration, *The Governor's Corrections Plans*, 68.

28. "Corrections Plan Funded," *Angolite*, July/August 1990, 8.

29. *Williams v. McKeithan* C.A 71–98 (M.D.La, 1975), Civil Docket List, n.p., HWVJM.

30. *Williams v. McKeithan* C.A 71–98 (M.D.La, 1975), Civil Docket List, n.p., HWVJM; "Prison Expansion Approved," *Angolite*, November/December 1990, 8.

31. "Sheriff Says Jail Should Get OK," *Advocate*, March 28, 1990; "Jail Won't Accept Any New Parish Prisoners," *Advocate*, April 24, 1990; "Rapides Sheriff in Need of a Jail," *Advocate*, June 9, 1990.

32. *Williams v. McKeithan* C.A 71–98 (M.D.La, 1975), Civil Docket List, n.p., HWVJM; Sheriff Errol Romero letter to Judge Polozola, April 27, 1992, *Williams v. McKeithan* C.A 71–98 (M.D.La, 1975), Box 13, Document 5396, HWVJM. For a sample of parishes voting down jail expansions, see Judi Provosty and Greg Thomas, "Nunez NO Jail Aid Plead," *Times-Picayune*, September 2, 1989; Allan Katz, "Voters Defeat Both Jail Millages," *Times-Picayune*, October 8, 1989; Bill Walsh, "Jeff Might House Inmates in N.O.: Prison Space Shortage Forcing a Decision," *Times-Picayune*, November 26, 1992; Steve Culpepper, "Voters Don't Like Paying for Jails," *Advocate*, August 16, 1992.

33. For instance, in both Caddo Parish, home to Shreveport, and East Carroll Parish, it took five attempts for voters to approve jail taxes. Culpepper, "Voters Don't Like Paying for Jails."

34. Culpepper, "Voters Don't Like Paying for Jails."

35. Sheriff Errol Romero letter to Judge Polozola, April 27, 1992, *Williams v. McKeithan* C.A 71–98 (M.D.La, 1975), Box 13, Document 5396, HWVJM; *Williams v. McKeithan* C.A 71–98 (M.D.La, 1975), Civil Docket List n.p., HWVJM.

36. *Williams v. McKeithan* C.A 71–98 (M.D.La, 1975), Civil Docket List, n.p., HWVJM.

37. Over the 1980s the New Orleans government went from covering 90 percent of the sheriff's budget to less than 50 percent. *The Criminal Justice Council and Office of Criminal Justice Coordination*, 32, Folder 2, Box 28, MMP.

38. As elected officials, maintaining their political position was of the utmost importance. And in Louisiana the sheriff is a particularly powerful state position. The role is structured to have extremely limited accountability to any state officials or agencies, is without term limits, and, in the two-thirds of the state's parishes governed without a parish president or mayor, the sheriff has historically been the most commanding elected position. In this context sheriffs organized not only to maintain the jail growth of the 1980s but also to expand their jails during the 1990s.

39. Simon, "Refugees in a Carceral Age," 579–583; Welch, *Detained*.

40. *Williams v. McKeithan* C.A 71–98 (M.D.La, 1975), Civil Docket List n.p., HWVJM; Bares and Nunez, *Highlight Legislation of the 1988 Regular Legislative Session*, 41, Box 2, LRL; "Foti Asks to Use Warf as Overflow Jail for 300," *Times-Picayune*, August 25, 1989. Records are mixed on the rate that federal authorities paid Louisiana sheriffs for imprisoning Washington, D.C., and INS prisoners; it ranged from $40 to $48 a day.

41. Bridges, "Costs Bars Solution to La. Jail Crowding;" David Snyder, "Out-of-State Prisoners Profitable for Sheriff," *Times-Picayune*, June 16, 1991.

42. Avoyelles Opinion, June 20, 1990, *Williams v. McKeithan* C.A 71–98 (M.D.La, 1975), KNPP.

43. Burk Foster, "The Oakdale Riot," *Angolite*, January/February 1990, 47–62. For more on the history of federal immigration detention siting in Louisiana and the Oakdale riot, see Loyd and Mountz, *Boats, Borders, and Bases*, 30–38.

44. Snyder, "Out-of-State Prisoners Profitable for Sheriff."

45. "Sheriffs Want Judge to Ease Prisoner Ruling," *Advocate*, May 31, 1990; Mark Lambert, "Sheriffs Ordered to Explain Violations," *Advocate*, August 17, 1990.

46. Response to Court Order of June 25, 1990, *Williams v. McKeithan* C.A 71–98 (M.D.La, 1975), Box 7, Document 3438A, HWVJM.

47. Appeal of Avoyelles, August 13, 1991, *Williams v. McKeithan* C.A 71–98 (M.D.La, 1975), KNPP.

48. *Williams v. McKeithan* C.A 71–98 (M.D.La, 1975), Civil Docket List n.p., HWVJM.

49. Ross Maggio memo to Judge Polozola, March 13, 1992, *Williams v. McKeithan* C.A 71–98 (M.D.La, 1975), Box 13, Document 5399, HWVJM.

50. Douglass Dennis, "Legislative Digest," *Angolite*, September/October 1992, 47.

51. Some of the first cooperative endeavor agreements include the Cooperative Endeavor Agreement Moorhouse Parish Law Enforcement Agreement, October 20, 1992, *Williams v. McKeithan* C.A 71–98 (M.D.La, 1975), KNPP; Vernon Parish Cooperative Endeavor Agreement, November 17, 1992, *Williams v. McKeithan* C.A 71–98 (M.D.La, 1975), KNPP; Cooperative Endeavor Agreement Rapides Parish, March 1, 1993, *Williams v. McKeithan* C.A 71–98 (M.D.La, 1975), KNPP; Louisiana Cooperative Endeavor Agreement Natchitoches Parish Jail Agreement, August 19, 1993, *Williams v. McKeithan* C.A 71–98 (M.D.La, 1975), KNPP; Cooperative Endeavor Agreement with St. Mary Parish Law Enforcement District January 7, 1994, *Williams v. McKeithan* C.A 71–98 (M.D.La, 1975), KNPP; Cooperative Endeavor Agreement with Calcasieu Parish Law Enforcement District, August 16, 1994, *Williams v.*

McKeithan C.A 71–98 (M.D.La, 1975), KNPP; Cooperative Endeavor Agreement Sabine Parish Law Enforcement District, September 8, 1994, KNPP.

52. Vernon Parish Cooperative Endeavor Agreement, November 17, 1992, *Williams v. McKeithan* C.A 71–98 (M.D.La, 1975), KNPP. Emphasis added.

53. Peter Shinke, "State to Add 1,500 Prison Beds," *Advocate*, June 21, 1995.

54. Ross Maggio memo to Judge Polozola, March 13, 1992, *Williams v. McKeithan* C.A 71–98 (M.D.La, 1975), Box 13, Document 5399, HWVJM.

55. Court Order DOC Prisoners in Parish Jails, March 8, 1994, *Williams v. McKeithan* C.A 71–98 (M.D.La, 1975), KNPP.

56. Court Order DOC Prisoners in Parish Jails, March 8, 1994, *Williams v. McKeithan* C.A 71–98 (M.D.La, 1975), KNPP.

57. "State Vouches for Jails: Safe, Sanitary, Constitutional," *Times-Picayune*, March 24, 1994; "Judge Imposes Tougher Rules on Jails in La.," *Times-Picayune*, April 16, 1994.

58. *Revised Highlights of the 1993 Regular Session of the Louisiana Legislature and Summary Constitutional Amendments*, 1, Box 2, LRL.

59. "More Jail Beds to Cost State," *Times-Picayune*, April 29, 1995; Chris Frink and Peter Shinkle, "Releasing Inmates for Work Criticized," *Advocate*, June 2, 1995.

60. Frink and Shinkle, "Releasing Inmates for Work Criticized."

61. Order Housing State Prisoners in Parish Prisons, May 31, 1995, *Williams v. McKeithan* C.A 71–98 (M.D.La, 1975), KNPP.

62. Shinkle, "State to Add 1,500 Prison Beds"; Louisiana House of Representatives, *State and Local Government in Louisiana: An Overview 2004–2008 Term*, 89–91, Box 1, LRLP.

63. Marsha Shuler, "Agency Gets Nod to Overspend Budget for Prison Beds," *Advocate*, July 20, 1995; James Minton, "Polozola Reclaims Prisons," *Advocate*, July 21, 1995; "Edwards: State Must Rely Less on Parish Jails," *Times-Picayune*, August 3, 1995.

64. "Polozola Plan OK'd Again," *Advocate*, June 20, 1996.

65. Gottschalk, *Caught*, 43–44.

66. *Williams v. McKeithan* C.A 71–98 (M.D.La, 1975), Civil Docket List n.p., HWVJM; James Minton and Marsha Shuler, "Partial Settlement OK'd in Prisoners' Lawsuit," *Advocate*, September 27, 1996.

67. Carr, "Crime Does Pay."

68. Louisiana Legislative Fiscal Office, *Adult Correctional Systems*, 79.

69. Walt Philbin, "The Man," *Times-Picayune*, November 29, 1981.

70. Steve Cannizaro, "Foti Is Among the Most Sued Sheriffs," *Times-Picayune*, February 20, 1990.

71. Dale Curry, "Inmate Population at Orleans Prison Growing; New Building Not Complete," *Morning Advocate*, January 9, 1976, Folder: January–March 1976, Box 4, DCNC; *Louis Hamilton et. al. v. Victor Schiro et al*. Civ. A. No. 89-2443. The name of the case changed as the New Orleans mayors changed: from *Hamilton v. Schiro* to *Hamilton v. Landrieu* to *Hamilton v. Morial*. The case is most often referred to as *Hamilton v. Morial*.

72. Peter M. Zollman, "Conditions Said Improved at Orleans Parish Prison," *Morning Advocate*, March 21, 1976, Folder: January–March 1976, Box 4, DCNC; "Orleans Prison Said Extension of Angola Facility," *Times-Picayune*, April 2, 1976, Folder: April–May 1976, Box 4, DCNC.

73. "Orleans Prison Said Extension of Angola Facility"; Curry, "Inmate Population at Orleans Prison Growing."

74. Walt Philbin, "The Sheriff," *Times-Picayune*, November 29, 1981.

75. Philbin, "The Sheriff."

76. Ed Anderson, "Old Prison to Help Ease Overload," *Times-Picayune*, October 28, 1981, Folder: 10/2/81–12/31/82, Box 8, DCNC.

77. Stipulation and Consent Decree Orleans Parish Prison, September 22, 1982, *Williams v. McKeithan* C.A 71–98 (M.D.La, 1975), Box 2, Document 472, HWVJM.

78. Residents letter to Charles Foti, Re: Temporary Prison Housing "Tent City," June 28, 1983, *Williams v. McKeithan* C.A 71–98 (M.D.La, 1975), Box 2, Document 757, HWVJM.

79. Residents letter to Charles Foti, Re: Temporary Prison Housing "Tent City," June 28, 1983, *Williams v. McKeithan* C.A 71–98 (M.D.La, 1975), Box 2, Document 757, HWVJM.

80. Charles M. Hargroder, "Senate OKs Plan to Ease Jail Crowding," *Times-Picayune*, June 9, 1983.

81. Susan Finch, "Birthday Cakes just the Icing of Foti's Extracurricular Work," *Times-Picayune*, March 21, 1989.

82. Katz, "Voters Defeat Both Jail Millages." Although this practice is illegal, there are hints in newspaper articles and in the stories that continue to be told that Sheriff Foti used his deputies in his reelection campaigns as well.

83. Don Everard, interview with author, April 20, 2016.

84. Ed Anderson, "Litter: Crew Keeps Carnival Clean," *Times-Picayune*, March 3, 1987; Roger Green, "A Model Program of Prisoner Art," *Times Picayune*, September 2, 1988.

85. Iris Kelso, "Audit Sheriff Foti," *Times-Picayune*, December 6, 1981; Finch, "Birthday Cakes just the Icing of Foti's Extracurricular Work"; Johanna Schindler, "Foti's Thanksgiving Feast Marks 25 Years," *Times-Picayune*, November 21, 1999. It is not surprising that incarcerated people chose to work in these programs given the good time benefit such work afforded or the appeal of breaking out of the monotony of jail life.

86. Keith Woods and Susan Finch, "Citizens Often Hire Inmates," *Times-Picayune*, January 25, 1989.

87. Walt Philbin, "Money Is the One Big Mystery in the Way Foti Runs His Office," *Times-Picayune*, November 30, 1981.

88. Philbin, "Money is the One Big Mystery"; Joe Massa, "Council to Probe Foti's Office, Books," *Times-Picayune*, March 3, 1981; Kelso, "Audit Sheriff Foti." It was common not only for former and currently employees of Foti but also city council members to give interviews on such issues only under the cloak of anonymity.

89. Louisiana Coalition on Jails and Prisons, "LCJP Sues Orleans Sheriff," *Inside*, April/May 1982, 8, Folder: Louisiana Coalition, Box 2, SCJPR.

90. Kelso, "Audit Sheriff Foti"; Philbin, "The Sheriff."

91. Kelso, "Audit Sheriff Foti."

92. ACLU Legal Panel Agenda, August 21, 1984, Folder: Legal Panel Agendas, Box 13, ALR; ACLU Legal Panel Agenda, October 23, 1984, Folder: Recent Legal Agendas, Box 13, ALR. Included in defendants on this issue was Norris Henderson of the Angola Special Civics Project while he had a short stay in OPP because of a court hearing.

93. Larry Cartwright Complaint to ACLU of Louisiana, RE: OPP, November 30, 1987, Folder: Prison Condition Complaints 1988, Box 14, ALR.

94. ACLU Legal Panel Agenda, October 23, 1984, Folder: Recent Legal Agendas, Box 13, ALR.

95. Tyrone Wells Complaint to ACLU of Louisiana, RE: Jail Conditions at Parish Prison, April 26, 1988, Folder: Prison Condition Complaints 1988, Box 14, ALR.

96. Cooper, "Foti's Wish Comes True."

97. Louisiana Coalition on Jails and Prisons, "S.I.D.—Orleans Jail Goon Squad?" Folder: Southern Coalition State Reports 1981, Box 3, SCJPR.

98. Ken Fealing, "Reform Group Protests 'Abuse' of Inmates," *Louisiana Weekly*, February 28, 1981, Folder: Southern Coalition State Reports 1981, Box 3, SCJPR; Southern Coalition on Jails and Prisons, "Orleans Prisoners Demand Rights," *Southern Coalition Report on Jails & Prisons*, Fall 1981, Folder: Newsletters 1979–1990, Box 2, SCJPR.

99. *Estevez et al. v. Foti*, Civil Action No. 88–01162, Folder: Correspondence 1989, Box 11, ALR; Sheila Grissett, "Inmates File Suit against Foti over Prison Conditions," *Times-Picayune*, March 22, 1989. Bill Quigley, interview with author, July 6, 2017. Although the services offered in prisons were more limited than plaintiffs imagined, it is true that jails provided much less than the scant programs offered by the DPSC.

100. Susan Finch and Michael Perlstein, "Foti Tries to Sell Voters on Cells," *Times-Picayune*, September 18, 1989.

101. Frank Donze, "Tax Increase Proposals Find Home on October Ballot," *Times-Picayune*, July 22, 1989.

102. Walt Philbin, "Foti Quits Taking Minor Offenders in Parish Prison," *Times-Picayune*, April 21, 1989; Bill Grady, "Lower Bond May Ease Jail Crowding," *Times-Picayune*, May 20, 1989; Bill Grady, "Foti Frees Felony Suspects as Inmate Count Rises," *Times-Picayune*, May 25, 1989; "Foti Releases Felons for Space," *Times-Picayune*, July 7, 1989.

103. Jonathan Eig, "44% of Freed Inmates End up Booked Again," *Times-Picayune*, September 29, 1989. His office's figure of 44% was based on a sample of 2,500 people who had been released and not an actual full accounting of the people released over the previous year. This does not address the ways that race, class, gender, and geography shaped policing patterns to overdetermine certain populations to have higher rates of contact with law enforcement, and thus higher rates of arrest than counterparts who were not targeted for policing.

104. Allen Katz, "The Freed Felons," *Times-Picayune*, October 1, 1989.

105. Tyler Bridges, "Foti Massaging Media for Jail Propositions," *Times-Picayune*, October 3, 1989.

106. Bridges, "Foti Massaging Media for Jail Propositions."

107. Eig, "44% of Freed Inmates End up Booked Again."

108. Katz, "Voters Defeat Both Jail Millages."

109. Katz, "Voters Defeat Both Jail Millages."

110. Susan Finch, "Foti Wants Jail Issue on Feb. 3 Ballot," *Times-Picayune*, December 15, 1989.

111. Susan Finch, "Foti Pushing Property Tax to Build Jails," *Times-Picayune*, January 29, 1990; Susan Finch, "Tax to Support Jails Backed by Judges," *Times-Picayune*, February 1, 1990; "Election Recommendations," *Times-Picayune*, February 2, 1990; Frank Donze, "Chamber Opposes Tax for Jails," *Times Picayune*, February 3, 1990.

112. Michael Perlstein, "Foti Wins Property Tax to Build Four Jails," *Times-Picayune*, February 4, 1990.

113. Susan Finch and Coleman Warner, "Judgement, Jail Suits Target City Budget," *Times-Picayune*, December 22, 1989.

114. Steve Cannizaro, "Foti to Get More N.O. Money for Jail," *Times-Picayune*, April 21, 1990; Susan Finch, "Sheriff, N.O. Make Pay Pact," *Times-Picayune*, August 18, 1990.

115. "Summary of Sheriff Foti's Plans before the New Orleans City Council," October 3, 1991, *Williams v. McKeithan* C.A 71–98 (M.D.La, 1975), Document 5003, Box 12, HWVJM.

116. Sheriff Charles Foti letter to Governor Roemer, RE: Constructing and Operating of 992 Bed DOC Facility in New Orleans, July 25, 1990, *Williams v. McKeithan* C.A 71–98 (M.D.La, 1975), Document 3470, Box 7, HWVJM.

117. Charles C. Foti Jr., "Position Paper on Corrections in Louisiana," 1–2, December 27, 1991, *Williams v. McKeithan* C.A 71–98 (M.D.La, 1975), Document 5151, Box 12, HWVJM. Foti suggested there should also be "special" localized prisons designed for juveniles, women, and the mentally ill or, in the words of Rose Braz, "kinder, gentler prisons" that would integrate punitive "treatment." These measures would be coupled with "alternatives to incarceration" that would *extend* the reach of criminal justice system through electronic monitoring systems, more stringent supervision for parolees, and drug testing for all arrestees so that the city could compel more people into mandatory drug treatment. Braz, "Kinder, Gentler, Gender Responsive Cages."

118. Suzy Mague memo to Councilmember Giarrusso, November 29, 1993, Folder: Criminal Sheriff 1992–1994, Box 15, CJG.

119. Bill Walsh, "Jeff to Consider Pay-per-Prisoner Deal from Foti," *Times-Picayune*, December 2, 1992; Manuel Roig-Franzia, "Jeff to Pay Premium to Send Foti Inmates," *Times-Picayune*, March 16, 1996; Martha Carr, "Cheaper Place to Hold Youths Needed—St. John Hunts Jail Alternatives," *Times-Picayune*, June 20, 1997.

120. Cooper, "Foti's Wish Comes True."

121. Cooper, "Foti's Wish Comes True."

122. Schept, *Progressive Punishment*.

123. In the first month of this collaboration, 125 people were arrested. Arthur Roane, "Cops on the Prowl for 150 Who Missed their Day in Court," *Times-Picayune*, January 7, 1991; Dan Bennett, "25 Arrested in Sweep to Catch Bond-Jumpers," *Times-Picayune*, January 26, 1991.

124. The first weekend more than 350 people were arrested. The following weekend another 101 people found law enforcement at their doors. Michael Perlstein, "Crime Force to Hunt Suspects, Bond-Jumpers, Ieyoub Says," *Times-Picayune*, February 1, 1992; Lynne Jensen, "Fugitives Caught in 8-Parish Sweep," *Times-Picayune*, February 9, 1992; Michael Perlstein, "More than 350 Suspects Booked in N.O. Crime Sweep," *Times-Picayune*, February 11, 1992; "Task Force Reels in 100 Suspects," *Times-Picayune*, February 16, 1992.

125. Chris Adams, "Tragedy Marks a Night of Crime," *Times-Picayune*, August 5, 1990; Sheila Grissett, "Murder Rate in N.O. Exceeds One a Day," *Times-Picayune*, July 17, 1993; Sheila Stroup, "When Will It All End?" *Times-Picayune*, July 26, 1994.

126. Walt Philbin, "Murder Rate May Break Record," *Times-Picayune*, July 6, 1990.

127. Mark Lorando, "Crime is Talk of the Town," *Times-Picayune*, December 14, 1993.

128. Meiners, *For the Children?*

129. Dan Bennett, "'Least Worst' Juveniles Go Free," *Times-Picayune*, November 21, 1989.

130. Wayne A. Collier, "Crime: See the Enemy Clearly and Take a Stand," *Times-Picayune*, September 4, 1990.

131. "Crackdown on Juveniles Vowed in N.O. Crime War," *Times-Picayune*, August 16, 1990.

132. International Association of Police Chiefs, *The New Orleans Police Department Revisited*, 2–8, Folder 1, Box 33, MMP.

133. International Association of Police Chiefs, *The New Orleans Police Department Revisited*, 14, Folder 1, Box 33, MMP.

134. International Association of Police Chiefs, *The New Orleans Police Department Revisited*, 5, Folder 1, Box 33, MMP.

135. *The Criminal Justice Council and the Office of Criminal Justice Coordination*, 20, Folder 2, Box 28, MMP.

136. Sheila Grissett, "Murder Rate down 16 Percent—Mayor Credits New Chief and Police Program," *Times-Picayune*, May 19, 1992; "Orleans Murders down 17%," *Times-Picayune*, July 2, 1992; Michael Perlstein, "Study: N.O. Safer than Baton Rouge," *Times-Picayune*, May 25, 1994.

137. Franklin Zimring is the most direct in his assessment that "the great American crime decline was a surprise when it began and is a mystery to this day.... Fifteen years after the decline began, there is little consensus among experts." Zimring, *The Great American Crime Decline*, v.

138. Dawn Ruth, "New Jails Deterring Crime, Foti Says," *Times-Picayune*, November 1, 1991.

139. Grissett, "Murder Rate down 16 Percent."

140. *Report of the Volunteer Transition Task Force on Criminal Justice*, 23–26, Folder 2, Box 28, MMP.

141. John Pope, "Residents Raise Cry over Crime," *Times-Picayune*, January 19, 1994.

142. Morial for Mayor Campaign, *Senator Marc Morial's Plan for Crime Prevention & Reform: "CPR for New Orleans,"* 24; Perkins, "Failing the Race," 38–40.

143. For more on the Zimbardo experiment and its willful misreading by Wilson and Kelling, see Ansfield, "The Broken Windows of the Bronx."

144. James Q. Wilson and George Kelling, "Broken Windows Theory," *Atlantic*, March 1982.

145. Smith, "Giuliani Time"; Delany, *Times Square Red, Times Square Blue*; Herbert, "Policing the Contemporary City"; Mitchell, *The Right to the City*, 195–226; Herbert and Brown, "Conceptions of Space and Crime"; Williams, *Our Enemies in Blue*, 197–222; Parenti, *Lockdown America*, 69–110; Camp and Heatherton, *Policing the Planet*.

146. Harcourt, *Illusion of Order*, 128.

147. Herbert and Brown, "Conceptions of Space and Crime"; Lipsitz, "Policing Place and Taxing Time."

148. Platt et al., *The Iron Fist and the Velvet Glove*; Hansford, "Community Policing Reconsidered," 215–25.

149. Story, *Prison Land*, especially 137–41; Schrader, "Against the Romance of Community Policing."

150. Harcourt, *Illusion of Order*; Tanya Erzen and Andrea McArdle, *Zero Tolerance*; Camp and Heatherton, *Policing the Planet*.

151. US Department of Justice, "President Clinton Announces New Crime Bill," Murakawa, 126–29.

152. Joseph Giarrusso letter to Senator Joseph Biden, November 15, 1993, Folder: Police Department, Box 7, CJG.

153. Federal discretionary funding to New Orleans plummeted under the Reagan and Bush administrations from $24.1 million in 1979 to $680,000 in 1989. Bureau of Governmental Research, *Financing City Government in New Orleans: Outlook '90*, 2, Folder 4, Box 27, MMP; Hirsch, "New Orleans: Sunbelt in the Swamp"; Taylor, *From #BlackLivesMatter to Black Liberation*, 92–100.

154. *City Debt*, 1994, 2, Folder 5, Box 27, MMP; Bureau of Governmental Research, *Financing City Government in New Orleans: Outlook '90*, 2, Folder 4, Box 27, MMP.

155. Bureau of Governmental Research, *Financing City Government in New Orleans: Outlook '90*, 13–14, Folder 4, Box 27, MMP.

156. Bureau of Governmental Research, *Financing City Government in New Orleans: Outlook '90*, 50, Folder 4, Box 27, MMP; Moody's Investors Service, "General Obligation/Special Tax," Folder 4, Box 27, MMP.

157. Moody's Investors Service, "General Obligation/Special Tax," 46, Folder 4, Box 27, MMP.

158. Moody's Investors Service, "General Obligation/Special Tax," Folder 4, Box 27, MMP; Souther, *New Orleans on Parade*, 180–191.

159. Gary Boulard, "Mintz, Morial Face Runoff in New Orleans Mayoral Race," *Los Angeles Times*, February 6, 1994; Ronald Smothers, "Hate Fliers Inflame Mayoral Race in New Orleans," *New York Times*, February 27, 1994; "Ex-Mayor's Son Wins Runoff in New Orleans," *Los Angeles Times*, March 6, 1994.

160. Morial for Mayor Campaign, *Senator Marc Morial's Plan*, 1, Folder 4, Box 32, MMP.

161. *The Criminal Justice Council and the Office of Criminal Justice Coordination*, 7–8, Folder 2, Box 28, MMP.

162. Morial for Mayor Campaign, *Senator Marc Morial's Plan for Crime Prevention & Reform*, 18, Folder 4, Box 32, MMP.

163. City of New Orleans Crime Plan, 1994, Folder 4, Box 33, MMP.

164. Muhammad, *The Condemnation of Blackness*; Moynihan, *The Negro Family*.

165. Although Morial stated that policing against violence and drug use would be focused on all neighborhoods, in actuality, the NOPD never focused on places like Tulane University's fraternity row—home to notorious levels of drinking, drug use, and sexual violence among of white middle- and upper-class youth. City of New Orleans Crime Plan, 1994, Folder 4, Box 33, MMP; Luft and Griffin, "A Status Report on Housing in New Orleans after Katrina: An Intersectional Analysis," 52.

166. *Report of the Volunteer Transition Task Force on the New Orleans Police Department*, 19, Folder 4, Box 33, MMP.

167. *Report of the Volunteer Transition Task Force on the New Orleans Police Department*, 10–20, Folder 4, Box 33, MMP.

168. *Report of the Volunteer Transition Task Force on the New Orleans Police Department*, 2–3, Folder 4, Box 33, MMP.

169. "First Draft Report of Citizen's Involvement Subcommittee, Mayor Elect's Transition Committee on the NOPD," Folder 4, Box 33, MMP.

170. "City of New Orleans Crime Plan," 1994, Folder 4, Box 33, MMP.

171. "High Homicide Rate Leaves New Orleans Fearful," *New York Times*, May 3, 1994.

172. "100 Days of Change: New Orleans in a New Direction," August 11, 1994, Folder 1, Box 27, MMP.

173. Although youth would not be arrested for violating the curfew, the law gave law enforcement probable cause to stop anyone who "looked" young, thereby opening the way for searches and running people's names on the police database. In addition, parents of curfew violators could be ordered to take parenting classes or perform community service. "100 Days of Change: New Orleans in a New Direction," August 11, 1994, Folder 1, Box 27, MMP; Frank Donze, "Curfew, Summer Jobs Await N.O. Teens," *Times-Picayune*, April 6, 1997.

174. "100 Days of Change: New Orleans in a New Direction," August 11, 1994, Folder 1, Box 27, MMP; Linda Nuss Russo, "Municipal Court and Traffic Court: A Report to Honorable Marc Morial, Mayoral-Elect," 2, April 1994, Folder 1, Box 28, MMP.

175. *Rebuilding New Orleans*, 10–11, Folder 7, Box 43, MMP.

176. "Len Davis, Eight Other New Orleans Police Officers, Charged in Drug Sting," *Times-Picayune*, December 8, 1994; "Richard Pennington Says He Was Warned about Len Davis," *Times-Picayune*, March 16, 1997.

177. "NOPD Reform Media Strategy," Folder 7, Box 53, MMP; Joseph Giarrusso letter to Governor Edwin Edwards, Folder 7, Box 53, MMP; The City of New Orleans, "New Orleans Police Chief Pennington Announces Complete Department Reorganization and Sweeping Reforms," January 11, 1995, Folder 7, Box 53, MMP.

178. It is worth noting that the incorporation of the FBI into the new PID was at least partially done to stave off a DOJ investigation into the NOPD.

179. The City of New Orleans, "New Orleans Police Chief Pennington," Folder 7, Box 53, MMP.

180. "New Orleans Police Reform Timeline," Folder 10, Box 47, MMP.

181. "New Orleans Police Reform Timeline," Folder 10, Box 47, MMP.

182. "New Orleans Police Reform Timeline," Folder 10, Box 47, MMP; "NOPD Chief Issues Progress Report Showing Police Reform Working: Murder and Police Corruption Down," October 10, 1995, Folder 1, Box 56, MMP.

183. "Stepped Up Security at NORD Playgrounds," June 19, 1995, Folder 2, Box 56, MMP.

184. "Vice President Al Gore Visits B.W. Cooper Community Policing Area," April 11, 1996, Folder 6, Box 56, MMP.

185. "New Orleans Police Reform Timeline," Folder 10, Box 47, MMP.

186. "Police Chief Pennington and Fire Chief McDaniels Launch 'Operation Chill Out' in Desire Housing Development," June 9, 1995, Folder 2, Box 56, MMP.

187. "City Officials Observe National Night Out against Crime," August 6, 1996, Folder 5, Box 56, MMP; "New Orleans Police Reform Timeline," Folder 10, Box 47, MMP.

188. Walt Philbin, "Deputies Help Police Boost Quarter Patrols," *Times-Picayune*, March 25, 1995; *Building New Orleans Together*, 8, Folder 7, Box 43, MMP.

189. Cassandra Sharpe letter to Oliver Thomas, June 27, 1995, Folder 28, Box 2, OTR; Lynne Hunter Uhalt letter to Councilman Oliver Thomas, November 15, 1995, Folder 28, Box 2, OTR; Downtown Development District, "Downtown," Folder 28, Box 2, OTR; Downtown Development District, "New Orleans Street Smart," March 1996, Folder 28, Box 2, OTR.

190. Like most crime in New Orleans during the 1990s, the slightly increased number of robberies from the previous year was still below the rate of robberies in the French Quarter over the majority of the preceding years. Walt Philbin, "NOPD Getting Help in Quarter—State Troopers, Sheriff Sign On," *Times-Picayune*, July 31, 1996.

191. Joseph A. Kirby, "Big Easy Gets Tough on Crime and Crooked Cops," *Chicago Tribune*, June 7, 1996.

192. Kirby, "Big Easy Gets Tough on Crime and Crooked Cops"; Walt Philbin, "Next Leap for Police," *Times-Picayune*, May 24, 1996; Adam Nossiter, "2 Crime Busters for New Orleans," *New York Times*, December 5, 1996.

193. Implementing CompStat was to be coupled with the NOPD deprioritizing its response to 911 calls.

194. "New Orleans Police Reform Timeline," Folder 10, Box 47, MMP; Michael Perlstein, "Pennington Promises Safe City, Safe Streets," *Times-Picayune*, October 15, 1996.

195. Mark Schleifstein, "Budget Battle Isn't Finished in N.O.," *Times-Picayune*, November 28, 1996.

196. "Coalition of the Concerned," *Times-Picayune*, December 11, 1996.

197. "Mayor Supports Financing Plan Recommended by Council Budget Committee," December 6, 1996, Folder 8, Box 56, MMP; "New Orleans Police Reform Timeline," Folder 10, Box 47, MMP.

198. *Building New Orleans Together*, 18, Folder 7, Box 43, MMP.

199. "New Orleans Police Reform Timeline," Folder 10, Box 47, MMP; Michael Perlstein, "Strength in Numbers," *Times-Picayune*, April 22, 1997.

200. Violent Crime Control and Law Enforcement Act of 1994, PL 103-322 § 20101 (b) (1); Ed Anderson, "'Good Time,' Parole Blasted by Connick," *Times-Picayune*, January 26, 1995; Justice Policy Center, *The Influences of Truth-in-Sentencing Reforms on Changes in States' Sentencing Practices and Prison Populations*, 11.

201. The Marc Morial archive is full of press releases heralding drops in crime, and they are a centerpiece of each of his annual reports on New Orleans. Two examples are "New Orleans Mayor's Initiatives Reduce Murder, Juvenile Crime and Spurs Local Economy to Highest Level in a Decade," May 24, 1995, Folder 3, Box 56, MMP; "City's Murder Rate Shows Consistent Decrease over Two Year Period," June 4, 1996, Folder 5, Box 56, MMP; *Rebuilding New Orleans*, Folder 7, Box 43, MMP.

202. Howell, Shaw, and Unter, *A Citizen Evaluation*, 3–5, Folder 5, Box 43, MMP.

203. Rick Bragg, "New Orleans Is Hopeful about Police Overhaul," *New York Times*, January 29, 1995; Sue Anne Presely, "The Big Easy Makes Serious Effort to Solve Sobering Crime Problem," *Washington Post*, July 5, 1997; Daniel Pedersen, "Go Get the Scumbags," *Newsweek*, October 20, 1997; Mimi Hall, "Clinton Sings Praises of Teen Curfews," *USA Today*, May 31, 1996. In addition, at the end of his first term, Morial was invited by the US Conference of Mayors to join the Juvenile Crime Task Force, paving the way for him to become the president of the Conference of Mayors in 2001 and later the president of the National Urban League in 2003. Marc H. Morial letter to Jerry Abramson, September 24, 1997, Folder 3, Box 18, MMP.

204. FBI, Uniform Crime Reporting New Orleans Historic Crime Trends 1985–2013.

205. Unter, "The New Orleans Police Department," 126–41.

206. Unter, "The New Orleans Police Department," 107.

207. Howell, Shaw, and Unter, *A Citizen Evaluation*, 6, Folder 5, Box 43, MMP.

208. Unter, "The New Orleans Police Department," 106–7.

209. Gilliard, *Prison and Jail Inmates at Midyear 1998*, 8, 4.

210. Lee, *1996 District Attorney's Race*, Folder 5, Box 48, MMP; Susan Finch, "Connick Wins Some, Loses One in Battle for Endorsements," *Times-Picayune*, September 14, 1996; Susan Finch, "Reed, Connick Fight to the Finish," *Times-Picayune*, October 31, 1996.

211. Many of these articles were written by the recently hired Lolis Eric Elie, son of New Orleans civil rights attorney Lolis Elie.

212. Kevin M. Davis #631011 letter to Oliver Thomas, November 10, 1995, Folder 17, Box 2, OTR.

213. "Residents Complain in Deputies' Search," *Times-Picayune*, December 11, 1996; Michael Perlstein, "Ex-Cop Faces Rape Charge—Prostitute Says It Can't Go On," *Times-Picayune*, July 14, 1997.

214. Pamela Coyle and Michaael Perlstein, "Cops Irked by Rape Arrests by Deputies—NOPD Wasn't Notified, Police Say," *Times-Picayune*, March 6, 1999.

215. Human Rights Watch, *Locked Away*, 1; Lolis Eric Elie, "Activists Rap Foti's Prison," *Times-Picayune*, May 30, 1997; Cielo Cruz, interview with author, April 15, 2016.

216. Human Rights Watch, *Locked Away*; Joan Treadway, "Rights Group Gives Orleans Jail Low Rating—INS Detainees Focus on Probe," *Times-Picayune*, September 10, 1998.

217. Human Rights Watch, *Locked Away*.

218. Human Rights Watch, *Locked Away*.

219. "Foti Says Detainee Reports False, Exaggerated," *Times-Picayune*, September 19, 1998; "Immigration Service Defends Detention Policy," *Times-Picayune*, October 5, 1998.

220. Michael Perlstein, "Diabetic Attack Killed Prisoner—Heart Stopped Coroner Says," *Times-Picayune*, April 8, 1998; "Death in Custody," *Times-Picayune*, April 9, 1999.

221. Michael Perlstein, "Dead Woman's Family Sues Cops—Diabetic Died in Custody," *Times-Picayune*, April 10, 1999.

222. Perlstein, "Dead Woman's Family Sues Cops."

223. "Death in Custody"; Lolis Eric Elie, "Who Protects?" *Times-Picayune*, April 9, 1999; Lolis Eric Elie, "Jailed Dads," *Times-Picayune*, June 23, 1999.

224. Walt Philbin, "FBI Reviewing Diabetic's Death," *Times-Picayune*, April 13, 1999.

225. Philbin, "FBI Reviewing Diabetic's Death."

226. Michael Perlstein, "ACLU Turns up Heat on Foti," *Times-Picayune*, April 29, 1999.

227. Michael Perlstein, "Hearing Set on Mothers in Jail; ACLU Reports Shackles in Labor," *Times-Picayune*, May 4, 1999.

228. Bruce Alpert, "Foti's Deputies Blasted for Using Stun Belts on HIV-Positive Inmates," *Times-Picayune*, June 9, 1999.

229. Leslie Williams, "Protesters Accuse Foti of Murder," *Times-Picayune*, June 18, 1999.

230. "Petition Drive to Recall Foti Gearing Up," *Times-Picayune*, April 21, 1999; Williams, "Protesters Accuse Foti of Murder."

231. Susan Finch, "Foti Delays Inmates' Release, Suit Says—Orleans Sheriff Accused of Ignoring Court Orders," *Times-Picayune*, September 29, 1999.

232. Michael Perlstein, "Sheriff Foti Seals Deal with Charity Hospital," *Times-Picayune*, December 21, 1999; Michael Perlstein, "Lawsuit in Death of Inmate Settled—Diabetic Woman Died from Lack of Insulin," *Times-Picayune*, June 17, 2000.

233. Bruce Eggler, "Sheriff Defends Need for New Jail," *Times-Picayune*, November 17, 1999; Michael Perlstein, "Campaign to Remove Criminal Sheriff Foti Fails," *Times-Picayune*, November 17, 1999; "Election Returns: Orleans," *Times-Picayune*, November 21, 1999.

234. Dixon, *Another Politics*.

235. Shana M. griffin, interview with author, April 21, 2016.

236. Griffin, interview; Melissa Burch, interview with author, March 22, 2016; Celeste, Bauer, Bervera, and Utter, "Just Shut It Down."

237. The activist and theoretical work on prison abolition is both deep and wide. Some key texts include Davis, *Are Prisons Obsolete?*; Critical Resistance Publications Collective, Critical Resistance to the Prison-Industrial Complex Special Issue; Shaylor and Chandler, "Reform and Abolition"; CR 10 Publications Collective, *Abolition Now!*; Bassichis, Lee, and Spade, "Building an Abolitionist Trans and Queer Movement"; Dan Berger, Mariame Kaba, and David Stein, "What Abolitionists Do"; Gilmore, "Abolition Geography and the Problem of Innocence."

238. Davis, *Are Prisons Obsolete?*; Foucault, *Discipline and Punish*.

239. Davis, *If They Come in the Morning*; Samuels, "Improvising on Reality"; Berger, *Captive Nation*; Thuma, "Lessons in Self-Defense."

240. Critical Resistance Publications Collective, "The History of Critical Resistance"; Brown et al., "Reflections on Critical Resistance"; "Perspectives on Critical Resistance," ed. Samuels and Stein.

241. Burch, interview.

242. Burch, interview.

243. Burch, interview.

244. Griffin, interview; Burch, interview; Education Not Incarceration Meeting Notes, February 18, 2001; SGPP.

245. NO PORC was modeled on the Prison Activist Resource Center based out of California. Griffin, interview; Burch, interview.

246. Griffin, interview.

247. Burch, interview.

248. Burch, interview; Griffin, interview.

249. Griffin, interview.

250. Burch, interview.

251. Burch, interview.

252. Burch, interview; Critical Resistance: Southern Conference and Strategy Session Program, April 4–6, 2003, CROP.

253. Tamika Middleton, interview with author, March 29, 2021.

254. Griffin, interview; Burch, interview.

255. Burch, interview.

256. Critical Resistance: Southern Conference and Strategy Session Program, April 4–6, 2003, CROP.

257. Critical Resistance: Southern Conference and Strategy Session Program, April 4–6, 2003, CROP.

258. Burch, interview.

259. Burch, interview.

260. Critical Resistance South Conference: Beyond the Prison Industrial Complex, Media Coverage Winter/Spring 2003, MBPP; Melissa Burch and Jason Ziedenberg, "Critical Resistance to Southern Prisons," 2003, MBPP; Allen G. Breed, "Packed Prisons: New Orleans Conference Addresses Reasons behind Rising Number of People behind Bars," *Associated Press*, April 4, 2003; Gwen Filosa, "Conference Targets Prison System," *Times-Picayune*, April 5, 2003; Katy Reckdahl, "Big Picture," *Gambit*, April 1, 2003; Lili LeGardeur, "Seeking Alternatives to Prison," *State Times/Morning Advocate*, May 3, 2003; Lili LeGardeur, "Restorative Justice: Mending the Fabric of Society," *National Catholic Reporter*, May 30, 2003.

261. Burch, interview.

262. Breed, "Packed Prisons"; Reckdahl, "Big Picture."

263. Reckdahl, "Big Picture."

264. Griffin, interview.

265. Burch, interview.

266. With the successes of CR South also came disadvantages. Most notably, the time and energy required to host a conference of this scope and size led to other political work being neglected. Once the conference was over, people's post-conference exhaustion and burnout led to most of the collective organizations within the Prison Coalition folding. Although members of ENI decided to remake their group into an official Critical Resistance chapter, tensions emerged in response to changes in paid staff. Melissa Burch moved away not long after the conference. Many local activists hoped that Althea Francois would be selected as the new staffer, but CR hired someone from out of town who ended up only staying for one year. Unable to find work in New Orleans, Francois took a position in Atlanta and would not return to New Orleans until after Hurricane Katrina.

267. Keaton, *Adult Correctional Systems*, 2000.

268. Stephanie Grace and Frank Donze, "Morial's Budget Speech Commends Federal Aid," *Times-Picayune*, November 4, 2000.

269. "Orleans Parish Criminal Sheriff's Office Transition Team Rehabilitation, Education, and Community Services, Data Collection/Rehabilitation Sub-Committee Report" January 4, 2005, Folder 4, Box 1, CJC.

270. Keaton, *Adult Correctional Systems*, 1999; Keaton, *Adult Correctional Systems*, 2000; Freeman, *Adult Correctional Systems*.

Chapter 4

1. US Senate Committee on Homeland Security and Governmental Affairs, *Situational Awareness*.

2. This organized abandonment and neoliberal restructuring were in dialectical relationship to one another. Neoliberal governance made the abdication of state responsibility to care for people in the face of disaster commonsense while the organized abandonment of the city created the conditions for the mass displacement of Black New Orleanians and the attendant post-Katrina land grab.

3. Popular narratives asserted that the government's inept response to the storm epitomized a failure of the state, rather than, as activists on the ground and radical scholars have asserted, an unsurprising series of actions by a state animated by racial capitalism. For mainstream news and writing that reiterated the notion of Katrina and a collapsed state, see "Editorial: Unprepared," *Washington Post*, September 5, 2005; "Government's Failures Doomed Many," *Seattle Times*, September 11, 2005; "Editorial: The Katrina Housing Debacle," *New York Times*, November 24, 2005; Horne, *Breach of Faith*. For scholarship on the "breakdown" of the New Orleans criminal legal system, see Allen-Bell, "Bridge over Troubled Waters"; Garrett and Tetlow, "Criminal Justice Collapse"; Vance, "Justice after Disaster." For counterarguments articulating the systematic organized abandonment of New Orleans and the broader Gulf Coast by the state, see Smith, "There's No Such Thing as a Natural Disaster"; Bullard and Wright, *Race, Place, and Environmental Justice*, 1–18; Woods, "Les Misérables of New Orleans"; Woods, *Development Drowned and Reborn*.

4. Woods, "Sittin' on Top of the World," 48.

5. Racial justice struggles also included environmental justice organizing in the Vietnamese communities of New Orleans East, as well as against the toxic and exploitative conditions immigrant day laborers and guest workers (mostly Latinx but also South Asian) were rebuilding under. Radical human rights also permeated these sectors of organizing. Naughton and Wallace, "Day Laborers in the Reconstruction of New Orleans"; Browne-Dianis et al., AND INJUSTICE FOR ALL; Tang, "A Gulf Unites Us."

6. Ursula Price, interview with author, March 19, 2016.

7. Xochitl Bervera, interview with author, April 12, 2022.

8. Norris Henderson, interview with author, May 15, 2016.

9. United States Social Forum, "Another World Is Possible, Another U.S. Is Necessary" June 27–July 1, 2007 program. In author's personal possession.

10. Mann, *Katrina's Legacy*; Flaherty, *Floodlines*.

11. kai lumumba barrow interview with author, June 18, 2016.

12. The People's Hurricane Relief Fund and the People's Institute for Survival and Beyond brought Laura van Deernoot Lipsky to facilitate trauma stewardship workshops in New Orleans. The impacts of those spaces resonated outward for years. For more on this approach see Lipsky with Burk, *Trauma Stewardship*.

13. Luft, "Men and Masculinities in the Social Movement for a Just Reconstruction After Hurricane Katrina."

14. I am indebted to Deborah Gould's *Moving Politics: Emotion and ACT UP's Fight against AIDS* for her discussion about how she was overcome by grief while researching her book, even though that was not the affective state she experienced while in ACT UP. This is the closest approximation I have found in the social movement literature to what it feels like to write about organizing after the storm.

15. Bill Quigley, "New Orleans Katrina Pain Index at 10: Who Was Left Behind," *Huffington Post*, July 20, 2015.

16. Luft, "Racialized Disaster Patriarchy," 10–14.

17. About 2,600 hospital workers were fired from Charity Hospital and more than 7,500 public school teachers and other school employees were fired, which decimated the teachers' union. Although there are no statistics on the displacement of former Charity Hospital employees, it seems fair to extrapolate that, given the extent to which pre-Katrina New Orleans school teachers did not return home, hospital workers were similarly pushed out of the labor market, and thus the city. Ott, "The Closure of New Orleans' Charity Hospital," 83; United Teachers of New Orleans, Louisiana Federation of Teachers, and American Federation of Teachers, *"National Model" or Flawed Approach?*, 5; Danielle Dreilinger, "Most Katrina Laid-Off Teachers Never Came Back, Study Confirms," *Times-Picayune*, May 31, 2017.

18. The best encapsulation of the post-Katrina public housing struggle remains the documentary *Land of Opportunity*, dir. Luisa Dantas. For more on the post-Katrina crisis of homelessness see Casper-Futterman, "The Operation Was Successful but the Patient Died."

19. What is more, organizers pointed out that the post-Katrina destruction of public housing and its antecedent the HOPE VI redevelopment of the St. Thomas housing project, served to atomize much of the collective infrastructure for organizing Black working-class and poor communities.

20. US Climate Prediction Center, *The 2005 North Atlantic Hurricane Season*; National Center for Atmospheric Research, "Global Warming Fueled Record 2005 Hurricane Season Conclude Scientists," *Mongabay*, June 22, 2006.

21. US National Weather Service, *Service Assessment Hurricane Katrina August 23–31, 2005*, 5–7.

22. Austin, "Coastal Exploitation, Land Loss, and Hurricanes"; Theriot, *American Energy, Imperiled Coast*.

23. US Department of Energy, Office of Electricity Delivery and Energy Reliability, *Comparing the Impacts of the 2005 and 2008 Hurricanes on U.S. Energy Infrastructure*, 11; US Geological Survey, National Wetlands Research Center, *Over 100 Years of Land Change for Coastal Louisiana*.

24. Danny Heitman, "Hurricane Katrina."

25. US Federal Emergency Management Agency, *High Water Mark Collection for Hurricane Katrina in Louisiana*, 32–35; US Geological Survey, *Temporal Analysis of Floodwater Volumes in New Orleans After Hurricane Katrina*, 59.

26. State reports note this official death toll is a bare minimum and does not account for the people who went missing during the storm and were never found or those whose lives were cut short by the ongoing health stressors in the months that followed. Louisiana Department of Health and Human Services, *Hurricane Katrina Deaths, Louisiana, 2005*.

27. Muhammad, "Hurricane Katrina: The Black Nation's 9/11!"

28. US 109th Congress, *A Failure of Initiative*, 248.

29. US 109th Congress, *A Failure of Initiative*, 254–256.

30. Garrett and Tetlow, "Criminal Justice Collapse," 145.

31. Congress passed laws to discipline New Orleans through disaster debt. As Brandon Garrett and Tania Tetlow write in "Criminal Justice Collapse," "Congress passed legislation prohibiting FEMA from providing operating expenses to local

government although it may provide money for repairing buildings and loans to homeowners and businesses. In the past the president forgave emergency loans to local government, but Congress amended the Katrina relief bill to prohibit forgiveness, and thus local governments signed loan applications with dubious promises of an ability to repay with repayments beginning immediately," 154.

32. Gwen Filsoa, "New Detention Center Opened," *Times-Picayune*, September 3, 2005.

33. Alex Berenson, "With Jails Flooded, Bus Station Fills the Void," *New York Times*, September 7, 2005.

34. Gilmore, "Race, Prisons, War," 80.

35. Garrett and Tetlow, "Criminal Justice Collapse," 145.

36. Gilmore, "Race, Prisons, War," 248; Edward Wyatt, "In Hurricane's Aftermath, Winfrey Calls for Apology," *New York Times*, September 7, 2005.

37. This is not to say that violence did not occur. Black women testified to experiencing sexualized violence in the days after the storm—which was then downplayed by state officials. Bierria, Liebenthal, and INCITE! Women of Color Against Violence, "To Render Ourselves Visible."

38. US 109th Congress, *A Failure of Initiative*, 249.

39. Flaherty, *Floodlines*; Berger, "Constructing Crime, Framing Disaster"; Allen-Bell, "Bridge Over Troubled Waters."

40. "Military Due to Move in to New Orleans," *CNN*, September 2, 2005.

41. "Military Due to Move in to New Orleans," *CNN*, September 2, 2005.

42. Sabrina Shankman et al., "After Katrina, New Orleans Cops Were Told They Could Shoot Looters," *ProPublica*, Aug 24, 2010.

43. Louisiana Disaster Act of 1974, Act 636, Folder 1, Box 704, DTP.

44. Office of State Police, *Tactical Units Procedure Order 415*, 1, Folder 1, Box 704, DTP.

45. Office of State Police, *Tactical Units Procedure Order 415*, 19, Folder 1, Box 704, DTP.

46. Office of State Police, *Tactical Units Procedure Order 415*, 6–9, Folder 1, Box 704, DTP.

47. Mayor Nagin letter to Governor Blanco, November 28, 2006, Folder 8, Box 19, MCRN.

48. Jim Letten, "Violent Crime and the Criminal Justice System in New Orleans Following Hurricane Katrina," statement to US Senate, June 20, 2007, Folder 18, Box 1, CJC.

49. Although A. C. Thompson was the first journalist to report on the vigilantes, their actions were not unknown. Malik Rahim routinely recounted stories of the white vigilantes to the thousands of volunteers cycling in and out of Common Ground Relief between 2005 and 2007. Rahim also testified about the killings at the People's Hurricane Relief Fund's International Tribunal on the second anniversary of Hurricane Katrina. A. C. Thompson, "Post-Katrina, White Vigilantes Shot African-Americans with Impunity," *ProPublica*, December 18, 2008.

50. Thompson, "Post-Katrina, White Vigilantes Shot African-Americans with Impunity."

51. Thompson, "Post-Katrina, White Vigilantes Shot African-Americans with Impunity."

52. Wells, "Mob Rule in New Orleans," 355.

53. Thompson, "Post-Katrina, White Vigilantes Shot African-Americans with Impunity."

54. Thompson, "Post-Katrina, White Vigilantes Shot African-Americans with Impunity," emphasis added.

55. *Welcome to New Orleans*, dir. Rasmus Holm.

56. Thompson, "Post-Katrina, White Vigilantes Shot African-Americans With Impunity."

57. A.C. Thompson, "Body of Evidence," *ProPublica*, December 19, 2008.

58. Campbell Robertson, "Jury Convicts 3 Officers in Post-Katrina Death," *New York Times*, December 9, 2010.

59. Laura Maggi, "NOPD Probe of Danziger Bridge Incident Lacks Key Proof, Witnesses," *Times-Picayune*, May 18, 2007; *United States of America v. Michael Lohman Criminal Action* 10–032 (E.D.La, 2010), Bill of Information for Conspiring to Obstruct Justice.

60. *United States of America v. Michael Lohman Criminal Action* 10–032 (E.D.La, 2010), Bill of Information for Conspiring to Obstruct Justice; New Orleans Police Department, "New Orleans Police Department Investigative Support Division Major Case Homicide Section J-05934–05;" Flaherty, *Floodlines*, 173.

61. Although some news outlets later admitted that much of the initial reporting of crime and violence in New Orleans was unsubstantiated, the fact that those stories were published weeks after national attention was focused on Katrina ensured they did not receive the level of circulation that the initial racist sensationalized reporting did. It is the initial stories, not the retractions, that are primarily remembered as truth. Brian Thevenot and Gordon Russell, "Rape. Murder. Gunfights," *Times-Picayune*, September 26, 2005; Jim Dwyer and Christopher Drew, "Fear Exceeded Crime's Reality in New Orleans," *New York Times*, September 29, 2005.

62. "Eastern New Orleans Shootout," *Times-Picayune*, September 4, 2005.

63. "Breaking News from The Times-Picayune and Nola.com—Hurricane Katrina—the aftermath Weblog for Day 9: Sunday, September 4, 2005," *Times-Picayune*, September 4, 2005; Ron Thibodeaux and Gordon Russell, "7th Day of Hell—A Week of Horror Ends with More Evacuations and Uncertainty," *Times-Picayune*, September 5, 2005.

64. One of the initial falsehoods was that the death toll at Danziger was higher (five to six casualties) than it was. This reporting fits in not only with the narratives of thousands dead in New Orleans but also with the cops' attempt to turn the Danziger Bridge shooting into a heroic story of an NOPD battle victory against violent looters. A selection of news articles that regurgitated the NOPD's cover-up story about the Danziger shooting is as follows: "Police Shoot 8 on New Orleans Bridge," *Associated Press*, September 4, 2005; "Police Kill 5 as Contractors Attacked," *Associated Press*, September 4, 2005; "At Least 5 Fatally Shot on New Orleans Bridge after Firing on Federal Contractors," *San Juan Star*, September 5, 2005; Chris Adams, Susannah A. Nesmith, and Martin Merzer, "Violence Continues—Police Kill

Suspected Looters Who Fired on Contractors Trying to Make Repairs," *Saint Louis Post-Dispatch*, September 5, 2005; Associated Press, "Police Fatally Shoot Five," *Bridgeton News*, September 5, 2005; David Zucchino, "New Orleans: The Flood Beat—Close Up," *Los Angeles Times*, September 28, 2005; Michael Hedges et. al, "Katrina's Aftermath—Rescuers Hit Obstacles," *Houston Chronicle*, September 5, 2005; Robert Tanner, "Gunfight in New Orleans Corps Contractors Shot at, at Least 5 Gunmen Killed," *Charleston Gazette*, September 5, 2005.

65. Daryn Kagan et al., "President Bush Visits Hurricane-Damaged Area-New Orleans Press Conference," *CNN Live Today*, September 5, 2005.

66. Rita Cosby et al., "Hurricane Katrina: Crisis, Recovery for September 4, 2005," *MSNBC Special Reports*, September 4, 2005.

67. John Burnett, "Evacuees Were Turned away at Gretna, La.," *NPR*, September 20, 2005; Brock N. Meeks, "Gretna Mayor Defends Bridge Blockade," *NBC News*, September 22, 2005.

68. Renee Sanchez, "Marchers: Jeff Wall Doesn't Stand a Chance," *Times-Picayune*, February 23, 1987, Folder: Harry Lee, Box 15, ALR.

69. ACLU National Prison Project, *Abandoned and Abused*, 20–23.

70. ACLU National Prison Project, *Abandoned and Abused*, 10, 29.

71. ACLU National Prison Project, *Abandoned and Abused*, 29–30.

72. ACLU National Prison Project, *Abandoned and Abused*, 23, 30.

73. ACLU National Prison Project, *Abandoned and Abused*, 23.

74. ACLU National Prison Project, *Abandoned and Abused*, 29.

75. ACLU National Prison Project, *Abandoned and Abused*, 35.

76. ACLU National Prison Project, *Abandoned and Abused*, 44.

77. ACLU National Prison Project, *Abandoned and Abused*, 39, 68.

78. ACLU National Prison Project, *Abandoned and Abused*, 39–43.

79. ACLU National Prison Project, *Abandoned and Abused*, 69.

80. ACLU National Prison Project, *Abandoned and Abused*, 34.

81. ACLU National Prison Project, *Abandoned and Abused*, 43.

82. ACLU National Prison Project, *Abandoned and Abused*, 52–53.

83. ACLU National Prison Project, *Abandoned and Abused*, 48.

84. ACLU National Prison Project, *Abandoned and Abused*, 52.

85. ACLU National Prison Project, *Abandoned and Abused*, 54.

86. ACLU National Prison Project, *Abandoned and Abused*, 69–70.

87. ACLU National Prison Project, *Abandoned and Abused*, 61.

88. ACLU National Prison Project, *Abandoned and Abused*, 65.

89. ACLU National Prison Project, *Abandoned and Abused*, 65.

90. I am borrowing from Evelyn Brooks Higginbotham's concept of the "metalanguage of race." Higginbotham, "African-American Women's History."

91. ACLU National Prison Project, *Abandoned and Abused*, 66.

92. "Breaking News from The Times-Picayune and Nola.com—Hurricane Katrina—the aftermath Weblog for Day 8: Sunday, September 3, 2005," *Times-Picayune*, September 3, 2005.

93. "Looters Taking Advantage of Katrina Devastation," *CTV News*, August 31, 2005.

94. Michael Perlstein, "Prison Became Island of Fear and Frustration—As Floodwaters Rose, Inmates and Guards Were in It Together—'It Was a Wild Ride,' Chief Deputy Says," *Times-Picayune*, September 23, 2005.

95. ACLU National Prison Project, *Abandoned and Abused*, 70, 73.

96. ACLU National Prison Project, *Abandoned and Abused*, 77.

97. ACLU National Prison Project, *Abandoned and Abused*, 76.

98. ACLU National Prison Project, *Abandoned and Abused*, 77.

99. ACLU National Prison Project, *Abandoned and Abused*, 76.

100. ACLU National Prison Project, *Abandoned and Abused*.

101. ACLU National Prison Project, *Abandoned and Abused*, 79.

102. Evelyn Lynn first called my attention to this incident and its parallels with Abu Ghraib. Lynn, interview. I want to note that such a connection should not surprise us given the circulation of white supremacist, colonial, and homophobic practices between the US's carceral state and imperial regimes, as well as the literal movements of US prison guards to the battlefronts of the US War on Terror and back again.

103. "Louisiana: Detainee Abuse Requires Federal Probe," *Human Rights News*, October 5, 2005.

104. Garrett and Tetlow, "Criminal Justice Collapse," 148.

105. ACLU National Prison Project, *Abandoned and Abused*, 36.

106. Garrett and Tetlow, "Criminal Justice Collapse," 156–57.

107. Garrett and Tetlow, "Criminal Justice Collapse," 147.

108. Gerharz and Hong, "Down by Law: Orleans Parish Prison before and after Hurricane Katrina," *Dollars & Sense*, March/April 2006.

109. Garret and Tetlow, "Criminal Justice Collapse," 151; Gerharz and Hong, "Down by Law."

110. Lynn, interview.

111. New Orleans healthcare activist Catherine Jones best captures the everyday criminalization of New Orleans post-storm in her blog *Floodlines*, http://floodlines.blogspot.com/.

112. Bervera, interview.

113. Barrow, interview.

114. Barrow, interview; Tamika Middleton, interview with author, March 29, 2021.

115. Middleton, interview.

116. For a more detailed discussion of the human rights framework as part of the Black radical tradition in post-Katrina organizing see Luft, "Beyond Disaster Exceptionalism."

117. For more on the Third Reconstruction framework see Muhammad, "Hurricane Katrina: The Black Nation's 9/11!"; Mann, *Katrina's Legacy*.

118. Civil Rights Congress, *We Charge Genocide*; Kelley, *Freedom Dreams*, 58–59. Although not a sponsor of the *We Charge Genocide* petition, the Black feminist communist organization Sojourners for Truth and Justice similarly articulated US anti-Black racism as a genocidal state project that a human rights political project had the potential to remedy. McDuffie, *Sojourning for Freedom*, 173–82.

119. I do not wish to discount the transnational feminist literature that critiques how human rights have been mobilized to justify Western imperialism and military intervention—often under the liberal feminist banner of "saving the women" of the Global South, and particularly the Middle East and North Africa. At the same time, I contend this is not the only lineage of human rights, and it is to our detriment if we forget the liberatory politics of human rights as used by radical antiracist and anticolonial movements throughout the Global South and by oppressed communities in the Global North (such as Black US southerners). For feminist scholarship critiquing imperial human rights, see Abu-Lughod, "Do Muslim Women Really Need Saving?"; Cornwall and Molyneux, "The Politics of Rights." For more on antiracist and decolonial human rights struggles see Prashad, *The Poorer Nations*; Getachew, *Worldmaking after Empire*.

120. Moreover, the "of" in right of return is significant, not to be lightly replaced with "to," in that the definition of "to" refers to one's movement or direction back to a place, whereas the definition of "of" refers to origin or belonging.

121. The organization was originally the People's Hurricane Relief Fund and Organizing Committee (PHRF-OC), but not long after its founding there was a split between PHRF and POC and much post-Katrina organizing was led by PHRF.

122. It would later change its name to the Louisiana Capital Assistance Center.

123. Price, interview.

124. Price, interview.

125. Lynn, interview; Bervera, interview.

126. Middleton, interview.

127. Sideris and the Amnesty Working Group, "Amnesty for Prisoners of Katrina," 1.

128. Middleton, interview.

129. Middleton, interview.

130. Barrow, interview.

131. Lynn, interview.

132. *I Won't Drown on That Levee and You Ain't Gonna Break My Back*, dir. Ashley Hunt.

133. *I Won't Drown on That Levee and You Ain't Gonna Break My Back*, dir. Ashley Hunt.

134. *I Won't Drown on That Levee and You Ain't Gonna Break My Back*, dir. Ashley Hunt.

135. *I Won't Drown on That Levee and You Ain't Gonna Break My Back*, dir. Ashley Hunt.

136. *I Won't Drown on That Levee and You Ain't Gonna Break My Back*, dir. Ashley Hunt.

137. *I Won't Drown on That Levee and You Ain't Gonna Break My Back*, dir. Ashley Hunt.

138. In my search of news archives, the only documentation I can find of the press conference is by local activist-journalist Jordan Flaherty. Jordan Flaherty, "Crime and New Orleans," *Left Turn Magazine*, October 12, 2005.

139. Lynn, interview.

140. Middleton, interview.

141. Middleton, interview; Mayaba Liebethal, interview with author, April 27, 2016.

142. Critical Resistance, "Media Kit," in author's possession.

Chapter 5

1. Although my periodization of these phases differs from Rachel Luft's, I am indebted to her thinking on the multitude of phases of organizing in those rapid but full years. Luft, "Beyond Disaster Exceptionalism."

2. Evelyn Lynn, interview with author, March 10, 2016.

3. "Definition of a Day Reporting Center" n.d. Folder 25, Box 1, CJC; "Criminal Justice System Analysis and Budget Proposal," September 16, 2006, Folder 10, Box 1, CJC.

4. Jack Cassidy is a pseudonym by request.

5. Norris Henderson, interview with author, May 15, 2016; Lynn, interview; Jack Cassidy, interview with author, March 16, 2016.

6. Safe Streets/Strong Communities pamphlet. n.p., 2007.

7. Cassidy, interview.

8. Xochitl Bervera, interview with author, April 12, 2022.

9. The exact language to describe these three campaigns were different across various Safe Streets documents and how former staffers articulated them. This language is my best attempt to encapsulate the spirit of each campaign. Henderson, interview; Lynn, interview; Cielo Cruz, interview with author, April 15, 2016; Cassidy, interview; Ursula Price, interview with author, March 19, 2016; Bervera, interview.

10. Lynn, interview.

11. Norris Henderson, interview with author, May 15, 2016.

12. Norris Henderson, interview with author, May 15, 2016.

13. Price, interview.

14. Bervera, interview.

15. Drew, "Louisiana's New Public Defender System," 957–69; Southern Center for Human Rights, *A Report on Pre- and Post-Katrina Indigent Defense in New Orleans*.

16. Safe Streets/Strong Communities, *Who Pays the Price*, 4.

17. Safe Streets/Strong Communities, *Who Pays the Price*; Southern Center for Human Rights, *A Report on Pre- and Post-Katrina Indigent Defense in New Orleans*.

18. Southern Center for Human Rights, *A Report on Pre- and Post-Katrina Indigent Defense in New Orleans*.

19. Safe Streets/Strong Communities, *Who Pays the Price*, 5.

20. Safe Streets/Strong Communities, *Who Pays the Price*.

21. Lynn, interview.

22. Drew, "Louisiana's New Public Defender System," 956–66.

23. Cassidy, interview.

24. Southern Center for Human Rights, *A Report on Pre- and Post-Katrina Indigent Defense in New Orleans*.

25. Lynn, interview; Cassidy, interview.

26. Lynn, interview.

27. Susan Finch, "Public Defense Absent, Group Says," *Times-Picayune*, March 10, 2006; Lynn, interview.

28. Laura Maggi, "Katrina Adds to Public Defender Woes," *Times-Picayune*, March 23, 2006.

29. James Gill, "The Case of Disappearing Lawyers," *Times-Picayune*, March 24, 2006.

30. Laura Maggi, "Indigent Office in for Nearly $3 Million," *Times-Picayune*, May 12, 2006.

31. Lynn, interview.

32. Laura Maggi, "Judge Takes Public Defense to Task," *Times-Picayune*, September 18, 2006.

33. Drew, "Louisiana's New Public Defender System," 972–80.

34. Cruz, interview.

35. For more on transformative organizing see Williams, *Demand Everything*.

36. Norris Henderson, interview with author, May 15, 2016.

37. Lynn, interview.

38. Norris Henderson, interview with author, May 15, 2016.

39. Norris Henderson, interview with author, May 15, 2016.

40. Price, interview; Gilmore, *Golden Gulag*.

41. Bervera, interview.

42. Bervera, interview.

43. Lynn, interview.

44. Lynn, interview.

45. Norris Henderson, interview with author, May 15, 2016.

46. Price, interview; Spatial Information Design Lab, *Justice Reinvestment New Orleans*, 18, 27–31.

47. Cruz, interview.

48. Price, interview.

49. Norris Henderson, interview with author, May 15, 2016.

50. Cruz, interview.

51. Cruz, interview.

52. Cruz, interview.

53. Cruz, interview.

54. Lynn, interview.

55. Norris Henderson, interview with author, May 15, 2016.

56. Norris Henderson, interview with author, May 15, 2016.

57. Bervera, interview.

58. Bervera, interview.

59. Mary Howell, "Draft Report of the Police-Civilian Review Task Force," n.d. Folder 17, Box 6, CCDDR; Bruce Eggler, "Independent Police Monitor Urged for N.O. Police—Brutality Complaints Revive 2002 Proposal," *Times-Picayune*, April 28, 2006.

60. Cassidy, interview.

61. Norris Henderson, interview with author, May 15, 2016.

62. Ken Bowen, "Mayor Betrays Loyal Officers," *Times-Picayune*, October 15, 2005; Flaherty, *Floodlines*, 174.

63. Cassidy, interview.

64. Cassidy, interview.

65. Cassidy, interview; Lynn, interview; Price, interview; Gwen Filosa, "Grand Jury to Review Cases Linked to Storm," *Times-Picayune*, January 26, 2006.

66. Soledad O'Brien, Miles O'Brien, Drew Griffin, Andy Serwer, Sibila Vargas, "Police Shooting—No Apologies," *CNN*, May 23, 2006; James Polk, Drew Griffin, and Kate Albright-Hanna, "Katrina Autopsy: Police Shot Mentally Disabled Man in Back," *CNN*, May 23, 2006.

67. Anderson Cooper, "In Depth Look at Violence and Looting Following Katrina," *CNN*, August 26, 2006; Michael Norris and Robert Siegel, "What Happened on New Orleans' Danziger Bridge?" *NPR*, September 13, 2006; Gwen Filosa, "Lawsuits Dispute Fatal Shooting," *Times-Picayune*, September 14, 2006; Jarvis DeBerry, "Why It's So Hard to Trust the Police," *Times-Picayune*, September 15, 2006; Jarvis DeBerry, "Police Supporters Fire Back at Columnist," *Times-Picayune*, September 22, 2006; Drew Griffin, "Shoot to Kill," *CNN*, October 14, 2006.

68. Price, interview.

69. Safe Streets Community Survey #1, 2006. In author's personal possession.

70. Norris Henderson, interview with author, May 15, 2016; Lynn, interview; Gwen Filosa, "Survey: NOPD Not Trusted—Residents Say They're Afraid to Report Crimes," *Times-Picayune*, October 25, 2006.

71. Safe Streets/Strong Communities, *Crisis of Confidence*, 2–6.

72. Safe Streets/Strong Communities, *Crisis of Confidence*, 5–6.

73. Safe Streets/Strong Communities, *Crisis of Confidence*, 7.

74. Safe Streets/Strong Communities, *Crisis of Confidence*, 9–10.

75. Safe Streets/Strong Communities, *Crisis of Confidence*, 7–11.

76. Filosa, "Survey: NOPD Not Trusted"; "Editorial: Earning People's Trust," *Times-Picayune*, October 26, 2006.

77. "Editorial: Earning People's Trust."

78. "Editorial: Earning People's Trust"; Safe Streets/Strong Communities, *Crisis of Confidence*, 5.

79. Safe Streets/Strong Communities, *Crisis of Confidence*, 8.

80. Cruz, interview; Kali Akuno, "Peoples' Justice: The International Tribunal on Hurricanes Katrina and Rita," Pambazuka News, August 30, 2007; Moorehead, *International Tribunal*.

81. Safe Streets/Strong Communities, "New Orleans Coming Home"; October 24, 2007.

82. Safe Streets/Strong Communities, "New Orleans Coming Home"; Cruz, interview.

83. Bruce Eggler, "Increase in Police Brutality in N.O. Alleged," *Times-Picayune*, March 17, 2006; Deborah Cotton, "From the Ground Up: Safe Streets/Strong Communities Pushes for Reform of New Orleans Police Department," *Beehive*, March 2, 2006.

84. They explicitly stated this money should not be located under the NOPD's operating budget. Bruce Eggler, "Independent Monitor Urged for N.O. Police," *Times-Picayune*, April 28, 2006.

85. Bruce Alpert, "Federal Crime Fighting Sought," *Times-Picayune*, August 4, 2006.

86. Lolis Eric Elie, "Someone to Watch over Them," *Times-Picayune*, October 8, 2007.

87. Price, interview; Lynn, interview; Bruce Eggler, "Council Ratifies Ethics Appointees," *Times-Picayune*, January 11, 2007; Michelle Krupa, "Inspector General Undaunted—City's Watchdog Accepts Challenge," *Times-Picayune*, June 22, 2007; Bruce Eggler, "Inspector General Puts Feet to Grindstone," *Times-Picayune*, September 6, 2007.

88. Lynn, interview.

89. Katy Reckdahl, "Culture, Change Collide in Treme," *Times-Picayune*, October 3, 2007.

90. Kerwin James was known for his arrangement of "Who Dat Called the Police?" a classic brass band song to play when cops attempt to break up a second line. Sakakeeny, *Roll with It*, 56.

91. Elie, "Someone to Watch over Them."

92. Chris Kirkham and Brenden McCarthy, "N.O. Cop Suspended in Scrap with Officer," *Times-Picayune*, July 8, 2008.

93. Price, interview.

94. Norris Henderson, interview with author, May 15, 2016. I contacted James Carter's office multiple times for his recollection of this event. Unfortunately, I never heard back from him.

95. Norris Henderson, interview with author, May 15, 2016.

96. David Hammer, "Police Monitor's Powers Approved," *Times-Picayune*, July 11, 2008.

97. Brian Friedman, "Officials Support Inspector General Ordinance," *Times-Picayune*, September 21, 2008; "Election Returns," *Times-Picayune*, October 5, 2008.

98. Lynn, interview.

99. Brenden McCarthy, "Committee Makes Choice for Police Monitor Nominee," *Times-Picayune*, August 6, 2009.

100. "Criminal Justice Committee Chair James Carter Calls for Halt," September 23, 2009.

101. Norris Henderson, interview with author, May 15, 2016; Lynn, interview; Brenden McCarthy, "Woman Chose to Keep an Eye on NOPD," *Times-Picayune*, April 24, 2010.

102. ACLU National Prison Project, *Abandoned and Abused*, 87–90. The "temporary" jailing tents imprisoned people for more than seven years. Naomi Martin, "After 7 Years, Sheriff Marlin Gusman Announces End of 'Temporary' Tents," *Times-Picayune*, February 25, 2014.

103. Garrett and Tetlow, "Criminal Justice Collapse."

104. Rene Lapeyrolerie, "What Really Happened at Orleans Parish Prison in the Aftermath of Hurricane Katrina," *New Orleans Tribune*, Feb/March 2006. During an

interview, Norris Henderson summed up and debunked this argument. "People are saying that nobody complained about Foti and I say straight up, I beg to differ. One, Foti was not the sheriff when I went off to prison. Louis Hyde was the sheriff. I came back and found Foti there. But the few times I passed through the jail on court orders, if you go check into federal court you would see Henderson v. Foti. I challenged Foti every time I ended up in that jail about something. I sued him about something. So y'all are the ones who allowed this to happen and now you're saying that because the Black man is in charge everyone wants to cry foul. Not so. Everyone should have been crying foul from the beginning. But y'all went along to get along because y'all wanted the perks that Foti had. Y'all wanted the turkey dinners. Y'all wanted the free tent. Or you wanted the food the jail cooked and sent to you." Norris Henderson, interview with author, May 15, 2016.

105. Price, interview.

106. Price, interview.

107. Gerharz and Hong, "Down by Law," 39–42.

108. Cassidy, interview.

109. Gerharz and Hong, "Down by Law," 43. In addition, the DPSC sent the New Orleans city government an invoice for $11 million for *municipal* OPP prisoners because FEMA argued it was not responsible for covering such costs. Richard Stadler letter to Mayor C. Ray Nagin, RE: Orleans Parish Evacuated Prisoners, January 30, 2007, Folder 2, Box 14, MCRN.

110. Gerharz and Hong, "Down by Law," 44.

111. ACLU National Prison Project, *Abandoned and Abused*, 11

112. ACLU National Prison Project, *Abandoned and Abused*, 20–27.

113. *Abandoned and Abused*, 66.

114. ACLU National Prison Project, *Abandoned and Abused*, 10–15. The labeling of prisoners as units calls forth the dehumanizing ideologies of slavery under which enslaved African were, in the words of Angela Davis, conceived of as nothing more than "labor units." Davis, *Women, Race, & Class*, 5.

115. ACLU National Prison Project, *Abandoned and Abused*, 87–93.

116. Laura Maggi, "ACLU Blasts Conditions at Parish Prison—But N.O. Sheriff Says Report Is 'Inaccurate,'" *Times-Picayune*, August 21, 2006.

117. Cruz, interview.

118. Lynn, interview.

119. Mayaba Liebenthal, interview with author, April 27, 2016.

120. Sideris and Amnesty Working Group, "Amnesty for Prisoners of Katrina," 18.

121. Sideris and Amnesty Working Group, "Amnesty for Prisoners of Katrina," 19; Liebenthal, interview.

122. Sideris and Amnesty Working Group, "Amnesty for Prisoners of Katrina," 19.

123. Liebenthal, interview.

124. Norris Henderson, interview with author. May 15, 2016.

125. Katy Reckdahl, "Residents Line up for A Fresh Start," *Times-Picayune*, March 30, 2008.

126. Norris Henderson, interview with author. May 15, 2016.

127. Price, interview.

128. Liebenthal, interview; Andrea Slocum, interview with author, May 9, 2016.

129. Adam Nossiter and Shaila Dewan, "Mayor Orders Evacuation of New Orleans," *New York Times*, August 30, 2008.

130. Cruz, interview.

131. Although New Orleans was largely spared, Baton Rouge did experience significant damage from Hurricane Gustav.

132. Cruz, interview.

133. Nadiene Van Dyke to Alexander Chenault, "Establishment of Law Enforcement Taxing Proposition," October 23, 2008, Folder 7, Box 1, CJC.

134. Laura Maggi, "Sheriff Seeks to Extend Tax for Jail," *Times-Picayune*, September 30, 2008.

135. Don Everard, interview with author, April 20, 2016; Norris Henderson, interview with author, May 15, 2016; Bill Quigley, interview with author, July 6, 2016.

136. Price, interview.

137. Everard, interview.

138. Norris Henderson, interview with author, May 15, 2016.

139. Cruz, interview.

140. Kai Lumumba Barrow, interview with author, June 18, 2006.

141. Reagon, "Coalition Politics," 359.

142. Jacinta Gonzalez, interview with author, April 19, 2022.

143. Gonzalez, interview.

144. Gonzalez, interview.

145. OPPRC Structure, Internal Document. In author's personal possession.

146. Barrow, interview; Pam Nath, interview with author, April 6, 2016.

147. While CR was the only abolitionist organization, there were several activists in OPPRC who identified as abolitionists but who represented organizations that held more reformist positions.

148. Barrow, interview.

149. OPPRC Structure, Internal Document, 1. In author's personal possession.

150. OPPRC Structure, Internal Document. In author's personal possession.

151. Cruz, interview.

152. Laura Maggi, "Sheriff to Close House of Detention," *Times-Picayune*, April 11, 2012.

153. Price, interview.

154. Civil Rights Division, US Department of Justice "Orleans Parish Prison Conditions of Confinement Investigation," September 11, 2009, Folder 7, Box 6, CSM.

155. The exact amount that FEMA allocated to rebuilding the jail is not clear. In 2010, it was widely said that FEMA had granted the city $270 million. Yet when the new jail opened in 2015, local media pegged the cost of the jail's rebuilding at $145 million and noted that it was not entirely financed from FEMA. I therefore conservatively guess that around $100 million came from FEMA and the remainder from existing jail millages, although because of the lack of transparency from Sheriff Gusman's office, I am unable to confirm or deny this through public record

requests. Jordan Flaherty, "ACLU of LA Seeks Sheriff's Records Related to FEMA Funding of Orleans Parish Prison Expansion," *Justice Roars*, November 4, 2010; Takei, "The $270 Million Lockup"; Jim Mustain, "As New $145 Million Jail Opens, City Closes Sordid Chapter with Shuttering of Old Parish Prison," *Advocate*, September 14, 2015.

156. Bruce Eggler, "Council Delays Vote on Prison," *Times-Picayune*, June 18, 2010; FEMA, "Justice Facilities Master Plan, Executive Summary," 9, September 15, 2007, Folder 18, Box 2, CJC.

157. Bruce Eggler, "N.O. Council Oks Plans for New Prison Complex," *Times-Picayune*, July 2, 2010.

158. Cruz, interview.

159. Campbell Robertson, "Landrieu Takes Mayoral Seat in New Orleans," *New York Times*, February 6, 2010; E. W. Lewis, "Landrieu's Police Chief Choice Controversial," *Louisiana Weekly*, May 10, 2010.

160. Barrow, interview.

161. Exec. Order No. MJL 10–06, 3 C.F.R. 2. 2010.

162. Don Everard, interview; Norris Henderson, interview with author, May 15, 2016.

163. Barrow, interview.

164. Cruz, interview.

165. Eggler, "Council Delays Vote on Prison."

166. Katy Reckdahl, "Jail Plan Reflects a Major Shift," *Times-Picayune*, December 19, 2010.

167. Laura Maggi, "Does New Orleans Need a Larger Prison?" *Times-Picayune*, September 19, 2010.

168. Stephen Singer and Katherine Mattes, "Look More Closely at Supersize Jail Plan," *Times-Picayune*, November 10, 2010.

169. Frank Barnes, "Open Jail Books, Stop Housing State Inmates," *Times-Picayune*, September 21, 2010.

170. American Civil Liberties Union, "President Obama Signs Bill Reducing Cocaine Sentencing Disparity."

171. Alexander, *The New Jim Crow*.

172. OPPRC Structure, Internal Document, 1. In author's personal possession.

173. Matt Davis, "Gusman's Courthouse Threat Looms as He Awaits Payment," *Lens*, November 2, 2010; Bruce Eggler and Katy Reckdahl, "Gusman Warns of Deficit even if Inmates Decrease," *Times-Picayune*, November 10, 2010.

174. For more on these public meetings and how racialized and patriarchal debates about epistemology structured them, see Colom and Pelot-Hobbs, "Constructing the Unruly Public."

175. Austin, Ware, and Ocker, *Orleans Parish Prison Ten-Year Inmate Population Projection*, 8.

176. Austin and Irwin, *It's about Time*; Austin et al., *Unlocking America*.

177. Austin et al., *Unlocking America*, 12, 33.

178. Austin et al., *Unlocking America*, 33.

179. Austin et al., *Unlocking America*, 24–29.

180. Austin et al., *Unlocking America*, 23.

181. Austin, Ware, and Ocker, *Policy Simulations of Alternative Options to Reduce the Orleans Parish Prison*. These reforms included the implementation of pretrial release for people with felony charges; the replacement of arrests with summons for marijuana possession and similarly categorized offenses; greater efficiency in processing cases; reduction in the time in which parole violators were imprisoned; and the almost total elimination of state prisoners at OPP.

182. One note on 1,438 as the specific bed count number. To this day, it widely circulates in New Orleans that this number was arrived at based on the Austin Report. However, the Working Group's resolution states that the Austin Report suggested 1,485, rather than 1,438, beds for OPP. Yet nowhere does the Austin Report offer 1,485 as the ideal size of OPP. No hard number is ever given for how many beds OPP should have were all five proposed reforms to be enacted. Reports only state that they could cut down the jail's size by an additional 1,300 beds from their "base projection," which would be at most 1,812 beds with a limited amount of state and federal prisoners or 717 without any state and federal prisoners. My hunch is that the 1,485 population limit was determined by the Criminal Justice Working Group based on a JFA Institute model that was not included in either report, but I have not been able to verify this. Regardless of how the JFA Institute decided on 1,485, it appears that the Criminal Justice Working Group recognized how close this bed count was to Gusman's *own proposal of 1,438 beds* for what he had hoped would be the first of many new buildings in the OPP redevelopment (so-called Phase I). Thus, the Criminal Justice Working Group apparently turned Gusman's proposal on its head to make it the entirety—not a piece—of the new OPP. Criminal Justice Working Group, *Resolution on Executive Order 10–06*.

183. Katy Reckdahl, "Jail Needs Flexibility to Hold All, Group Says," *Times-Picayune*, November 23, 2010.

184. Katy Reckdahl, "Mayor Supports Smaller Size for Jail," *Times-Picayune*, December 10, 2010.

185. Maggie Zambolla, "Smaller Jail a Step in the Right Direction," *Times-Picayune*, December 3, 2010.

186. Matt Davis, "New Jail Building Approved by City Council; Sheriff Must Close Others When It's Built," *Lens*, February 3, 2011; Ordinance, City of New Orleans, CALENDAR NO. 28,291.

187. *Cacho and Ocampo*, US District Court for Eastern District of Louisiana.

188. Gonzalez, interview.

189. Gonzalez, interview.

190. Richard Rainey, "Council Attacks Sheriff's Immigrant Policy at Jail—Officials Demand Updated Policy," *Times-Picayune*, May 17, 2013.

191. There was significant back-and-forth about these carve-outs. Initially Gusman wanted the carve-outs to include anyone charged with assault with a weapon—which Congreso members challenged as too vague and got further refined. The eventual decision to agree to carve-outs related to convictions around homicides, aggravated rape, and robbery with a firearm was based on the idea that if people were found guilty, they were not going to be held in OPP anyway

and would be run through similar checks in the state prison system. Gonzalez, interview.

192. Juliet Linderman, "Sheriff Ends ICE holds—Change Related to Lawsuit Filed by Immigration Groups," *Times-Picayune*, August 14, 2013. For a video of Gusman making this announcement to Congreso see https://www.youtube.com/watch?v=XI2RofstcvE&ab_channel=CongressofDayLaborers%2FCongresodeJornaleros.

193. Kevin Allman, "Orleans Parish Prison Reform Coalition Meeting Tonight," *Gambit*, September 20, 2011.

194. Laura Maggi, "10 Inmates Sue N.O. Jail over Safety, Healthcare," *Times-Picayune*, April 3, 2012.

195. "Editorial: Serious Problems at OPP," *Times-Picayune*, April 7, 2012; Danny Monteverde "N.O. Jail Sheds Inmates," *Times-Picayune*, August 13, 2012.

196. Maggi, "Sheriff to Close House of Detention."

197. Bruce Eggler, "Report: Jail Adequately Funded," *Times-Picayune*, June 7, 2013.

198. Naomi Martin, "OPP Consent Decree Could End Per Diem Funding System," *Times-Picayune*, July 26, 2013; Naomi Martin, "Sheriff Must Give Details of How Money Is Spent," *Times-Picayune*, October 22, 2013; Charles Maldonado, "Mayor, Sheriff Quietly End Much-Criticized Per Diem Method for Paying for Prisoners," *Lens*, October 27, 2014.

199. Katy Reckdahl, "N.O. Group Considering 2nd New Jail," *Times-Picayune*, August 13, 2012.

200. "Editorial: The Right Size for the Jail," *Times-Picayune*, August 19, 2012.

201. Richard Rainey, "OPP Consent Decree Costs Shape City Budget Hearing," *Times-Picayune*, November 1, 2013.

202. Richard Rainey, "New Orleans City Council Advances 89-Bed Jail Expansion Plans," *Times-Picayune*, May 18, 2017; Mike Ludwig, "New Orleans Activists Clash with Sheriff over Jail Expansion," *Truthout*, December 7, 2019; Matt Sledge, "New Orleans Asks Court to 'Indefinitely Suspend' Jail Expansion Plan," *Advocate*, June 29, 2020; Nicholas Chrastil, "Federal Judge Has Authority to Order Phase III of New Orleans Jail, Civil Rights Attorneys Argue," *Lens*, September 9, 2020; Michael Isaac Stein, "Council Considers Measures to Stop Phase III Jail Expansion, but It's Unclear whether They Will Succeed," *Lens*, July 27, 2021. For more on the Phase III struggle see Lexi Peterson-Burge, "Federal Courts, FEMA Dollars, and Local Elections in the Struggle Against Phase III in New Orleans," interviewed by Pelot-Hobbs.

203. Cruz, interview.

204. Liebenthal, interview.

205. Cruz, interview.

206. Gonzalez, interview.

Chapter 6

1. Here I am following the work of Roderick Ferguson who poses that we attend to the figure of the racialized gender non-conforming sex worker as a key location to critique capital. Ferguson, *Aberrations in Black*, 1–2.

2. McKittrick, *Demonic Grounds*, xiii; McKittrick, "On Plantations, Prisons, and a Black Sense of Place."

3. Muñoz, *Cruising Utopia*, 91.

4. Lefebvre, *Writings on Cities*, 158.

5. Civil Rights Division, *Investigation of the New Orleans Police Department*, xxvi.

6. Wes Ware, interview with author, January 20, 2015.

7. Ware, *Locked Up & Out*.

8. Ware, interview; Milan Sherry, interview with author, November 18, 2015; Lhundyn Palmer, interview with author, December 2, 2015; Kenisha Harris, letter to author, September 23, 2015.

9. Ware, interview.

10. While their first meetings were under the banner of the LGBTQ Project of JJPL, they adopted the name BreakOUT! by the beginning of 2011. For clarity, I refer these initial meetings as BreakOUT! although not all these activities were under that official moniker.

11. Palmer, interview.

12. Sherry, interview.

13. Hobson, "Policing Gay L.A.," 192.

14. Davis, "Reflections on the Black Woman's Role in the Community of Slaves"; Davis, "JoAnne Little"; Hartman, *Scenes of Subjection*, 82–90; Collins, *Black Feminist Thought*, 146–48; Haley, *No Mercy Here*; Ritchie, *Invisible No More*.

15. BreakOUT! Internal Document. In author's personal possession.

16. When I asked if naming the campaign "We Deserve Better" was a strategic messaging choice to link with the popularity of Dan Savage's "It Gets Better" YouTube campaign around LGBTQ youth suicide, Ware shared "I don't think any of our young people knew what It Gets Better was which shows you how irrelevant and narrow of a reach it had. Most of our young people were street involved, involved in underground street economies, and homeless or marginally housed. I mean really our entire membership was at that point packed into these few motel rooms. They're not watching Youtube videos about how 'It Gets Better.' No, they're surviving." Ware, interview.

17. Ware, interview.

18. *The People's Statement*, 4,7, 10–11.

19. Civil Rights Division, *Investigation of the New Orleans Police Department*, v–vi.

20. Civil Rights Division, *Investigation of the New Orleans Police Department*, x.

21. Civil Rights Division, *Investigation of the New Orleans Police Department*, 35.

22. Civil Rights Division, *Investigation of the New Orleans Police Department*, 35–37.

23. BreakOUT!, *We Deserve Better*.

24. Palmer, interview.

25. Sherry, interview.

26. Ritchie, *Invisible No More*, 110.

27. Ware, interview.

28. *We Deserve Better.*
29. *We Deserve Better.*
30. *We Deserve Better.*
31. BreakOUT! and Streetwise and Safe, *Get Yr Rights*, 42.
32. Wesley Ware, "Consent Decree between NOPD and DOJ Includes Unprecedented Victory for LGBT Youth," *Bridge The Gulf Project*, July 31, 2012. This is not to say that the NOPD consent decree went far enough. For many local racial justice activists, the NOPD consent decree was not as strong as they had hoped, particularly in relation to civilian oversight. Edmund W. Lewis, "CUC Files a Notice of Appeal in NOPD Consent-decree Case," *Louisiana Weekly*, October 29, 2012.
33. Civil Rights Division, *Consent Decree Regarding the New Orleans Police Department*, 50.
34. Civil Rights Division, *Consent Decree Regarding the New Orleans Police Department*.
35. BreakOUT!, "BreakOUT! in City Council."
36. City of New Orleans, "Statement from Mayor Landrieu"; Charles Maldanado, "NOPD Consent Decree: Update on the Monitor RFP plus More on BreakOUT! and the LGBT Policy," *Gambit*, January 24, 2013.
37. BreakOUT!, "Chief Ronal Serpas: Keep Your Promise."
38. Derwin Wilright, Jr., Milan Sherry, and Wesley Ware on behalf of BreakOUT!, "Stop & Frisk: An LGBTQ Issue," *Ambush Magazine*, April 16–29, 2013.
39. Mallory Faulk, interview with Milan Nicole Sherry, Nate Faulk, and Derwin Wilright, Jr., *Bridge The Gulf*, podcast audio, May 26, 2013. In author's possession.
40. Wesley Ware and BreakOUT!, letter to Ronal Serpas, March 20, 2013.
41. Wesley Ware and BreakOUT!, letter to Ronal Serpas, March 20, 2013.
42. Unknowingly to the city, the release of Policy 402 was on the 44th anniversary of the Stonewall riots. BreakOUT!, "New Orleans Police Department Issues LGBTQ Policy."
43. BreakOUT!, "New Orleans Police Department Issues LGBTQ Policy."
44. BreakOUT!, *We Deserve Better.*
45. BreakOUT!, *We Deserve Better.*
46. BreakOUT!, *We Deserve Better.*
47. BreakOUT!, *We Deserve Better.*
48. BreakOUT!, *We Deserve Better.*
49. Mallory Faulk, interview with Milan Nicole Sherry, Nate Faulk, and Derwin Wilright, Jr., *Bridge The Gulf*, podcast audio, May 26, 2013. In author's possession.
50. Long, *Great Southern Babylon*, 1.
51. Long, *Great Southern Babylon*, 102–30. The city used as precedent the *Homer Plessy v. Judge Ferguson* ruling of "separate but equal" to justify their residential segregation of "prostitutes" in 1897. Long argues that the same moralizing arguments were then made to legitimize the corralling of Black New Orleanians into substandard neighborhoods a few years later.
52. Long, *Great Southern Babylon*, 226–27.
53. Souther, *New Orleans on Parade*, 46–49.

54. Souther, *New Orleans on Parade*, 49.

55. Nan Perales, "War on Prostitution Nets 27 During Raid in French Quarter," *Times-Picayune*, January 31, 1983; "63 Arrested in Police Raid in Quarter," *Times-Picayune*, June 21, 1983; Bob Ross, "Crew Looks Unlikely but Reaches Its Goal on Raid in Quarter," *Times-Picayune*, July 11, 1983; Jason DeParle, "Connick Crackdown is Blasted by ACLU," *Times-Picayune*, May 1, 1984.

56. Patricia Behre, "Gays Vow Fight Against Harassment," *Times-Picayune*, June 4, 1984.

57. "Mayor Landrieu, Aviation Board and Regional Leaders Announce Plans," April 17, 2013; "Mayor Landrieu Touts New Orleans 2016 Successes," December 27, 2016; Jeff Adelson, "City Council Approves New Short-Term Rental Rules," *Advocate*, October 20, 2016.

58. "New Orleans Breaks Tourism Records for Visitation, Visitor Spending in 2016," *Biz New Orleans*, March 23, 2017.

59. Jeff Adelson and Dan Swenson, "A First since Katrina: More People Leaving New Orleans for Other Parts of U.S. than Moving from Them," *Advocate*, March 23, 2017.

60. Emily Hobson's work on the history of policing gay Los Angeles demonstrates such racialized and sexualized policing did not originate with the beginning of neoliberalism but was embedded in earlier urban redevelopment projects as well. Yet the era of neoliberalism has led to a surge of such policing initiatives, that mark that it is important to attend to as a period. Hobson, "Policing Gay L.A," 199–203.

61. Hanhardt, "Broken Windows at Blue's," 45.

62. Hanhardt, "Broken Windows at Blue's."

63. Delany, *Times Square Red, Times Square Blue*; Hubbard, "Cleansing the Metropolis"; Amar, "Operation Princess in Rio de Janeiro."

64. Williams, "Sex Work and Exclusion," 4.

65. Grant, "Beyond Strange Bedfellows."

66. Musto, *Control and Protect*; Department of Justice, "Human Trafficking: Key Legislation"; "Report to Congress from Attorney General Alberto R. Gonzales."

67. Department of Justice, "Human Trafficking: Key Legislation"; Immigration and Customs Enforcement, *DHS Blue Campaign*.

68. Naomi Martin, "Former Sex Trafficking Victim Shines Light on Dark Underworld of Super Bowl," *Times-Picayune*, February 2, 2013; Eleanor Goldberg, "Attorney General: Super Bowl Is Largest Human Trafficking Incident in U.S.," *Huffington Post*, February 6, 2013.

69. Naomi Martin, "Authorities Nab 85 in an Effort to Combat Super Bowl Sex Trafficking," *Advocate*, February 8, 2013; Allen Powell II, "More than 80 Booked in Super Bowl Crackdown on Prostitution, Human Trafficking," *Advocate*, February 10, 2013; Lucy Tiven, "Here's Who Really Profits Off Sex Trafficking at The Super Bowl," *Attn:*, February 3, 2016.

70. Richard Rainey, "Civilian NOLA Patrol for French Quarter Clears the City Council," *Times-Picayune*, November 7, 2014.

71. Prescotte Stokes III, "After Bourbon Street Shooting, State Troopers Will Help Patrol on Temporary Basis," *The Times-Picayune*, July 10, 2014; FBI, *New Orleans Historic Crime Trends 1985–2013*; City of New Orleans, "NOPD News," 2018, accessed July 10, 2018, http://nopdnews.com/transparency/ucr/.".

72. This protest came only a few months after the police killing of Mike Brown in the St. Louis suburb of Ferguson, MO catapulted #BlackLivesMatter. While anti-racist organizers contested police violence, broken windows policing, and anti-Black racism, this collective of white wealthy individuals were re-entrenching the argument that police equaled safety.

73. The Landrieuville signs also said in smaller font "(Oh murderers too . . . but those are down)" demonstrating how pro-police residents tended to foreground areas where statistics pointed to rising crime while underplaying statistics that undermined their arguments.

74. *Keep the French Quarter Safe*, dir. Sidney Torres, IV.

75. Alex Woodward, "Drawn and (French) Quartered: A spate of violent crime in the Vieux Carre has some blaming Mayor Mitch Landrieu," *Gambit*, January 8, 2015.

76. John Simerman, "Hodgepodge of French Quarter Security Arrangements Still in Flux as Vote on Tax Approaches," *Advocate*, September 28, 2015.

77. David Amsden, "Who Runs the Streets of New Orleans?" *New York Times*, July 30, 2015.

78. Jonathan Bullington, "New French Quarter Police Patrol, Crime App Taking Shape," *Times-Picayune*, February 20, 2015.

79. French Quarter Management District Security Task Force. Meeting Minutes, June 17, 2015. In author's personal possession.

80. *New York Times Magazine* profile on Torres and the private patrol promoted the idea of Torres rescuing the French Quarter from out-of-control crime on a national stage, a narrative which then trickled down into local conversations in New Orleans.

81. The main proponent of the FQMD was state senator Edwin Murray who represented the French Quarter through 2015. French Quarter Management District, "Purpose & History."

82. Ward, "Business Improvement Districts."

83. French Quarter Management District, "Bylaws"; French Quarter Management District, "Board of Commissioners."

84. At the tail-end of my attendance at the Security Task Force meetings, the committee's name was changed to the Security Enforcement Committee.

85. LA Rev Stat § 25:799. Other work of the FQMD includes surveys of the neighborhood's sidewalks, increasing parking regulations, and the creation of "hospitality zones" around Bourbon and Frenchmen streets.

86. French Quarter Management District, "Accomplishments"; City of New Orleans, M.C.S., Ord. No. 24636, § 1, 10–20–11.

87. French Quarter Management District, "SafeCam."

88. The funds were to be divvied up with the state troopers getting the vast majority and the French Quarter Task Force receiving $75,000 a year. French

Quarter Economic Development District, Quarter for Quarter Presentation, October 15, 2015, Presentation handouts in author's possession; French Quarter Management District, "Economic Development District"; Simerman, "Hodgepodge of French Quarter Security Arrangements."

89. French Quarter Economic Development District, Quarter for Quarter Presentation, October 15, 2015, Presentation handouts in author's possession; "Our Views: French Quarter Tax Vital to Protecting Entire City," *Advocate*, October 24, 2015.

90. Bureau of Governmental Research, "On the Ballot," October 24, 2015.

91. French Quarter Economic Development District, Quarter for Quarter Presentation.

92. These arrests came from responses to calls, traffic stops that were "utilized as a tool for discovery of other criminal activity," stops and frisks, and the work of undercover state troopers working the Quarter. French Quarter Management District Security Task Force, Meeting Minutes, September 16, 2015. In author's personal possession.

93. Meg Gatto, "French Quarter Residents Second Line for Safety," *New Orleans Fox 8*, October 3, 2015. Unlike any Black second line, the dozens of white paraders *paid* to participate in the parade, with the money raised going into the coffers of the FQMD.

94. John Simerman, "French Quarter Sales Tax Increase to Fund State Police Contingent Wins Handily," *Advocate*, October 25, 2015.

95. In the years after I concluded my fieldwork, a local Black business owner was appointed to the FQMD Board of Commissioners by Mayor LaToya Cantrell and served as an active member on the Security and Enforcement Committee.

96. Ironically, the much-publicized dispute between Torres and Simms emerged following Torres going to the press to declare that the Security Task Force had become too lax as it aligned with the NOPD and became less business-like. Along with the two news stations that filmed that particularly heated meeting was a camera crew Torres personally hired to have his own record of the meeting—demonstrating an unwavering ideological consistency in his belief in the importance of filming almost everything that happened in the French Quarter.

97. This was in diametrical opposition to my own experiences in the French Quarter over the preceding ten-plus years. Having spent countless hours in the French Quarter working as a server, seeing music, attending parades and parties, eating and drinking with friends, my sense of the French Quarter—whether at 9:30 in the morning, 4 in the afternoon, or 2 A.M.—had always been as a place that was relatively safe as long as common-sense precautions were taken. This does not mean that I would suggest that anyone wander around drunk in the middle of the night by themselves—but I wouldn't recommend anyone do that in any neighborhood in any city.

98. Weber, "Politics as a Vocation," 212–25.

99. The shoeshine hustlers in New Orleans are ubiquitous. They begin by saying, "I bet I can tell you where you got your shoes." To which their answer is, "On your feet." After this, they will rub a rag on one's shoes and then demand payment for the "bet" and "service."

100. While race was never mentioned in the retelling of this urban legend, this story was racially coded. Anyone familiar with the French Quarter shoeshine hustle (which is practically everyone in the city of New Orleans) knows that the people running this hustle are primarily, if not entirely, Black poor and working class men. It also takes no stretch of the imagination to assume that this family, sometimes from Biloxi, Mississippi, and sometimes from Mobile, Alabama, were conceived as white by storytellers and listeners.

101. This logic has been part of the appeal of broken windows policing since its inception. Harcourt, *Illusion of Order*.

102. The FQMD's power to turn their winding conversations into police sweeps and partitions went beyond targeting specific corners or blocks. Owners of the antique shops and art galleries that line Royal Street complained to the FQMD about how the crowds attracted to street performers on the Royal Street pedestrian mall obstructed easy access to their businesses, which they claimed undermined their profits. FQMD Board members brainstormed how to shut down the Royal Street pedestrian mall and if the mayor or council would be amenable to such a proposal. A few weeks after this particular meeting, musicians and other street performers were stunned to find the NOPD had shut down the pedestrian mall—with the local news reporting that no one knew who was responsible for this decision. I shared my hunch that the FQMD was behind this move with the local musician and cultural workers' advocacy organization, and they soon confirmed that it was the FQMD who had closed down the pedestrian mall. While the pedestrian mall was quickly reopened, this event points to the ease with which the FQMD leveraged punitive state capacity to fulfill their desires.

103. The Security Task Force also set the stage for putting cameras along Elysian Fields, if fiber optics infrastructure was installed.

104. Harvey, *The New Imperialism*; Woods, "Asset Stripping Blues."

105. Smith, "Contours of a Spatialized Politics"; Smith, "Giuliani Time"; Mitchell, *The Right to the City*; Lipsitz, "Policing Place and Taxing Time on Skid Row."

106. Willse, *The Value of Homelessness*.

107. French Quarter Management District Security Task Force, Meeting Minutes, September 16, 2015. In author's personal possession.

108. Browne, *Dark Matters*, 16.

109. NOPD Eighth District Arrests, 2015–2016.

110. Jonathan Bullington, "Mayor Landrieu proposes $10.5 million NOPD budget increase for 2016," *Times-Picayune*, October 15, 2015; John Simerman, "New Orleans Mayor, Police Chief, Stump for Millage to Pay for More Cops," *Advocate*, April 6, 2016.

111. Political Education Working Group of European Dissent, "FAQ on the April 9 Policing Millage Vote."

112. "Mayor Landrieu Announces Deal with Firefighters and Says 'We're Gonna Have to Pay It Together,'" *WGNO New Orleans*, October 16, 2015.

113. "'Yes' for more money for New Orleans police, firefighters and streets: Editorial," *Times-Picayune*, March 20, 2016; "Editorial: It Takes a Millage," *Gambit*, March 24, 2016; Bureau of Governmental Research, "On the Ballot," April 2016; "Business groups endorse proposed tax hike for public safety in New Orleans," *Advocate*, March 22, 2016.

114. For a discussion of trying to organize people to take a tax vote seriously as a question of racial justice see Pelot-Hobbs, "How Do We Actually Put Abolition into Practice?"

115. Richard Rainey, "Who Voted Against Mayor Landrieu's New Orleans Tax Hike Plan?" *Times-Picayune*, April 11, 2016.

116. The Black New Orleans newspaper *Louisiana Weekly* came out against the public safety millage, not inspired by the politics of Black Lives Matter but as people against higher taxes. "City Seeks More Taxes on April 9," *Louisiana Weekly*, April 4, 2016.

117. In thinking through the idea of BreakOUT! as embodying a specifically Black trans feminist politic in their organizing, I am indebted to theorizations of the linkages between Black feminism and trans feminist politics. Sudbury, "Maroon Abolitionists," 1–29; Green, "Troubling the Waters"; Green and Bey, "Where Black Feminist Thought and Trans* Feminism Meet."

118. Harvey, "The Right to the City," 23.

119. "Support CeCe!"; Nicole Pasulka, "The Case of CeCe McDonald: Murder-or Self-Defense Against a Hate Crime?" *Mother Jones*, May 22, 2012.

120. Mock, *Redefining Realness*; Cox, "Laverne Cox Explains the Intersection of Transphobia, Racism, and Misogyny"; Mock, "A Note on Visibility."

121. Garza, "A Herstory of the #BlackLivesMatter Movement."

122. This is not to imply that the number of police killings of Black people during this time was unique. Rather that the spark of Ferguson transformed individualized outrage at such racist murders into a collective and public condemnation which not only increased attention on each instance of police violence but located these killings within a matrix of structural state violence. Taylor, *From #BlackLivesMatter to Black Liberation*, 153–90.

123. Sherry, interview.

124. Snorton, *Black on Both Sides*, 195.

125. Sherry, interview.

126. Snorton, *Black on Both Sides*, 185.

127. "Pumping silicone" refers to the practice of people without access to gender-affirming healthcare to inject silicone into their body for curves, which can have grave medical consequences.

128. Harkening to the politicized concept of British Black, BreakOUT! articulated during the rally that by Black they meant "anything not white."

129. BreakOUT!, "Platform for a Safer City."

130. Jai Shavers, interview with author, January 30, 2016.

131. Tuzzolo and Hewitt, "Rebuilding Inequity."

132. Anthoni/Kym Johnson, interview with author, January 6, 2016.

133. This logic also influenced my fieldwork as part of my agreements with BreakOUT! was that I would compensate every interviewee for taking the time to talk with me.

134. Nia Faulk, interview with author, January 29, 2016.

135. Faulk, interview.

136. Faulk, interview.

137. Over time Congreso became a multi-gendered organization with many families making up their base.

138. Cohen, "Punks, Bulldaggers, and Welfare Queens," 458.

139. Westley also built a relationship with one of BreakOUT!'s founders who was also doing time at the same facility. Arely Westley, interview with author, January 6, 2016.

140. Westley, interview.

141. BreakOUT!, "The Moment We've Been Waiting For," emphasis in original.

142. Landrieu, *New Orleans*, 5–9.

143. Cohen, "Punks, Bulldaggers, and Welfare Queens," 457.

Conclusion

1. Nick Chrastil, "Sheriff's Office Confirms 15 New Orleans Inmates Positive for Coronavirus, Advocates in Motorcade Protest for More Releases" *Lens*, April 6, 2020.

2. Orleans Parish Prison Reform Coalition letter to New Orleans elected officials, "Community Demands for Decarceration in the Response to the Coronavirus COVID-19," March 18, 2020, https://opprcnola.org/blog/opprc-covid19-letter.

3. For more on the connections between organizing to "free them all" at the beginning of the COVID-19 pandemic and abolitionist organizing around OPP after Hurricane Katrina see Pelot-Hobbs, "Amnesty for All."

4. "New Orleans Jail Population Snapshot," https://council.nola.gov/committees/criminal-justice-committee/#jail-dashboard. This early pandemic population drop was not unique to New Orleans but occurred in carceral facilities across the United States. Emily Widra, "State Prisons and Local Jails Appear Indifferent to COVID Outbreaks, Refuse to Depopulate Dangerous Facilities" *Prison Policy Initiative*, February 10, 2022, https://www.prisonpolicy.org/blog/2022/02/10/february2022_population.

5. Nicholas Chrastil, "Federal Judge Has Authority to Order Phase III of New Orleans Jail, Civil Rights Attorneys Argue," *Lens*, September 9, 2020.

6. Nicholas Chrastil, "Federal Magistrate Judge Demands Answers regarding Ongoing Discussions of Jail Retrofit Alternative to Phase III," *Lens*, August 10, 2022.

7. Matt Sledge, "As Jail Population Drops, New Orleans Prosecutors Say Inmate Release Could Be Coronavirus 'Threat,'" *Times-Picayune*, March 19, 2020; "Louisiana Leaders Disagree on Prisoner Releases," *Crime Report*, April 6, 2020; David Jacobs, "Oil Price Crash Bad News for Louisiana Industry, State Budget," *New Orleans City Business*, April 21, 2020.

8. LeBrón, *Policing Life and Death*.

9. Against the claim that Edwards's reforms were bold and historic, they do not come even close to reducing the buildup of Louisiana's carceral infrastructure since the 1970s, with most sentencing reforms reserved for what Marie Gottschalk has termed the "non, non nons" and some laws extending punitive power—such as a new mandatory minimum sentence for opioid possession. Gottschalk, *Caught*, 165; Julia O'Donoghue, "Here's How Louisiana Parole Will Change under Criminal

Justice Reform," *Times-Picayune*, June 23, 2017; Julia O'Donoghue, "Here's How Louisiana Sentencing Laws Will Change under Criminal Justice Reform," *Times-Picayune*, June 26, 2017.

10. Grey Larose, "Bond Commission Sits on Power Plant Financing until New Orleans Rescinds Abortion Policy," *Louisiana Illuminator*, August 18, 2022.

11. To say nothing of the racial politics of finance capital as Destin Jenkins reminds us in *Bonds of Inequality*.

12. Gilmore, "Abolition Geography and the Problem of Innocence."

13. Olsavsky, *The Most Absolute Abolition*; Davis, *The Emancipation Circuit*; Prashad, *Darker Nations*; Getachew, *Worldmaking after Empire*.

14. A case in point: Oliver Thomas advocated for tough-on-crime policies during his time on the New Orleans City Council until 2007 when he went to federal prison to serve his sentence for corruption charges. After his release and several years back home, he was reelected to the New Orleans City Council in 2021; since resuming office, he has been a staunch proponent for law and order without much, if any, critique of the prison system.

15. Kai Lumumba Barrow, interview with author, June 18, 2016.

16. Gorz, *Strategy for Labor*.

17. Gilmore, "Abolition Geography and the Problem of Innocence," 230.

18. Care Collective, *The Care Manifesto*.

19. Reagon, "Coalition Politics," 359.

Bibliography

Primary Sources

Interviews by the Author
kai lumumba barrow, New Orleans, June 18, 2016
Xochitl Bervera, video call interview, April 12, 2022
Melissa Burch, telephone interview, March 22, 2016
Jack Cassidy*, New Orleans, March 16, 2016
Cielo Cruz, New Orleans, April 15, 2016
Eugene Dean, New Orleans, December 31, 2010
Don Everard, New Orleans, April 20, 2016
Naomi Farve, New Orleans, March 21, 2011
Nia Faulk, New Orleans, January 29, 2016
Jacinta Gonzalez, video call interview, April 19, 2022
Shana M. griffin, New Orleans, April 21, 2016
Kenisha Harris, letters to author, September 23, 2015; October 29, 2016
Norris Henderson, New Orleans, October 7, 2010; December 14, 2010; May 15, 2016
Anthoni/Kym Johnson, New Orleans, January 6, 2016
Shaena Johnson, New Orleans, January 6, 2016
Kenneth "Biggy" Johnston, New Orleans, January 15, 2011, March 25, 2016
Mayaba Liebethal, New Orleans, April 27, 2016
Evelyn Lynn, telephone interview, March 10, 2016
Tamika Middleton, video call interview, March 29, 2021
Cobella Moore, New Orleans, January 10, 2016
Pam Nath, New Orleans, April 6, 2016
Keith Nordyke, Baton Rouge, April 7, 2016
Lhundyn Palmer, New Orleans, December 2, 2015
Ursula Price, New Orleans, March 19, 2016
Ted Quant, telephone interview, February 9, 2011
Bill Quigley, New Orleans, July 6, 2017
Jai Shavers, New Orleans, January 30, 2016
Milan Sherry, New Orleans, November 18, 2015
Andrea Slocum, New Orleans, May 9, 2016
Wes Ware, New Orleans, January 20, 2015
Arely Westley, New Orleans, January 6, 2016
Checo Yancy, Baton Rouge, January 7, 2011

*Pseudonym by request.

Archival and Manuscript Collections

Amistad Research Center, Tulane University, New Orleans, LA
    ACLU of Louisiana Records, 1970-1985
    Ernest "Dutch" Morial Papers, 1929-1995
    Marc H. Morial Papers, 1994-2002

Hill Memorial Library, Louisiana State University, Baton Rouge, LA
    James L. Stovall Papers, 1943-1997

Louisiana Research Collection, Howard-Tilton Memorial Library, Tulane University, New Orleans, LA
    David Treen Papers

Louisiana State Archives, Baton Rouge, LA
    Department of Corrections Board Records, 1977-1979
    Department of Corrections News Clippings, 1972-1984
    Economic Development Publications, 1962-1976
    Governor's Office Long Range Prison Study Files, 1972-1980
    Legislative Research Library, 1982-1998
    Legislative Research Library Publications, 1992-2004
    Louisiana State Penitentiary Correspondence, 1952-1964
    Louisiana State Penitentiary Records, 1952-1962
    State Budget Reports, 1970-1989

National Archives and Records Southwest Region, Fort Worth, TX
    Hayes Williams et al. v. John McKeithan et al., No. Civil Action 71-98 (M.D.La 1975)

Southern Historical Collection, Louis Round Wilson Special Collections Library, University of North Carolina, Chapel Hill, NC
    Southern Coalition on Jails and Prisons Records, 1974-1980

Special Collections and City Archives, New Orleans Public Library, New Orleans, LA
    City Council District D Records
    Councilman-at-Large Joseph I. Giarrusso
    Councilmember Shelly S. Midura—District A Records, 2006-2010
    Mayor C. Ray Nagin—Mayor's Office Administration Subject/Correspondence Files
    Mayor Ernest N. Morial Records, 1977-1986
    Oliver Thomas Records

Private Collections

Critical Resistance Organizational Papers, Oakland, CA
Melissa Burch Personal Papers, Ann Arbor, MI
Shana M. griffin Personal Papers, New Orleans, LA
Keith Nordyke Personal Papers, Baton Rouge, LA

Government Publications

Carroll, Stuart P., and Linda Marye. *The New Orleans Criminal Justice System 1983*. Office of Criminal Justice Coordination, 1983.

Carter, James. "Criminal Justice Committee Chair James Carter Calls for Halt to Independent Police Monitor Selection Process and Requests Office of Inspector General and the Ethics Review Board Comply with Its Enabling Legislation." News release, New Orleans City Council, September 23, 2009.

City of New Orleans. "Mayor Landrieu, Aviation Board and Regional Leaders Announce Plans to Build New, World Class Airport on North Side of MSY." Press release, April 17, 2013.

———. "Mayor Landrieu Touts New Orleans 2016 Successes and Unveils New Year Holiday Public Safety Plan." Press release, December 27, 2016.

———. "Statement from Mayor Landrieu." News release, January 11, 2013.

City of New Orleans, Office of Criminal Justice Coordination. *Grants in the War on Crime: The New Orleans Experience 1968–1988*. By Stuart P. Carroll and Linda Marye. December 1988.

Criminal Justice Working Group. *Resolution on Executive Order 10–06*. November 22, 2010.

Landrieu, Mitchell J. *New Orleans: Citywide Public Safety Improvements*. January 23, 2017.

Louisiana Board of Pardons & Committee on Parole. *2021 Annual Report*. https://s32082.pcdn.co/wp-content/uploads/2022/03/2021-Annual-Report.pdf.

Louisiana Department of Health and Human Services. *Hurricane Katrina Deaths, Louisiana, 2005*. By Joan Brunkard, Gonza Namulanda, and Raoult Ratard. Baton Rouge. August 28, 2008. http://www.dhh.louisiana.gov/assets/docs/katrina/deceasedreports/KatrinaDeaths_082008.pdf.

Louisiana Department of Natural Resources, Office of Conservation. *First Oil Well in Louisiana*. http://dnr.louisiana.gov/index.cfm?md=pagebuilder&tmp=home&pid=48.

Louisiana Department of Natural Resources, Technology Assessment Division. *Louisiana Severance Tax*. 2016. http://dnr.louisiana.gov/assets/TAD/data/severance/la_severance_tax_rates.pdf.

Louisiana Department of Public Safety and Corrections. *Transitional Work Program Facilities*. September 16, 2014. http://doc.louisiana.gov/media/1/twp-contact-info-sept-2014.pdf.

Louisiana Division of Administration, Office of Planning and Budget. *The Governor's Corrections Plan: A Balanced Comprehensive Approach to Corrections*. April 1990.

Louisiana Legislative Auditor. *State Mineral and Energy Board Mineral Lease Royalty Rates*. By Daryl G. Purpera. April 2013. http://app1.lla.state.la.us/PublicReports.nsf/DB918AD8E33411F286257B490074B82A/$FILE/00031C97.pdf.

Louisiana Legislative Fiscal Office. *Adult Correctional Systems: A Report Submitted to the Fiscal Affairs and Government Operation Committee*. By Christopher A. Keaton. Baton Rouge, 1999.

———. *Adult Correctional Systems: A Report Submitted to the Fiscal Affairs and Government Operation Committee*. By Christopher A. Keaton. Baton Rouge, 2000.

———. *Adult Correctional Systems: A Report Submitted to the Fiscal Affairs and Government Operation Committee.* By Kristy Freeman. Baton Rouge, 2002.

———. *Direct Mineral Revenue, 1969–2014.* By Gregory Albrecht.

———. *Louisiana Relative Unemployment Rates.* By Gregory Albrecht. 2015.

New Orleans City Council, Criminal Justice Committee. "New Orleans Jail Population Snapshot." https://council.nola.gov/committees/criminal-justice-committee/#jail-dashboard.

New Orleans Police Department. "New Orleans Police Department Investigative Support Division Major Case Homicide Section J-05934–05." October 14, 2005. https://www.documentcloud.org/documents/548-nopd-report-on-the-danziger-bridge-shooting.html.

US 109th Congress. *A Failure of Initiative.* By Select Bipartisan Committee to Investigate the Preparation for and Response to Hurricane Katrina. Washington DC, 2006. https://www.gpo.gov/fdsys/pkg/CRPT-109hrpt377/pdf/CRPT-109hrpt377.pdf.

US Climate Prediction Center. *The 2005 North Atlantic Hurricane Season: A Climate Perspective.* By Gerald D. Bell, Eric S. Blake, Christopher W. Landsea, Kingtse C. Mo, Richard J. Pasch, Muthuvel Chelliah, and Stanley B. Goldenberg. n.d. https://www.cpc.ncep.noaa.gov/products/expert_assessment/hurrsummary_2005.pdf.

US Department of Energy, Office of Electricity Delivery and Energy Reliability. *Comparing the Impacts of the 2005 and 2008 Hurricanes on U.S. Energy Infrastructure.* February 2009. https://www.oe.netl.doe.gov/docs/HurricaneComp0508r2.pdf.

US Department of Justice. "Human Trafficking: Key Legislation." https://www.justice.gov/humantrafficking/key-legislation.

———. "President Clinton Announces New Crime Bill Grants to Put Police Officers on the Beat." October 12, 1994. https://www.justice.gov/archive/opa/pr/Pre_96/October94/590.txt.html.

———. "Report to Congress from Attorney General Alberto R. Gonzales on U.S. Government Efforts to Combat Trafficking in Persons in Fiscal Year 2004." July 2005. https://www.justice.gov/archive/ag/annualreports/tr2004/agreporthumantrafficing.pdf.

US Department of Justice, Bureau of Justice Statistics. *Correctional Populations in the United States, 1985.* 1987.

———. *Prison and Jail Inmates at Midyear 1998.* By Darrell K. Gilliard. 1999. https://www.bjs.gov/content/pub/pdf/pjim98.pdf.

———. *Prisoners in 1980.* By Carol B. Kalish. 1981. http://www.bjs.gov/index.cfm?ty=pbdetail&iid=3365.

———. *Prisoners in 2013.* By E. Ann Carson. 2014. https://www.bjs.gov/content/pub/pdf/p13.pdf.

———. *Prisoners in 2019.* By E. Ann Carson. 2020. https://bjs.ojp.gov/content/pub/pdf/p19.pdf.

———. *Prisoners in 2021.* By E. Ann Carson. 2022. https://bjs.ojp.gov/sites/g/files/xyckuh236/files/media/document/p21st.pdf.

US Department of Justice, Civil Rights Division. *Consent Decree Regarding the New Orleans Police Department*. 2012.
———. *Investigation of the New Orleans Police Department*. 2011. https://www.justice.gov/sites/default/files/crt/legacy/2011/03/17/nopd_report.pdf.
US Department of Labor, Bureau of Labor Statistics. *The Economics Daily: Unemployment Rate and Employment-Population Ratio Vary by Race and Ethnicity*. 2017. https://www.bls.gov/opub/ted/2017/unemployment-rate-and-employment-population-ratio-vary-by-race-and-ethnicity.htm.
US Department of Labor, Office of Policy, Planning, and Research. *The Negro Family: The Case for National Action*. By Daniel Patrick Moynihan. 1965.
US Federal Bureau of Investigation. *New Orleans Historic Crime Trends 1985–2013*. 2014.
US Federal Emergency Management Agency. *High Water Mark Collection for Hurricane Katrina in Louisiana*. By URS Group, Inc. 2006. https://www.fema.gov/pdf/hazard/flood/recoverydata/katrina/katrina_la_hwm_public.pdf.
US Geological Survey. *Temporal Analysis of Floodwater Volumes in New Orleans after Hurricane Katrina*. By Jodie Smith and James Rowland. 2007. https://pubs.usgs.gov/circ/1306/pdf/c1306_ch3_h.pdf.
US Geological Survey, National Wetlands Research Center. *Over 100 Years of Land Change for Coastal Louisiana*. By Louisiana Coastal Area (LCA) Land Change Study Group. 2005.
US Immigration and Customs Enforcement. *DHS Blue Campaign*. June 6, 2013. https://www.ice.gov/factsheets/dhs-blue-campaign.
US National Weather Service. *Service Assessment Hurricane Katrina August 23–31, 2005*. By David L. Johnson. Silver Spring, MD, June 2006. https://www.weather.gov/media/publications/assessments/Katrina.pdf.
US Senate Committee on Homeland Security and Governmental Affairs. *Situational Awareness: The Day of Landfall*. February 9, 2006. https://www.npr.org/documents/2006/feb/katrina/awareness_timeline.pdf.

Newspapers and Periodicals

Advocate (Baton Rouge, LA)
Alexandria Daily Town Talk (Alexandria, LA)
Ambush Magazine
American Press (Lake Charles, LA)
Angolite
Associated Press
Atlantic
Attn:
Beehive (New Orleans, LA)
Biz New Orleans
Bridgeton News (Bridgeton, NJ)
Charleston Gazette (Charleston, WV)
CNN
Collier's Magazine
Comet (Thibodaux, LA)
CTV News
Daily Advertiser (Lafayette, LA)
Daily Courier (Homer, LA)
Daily Enterprise (Mansfield, LA)
Daily News (Bogalusa, LA)
Daily Reveille (Baton Rouge, LA)
Dallas Morning News
Eunice Gazette (Eunice, LA)
Gambit (New Orleans, LA)
Gazette (Farmersville, LA)
Houston Chronicle (TX)
Huffington Post

Human Rights News
Inside
Jericho
Justice Roars
Lafayette Advertiser (Lafayette, LA)
Lake Charles American Press
Lens (New Orleans, LA)
Los Angeles Times (Los Angeles, CA)
Louisiana Weekly (New Orleans, LA)
Mongabay
Monroe Morning World (Monroe, LA)
Morning Advocate (Baton Rouge, LA)
MSNBC Special Reports
National Catholic Reporter
NBC News
New Orleans Fox 8
New Orleans Tribune
New York Times (New York, NY)
NPR
Pambazuka News
ProPublica
Red River Journal (Pineville, LA)
Saint Louis Post-Dispatch
San Juan Star (San Juan, Puerto Rico)
Seattle Times
Shreveport Journal (Shreveport, LA)
Shreveport Times
St. Francisville Democrat (St. Francisville, LA)
States-Item (New Orleans, LA)
States Times (Baton Rouge, LA)
Times Picayune (New Orleans, LA)
Truthout
Vindicator (Hammond, LA)
Washington Post
WGNO New Orleans
Winn Parish Enterprise (Winnfield, LA)

Nongovernmental Organizations Reports and Publications

American Civil Liberties Union. *Abandoned and Abused: Complete Report.* By National Prison Project of the ACLU, ACLU of Louisiana, ACLU Human Rights Program, ACLU Racial Justice Program, Human Rights Watch, Juvenile Justice Project of Louisiana, NAACP Legal Defense and Education Fund, and Safe Streets/Strong Communities. 2006. https://www.aclu.org/report/abandoned-abused-complete-report.

Austin, James, Todd Clear, Troy Duster, David F. Greenberg, John Irwin, Candace McCoy, Alan Mobley, Barbara Owen, and Joshua Page. *Unlocking America: Why and How to Reduce America's Prison Population.* Washington DC: JFA Institute, 2007.

Austin, James, Wendy Ware, and Roger Ocker. *Orleans Parish Prison Ten-Year Inmate Population Projection.* Washington DC: JFA Institute, 2010.

——. *Policy Simulations of Alternative Options to Reduce the Orleans Parish Prison Ten-Year Projection.* Washington DC: JFA Institute, 2010.

BreakOUT! "BreakOUT! in City Council." News release, October 26, 2012.

——. "Platform for a Safer City." November 2015.

——. *We Deserve Better: A Report on Policing in New Orleans by and for Queer and Trans Youth.* 2014.

BreakOUT! and Streetwise and Safe. *Get Yr Rights: A Toolkit for LGBTQTS Youth and LGBTQTS Youth-Serving Organizations.* 2015.

Browne-Dianis, Judith, Jennifer Lai, Marielena Hincapie, and Saket Soni. AND INJUSTICE FOR ALL: *Workers Lives in the Reconstruction of New Orleans.* Advancement Project, 2007.

Bureau of Governmental Research. "On the Ballot." October 24, 2015.

———. "On the Ballot." April 2016.

Celeste, Gabriella, Grace Bauer, Xochitl Bervera, and David Utter. "Just Shut It Down: Bringing down a Prison while Building a Movement." Friends and Families of Louisiana's Incarcerated Children. http://www.fflic.org/wp-content/uploads/2010/03/Just-Shut-It-Down.pdf.

Civil Rights Congress. *We Charge Genocide: The Historic Petition to the United Nations for Relief from a Crime of the United States Government against the Negro People.* New York, 1951.

Critical Resistance. "Media Kit: Amnesty for Prisoners of Katrina Weekend." December 2006.

Human Rights Watch. *Locked Away: Immigration Detainees in Jails in the United States.* September 1998. https://www.refworld.org/docid/3ae6a8400.html.

Justice Policy Center. *The Influences of Truth-in-Sentencing Reforms on Changes in States' Sentencing Practices and Prison Populations.* By William J. Sabol, Katherine Rosich, Kamala Mallik Kane, David P. Kirk, and Glenn Dubin. Urban Institute, April 2002. https://www.urban.org/sites/default/files/publication/60401/410470-The-Influences-of-Truth-in-Sentencing-Reforms-on-Changes-in-States-Sentencing-Practices-and-Prison-Populations.PDF.

Louisiana Budget Project. *Poverty in Louisiana: Census 2019.* September 2020. https://www.labudget.org/wp-content/uploads/2020/09/LBP-Census-2019.pdf.

People's Consent Decree. *The People's Statement and Terms and Conditions for a Consent Decree by and between the US Department of Justice and the City of New Orleans/New Orleans Police Department.* 2010.

People's Hurricane Relief Fund. *International Tribunal: Our Demand for Justice and Restitution from the U.S. Government.* Program. New Orleans: People's Hurricane Relief Fund, August 29–September 2, 2007.

Political Education Working Group of European Dissent. "FAQ on the April 9 Policing Millage Vote." April 2016.

Prison Policy Initiative. "Era of Mass Expansion: Why State Officials Should Fight Jail Growth." By Joshua Aiken. May 31, 2017. https://www.prisonpolicy.org/reports/jailsovertime_table_5.html.

———. "State Prisons and Local Jails Appear Indifferent to COVID Outbreaks, Refuse to Depopulate Dangerous Facilities." By Emily Widra. February 10, 2022. https://www.prisonpolicy.org/blog/2022/02/10/february2022_population.

Safe Streets/Strong Communities. *Crisis of Confidence: Persistence Problems within the New Orleans Police Department: Voices and Solutions from Communities Most Impacted by Violent Crime.* October 22, 2006.

———. *New Orleans Coming Home: A National Panel Hearing on Law Enforcement in the Reconstruction.* October 24, 2007.

———. *Who Pays the Price for Orleans Parish's Broken Indigent Defense System? A Summary of Investigative Findings.* March 2006.

Sakala, Leah. *Breaking down Mass Incarceration in the 2010 Census*. Prison Policy Initiative, 2014. https://www.prisonpolicy.org/reports/rates.html.

Sideris, Marina, and Amnesty Working Group. "Amnesty for Prisoners of Katrina: A Critical Resistance Special Report." In *Hurricane Katrina and Criminal Justice: Response to the Periodic Report of the United States to the United Nations Committee on the Elimination of Racial Discrimination*. November 2007.

Southern Center for Human Rights. *A Report on Pre- and Post-Katrina Indigent Defense in New Orleans*. March 2006.

Spatial Information Design Lab. *Justice Reinvestment New Orleans*. New York: Columbia University Graduate School of Architecture, Planning and Preservation, February 2009.

United Teachers of New Orleans, Louisiana Federation of Teachers, and American Federation of Teachers. *"National Model" or Flawed Approach? The Post-Katrina New Orleans Public Schools*. Self-published, United Teachers of New Orleans, 2006.

Ware, Wesley. *Locked Up & Out: Lesbian, Gay, Bisexual, & Transgender Youth in Louisiana's Juvenile Justice System*. New Orleans: Juvenile Justice Project of Louisiana, 2010.

Films, Documentaries, Podcasts

Dantas, Luisa, dir. *Land of Opportunity*. JoLu Productions, 2010.

Falk, Mallory. Interview with Milan Nicole Sherry, Nia Faulk and Derwin Wilright, Jr. *Bridge the Gulf*. Podcast audio. May 26, 2013.

Holm, Rasmus, dir. *Welcome to New Orleans*. Fridthjof Film, 2006. https://www.youtube.com/watch?v=V__lSdR1KZg.

Hunt, Ashley, dir. *I Won't Drown on That Levee and You Ain't Gonna Break My Back*. Corrections Documentary Project, 2006. https://vimeo.com/17174758.

Torres, Sidney, dir. *Keep the French Quarter Safe*. 2015. https://www.youtube.com/watch?v=EGahOQUzSPo.

We Deserve Better. BreakOUT! and FosterBear Films, 2012. https://vimeo.com/35268253.

Secondary Sources

Abu-Lughod, Lila. "Do Muslim Women Really Need Saving? Anthropological Reflections on Cultural Relativism and Its Others." *American Anthropologist* 104, no. 3 (2002).

Adams, Jessica. "'The Wildest Show in the South': Tourism and Incarceration at Angola." *TDR/The Drama Review* 45, no. 2 (Summer 2001).

Adamson, Christopher R. "Punishment after Slavery: Southern State Penal Systems, 1865–1890." *Social Problems* 30, no. 5 (1983).

Akuno, Kali. "Peoples' Justice: The International Tribunal on Hurricanes Katrina and Rita." Pambazuka News, August 30, 2007. https://www.pambazuka.org/governance/peoples-justice-international-tribunal-hurricanes-katrina-and-rita.

Alexander, Michelle. *The New Jim Crow: Mass Incarceration in the Age of Colorblindness*. New York: New Press, 2010.

Allen-Bell, Angela A. "Bridge over Troubled Waters and Passageway on a Journey to Justice: National Lessons Learned about Justice from Louisiana's Response to Hurricane Katrina." *California Western Law Review* 46, no. 2 (Spring 2010).

Amar, Paul. "Operation Princess in Rio de Janeiro: Policing 'Sex Trafficking,' Strengthening Worker Citizenship, and the Urban Geopolitics of Security in Brazil." *Security Dialogue* 40, no. 4–5 (2009).

Ansfield, Bench. "The Broken Windows of the Bronx: Putting the Theory in Its Place." *American Quarterly* 72, no. 1 (2020).

Arend, Orissa. *Showdown in Desire: The Black Panthers Take a Stand in New Orleans*. Fayetteville: University of Arkansas Press, 2009.

Arrighi, Giovanni. *The Long Twentieth Century: Money, Power, and the Origins of Our Times*. London: Verso, 1994.

Austin, Diane E. "Coastal Exploitation, Land Loss, and Hurricanes: A Recipe for Disaster." *American Anthropologist* 108, no. 4 (December 2006).

Austin, James, and John Irwin. *It's about Time: America's Imprisonment Binge*. Australia: Wadsworth, 2001.

Ayers, Edward L. *Vengeance and Justice: Crime and Punishment in the 19th-Century American South*. New York: Oxford University Press, 1984.

Balto, Simon. *Occupied Territory: Policing Black Chicago from Red Summer to Black Power*. Chapel Hill: The University of North Carolina Press, 2019.

Bassichis, Morgan, Alexander Lee, and Dean Spade. "Building an Abolitionist Trans and Queer Movement with Everything We've Got." In *Captive Genders: Trans Embodiment and the Prison Industrial Complex*, edited by Eric A. Stanley and Nat Smith. Oakland: AK Press, 2011.

Beckett, Katherine. *Making Crime Pay: Law and Order in Contemporary American Politics*. New York: Oxford University Press, 1997.

Bell, Caryn Cossé. *Revolution, Romanticism, and the Afro-Creole Protest Tradition in Louisiana, 1718–1868*. Baton Rouge: Louisiana State University Press, 1997.

Benns, Whitney. "American Slavery, Reinvented." *Atlantic*. September 21, 2015. https://www.theatlantic.com/business/archive/2015/09/prison-labor-in-america/406177/.

Berger, Dan. *Captive Nation: Black Prison Organizing in the Civil Rights Era*. Chapel Hill: The University of North Carolina Press, 2014.

———. "Constructing Crime, Framing Disaster: Routines of Criminalization and Crisis in Hurricane Katrina." *Punishment & Society* 11, no. 4 (2009).

Berger, Dan, Mariame Kaba, and David Stein. "What Abolitionists Do." *Jacobin*. August 24, 2017. https://www.jacobinmag.com/2017/08/prison-abolition-reform-mass-incarceration.

Bergner, Daniel. *God of the Rodeo: The Quest for Redemption in Louisiana's Angola Prison*. New York: Ballantine Books, 1999.

Bernstein, Elizabeth. "Militarized Humanitarianism Meets Carceral Feminism: The Politics of Sex, Rights, and Freedom in Contemporary Antitrafficking Campaigns." *Signs: Journal of Women in Culture and Society* 36, no. 1 (2010).

Bhandar, Brenna. *Colonial Lives of Property: Law, Land, and Racial Regimes of Ownership*. Durham, NC: Duke University Press, 2018.

Bierria, Alisa, Mayaba Liebenthal, and INCITE! Women of Color against Violence. "To Render Ourselves Visible: Women of Color Organizing and Hurricane Katrina." In *What Lies Beneath: Katrina, Race, and the State of the Nation*, edited by South End Press Collective. Cambridge, MA: South End Press, 2007.

Bissonette, Jamie. *When the Prisoners Ran Walpole: A True Story in the Movement for Prison Abolition*. Cambridge, MA: South End Press, 2008.

Black, William G. "Louisiana State Expenditures: An Overview." In *Louisiana's Fiscal Alternatives: Finding Permanent Solutions to Recurring Budget Crises*, edited by James A. Richardson. Baton Rouge: Louisiana State University Press, 1988.

Blackmon, Douglas A. *Slavery by Another Name: The Re-Enslavement of Black Americans from the Civil War to World War II*. New York: Doubleday, 2008.

Bonds, Anne. "Discipline and Devolution: Constructions of Poverty, Race, and Criminality in the Politics of Rural Prison Development." *Antipode* 41, no. 3 (2009).

——. "Economic Development, Racialization, and Privilege: 'Yes in My Backyard' Prison Politics and the Reinvention of Madras, Oregon." *Annals of the Association of American Geographers* 103, no. 6 (2013).

Braz, Rose. "Kinder, Gentler, Gender Responsive Cages: Prison Expansion Is Not Prison Reform." *Women, Girls, & Criminal Justice* (October/November 2006).

Brown, Michelle. "ICE Comes to Tennessee: Violence Work and Abolition in the Appalachian South." *Citizenship Studies* 25, no. 2 (2021).

Brown, Rita (Bo), Terry Kupers, Andrea Smith, and Julia Sudbury. "Reflections on Critical Resistance." Interviewed by Dylan Rodriguez and Nancy Stoller. *Social Justice* 27, no. 3 (Fall 2000).

Browne, Jaron. "Rooted in Slavery: Prison Labor Exploitation." *Race, Poverty & the Environment* 14, no. 1 (2007).

Browne, Simone. *Dark Matters: On the Surveillance of Blackness*. Durham, NC: Duke University Press, 2015.

Bullard, Robert D., and Beverly Wright, eds. *Race, Place, and Environmental Justice after Hurricane Katrina: Struggles to Reclaim, Rebuild, and Revitalize New Orleans and the Gulf Coast*. Boulder: Westview Press, 2009.

Burton, Orisanmi. "Organized Disorder: The New York City Jail Rebellion of 1970." *Black Scholar* 48, no. 4 (2018).

Cacho, Lisa Marie. *Social Death: Racialized Rightlessness and the Criminalization of the Unprotected*. New York: New York University Press, 2012.

Camp, Jordan T. *Incarcerating the Crisis: Freedom Struggles and the Rise of the Neoliberal State*. Berkeley: University of California Press, 2016.

Camp, Jordan T., and Christina Heatherton, eds. *Policing the Planet: Why the Policing Crisis Led to Black Lives Matter*. London: Verso, 2016.

Canaday, Margot. *The Straight State: Sexuality and Citizenship in Twentieth Century America*. Princeton: Princeton University Press, 2009.

Carby, Hazel V. "'On the Threshold of Woman's Era': Lynching, Empire, and Sexuality in Black Feminist Theory," *Critical Inquiry* 12, no. 1 (Autumn 1985).

Care Collective. *The Care Manifesto: The Politics of Interdependence*. London: Verso, 2020.

Carleton, Mark T. *Politics and Punishment: The History of the Louisiana State Penal System*. Baton Rouge: Louisiana State University Press, 1971.

Casper-Futterman, Evan. "The Operation Was Successful but the Patient Died: The Politics of Crisis and Homelessness in Post-Katrina New Orleans." Master's thesis, University of New Orleans, 2011.

Césaire, Aimé. *Discourse on Colonialism*. New York: Monthly Review Press, 2001.

Chase, Robert. *We Are Not Slaves: State Violence, Coerced Labor, and Prisoners' Rights in Postwar America*. Chapel Hill: The University of North Carolina Press, 2020.

Childs, Dennis. *Slaves of the State: Black Incarceration from the Chain Gang to the Penitentiary*. Minneapolis: University of Minnesota Press, 2015.

Cobb, James C. *The Most Southern Place on Earth: The Mississippi Delta and the Roots of Regional Identity*. New York: Oxford University Press, 1994.

Cohen, Cathy. "Punks, Bulldaggers, and Welfare Queens: The Radical Potential of Queer Politics?" *GLQ* 3 (1997).

Colom, Siri, and Lydia Pelot-Hobbs. "Constructing the Unruly Public: Governing Affect & Legitimate Knowledge in Post-Katrina New Orleans." *Gender, Place, and Culture* 29, no. 9 (2021).

Collins, Patricia Hill. *Black Feminist Thought: Knowledge, Consciousness, and the Politics of Empowerment*. New York: Routledge, 2000.

Colten, Craig E. "An Incomplete Solution: Oil and Water in Louisiana." *Journal of American History* 99, no. 1 (2012).

Cornwall, Andrea, and Maxine Molyneux. "The Politics of Rights: Dilemmas for Feminist Praxis: An Introduction." *Third World Quarterly* 27, no. 7 (2006).

Cox, Laverne. "Laverne Cox Explains the Intersection of Transphobia, Racism, and Misogyny (and What to Do about It)." *Everyday Feminism*, December 7, 2014. https://everydayfeminism.com/2014/12/laverne-cox-intersection-what-to-do/.

Cleaver, Harry. *Reading Capital Politically*. Leeds: Anti/Theses, 2000.

CR 10 Publications Collective. *Abolition Now! Ten Years of Strategy and Struggle against the Prison Industrial Complex*. Chico: AK Press, 2008.

Critical Resistance Publications Collective. "Critical Resistance to the Prison-Industrial Complex Special Issue." *Social Justice* 27, no. 3 (Fall 2000).

———. "The History of Critical Resistance." *Social Justice* 27, no. 3 (Fall 2000).

Critical Resistance and INCITE! Women of Color against Violence. "Gender Violence and the Prison-Industrial Complex." In *Color of Violence: The INCITE! Anthology*, edited by INCITE! Women of Color against Violence. Cambridge, MA: South End Press, 2006.

Curtin, Mary Ellen. *Black Prisoners and their World, Alabama, 1865–1900*. Charlottesville: University of Virginia Press, 2000.

Davis, Angela Y. *Are Prisons Obsolete?* New York: Seven Stories Press, 2003.

———. "From the Prison of Slavery to the Slavery of Prison: Fredrick Douglass and the Convict Lease System." In *The Angela Y. Davis Reader*, edited by Joy James. Malden: Blackwell, 1998.

———, ed. *If They Come in the Morning: Voices of Resistance*. London: Verso, 2016.

———. "JoAnne Little: The Dialectics of Rape." In *The Angela Y. Davis Reader*, edited by Joy James. Malden, MA: Blackwell, 2008.

———. "Racialized Punishment and Prison Abolition." In *The Angela Y. Davis Reader*, edited by Joy James. Malden, MA: Blackwell, 1998.

———. "Reflections on the Black Woman's Role in the Community of Slaves." In *The Angela Y. Davis Reader*, edited by Joy James. Malden, MA: Blackwell, 2008 (1971).

———. *Women, Race & Class*. New York: Vintage Books, 1983.

Davis, Thulani. *The Emancipation Circuit: Black Activism Forging a Culture of Freedom*. Durham, NC: Duke University Press, 2022.

Delany, Samuel R. *Times Square Red, Times Square Blue*. New York: New York University Press, 2001.

Dixon, Chris. *Another Politics: Talking across Today's Transformative Movements*. Berkeley: University of California Press, 2014.

Drew, Richard. "Louisiana's New Public Defender System: Origins, Main Features, and Prospects for Success." *Louisiana Law Review* 69, no. 4 (Summer 2009).

Du Bois, W. E. B. *Black Reconstruction in America, 1860–1880*. New York: Free Press, 1998.

Erzen, Tanya, and Andrea McArdle, eds. *Zero Tolerance: Quality of Life and the New Police Brutality in New York City*. New York: New York University Press, 2001.

Federici, Silvia. *Caliban and the Witch: Women, the Body, and Primitive Accumulation*. Brooklyn: Autonomedia, 2009.

Felber, Garrett. *Those Who Know Don't Say: The Nation of Islam, the Black Freedom Movement, and the Carceral State*. Chapel Hill: The University of North Carolina Press, 2020.

Felker-Kantor, Max. *Policing Los Angeles: Race, Resistance, and the Rise of the LAPD*. Chapel Hill: The University of North Carolina Press, 2018.

Ferguson, Roderick. *Aberrations in Black: Toward a Queer of Color Critique*. Minneapolis: University of Minnesota Press, 2004.

Fields, Barbara Jeanne. "The Nineteenth-Century American South: History and Theory." *Plantation Society* 2, no. 1 (April 1983).

Fierce, Milfred C. *Slavery Revisited: Blacks and the Southern Convict Lease System, 1865–1933*. New York: Africana Studies Research Center, Brooklyn College, City University of New York, 1994.

Flaherty, Jordan. "Crime and New Orleans." *Left Turn Magazine*, October 12, 2005. http://www.leftturn.org/crime-and-new-orleans.

———. *Floodlines: Community and Resistance from Katrina to the Jena Six*. Chicago: Haymarket Books, 2010.

Foster, Burk. "What Is the Meaning of Life: The Evolution of Natural Life Sentences in Louisiana, 1973–1994." Lecture, Academy of Criminal Justice Sciences Annual Meeting, Boston, MA, May 9, 1995. www.burkfoster.com/MeaningofLife.htm.

Foucault, Michel. *Discipline and Punish: The Birth of the Prison*. New York: Vintage Books, 1995.
Garrett, Brandon L., and Tania Tetlow. "Criminal Justice Collapse: The Constitution after Hurricane Katrina." *Duke Law Journal* 56 (2006).
Garza, Alicia. "A Herstory of the #BlackLivesMatter Movement." *Feminist Wire*, October 7, 2014. http://www.thefeministwire.com/2014/10/blacklivesmatter-2/.
Gerharz, Barry, and Seung Hong. "Down by Law: Orleans Parish Prison before and after Hurricane Katrina." *Dollars & Sense* (March/April 2006).
Getachew, Adom. *Worldmaking after Empire: The Rise and Fall of Self-Determination*. Princeton: Princeton University Press, 2019.
Gillespie, Kathryn. "Placing Angola: Racialisation, Anthropocentrism, and Settler Colonialism at the Louisiana State Penitentiary's Angola Rodeo." *Antipode* (April 2018).
Gilmore, Craig. "An Interview with James Kilgore." *Abolitionist* (Fall 2014).
Gilmore, Ruth Wilson. "Abolition Geography and the Problem of Innocence." In *Futures of Black Radicalism*, edited by Gaye Theresa Johnson and Alex Lubin. London: Verso, 2017.
———. "Forgotten Places and the Seeds of Grassroots Planning." In *Engaging Contradictions: Theory, Politics, and Methods of Activist Scholarship*, edited by Charles R. Hale. Berkeley: University of California Press, 2008.
———. "Globalisation and US Prison Growth: From Military Keynesianism to Post-Keynesian Militarism." *Race & Class* 40, no. 2–3 (1999).
———. *Golden Gulag: Prisons Surplus, Crisis, and Opposition in Globalizing California*. Berkeley: University of California Press, 2007.
———. "Race, Prisons, War: Scenes from the History of US Violence." In *Socialist Register: Violence Today, Actually Existing Barbarism*, edited by Leo Panich and Colin Leys. New York: Monthly Review Press, 2009.
———. "The Worrying State of the Anti-Prison Movement." *Social Justice*. February 23, 2015. http://www.socialjusticejournal.org/the-worrying-state-of-the-anti-prison-movement/.
Gilmore, Ruth Wilson, and Craig Gilmore. "Restating the Obvious." In *Indefensible Space: The Architecture of the National Insecurity State*, edited by Michael Sorkin. New York: Routledge Press, 2008.
Gindin, Sam, and Leo Panitch. *The Making of Global Capitalism: The Political Economy of American Empire*. London: Verso, 2012.
Glenn, Evelyn Nakano. *Unequal Freedom: How Race and Gender Shaped American Citizenship and Labor*. Cambridge, MA: Harvard University Press, 2004.
Goldberg, David Theo. *The Racial State*. Malden, MA: Blackwell, 2001.
Goodwin, Jeff, and James M. Jasper. "Caught in a Winding, Snarling Vine: The Structural Bias of Political Process Theory." *Sociological Forum* 14, no. 1 (March 1999).
Gorz, André. *A Strategy for Labor: A Radical Proposal*. Boston: Beacon Press, 1967.
Gotham, Kevin Fox. "Tourism Gentrification: The Case of New Orleans' Vieux Carre." *Urban Studies* 42, no. 7 (June 2005).

Gottschalk, Marie. *Caught: The Prison State and the Lockdown of American Politics.* Princeton: Princeton University Press, 2016.

———. *The Prison and the Gallows: The Politics of Mass Incarceration in America.* Cambridge: Cambridge University Press, 2006.

Gould, Deborah B. *Moving Politics: Emotion and ACT UP's Fight against AIDS.* Chicago: University of Chicago Press, 2009.

Gramsci, Antonio. *Selections from the Prison Notebooks.* New York: International Publishers, 1999.

Grant, Melissa Gira. "Beyond Strange Bedfellows: How the 'War on Trafficking' Was Made to Unite the Left and Right." *Public Eye,* 2018. https://politicalresearch.org/2018/08/13/beyond-strange-bedfellows.

Green, Kai M. "Troubling the Waters: Mobilizing a Trans* Analytic." In *No Tea, No Shade: New Writings in Black Queer Studies,* edited by E. Patrick Johnson. Durham, NC: Duke University Press, 2016.

Green, Kai M., and Marquis Bey. "Where Black Feminist Thought and Trans* Feminism Meet: A Conversation." *Souls* 19, no. 4 (2017).

Hackworth, Jason. *The Neoliberal City: Governance, Ideology, and Development in American Urbanism.* Ithaca: Cornell University Press, 2007.

Hair, William Ivy. *Bourbonism and Agrarian Protest: Louisiana Politics, 1877–1900.* Baton Rouge: Louisiana State University Press, 1969.

Haley, Sarah. *No Mercy Here: Gender, Punishment, and the Making of Jim Crow Modernity.* Chapel Hill: The University of North Carolina Press, 2016.

Hall, Gwendolyn Midlo. *Africans in Colonial Louisiana: The Development of Afro-Creole Culture in the Eighteenth Century.* Baton Rouge: Louisiana State University Press, 1992.

Hall, Stuart. "The State in Question." In *The Idea of the Modern State,* edited by G. McLennan, D. Held, and S. Hall. Open University Press, 1984.

Hall, Stuart, Chas Critcher, Tony Jefferson, John Clarke, and Brian Roberts. *Policing the Crisis: Mugging, the State and Law and Order.* London: Palgrave Macmillan, 2013.

Hamilton, Anne Butler, and C. Murray Henderson. *Angola: Louisiana State Penitentiary, a Half-Century of Rage and Reform.* Lafayette: Center for Louisiana Studies, University of Southwestern Louisiana, 1990.

Hanhardt, Christina. "Broken Windows at Blue's: A Queer History of Gentrification and Policing." In *Policing the Planet: Why the Policing Crisis Led to Black Lives Matter,* edited by Jordan T. Camp and Christina Heatherton. London: Verso, 2016.

———. *Safe Space: Gay Neighborhood History and the Politics of Violence.* Durham, NC: Duke University Press, 2013.

Hansford, Justin. "Community Policing Reconsidered: From Ferguson to Baltimore." In *Policing the Planet: Why the Policing Crisis Led to Black Lives Matter,* edited by Jordan T. Camp and Christina Heatherton. London: Verso, 2016.

Harcourt, Bernard E. *Illusion of Order: The False Promise of Broken Windows Policing.* Cambridge, MA: Harvard University Press, 2001.

Hartman, Saidiya V. *Scenes of Subjection: Terror, Slavery, and Self-Making in Nineteenth-Century America.* New York: Oxford University Press, 1997.

Harvey, David. *A Brief History of Neoliberalism*. Oxford: Oxford University Press, 2005.
———. *The Limits to Capital*. Chicago: University of Chicago Press, 1982.
———. *The New Imperialism*. Oxford: Oxford University Press, 2003.
———. "The Right to the City." *New Left Review* 53 (September/October 2008).
———. "The Spatial Fix–Hegel, von Thunen, and Marx." *Antipode* 13, no. 3 (1981).
Herbert, Steve. "Policing the Contemporary City: Fixing Broken Windows or Shoring Up Neo-Liberalism?" *Theoretical Criminology* 5, no. 4 (2001).
Herbert, Steve, and Elizabeth Brown. "Conceptions of Space and Crime in the Punitive Neoliberal City." *Antipode* 38, no. 4 (2006).
Higginbotham, Evelyn Brooks. "African-American Women's History and the Metalanguage of Race." *Signs: Journal of Women in Culture and Society* 17, no. 2 (1992).
Hinton, Elizabeth K. *From the War on Poverty to the War on Crime: The Making of Mass Incarceration in America*. Cambridge, MA: Harvard University Press, 2017.
Hirsch, Arnold. "New Orleans: Sunbelt in the Swamp." In *Sunbelt Cities: Politics and Growth since World War II*, edited by Richard M. Bernard and Bradley Robert Rice. Austin: University of Texas Press, 1988.
Hobson, Emily K. "Policing Gay L.A.: Mapping Racial Divides in the Homophile Era, 1950–1967." In *The Rising Tide of Color: Race, State Violence, and Radical Movements across the Pacific*, edited by Moon-Ho Jung. Seattle: University of Washington Press, 2015.
Hodes, Martha. "The Sexualization of Reconstruction Politics: White Women and Black Men in the South after the Civil War." *Journal of the History of Sexuality* 3, no. 3 (January 1993).
Horne, Jed. *Breach of Faith: Hurricane Katrina and the Near Death of a Great American City*. New York: Random House, 2006.
Houzeau, Jean-Charles. *My Passage at the New Orleans Tribune: A Memoir of the Civil War Era*, edited by David C. Rankin. Baton Rouge: Louisiana State University Press, 1984.
Hubbard, Phil. "Cleansing the Metropolis: Sex Work and the Politics of Zero Tolerance." *Urban Studies* 4, no. 9 (2004).
James, C. L. R. *The Black Jacobins: Toussaint L'Ouverture and the San Domingo Revolution*. New York: Random House, 1989.
James, Selma. *Sex, Race, Class: The Perspective of Winning*. Oakland: PM Press, 2012.
Jasper, James M. "Social Movement Theory Today: Toward a Theory of Action?" *Sociology Compass* 4, no. 11 (November 2010).
Jenkins, Destin. *The Bonds of Inequality: Debt and the Making of the American City*. Chicago: University of Chicago Press, 2021.
Jones, Catherine. *Floodlines* (blog). http://floodlines.blogspot.com/.
Jung, Moon-Ho. *Coolies and Cane: Race, Labor, and Sugar in the Age of Emancipation*. Baltimore: Johns Hopkins University Press, 2006.
Kelley, Robin D. G. *Freedom Dreams: The Black Radical Imagination*. Boston: Beacon Press, 2002.

———. "'We Are Not What We Seem': Rethinking Black Working Class Opposition in the Jim Crow South." *Journal of American History* 80, no. 1 (June 1993).

Kennedy, Liam. "'Today They Kill with the Chair instead of the Tree': Forgetting and Remembering Slavery at a Plantation Prison." *Theoretical Criminology* 21, no. 2 (2016).

Kilgore, James. "The Myth of Prison Slave Labor Camps in the U.S." *Counterpunch*. August 9, 2013. https://www.counterpunch.org/2013/08/09/the-myth-of-prison-slave-labor-camps-in-the-u-s/.

Kohler-Hausman, Julilly. *Getting Tough: Welfare and Imprisonment in 1970s America*. Princeton: Princeton University Press, 2017.

Kunzel, Regina. *Criminal Intimacy: Prison and the Uneven History of Modern American Sexuality*. Chicago: University of Chicago Press, 2008.

LeBrón, Marisol. *Policing Life and Death: Race, Violence, and Resistance in Puerto Rico*. Oakland: University of California Press, 2019.

Lefebvre, Henri. *Writings on Cities*. Oxford: Blackwell, 1996.

LeFlouria, Talitha L. *Chained in Silence: Black Women and Convict Labor in the New South*. Chapel Hill: The University of North Carolina Press, 2015.

Lichtenstein, Alex. "Good Roads and Chain Gangs in the Progressive South: 'The Negro Convict Is a Slave.'" *Journal of Southern History* 59, no. 1 (1993).

———. *Twice the Work of Free Labor: The Political Economy of Convict Labor in the New South*. London: Verso, 1996.

Linebaugh, Peter. *The London Hanged: Crime and Civil Society in the Eighteenth Century*. London: Verso, 2006.

Linebaugh, Peter, and Marcus Rediker. *The Many-Headed Hydra: Sailors, Slaves, Commoners, and the Hidden History of the Revolutionary Atlantic*. Boston: Beacon Press, 2013.

Lipsitz, George. "Policing Place and Taxing Time on Skid Row." In *Policing the Planet: Why the Policing Crisis Led to Black Lives Matter*, edited by Jordan T. Camp and Christina Heatherton. London: Verso, 2016.

Lipsky, Laura Van Dernoot, with Connie Burk. *Trauma Stewardship: An Everyday Guide to Caring for Self While Caring for Others*. San Francisco: Berrett-Koehler, 2009.

Long, Alecia P. *The Great Southern Babylon: Sex, Race, and Respectability in New Orleans, 1865–1920*. Baton Rouge: Louisiana State University Press, 2004.

Loyd, Jenna M., and Alison Mountz. *Boats, Borders, and Bases: Race, the Cold War, and the Rise of Migration Detention in the United States*. Oakland: University of California Press, 2018.

Luft, Rachel E. "Beyond Disaster Exceptionalism: Social Movement Developments in New Orleans after Hurricane Katrina." *American Quarterly* 61, no. 3 (September 2009).

———. "Men and Masculinities in the Social Movement for a Just Reconstruction after Hurricane Katrina." In *Men, Masculinities and Disaster*, edited by Elaine Enarson and Bob Pease. New York: Routledge, 2016.

———. "Racialized Disaster Patriarchy: An Intersectional Model for Understanding Disaster Ten Years after Hurricane Katrina." *Feminist Formations* 28, no. 2 (Summer 2016).

Luft, Rachel E., and Shana griffin. "A Status Report on Housing in New Orleans after Katrina: An Intersectional Analysis." In *Katrina and the Women of New Orleans*, edited by Beth Willinger. New Orleans: Newcomb College Center for Research on Women, 2008.

Lynch, Mona. *Sunbelt Justice: Arizona and the Transformation of American Punishment*. Redwood City, CA: Stanford University Press, 2009.

Maginnis, John. *The Last Hayride*. Baton Rouge: Darkhorse Press, 1984.

Mancini, Matthew J. *One Dies, Get Another: Convict Leasing in the American South, 1866–1928*. Columbia: University of South Carolina Press, 1996.

Mann, Eric. *Katrina's Legacy: White Racism and Black Reconstruction in New Orleans and the Gulf Coast*. Los Angeles: Frontlines Press, 2006.

Mann, Michael. *States, War, and Capitalism: Studies in Political Sociology*. New York: Blackwell, 1988.

Marable, Manning. *How Capitalism Underdeveloped Black America: Problems in Race, Political Economy, and Society*. Boston: South End Press, 2000.

Martin, Lori Latrice, Kenneth Fasching-Varner, Molly Quinn, and Melinda Jackson. "Racism, Rodeos, and the Misery Industries of Louisiana." *Journal of Pan African Studies* 47, no. 6 (November 2014).

Marx, Karl. *Capital*, vol. 1. New York: Penguin Classics, 1976.

Marx, Karl, and Fredrick Engels. *The Communist Manifesto*. New York: International Publishers, 2009.

Mauer, Marc. *Race to Incarcerate*. New York: New Press, 2006.

McAdam, Doug. *Political Process and the Development of Black Insurgency, 1930–1970*. Chicago: University of Chicago Press, 1982.

McDuffie, Erik S. *Sojourning for Freedom: Black Women, American Communism, and the Making of Black Left Feminism*. Durham, NC: Duke University Press, 2011.

McGirr, Lisa. *Suburban Warriors: The Origins of the New American Right*. Princeton: Princeton University Press, 2001.

McKittrick, Katherine. *Demonic Grounds: Black Women and the Cartographies of Struggle*. Minneapolis: University of Minnesota Press, 2006.

———. "On Plantations, Prisons, and a Black Sense of Place." *Social & Cultural Geography* 12, no. 8 (December 2011).

McTighe, Laura, and Deon Haywood. "'There Is NO Justice in Louisiana': Crimes against Nature and the Spirit of Black Feminist Resistance." *Souls* 19, no. 3 (January 2018).

Meiners, Erica R. *For the Children? Protecting Innocence in a Carceral State*. Minneapolis: University of Minnesota Press, 2016.

Melamed, Jodi. *Represent and Destroy: Rationalizing Violence in the New Racial Capitalism*. Minneapolis: University of Minnesota Press, 2011.

Mitchell, Don. *The Right to the City: Social Justice and the Fight for Public Space*. New York: Guilford, 2003.

Mitchell, Timothy. *Carbon Democracy: Political Power in the Age of Oil*. Brooklyn: Verso, 2011.

Mock, Janet. "A Note on Visibility in the Wake of 6 Trans Women's Murders in 2015." *Janet Mock*, January 16, 2015. https://janetmock.com/2015/02/16/six-trans-women-killed-this-year/.

———. *Redefining Realness: My Path to Womanhood, Identity, Love & so Much More*. New York: Simon & Schuster, 2014.

Muhammad, Khalil Gibran. *The Condemnation of Blackness: Race, Crime, and the Making of Modern Urban America*. Cambridge, MA: Harvard University Press, 2009.

Muhammad, Saladin. "Hurricane Katrina: The Black Nation's 9/11! A Strategic Perspective for Self-Determination." *Socialism and Democracy* 20, no. 2 (July 2006).

Muñoz, José Esteban. *Cruising Utopia: The Then and There of Queer Futurity*. New York: New York University Press, 2009.

Murakawa, Naomi. *The First Civil Right: How Liberals Built Prison America*. Oxford: Oxford University Press, 2014.

Musto, Jennifer. *Control and Protect: Collaboration, Carceral Protection, and Domestic Sex Trafficking in the United States*. Oakland: University of California Press, 2016.

Naughton, Aoife, and Wes Wallace. "Day Laborers in the Reconstruction of New Orleans." *Callaloo* 29, no. 4 (2006).

Ngai, Mae. *Impossible Subjects: Illegal Aliens and the Making of Modern America*. Princeton: Princeton University Press, 2004.

Nore, Petter. "Oil and the State: A Study of Nationalization in the Oil Industry." In *Oil and Class Struggle*, edited by Petter Nore and Terisa Turner. London: Zed Press, 1980.

Nore, Petter, and Terisa Turner, eds. *Oil and Class Struggle*. London: Zed Press, 1980.

Norton, Jack. "Little Siberia, Star of the North: Prisons, Crisis, and Development in Rural New York, 1968–1994." PhD diss., City University of New York, 2018.

Olsavsky, Jesse. *The Most Absolute Abolition: Runaways, Vigilance Committees, and the Rise of Revolutionary Abolitionism, 1835–1861*. Baton Rouge: Louisiana State University Press, 2022.

Omi, Michael, and Howard Winant. *Racial Formation in the United States*. New York: Routledge, 1994.

Oshinsky, David M. *Worse than Slavery: Parchman Farm and the Ordeal of Jim Crow Justice*. New York: Free Press, 1996.

Ott, K. Brad. "The Closure of New Orleans' Charity Hospital after Hurricane Katrina: A Case of Disaster Capitalism." Master's thesis, University of New Orleans, 2012.

Painter, David S. "Oil and the American Century." *Journal of American History* 99, no. 1 (2012).

Parenti, Christian. *Lockdown America: Police and Prisons in the Age of Crisis*. London: Verso, 2008.

Parker, Brenda. *Masculinities and Markets: Raced and Gendered Urban Politics in Milwaukee*. Athens: University of Georgia Press, 2017.

Pasulka, Nicole. "The Case of CeCe McDonald: Murder-or Self-Defense against a Hate Crime?" *Mother Jones*, May 22, 2012. https://www.motherjones.com/politics/2012/05/cece-mcdonald-transgender-hate-crime-murder/.

Payne, Charles M. *I've Got the Light of Freedom: The Organizing Tradition and the Mississippi Freedom Struggle*. Berkeley: University of California Press, 2007.

Pelot-Hobbs, Lydia. "Amnesty for All: Organizing against Criminalization in Post-Katrina New Orleans." *Southern Cultures* 27, no. 3 (2021), 98–118.

———. "How Do We Actually Put Abolition into Practice? Some Reflections on the April 9 Policing Tax Vote." *Thinking about Freedom*, April 6, 2016. https://abolitiondemocracy.wordpress.com/2016/04/06/how-do-we-actually-put-abolition-into-practice/.

Peterson-Burge, Lexi. "Federal Courts, FEMA Dollars, and Local Elections in the Struggle Against Phase III in New Orleans." Interviewed by Lydia Pelot-Hobbs. In *The Jail Is Everywhere: Organizing Against the New Geography of Mass Incarceration*, edited by Jack Norton, Lydia Pelot-Hobbs, and Judah Schept. London: Verso, 2024.

Perkinson, Robert. *Texas Tough: The Rise of America's Prison Empire*. New York: Holt, 2010.

Platt, Tony, Jon Frappier, Gerda Ray, Richard Schauffler, Larry Trukillo, Lynn Cooper, Elliott Currie, and Sidney Harring. *The Iron Fist and the Velvet Glove: An Analysis of the U.S. Police*. Berkeley: Center for Research on Criminal Justice, 1977.

Prasad, Monica. "The Popular Origins of Neoliberalism in the Reagan Tax Cut of 1981." *Journal of Policy History* 24, no. 3 (2012).

Prashad, Vijay. *The Darker Nations: A People's History of the Third World*. New York: New Press, 2008.

———. *The Poorer Nations: A Possible History of the Global South*. London: Verso, 2014.

Pulido, Laura. "Flint, Environmental Racism, and Racial Capitalism." *Capitalism Nature Socialism* 27, no. 3 (2016).

Quan, H. L. T. "Emancipatory Social Inquiry: Democratic Anarchism and the Robinsonian Method." *African Identities* 11, no. 2 (2013).

Ransby, Barbara. *Ella Baker and the Black Freedom Movement: A Radical Democratic Vision*. Chapel Hill: The University of North Carolina Press, 2003.

Reagon, Bernice Johnson. "Coalition Politics: Turning the Century." In *Home Girls: A Black Feminist Anthology*, edited by Barbara Smith. New York: Kitchen Table Press, 1983.

Richardson, James A., and Loren C. Scott. "Mineral Resources and Revenues and Budgetary Stability." In *Louisiana's Fiscal Alternatives: Finding Permanent Solutions to Recurring Budget Crises*, edited by James A. Richardson. Baton Rouge: Louisiana State University Press, 1988.

Richie, Beth. *Arrested Justice: Black Women, Violence and America's Prison Nation*. New York: New York University Press, 2012.

Rideau, Wilbert. *In the Place of Justice: A Story of Punishment and Deliverance.* New York: Alfred A. Knopf, 2010.

Rideau, Wilbert, and Ron Wikberg. *Life Sentences: Rage and Survival behind Bars.* New York: Times Books, 1992.

Riofrancos, Thea. *Resource Radicals: From Petro-Nationalism to Post-Extractivism in Ecuador.* Durham, NC: Duke University Press, 2020.

Ritchie, Andrea J. *Invisible No More: Police Violence against Black Women and Women of Color.* Boston: Beacon, 2017.

Robinson, Cedric J. *Black Marxism: The Making of the Black Radical Tradition.* Chapel Hill: The University of North Carolina Press, 2000.

——. *Black Movements in America.* New York: Routledge, 1997.

——. *Forgeries of Memory and Meaning: Blacks and the Regimes of Race in American Theater and Film before World War II.* Chapel Hill: The University of North Carolina Press, 2012.

Rodriguez, Dylan. *Forced Passages: Imprisoned Radical Intellectuals and the US Prison Regime.* Minneapolis: University of Minnesota Press, 2006.

Rothman, Adam. *Slave Country: American Expansion and the Origins of the Deep South.* Cambridge, MA: Harvard University Press, 2005.

Rothman, Joshua D. *The Ledger and the Chain: How Domestic Slave Traders Shaped America.* New York: Basic Books, 2021.

Ruttenberg, Miriam H. "A Feminist Critique of Mandatory Arrest: An Analysis of Race and Gender in Domestic Violence Policy." *Gender and the Law* 171, no. 2 (1994).

Sakakeeny, Matt. *Roll with It: Brass Bands in the Streets of New Orleans.* Durham: Duke University Press, 2013.

Samuels, Liz. "Improvising on Reality: The Roots of Prison Abolition." In *The Hidden 1970s: Histories of Radicalism*, edited by Dan Berger. New Brunswick, NJ: Rutgers University Press, 2010.

Samuels, Liz, and David Stein, eds. "Perspectives on Critical Resistance." In *Abolition Now!: Ten Years of Strategy and Struggle against the Prison Industrial Complex*, edited by Critical Resistance Publications Collective. Oakland: AK Press, 2008.

Sanson, Jerry P. "'What He Did and What He Promised to Do . . .': Huey Long and the Horizons of Louisiana Politics." *Louisiana History* 47, no. 3 (Summer 2006).

Schept, Judah. *Coal, Cages, Crisis: The Rise of the Prison Economy in Central Appalachia.* New York: New York University Press, 2022.

——. *Progressive Punishment: Job Loss, Jail Growth, and the Neoliberal Logic of Carceral Expansion.* New York: New York University Press, 2016.

Schoenfeld, Heather. *Building the Prison State: Race and the Politics of Mass Incarceration.* Chicago: University of Chicago Press, 2018.

Schrader, Stuart. "Against the Romance of Community Policing." *Stuart Schrader* (blog). August 10, 2016. https://stuartschrader.com/blog/against-romance-community-policing.

Schrift, Melissa. "The Wildest Show in the South: The Politics and Poetics of the Angola Prison Rodeo and Inmate Arts Festival." *Southern Cultures* 14, no. 1 (2008).

Scott, Loren C. "The Structure of the Louisiana Economy." In *Louisiana's Fiscal Alternatives: Finding Permanent Solutions to Recurring Budget Crises*, edited by James A. Richardson. Baton Rouge: Louisiana State University Press, 1988.

Shaylor, Cassandra, and Cynthia Chandler. "Reform and Abolition: Points of Tension and Connection." In *Defending Justice: An Activist Resource Kit*, edited by Palak Shah. Boston: Political Research Associates, 2011.

Shugg, Roger W. *Origins of Class Struggle in Louisiana: A Social History of White Farmers and Laborers during Slavery and After, 1840–1875*. Baton Rouge: Louisiana State University Press, 1972.

Shulman, Steven. "Why Is the Black Unemployment Rate always Twice as High as the White Unemployment Rate?" In *New Approaches to Economic and Social Analyses of Discrimination*, edited by Richard R. Cornwall and Phanindra V. Wunnava. New York: Praeger, 1992.

Silverstein, Ken. *The Secret World of Oil*. New York: Verso, 2015.

Simon, Jonathan. "Refugees in a Carceral Age: The Rebirth of Immigration Prisons in the United States." *Public Culture* 10, no. 3 (1998): 579–583.

Sindler, Allan P. *Huey Long's Louisiana: State Politics, 1920–1952*. Baltimore: Johns Hopkins University Press, 1968.

Singh, Nikhil Pal. *Black Is a Country: Race and the Unfinished Struggle for Democracy*. Cambridge, MA: Harvard University Press, 2004.

Smallwood, Stephanie E. *Saltwater Slavery: A Middle Passage from Africa to American Diaspora*. Cambridge, MA: Harvard University Press, 2007.

Smith, Neil. "Contours of a Spatialized Politics: Homeless Vehicles and the Production of Geographical Scale." *Social Text*, no. 33 (1992).

———. "Giuliani Time: The Revanchist 1990s." *Social Text* 57 (1998): 1–20.

———. "There's No Such Thing as a Natural Disaster." Social Science Research Council, June 11, 2006. https://items.ssrc.org/understanding-katrina/theres-no-such-thing-as-a-natural-disaster/.

———. *Uneven Development: Nature, Capital and the Production of Space*. Athens: University of Georgia Press, 1990.

Snorton, C. Riley. *Black on Both Sides: A Racial History of Trans Identity*. Minneapolis: University of Minnesota Press, 2017.

Sommerville, Diane. "The Rape Myth in the Old South Reconsidered." *Journal of Southern History* 61, no. 3 (August 1995): 481–518.

Souther, J. Mark. *New Orleans on Parade: Tourism and the Transformation of the Crescent City*. Baton Rouge: Louisiana State University Press, 2006.

Stein, David P. "Still Bringing the State back In: Private Prisons and Mass Incarceration." *Process: A Blog for American History*. July 18, 2017. http://www.processhistory.org/stein-private-prisons/.

Stein, Judith. *Pivotal Decade: How the United States Traded Factories for Finance in the Seventies*. New Haven: Yale University Press, 2010.

Stein, Samuel. *Capital City: Gentrification and the Real Estate State*. Brooklyn: Verso, 2019.

Story, Brett. *Prison Land: Mapping Carceral Power Across Neoliberal America*. Minneapolis: University of Minnesota, 2019.

Sudbury, Julia. "Introduction: Feminist Critiques, Transnational Landscapes, Abolitionist Visions." In *Global Lockdown: Race, Gender, and the Prison-industrial Complex*, edited by Julia Sudbury. New York: Routledge, 2004.

———. "Maroon Abolitionists: Black Gender-Oppressed Activists in the Anti-Prison Movement in the US and Canada." *Meridians* 9, no. 1 (2009): 1–29.

Takei, Carl. "The $270 Million Lockup: Will New Orleans' Sheriff Stand in the Way of Rebuilding a Smaller and Smarter Orleans Parish Prison?" *American Civil Liberties Union Blog*, February 4, 2011. https://www.aclu.org/blog/mass-incarceration/270-million-lockup-will-new-orleans-sheriff-stand-way-rebuilding-smaller-and?redirect=blog/270-million-lockup-will-new-orleans-sheriff-stand-way-rebuilding-smaller-and-smarter-orleans.

Tang, Eric. "A Gulf Unites Us: The Vietnamese Americans of Black New Orleans East." *American Quarterly* 63, no. 1 (2011).

Taylor, Keeanga-Yamahtta. *From #BlackLivesMatter to Black Liberation*. Chicago: Haymarket Press, 2016.

Theriot, Jason P. *American Energy, Imperiled Coast: Oil and Gas Development in Louisiana's Wetlands*. Baton Rouge: Louisiana State University Press, 2014.

Thompson, Heather Anne. "Blinded by a 'Barbaric' South: Prison Horrors, Inmate Abuse, and the Ironic History of American Penal Reform." In *The Myth of Southern Exceptionalism*, edited by Matthew D. Lassiter and Joseph Crespino. Oxford: Oxford University Press, 2010.

Thompson, Krissah. "From a Slave House to a Prison Cell: The History of Angola Plantation." *Washington Post*, September 21, 2016.

Thuma, Emily. *All Our Trials: Prisons, Policing, and the Feminist Fight Against Violence*. Champaign, IL: University of Illinois Press, 2019.

———. "Lessons in Self-Defense: Gender Violence, Racial Criminalization, and Anticarceral Feminism." *Women's Studies Quarterly* 43, no. 3/4 (Fall/Winter 2015).

Tuzzolo, Ellen, and Damon T. Hewitt. "Rebuilding Inequity: The Re-Emergence of the School-to-Prison Pipeline in New Orleans." *High School Journal* 90, no. 2 (2006).

Unter, Kevin A. "The New Orleans Police Department: Melding Police and Policy to Dramatically Reduce Crime in the City of New Orleans." PhD diss., University of New Orleans, 2007.

Vance, Sarah S. "Justice after Disaster—What Hurricane Katrina Did to the Justice System in New Orleans." *Howard Law Journal* 51, no. 3 (2008).

Wacquant, Loic. *Punishing the Poor: The Neoliberal Government of Social Insecurity*. Durham, NC: Duke University Press, 2009.

Ward, Kevin. "Business Improvement Districts: Policy Origins, Mobile Policies and Urban Liveability." *Geography Compass* 1, no. 3 (May 2007).

Ware, Wesley. "Consent Decree between NOPD and DOJ Includes Unprecedented Victory for LGBT Youth." *Bridge the Gulf Project*, July 31, 2012. http://bridgethegulfproject.org/blog/2012/consent-decree-between-nopd-and-doj-includes-unprecedented-victory-lgbt-youth.

Watts, Michael. "Resource Curse? Governmentality, Oil, and Power in the Niger Delta, Nigeria." *Geopolitics* 9, no. 2 (2004).
Weber, Max. "Politics as a Vocation." In *Max Weber: Selections in Translation*, edited by W. G. Runciman. Cambridge: Cambridge University Press, 1978.
Weber, Ronald E. "Historical Development of the Louisiana State Tax Structure." In *Louisiana's Fiscal Alternatives: Finding Permanent Solutions to Recurring Budget Crises*, edited by James A. Richardson. Baton Rouge: Louisiana State University Press, 1988.
Welch, Michael. *Detained: Immigration Laws and the Expanding I.N.S. Jail Complex*. Philadelphia: Temple University Press, 2002.
Wells, Ida B. "Bishop Tanner's Ray of Light." In *The Light of Truth: Writings of an Anti-Lynching Crusader*, edited by Mia Bay and Henry Louis Gates. New York: Penguin Books, 2014.
———. "Mob Rule in New Orleans." [1900]. In *The Light of Truth: Writings of an Anti-Lynching Crusader*, edited by Mia Bay. New York: Penguin Books, 2014.
———. "Southern Horrors: Lynch Law in All Its Phases." In *The Light of Truth: Writings of an Anti-Lynching Crusader*, edited by Mia Bay and Henry Louis Gates. New York: Penguin Books, 2014.
Wiegman, Robyn. "The Anatomy of Lynching." *Journal of the History of Sexuality* 3, no. 3 (January 1993): 445–467.
Williams, Erica L. "Sex Work and Exclusion in the Tourist Districts of Salvador, Brazil." *Gender, Place, & Culture* 21, no. 4 (2014).
Williams, Kristian. *Our Enemies in Blue: Police and Power in America*. Cambridge, MA: South End Press, 2007.
Williams, Steve. *Demand Everything: Lessons of the Transformative Organizing Model*. New York: Rosa Luxemburg Stiftung, March 2013.
Willse, Craig. *The Value of Homelessness: Managing Surplus Life in the United States*. Minneapolis: University of Minnesota Press, 2015.
Wilson, Bobby M. *America's Johannesburg: Industrialization and Racial Transformation in Birmingham*. Lanham, MA: Rowman & Littlefield, 2000.
Wilson, James Q., and George Kelling. "Broken Windows Theory." *Atlantic* (March 1982).
Woods, Clyde. *Development Arrested: The Blues and Plantation Power in the Mississippi Delta*. London: Verso, 1998.
———. *Development Drowned and Reborn: The Blues and Bourbon Restorations in Post-Katrina New Orleans*, edited by Jordan T. Camp and Laura Pulido. Athens: University of Georgia Press, 2017.
———. "Les Misérables of New Orleans: Trap Economics and the Asset Stripping Blues, Part 1." *American Quarterly* 61, no. 3 (2009).
———. "'Sittin' on Top of the World': The Challenges of Blues and Hip Hop Geography." In *Black Geographies and the Politics of Place*, edited by Katherine McKittrick and Clyde Woods. Cambridge, MA: South End Press, 2007.
Woodward, C. Vann. *Origins of the New South: 1877–1913*. Baton Rouge: Louisiana State University Press, 1971.

———. *The Strange Career of Jim Crow.* New York: Oxford University Press, 1974.
Wurtzburg, Susan, and Thurston H. G. Hahn III. *Hard Labor: History and Archaeology at the Old Louisiana State Penitentiary, Baton Rouge, Louisiana.* United States District Court Middle District of Louisiana, 1991.
Zimring, Franklin E. *The Great American Crime Decline.* New York: Oxford University Press, 2009.

Index

Abandoned and Abused (ACLU publication), 187–88, 195. *See also* American Civil Liberties Union; Safe Streets/Strong Communities
abolition, 12–13, 16, 48, 100, 134–38, 161; abolitionist infrastructures, 17, 194, 257–63; abolitionist reforms, 11–13, 250
abortion, 256–57
Acadia Legal Services, 103
Act 394, 109
Administration of Criminal Justice (LCLE), 35
Advocates for Environmental Human Rights, 162
AFL-CIO, 49
Africk, Lance, 204, 251–252
Agricultural Administration Act, 27
Alexander, Amhari, 210
Alexander, Michelle, 199
Algiers, New Orleans, 133, 151–53, 179
All Congregations Together alliance, 127
Allen Correctional Center, 99, 107
Ambush (publication), 219
American Civil Liberties Union (ACLU), 40, 103–4, 117, 133, 163–64, 186–88, 191
American Correctional Association, 30, 111
amnesty campaigns, 18, 166–67. *See also* Critical Resistance (CR)
Amnesty International, 132–33, 162
anarchism, 134
Angola (Louisiana State Penitentiary): Closed Cell Restriction (CCR) at, 28; Hayes Williams lawsuit against, 1, 15–16, 19, 22–23, 29, 35–36, 253; law library in, 85; overcrowding in, 22, 36, 40; prison rodeo of, 14; protests at, 27, 60; publication on (See *Angolite* [publication]); purchase of, 26; racially coded language on, 45–46; reforms at, 29–30, 37–38, 40; revitalization funding for, 41; segregation of, 22, 36, 38–39, 59; solitary confinement at, 28, 30. *See also* Angola Special Civics Project, Louisiana penal system
Angola (convict leasing), 1, 26–27, 47, 271n25
Angola Lifers' Association, 48, 81, 86, 93, 136
Angola Special Civics Project, 16, 20, 63, 84–99, 171, 254, 258
Angola Three, 134, 136, 138
Angolite (publication): on Angola lawsuit, 29, 61; on Angola reforms, 58, 66; collective activism and, 87, 89; on inmate labor bill, 79–80; on life sentences, 62; as key source, 19–20; on political economy, 61, 80, 83; on prison expansion, 69, 73; on private prisons, 99; on racial violence, 73; restrictions on, 67, 97
antiauthoritarian current, 134
Anti-Drug Abuse Act (1986), 103
Anti-Drug Abuse Act (1988), 103
antijail activism, 117, 132–134, 186–188, 190–206, 251–52. *See also* abolition; ACLU; Congreso de Jornaleros; Critical Resistance (CR); Human Rights Watch; JoAnn Johnson Justice Committee; Louisiana Coalition on Jails and Prisons; Orleans Parish

Prison Reform Coalition (OPPRC); Safe Streets/Strong Communities
antipolicing activism, 132–41, 252. *See also* abolition; Black Lives Matter movement; BreakOUT!; Safe Streets/Strong Communities
antiprison activism, 135–36, 168–69. *See also* abolition; Angola Special Civics Project; Louisiana Coalition on Jails and Prisons; New Orleans Prison Coalition
antiracist activism, 11–13, 84–99, 145–48, 160–68, 199, 205–6, 208–22, 240–50, 294n219; Black Left organizations, 145–46, 161; racial justice activism, 17, 143, 179, 193, 214, 311n5. *See also* Angola Special Civics Project; Black Lives Matter movement; Black radical tradition; BreakOUT!; Community Labor United; Congreso de Jornaleros; Critical Resistance (CR); Human Rights Watch; INCITE! Women of Color Against Violence; Louisiana Coalition on Jails and Prisons; Orleans Parish Prison Reform Coalition (OPPRC); People's Hurricane Relief Fund; Safe Streets/Strong Communities; VOTE
antisex trafficking politics, 224–26, 234–38. *See also* LGBTQ policing; sex work, criminalization of
anti-state state, 63, 79, 284n8
Antoine's Restaurant, New Orleans, 230
Attica prison uprising (1971), 29, 47
austerity measures. *See* law-and-order austerity
Austin, James, 202
Austin Report (publication), 201–2, 325n182
Avoyelles Correctional Center, 99, 104, 107

Baker, Ella, 11
Bargain of 1876, 25

barrow, kai lumumba, 146, 161, 192, 194, 196, 239, 259
Bartholomew family, 153
Baton Rouge, 44. *See also* Louisiana State Penitentiary in Baton Rouge
Baton Rouge Stop Rape Crisis Center, 75
Bervera, Xochitl, 145, 161, 166, 171–72, 176, 178, 209
Blackburn, Frank, 87–88
Black Codes, 24–26
Black cultural traditions, 8–9, 184, 230
Black Lives Matter movement, 241–42, 329n72, 332n116
Black Marxism, 136, 162, 268n31
Black Panther Party (BPP), 33, 134, 152, 210, 245
Black radical tradition, 11, 30, 135, 136, 146, 161–62, 268n28. *See also* antiracist activism; Radical Reconstruction
#BlackTransLivesMatter campaign, 208, 240–48. *See also* Black Lives Matter movement
Blanco, Kathleen, 150, 151, 183
Board of Control, 26
Board of Pardons, 65
bonds: general obligation bonds (GOBs), 69, 82, 277n142, 289n113; lease revenue bonds (LRBs), 81–84, 99; 120; municipal, 102, 112, 134, 191; ratings, 105–106, 109, 126; prison construction, 25, 41, 42, 73, 105–107, 260. *See also* Louisiana Correctional Facilities Corporation; millages
Bossier Parish Maximum Security Jail, 159
Bourbon Democrats, 25–26
Bratton, William, 224, 254
BreakOUT!, 17, 207, 208, 209–22, 225, 238–50, 327n10; Trans March of Resilience (TMOR), 242–44, 24; Vice to ICE program, 247–48; We Deserve Better campaign, 208, 213–22, 327n16; "Your Guide to Street Safety & Preserving Your Rights with the Police" (manual), 215, 216, 220

Bretton Woods monetary system, 30
Brissette, James, 153
broken windows policing, 16, 102, 124–25, 131–32, 140, 224, 227, 232–33, 254
Brown, Mike, 241, 329n72
Brown, Ossie, 75
Brown v. Board of Education, 39
Building Our Power (BOP) program, 246, 248
Burch, Melissa, 135, 139
Bureau of Governmental Research, 119
Bush (GWB) administration, 145, 149, 161, 225, 304n153

Caddo Parish jail, 41, 42, 107, 111, 140
Caddo Parish School Board, 42
Cain, Burl, 97
Camp Greyhound, 149
Camp J, 59–60
Cannizzaro, Leon, 197, 202
capitalism. *See* racial capitalism
carceral cooperation, 4–5, 66, 101, 109–11, 139, 250, 254. *See also* Louisiana penal system
carceral expansion, 22–23, 46, 71–76, 102–21, 168, 170, 195. *See also* Louisiana penal system
carceral futures, 23, 53–58, 201–2
carceral geography, 14–15
carceral infrastructure, as term, 4
carceral logics, 10–12, 166, 168, 236, 259
carceral state-making, 3–4, 7, 23–28, 72, 196–97, 253–60. *See also* Louisiana penal system; state racism
Career Criminal Bureau, 33, 65
Carter, James, 184
Cassidy, Jack, 170, 179, 180, 187
Catholic Legal Immigration Network, 132
Cerasoli, Bob, 184, 185
chain gangs, 14. *See also* prison labor
Charity Hospital, 147, 190, 311n17
Chevalier, Fred L., 82

Citibank, 73
Citizens Rally to End Crime in the Quarter (2015), 226
Citizens United for the Rehabilitation of Errants, 95
Civics Project. *See* Angola Special Civics Project
Civil Rights Act (1871), 29
Civil Rights Congress, 162
Civil War, 24–25
Clemency, 65–66, 81, 92–93, 189, 285n18, 295n244
Clinton, Hillary, 122
Clinton administration, 102, 110, 125, 131, 140
Close Cell Restriction (CCR), 28
Cohen, Cathy, 250
Colten, Craig, 31
cooperative endeavor agreements, 106–107, 109–110, 111, 120, 298n51
Community Corrections Act, 56
Community Labor United (CLU), 136, 145, 162, 164
Compass, Eddie, 150, 180
CompStat, 130
conditions of confinement lawsuits: 11, 12, 55, 69, 117, 204; *Hamilton v. Morial,* 112–113, 133, 195; *Hayes Williams v. McKeithan,* 1, 5, 15–16, 19, 22–23, 29, 35–40, 85, 103, 108–109, 110, 111; limits of, 58–60, 88, 104, 251–252; Prison Litigation Reform Act, 111
Congreso de Jornaleros, 191, 193, 203, 220, 244, 253; Vice to ICE program, 247–48
Connick, Harry, 33–35, 41, 50, 65, 68, 121, 131, 132, 223, 280n195
convict leasing, 14, 24–26, 98, 271n19. *See also* Angola (Louisiana State Penitentiary); prison labor
Cook, Joe, 164
COPS program (Clinton administration), 129, 130, 140
COVID-19 pandemic, 204, 251–52, 256

Index 363

Cox, Laverne, 241, 243
Craig Elementary School, 137–38, 139
Criminal Justice Coordinating Council (CJCC), 35, 126
Criminal Justice Working Group, 196–97, 201, 202, 204, 325n182
criminal menopause, 95
crisis: 6, 252; crisis management, 9–10; economic crisis, 70–80, 105–106, 125–126, 252; and Hurricane Katrina, 148–160; of legitimacy, 6, 121, 127–128, 209; of overcrowding, 36, 41, 48, 50–52, 98, 105, 108
Crisis of Confidence (report; 2006), 181, 182
Critical Resistance (CR): 18, 102, 135, 145, 161, 163–67, 188–89, 194, 205, 259; Critical Resistance: Beyond the Prison Industrial Complex conference (1998), 135; Critical Resistance East Conference (2001), 136; Critical Resistance South Conference (2003), 100, 102, 136–37, 138–39, 141, 310n266. *See also* abolition; amnesty campaign
cruel and unusual punishment, as concept, 253
Cruz, Cielo, 172, 174–75, 177, 188, 191, 192, 195, 196, 206
curfew, 127, 131, 161, 228, 305n173

Danziger Bridge shooting (2005), 153–54, 176, 179, 180, 314n64
David Wade Correctional Center, 140
Davis, Angela, 24, 167, 322n114
Davis, Len, 128, 179
Dean, Eugene, 89
decentralization, 22, 30, 38, 40–48. *See also* liberalism; reformist reforms; satellite prisons
Democratic Party, 25, 64, 83
Department of Corrections. *See* Louisiana Department of Corrections (DOC); Louisiana Department of Public Safety and Corrections

Department of Health and Hospitals, 107
deportations, 193, 244, 247, 248. *See also* immigrant prisoners
DeSalvo, Frank, 173
Disaster Act (1974), 150
disaster response, 16–17, 148–50, 160–61. *See also* Hurricane Katrina (2005); state racism
Dixiecrats, 32, 269n42
Dixon, Chris, 134
Dixon Correctional Institute, 49–50, 68–69
Dollars & Sense (publication), 186–87
domestic violence, 135, 203
double-bunking, 72–73, 110–11. *See also* overcrowding
"Down by Law" (report), 186–87
drug courts, 9, 103
drunk tanks, 103
Du Bois, W.E.B., 13, 162
Duke, David, 97

East Louisiana State Hospital, 49
Economic Development District (EDD), 228–29
economic recessions, 1, 8, 30–31, 32, 62, 70–71, 72, 76–77, 79, 82. *See also* unemployment; petro capitalism; surplus populations
Economic Recovery Tax Act (1981), 71
Education Not Incarceration (ENI), 136
Edwards, Edwin, 23, 29, 30, 32, 40, 41, 42, 44, 47, 50, 52, 53, 54, 80–81, 82–83, 87, 91–92, 97
Edwards, John Bel, 249, 255, 334n9
Edwards, Nolan, 81
Ehrenkrantz Group, 55
elderly prisoners, 42, 44
electoral organizing, 89–92
Elie, Lolis Eric, 184, 199, 307n211
Emancipation Proclamation, 24
escape, 28, 92
ethnic cleansing, 30, 162
Evangeline, Louisiana, 31

Everard, Don, 115, 191–92, 205
Expungement Day, 189–90

Faulk, Nia, 246–47
FBI (Federal Bureau of Investigation), 117, 128, 133, 149, 151, 225, 306n178
FEMA (Federal Emergency Management Agency): denial of funding by, 187, 322n109; funding for jail expansion, 167, 168, 169, 195, 198, 261, 323n155; legislative ruling on, 312n31; property taxes and, 191; response to Hurricane Katrina by, 150
feminist politics: Black feminism, 134, 135, 161, 208, 209, 241, 289n99, 316n118; Black trans feminism, 17, 208, 250, 289n99, 333n117; carceral, 75–76, 102, 289n99; on emotional care, 177; on pornography, 224; on sexual violence, 39; transnational, 316n119
The First Boston Corporation, 73
First National Bank of Minneapolis, 83
flooding, 143, 148–49. *See also* Hurricane Katrina (2005)
Floyd, George, 252
Forgotten Man Committee, 87
Foster, Mike, 111, 295n243
FosterBear Films, 217
Foti, Charles, 6, 51, 69, 101, 112–120, 133–34, 141, 275n87. *See also* Orleans Parish Prison (OPP)
Foucault, Michel, 267n19
Francois, Althea, 134, 164–66, 172, 176, 209
"Free Them All" campaign, 251, 252
French Quarter, New Orleans, 208, 213, 222, 223–39
French Quarter Advocates (organization), 230
French Quarter Management District (FQMD), 17, 208, 227–33, 332n102. *See also* Security Task Force (FQMD)
Friends and Families of Louisiana's Incarcerated Children, 141, 163, 172

gender policing, 207, 208, 209–22
gendered segregation, 26–27, 294n220
gentrification: criminalization and, 183, 224, 235; in New Orleans, 9, 68, 124, 126, 235; threats to, 124, 184. *See also* tourism economy
Gerharz, Barry, 170
gerrymandering, 25
Giarrusso, Clarence, 51
Giarrusso, Joseph, Sr., 125
Gill, James, 174
Gilmore, Ruth Wilson, 6, 149, 260–61, 284n8
Giuliani, Rudy, 125, 232, 254
Glover, Henry, 153, 176, 179, 180
Goldberg, David Theo, 10
Gonzalez, Alberto, 151, 203
Gonzalez, Jacinta, 193, 206, 260
Goodman, Robert, 172, 192
Gottshalk, Marie, 75
Governor's Commission on Criminal Justice (Treen), 66, 80
The Governor's Corrections Plan, 62, 105–6
Governor's Pardon, Parole, and Rehabilitation Commission (GPPRC), 53–55
Greenwell Springs Hospital, 44
Gretna, New Orleans, 154–55
Griffin, Shana M., 100, 135, 139
Groves, Kim, 128, 179
Gusman, Marlin: abuse and accountability of, 142–43, 188; Camp Greyhound and Camp Amtrak by, 149; hurricane response by, 142, 155–56, 164, 166, 191;—Landrieu feud, 199–201; OPP expansion and, 186, 195–96, 198–99, 203–4, 261; OPPRC and, 141

habitual offenders, 41
Hall, Eddie, 86
Hall, Gwendolyn Midlo, 24
Hall, Stuart, 6
Hamilton v. Morial, 133, 195

Index   365

Hanhardt, Christina, 224
Harris, Kenisha, 210
Hayes Williams v. McKeithan, 19, 22–23, 29, 35–40, 85, 103, 108–109, 110, 111
healing justice, 246–47
Hedge-Morrell, Cynthia, 184–85
Henderson, Norris: as Angola lifer, 66; Angola Special Civics Project and, 84, 88; on collective activism, 145, 168, 170, 171; Safe Streets organizing by, 175–76, 177, 178, 189; VOTE organizing by, 192. *See also* Angola Special Civics Project
Herrington, Donnell, 151–52
Hobson, Emily, 211
Holmes, Jose, Jr., 153
homelessness, criminalization of, 129, 212, 222, 232–33, 235–36
Homer Plessy v. Judge Ferguson, 328n51
HOPE VI, 127, 147, 176, 312n19. *See also* St. Thomas housing development
hotel industry, 226–27, 228. *See also* tourism economy
Howard, Weil, Labouisse, and Friedrichs, Inc., 73
Howells, Mary, 176
human rights rhetoric, 30, 162, 316n119
Human Rights Watch, 132–33, 162
Hunt, Elayn, 29–30, 36, 40, 42, 47
Hunt Correctional Center, 53, 69, 80, 158–59
Hurricane Gustav (2008), 190–91
Hurricane Katrina (2005), 16, 142–43, 148–49, 205, 251, 312n26. *See also* Katrina Time; New Orleans; state racism
Hutson, Susan, 186, 252, 254

Iberia Parish jail, 107
ICE (Immigration and Customs Enforcement), 17, 149, 193, 203, 222, 248, 251, 253, 259
immigrant prisoners, 101, 102, 108–9, 132–33, 155, 193, 203–4, 244. *See also* deportation

incarceration rates: of Angola, 27; of Louisiana, 23, 26, 55, 62, 104–5; of Louisiana parish jails, 112, 140; of Mississippi, 6, 266n2
INCITE! Women of Color Against Violence, 135, 141, 145, 162
independent police monitor (IPM), 179–86, 205. *See also* Safe Streets/Strong Communities
indigent defense campaign, 169, 170, 171, 172–74. *See also* Safe Streets/Strong Communities
INS (Immigration and Naturalization Service), 16, 101, 108–9, 133
International Association of Chiefs of Police (IACP), 123
International Tribunal on Hurricanes Katrina and Rita, 182
In the Place of Justice (Rideau), 19

Jackson, Dee Dee, 210
jail system, 3. 101–12; changes from temporary to long-term system of, 16, 23, 68–70; conditions and regulation of, 5. *See also* Bossier Parish Maximum Security Jail; Caddo Parish jail; Iberia Parish jail; cooperative endeavor agreements; Jefferson Parish jail; Lafayette Parish jail; Orleans Justice Center; Orleans Parish Prison (OPP); Plaquemines Parish jail; Rapides Parish jail; Slidell jail; St. Bernard Parish jail; St. Charles Parish jail; St. John the Baptist Parish jail; St. Tammany jail; West Feliciana Parish jail
James, Samuel, 25, 26
Janak, Wayne, 152
Jasper, James M., 85
Jefferson Parish jail, 103, 104, 105, 120, 121, 197
Jena Correctional Facility, 159
Jetson Center for Youth, 158
JFA Institute, 201
Jindal, Bobby, 189, 226

JoAnn Johnson Justice Committee, 134
Johnson, Andrew, 24, 32
Johnson, Calvin, 160, 199
Johnson, JoAnn, 133
Johnston, Kenneth "Biggy," 29, 35, 61, 65, 85, 87. *See also* Angola Special Civics Project
Joseph, Andrew, 86
Joseph, Lazarus, 22, 28
Juvenile Justice Center, 251
Juvenile Justice Project of Louisiana (JJPL), 134, 141, 159, 163, 170, 194, 209

Kaplan, Dana, 194
Katrina (hurricane). *See* Hurricane Katrina (2005)
Katrina Time, 159, 162–66, 172–74, 187, 261. *See also* Louisiana penal system
Kelling, George L., 124
Kemp-Roth Bill, 71
King, John T., 67
Kopplin, Andy, 201
Kunzel, Regina, 39

labor. *See* prison labor; slave labor; surplus populations
Laborde, Raymond, 83, 99
Lafayette Parish jail, 51, 103, 108
Lambert, Louis, 64
Landrieu, Mary, 183
Landrieu, Mitch, 196, 199–201, 202, 204–5, 207, 218, 224, 226, 238
Landry, Jeff, 257
Latinx community, 13, 17, 193, 203, 214, 224, 247–48, 311n5
law-and-order austerity, 7, 16, 63–74, 98, 121, 256, 262. *See also* Louisiana penal system; economic recessions; petro capitalism; tourism economy; unemployment
Law Enforcement Administration Act (LEAA), 1, 23, 32–35, 41, 44, 55, 66, 74–75, 112; *Omnibus* Crime Control and Safe Streets Act (1968), 32

law library, 85
Lawson, Arthur, 154
League of Women Voters, 98
Lee, Harry, 154
Lefebvre, Henri, 208
Legal Defense Fund (NAACP), 164
The Lens (publication), 198–99
Letten, Jim, 151
levee work, 24
LGBTQ policing, 10, 11, 17, 207, 208–22, 225–26, 237–38, 240–50, 329n60. *See also* antisex trafficking politics; New Orleans Police Department (NOPD)
liberalism, 2, 4, 8, 9–10, 11, 15–16, 23, 29–30, 32, 38–40, 47, 53–57, 58–59, 81, 95, 121, 125, 170, 182, 197–198, 199, 239, 253, 272n45. *See also* decentralization; reformist reforms
Liebenthal, Mayaba, 188, 205
lifers, 48, 62, 84–86, 88, 97–98. *See also* Angola Lifers' Association; Angola Special Civics Project; long-termers
Lil Wayne, 142
Linebaugh, Peter, 251
Locked Up and Out (report; 2010), 209
Lombard, Ed, 101
Long, Alecia P., 223
Long, Earl, 87
Long, Huey, 7–8, 31, 32
long-termers, 48, 61–62, 92. *See also* lifers
Louisiana Association of Criminal Defense Lawyers, 163
Louisiana Bond Commission, 73, 257
Louisiana Capital Assistance Center, 160
Louisiana Coalition in Support of Penal Reform (LCSPR), 95–96
Louisiana Coalition on Jails and Prisons (LCJP), 1, 48, 53, 67, 74, 98, 100, 104, 283n246
Louisiana Commission on Law Enforcement, 35
Louisiana Correctional and Industrial School, 72–73, 80

Index 367

Louisiana Correctional Facilities Corporation (LCFC), 83, 105–7. *See also* bonds

Louisiana Correctional Institute for Women at St. Gabriel, 3, 52, 80, 136

Louisiana Crisis Assistance Center (LCAC), 162–63

Louisiana Department of Corrections (DOC), 5, 22, 29, 41–45, 255. *See also* Board of Control; Louisiana Department of Public Safety and Corrections

Louisiana Department of Public Safety and Corrections (DPSC), 62, 73–74, 81, 83, 87, 92, 101–11, 120, 131, 142–43, 155–59. *See also* Louisiana Department of Corrections

Louisiana District Attorneys Association, 54

Louisiana Fraternal Order of Police, 185

Louisiana Indigent Defense Assistance Board, 173

Louisiana penal system: about, 1–13, 253–57; carceral future of, 23, 53–58; decentralization of, 22, 30, 38, 40–48; expansion of, 22–23, 46, 71–76, 104–5, 112–21, 168, 170, 195; formation of, 23–28; Katrina Time in, 159, 162–66, 172–74, 187, 261; law-and-order austerity, 6, 16, 62–70; overcrowding in, 15, 22, 36, 40, 50–52, 68–70, 102–4; per diem payment system of, 5, 17, 51–52, 69, 103, 108–9, 120, 169, 187, 198–99, 202–5; punitive governance and, 65–70. *See also* Angola (Louisiana State Penitentiary); cooperative endeavor agreements; jail system; *Hayes Williams v. McKeithan*; prison reforms

Louisiana Prison System Study Commission, 55–58, 62

Louisiana Senate Committee on Revenue and Fiscal Affairs, 74

Louisiana Sheriffs' Association, 5, 70, 109, 115, 253

Louisiana State Penitentiary. *See* Angola (Louisiana State Penitentiary)

Louisiana State Penitentiary in Baton Rouge, 24, 26, 271n21

Louisiana States' Rights Party, 64

Louisiana World's Fair (1984), 68, 126, 223–24, 288n79

Loyola University Institute for Human Relations, 90

Lynn, Evelyn, 160, 166, 169, 170, 173, 175, 178, 192

Madison family, 153, 176, 185

Maggio, Ross, Jr., 67, 92

magic, 246–47

martial law, 150

Martin, Trayvon, 241

Marx, Karl, 77–78

McAdam, Doug, 268n32

McCollister, McCleary, Fazio, & Holliday, 82

McCormick, John, 35

McDonald, CeCe, 241

McGruder, Lionel, 79

McHatton, James A., 24

McKittrick, Katherine, 208

medical jail facility, 204, 251–52

medical neglect of incarcerated persons, 29, 44, 103, 117, 132–34, 156, 158–59, 195. *See also* prisoner neglect and abuse

mental illness, 236, 251–52

Mid-City Neighborhood Association, 198

Middleton, Tamika, 138, 161, 163, 166

millages, for jails, 109, 115, 117, 119–20, 191, 323n155; for law enforcement, 127, 238–9, 332n116

militia, 151–52

Minyard, Frank, 275n87

Mississippi, 6, 25, 41, 266n2

Mitchell, Arthur, 22, 28–29, 59

Mock, Janet, 241

Morial, Ernest "Dutch," 67, 68, 126, 286n50

Morial, Marc, 100, 102, 121, 126, 133, 140
Morial Administration Crime Initiatives (MAC I), 127–28
Moynihan, Daniel Patrick, 127
Muhammad, Curtis, 136
Muñoz, Jose Esteban, 208
Murray, Charles, 122

NAACP, 87–88, 164
Nagin, C. Ray, 141, 148, 149, 150, 151, 182, 183
National Coalition to Free the Angola 3, 136
National Guard, 149, 150–52, 193
National Prison Project (ACLU), 133, 163, 186, 187–88
Nation of Islam activists, 29
natural life, as concept, 285n28
The Negro Family (Moynihan), 127
The New Jim Crow (Alexander), 199
New Orleans: BreakOUT!'s activism on LGBTQ policing in, 17, 207, 208, 209–22, 225, 238–50; colonial jail in, 24; history of racial policing in, 270n4; Hurricane Gustav and, 190–91; law-and-order austerity in, 67–68; LEAA funds in, 32–35; Policy 402, 220, 222, 328n42; post-Katrina state violence in, 148–60; prison construction plans in, 42; punishment regime in, 132–39; Security Task Force (FQMD) in, 17, 208, 228–38, 249, 330n84, 331n96, 332n103; tourism industry of, 8–9, 17, 67, 68, 207–9, 288n79. *See also* BreakOUT!; Critical Resistance South; French Quarter, New Orleans; French Quarter Management District (FQMD); Hurricane Katrina (2005); New Orleans Police Department (NOPD); Orleans Parish Prison (OPP); Orleans Parish Prison Reform Coalition (OPPRC); Safe Streets/Strong Communities
New Orleans Business Council, 126

New Orleans City Council, 32, 116, 168, 335n14
New Orleans City Crime Summit, 123
New Orleans City Hall, 251
New Orleans Comprehensive Zoning Ordinance, 44
New Orleans Convention and Visitor's Bureau, 226, 228–30
New Orleans Convention Center, 68
New Orleans Indigent Defense Office, 33
New Orleans Police Department (NOPD): broken windows policing by, 16, 102, 124–25, 131–32, 140, 227, 232–33, 254; collusion with ICE, 214, 222, 260; community policing by, 125, 127, 128–129, 131, 140, consent decree, 209, 217–218, 219, 222; DOJ report on, 214; Hurricane Katrina and, 149–54; murders and coverups by, 152–54, 176, 179; reforms of, 121–32, 179–86, 238–39; stop-and-frisk tactics of, 32, 125, 129, 211, 212, 218, 219, 331n92; policing of LGBTQ residents by, 25, 208–22, 237–38, 240–50; tourist economy and policing by, 223–39. *See also* Orleans Parish Prison (OPP); Security Task Force (FQMD); state troopers
New Orleans Police Foundation, 129–30
New Orleans Prison Coalition, 136
New Orleans Prison Organizing Resource Center (NO PORC), 136
New York City, 125, 130, 159, 224, 232, 254
Night Out Against Crime initiative, 129
NIMBYism, 40–48, 198
NOLA Patrol, 226
NOLA Trans March (2015), 240
Nowe Miasto, 134
nursing homes, 42, 44

Oakdale Detention Center, 108–9
Obama administration, 199, 225, 244, 250

Office of Municipal Investigations (OMI), 179
Office of the Independent Police Monitor (OIPM), 17, 169, 183–85, 192, 255. *See also* independent police monitor (IPM)
Office of the Inspector General (OIG), 183–85
oil industry, 1, 7–8, 16, 30–32, 62, 70–72, 76, 91, 148, 252. *See also* petro capitalism
O'Neal, John, 136
one-party state, 25
Operation Chill Out, 129
Operation Crime Sweep, 121–22
Operation Innocence Lost, 225
Operation Relentless Pursuit, 238
OPP. *See* Orleans Parish Prison (OPP)
OPPRC. *See* Orleans Parish Prison Reform Coalition (OPPRC)
organization building, 11–13, 84–97, 144–48, 160–67, 205–6, 209–10, 258–63
organized abandonment, 143, 155–60, 163, 167, 251, 267n10
Orleans Indigent Defense (OID), 173
Orleans Justice Center, 251. *See also* Orleans Parish Prison (OPP)
Orleans Parish Prison (OPP): activism on, 18, 20, 168, 169, 191–205, 218, 251, 255, 261; expansion of, 101, 102, 105, 112–21, 132–34; FEMA funds for rebuilding, 167, 168, 169, 195, 198, 261, 323n155; flooding and state violence against prisoners of, 143, 155–60, 167, 251; increased incarceration in, 6, 16, 50–51; lawsuits against, 203–4; Phase III of, 251–52, 254; revised disaster policy of, 204–5; Safe Streets activism on, 186–90. *See also Hamilton v. Morial;* jail system; Orleans Justice Center, New Orleans
Orleans Parish Prison Reform Coalition (OPPRC), 17, 18, 20, 168, 169, 191–205, 218, 251, 255, 261. *See also* Orleans Parish Prison (OPP)

overcrowding, 15, 22, 36, 40, 50–52, 68–70, 102–4. *See also* crisis; Louisiana penal system

Palestine, 30, 162
Palmer, Lhundyn, 210, 214–15, 243
pardons. *See* clemency
Parenti, Christian, 78
Patterson, William, 162
Penn Center, 164
Pennington, Richard, 102, 121, 128, 130, 141, 182, 234
Pennington Plan, 102, 128–31, 254
People's Consent Decree, 214
People's Hurricane Relief Fund, 146, 164, 182, 311n12, 313n49, 317n121
People's Institute for Survival and Beyond, 311n12
per diem payment system, 5, 17, 51–52, 69, 103, 108–9, 120, 169, 187, 198–99, 202–5. *See also* Orleans Parish Prison (OPP), jail system
Pervel, Vinnie, 152
petro capitalism, 1, 7–8, 23, 31–32, 70, 71, 76–78, 148, 256, 274n78. *See also* oil industry
petro populism, 7–8
Phelps, C. Paul, 19, 52, 54, 67, 81, 103
philanthropy, 93–94
Plan for Crime Prevention & Reform (Morial), 100
plantation bloc, 25, 26
Plaquemines Parish jail, 105
plea bargaining, 61, 85
police accountability, 17, 179–86, 205
Police-Civilian Task Force (NOPD), 179
Police Early Warning System (PEWS), 128
police jury, 277n137
police violence, 147, 152–60, 176, 179, 241, 252, 329n72, 333n122. *See also* LGBTQ policing
policing reforms, 121–32. *See also* abolition; reformist reforms
Policing the Crisis (Hall et al.), 6

Policy 402 (New Orleans), 220, 222, 328n42
political education, 85, 89, 246, 248. *See also* abolition
political process theory, 268n32
Polozola, Frank, 22, 35–37, 40, 67, 72, 73, 92, 103–4, 106–107, 108, 110–11, 113, 141. See also *Hayes Williams v. McKeithan*
POSH Academy, 245
Pratt, William, 24
Price, Ursula, 163, 168, 171–72, 176, 177, 184, 186, 192
prisoner neglect and abuse, 133–34, 143, 155–60, 167, 195, 203–4, 316n102. *See also* medical neglect of incarcerated persons
prison-financing schemes, 81–84, 99. *See also* bonds; Louisiana Correctional Facilities Corporation
prison labor, 24, 26–27, 78–80, 270n7, 272n39; reproductive labor, 26–27, 290n128. *See also* convict leasing
Prison Litigation Reform Act (1996), 111, 186
Prison Reform Association of Louisiana, 26, 271n29
prison reforms: from 1971–75, 28, 29–35, 37; decentralization, 22, 30, 38, 40–48; downsizing OPP, 190–206; due to *Hayes Williams* lawsuit, 22, 29–30, 35–36; expansion, 22–23, 46, 71–76, 102–21, 168, 170. *See also* Louisiana penal system; Orleans Parish Prison (OPP); reformist reforms
prison riots, 33, 47, 88, 103, 108, 158; prisoner revolts, 27. *See also* Angola protests; prison revolts
prison ship, 44
prison violence, 29, 36–38, 92, 203, 273n57
Program for Older Prisoners (Tulane University), 95
pro-prison advocacy, 47–48
ProPublica, 180
protests, 27, 223–24, 226, 247–48, 252. *See also* antiracist activism; prison riots
Proud, Penny, 240, 242
public housing redevelopment programs, 127–28, 147, 176–77, 312n19. *See also* HOPE VI
Public Integrity Bureau (PIB), 179
Public Integrity Division (PID), 128

Quan, H.L.T., 269n44
Quant, Ted, 90, 193
queer futurity, 208
queerness and prison segregation, 39–40
queer youth of color, 10, 11, 17, 207, 208–22

racial capitalism, overview, 10, 46, 76–78, 272n45
racial segregation, 26–27, 36
racism by the state, 8–10, 148–60. *See also* carceral state-making; state racism
racist narratives, 74–76, 122, 126–27, 150–55
racist sentencing, 86–87
Rahim, Malik, 134, 152, 313n49
Rapides Parish jail, 106, 107
Rapping, Jon, 174
Reagan administration, 70, 71, 103, 108, 286n50, 304n153
Reagon, Bernice Johnson, 262
Reconstruction, 13, 17, 24, 25, 143, 160–67, 247
record expungement, 189–90, 249
Red Hat solitary confinement, 28, 30, 59
reformist reforms, 9–10, 11, 22–23, 29–30, 47, 53–58, 125, 128–131, 170, 260. *See also* decentralization, liberalism
reforms. *See* abolitionist reforms; policing reforms; prison reforms; reformist reforms
Republican Party, 25, 64, 83, 284n9
research methods, 18–20, 270n50
Rideau, Wilbert, 19, 22, 40, 87, 97, 138

Index   371

Riley, Warren, 154, 184
Ritchie, Andrea, 215
Robeson, Paul, 162
Robinson, Cedric, 1, 10, 14, 268n28
Roemer, Buddy, 91–92, 104–7
Roe v. Wade, 257
Roper, Nathan, 152
Ruffins, Kermit, 199

SafeCam, 228
Safe Streets/Strong Communities, 17, 18, 144, 169, 170–91, 205, 252. *See also* antiracist activism; Hurricane Katrina, Orleans Parish Prison Reform Coalition (OPPRC)
Sakakeeny, Matt, 184
Sanders, Joe, 65
satellite prisons, 22, 23, 42, 44. *See also* decentralization
Savoy, Michael, 72
Schept, Judah, 55, 121
Schrader, Stuart, 125
Scott, James, 150
Screaming Mothers of New Orleans, 133–34
Second Line for Safety, 230, 331n93
Security Task Force (FQMD), 17, 208, 228–38, 249, 330n84, 331n96, 332n103. *See also* French Quarter Management District (FQMD); New Orleans; tourism economy
Sens, Paul, 202
Serpas, Ronal, 197, 219
Sessions, Jeff, 250
sexual violence, 38, 39–40, 59, 75–76, 159, 195, 211, 212, 313n37
sex work, criminalization of, 66, 124, 132, 211, 213, 223–25, 232, 234–38, 243. *See also* antisex trafficking politics
shadow jailing, 103
Shavers, Jai, 244
Sherry, Milan Nicole, 209, 211, 219, 242
shoeshine hustlers, 232, 331nn99–100
Simms, Bob, 207, 231, 232, 233, 237, 238
slave labor, 26

Slidell jail, 105
Smith, Jerome, 137–38
Snorton, C. Riley, 242
solitary confinement, 28, 30, 36–37, 38, 59, 261
Soros Foundation, 171–72
Southern Center for Human Rights (SCHR), 162, 163, 164, 172
Southern Coalition on Jails and Prison, 48, 117
Southern Policy Law Center, 203
spadework, as term, 11
spatial fix, as concept, 295n3
state budgets, 32, 41, 42, 49–50, 52, 62, 64, 69, 71–74, 80, 83, 140. *See also* economic recessions; petro capitalism
state of emergency declaration, 41–42, 92, 104, 150
state racism, 8–10, 148–60, 249, 251–253, 255. *See also* Angola (Louisiana State Penitentiary); carceral state-making; Hurricane Katrina; LGBTQ policing; Louisiana penal system; Orleans Parish Prison (OPP); police violence; New Orleans Police Department (NOPD); racism
St. Bernard Parish jail, 105, 155
St. Charles Parish jail, 105
Stevenson, Lee, 22, 28
St. John the Baptist Parish jail, 105
St. Landry Parish, 66
state troopers, 6, 33, 66, 67, 121, 129, 130, 149, 150, 151, 170, 190, 222, 223, 226–227, 228–230, 233–4, 238, 250, 255, 330n88, 331n92,
stop-and-frisk tactics, 32, 125, 129, 211, 212, 218, 219, 331n92
Stovall, James, 53, 83–84
St. Tammany Parish jail, 105
St. Thomas public housing project, 127, 176–77, 312n19. *See also* HOPE VI
suicide, 92
surplus populations, 78, 236, 257. *See also* crisis, economic recessions, law-and-order austerity, unemployment

surveillance, 9, 37, 59, 208, 228, 230, 234, 249–50. *See also* New Orleans Police Department (NOPD); Security Task Force (FQMD)

Tallulah youth prison, 134, 137, 141, 159, 171
Tanner, William, 153, 176
Taylor, Breonna, 252
Taylor, Dorothy Mae, 29
10/6 law, 65, 85–86, 87, 88, 97
Texas, 69, 73
Thomas, Oliver, 158, 335n14
Thompson, A. C., 151, 152, 153, 180, 313n49
Times-Picayune (publication), 78–79, 105, 111, 116, 123, 133, 154, 180, 184, 198–99, 204
Tocqueville, Alexis de, 24
Torres, Sidney, IV, 226, 228, 231, 330n80, 331n96
tough-on-crime politics, 6, 9–10, 74–76, 86, 196
tourism economy, 8–9, 17, 67–68, 121, 126, 129, 207–9, 223–39, 288n79. *See also* French Quarter Management District (FQMD); gentrification; Security Task Force (FQMD)
Trans Defense Fund, 249
trans youth of color, 10, 11, 207, 208–22
Treen, David, 8, 16, 61, 62–70, 71–75, 77–82
Treme Community Center, 137–38, 189, 190
Trump administration, 249, 250
truth-in-sentencing, 131
Tulane University, 116, 305n165
Turley, John, 95
20/45 law, 96

unemployment, 13, 48, 53, 76–79, 289n115, 292n155. *See also* economic recessions, surplus populations
unemployment compensation program, 61, 72

University of New Orleans, 131, 134
Unter, Kevin, 131
US Department of Health and Human Services, 5
US Department of Homeland Security (DHS), 4, 225, 233–34, 250
US Department of Justice (DOJ), 17, 40, 195, 203, 204; BreakOUT! and, 207, 209–10, 213, 214, 217–19
US Human Rights Network, 162
US Parole Commission, 54
US Social Forum (2007), 145–46

Vera Institute, 191
Victims of Crime Act, 76
Victims of Trafficking and Violence Protection Act (2000), 225
victims' rights, 74–76
Vodicka, John, 48, 283n246
Voice of the Experienced (VOTE), 141, 171, 192

Wade Correctional Institute, 80
wage theft, 247
Ware, Wes, 209–10, 213, 217, 223, 327n16
Warmouth, Henry Clay, 25
War on Drugs, 103–4, 118
Washington Correctional Center, 73
Watters, Robert, 232, 236–37
We Charge Genocide (petition), 162
Welcome to New Orleans (film), 152
Wells, Ida B., 1, 76, 152
West Feliciana Parish jail, 107–8
Westley, Arely, 248, 333n139
Wharton School of Business, 55
white flight, 67–68
white supremacy, 11, 14, 15, 25, 39, 76, 122, 143, 146, 151–53, 226, 249, 313n49. *See also* state racism
Wikberg, Ron, 97
Willard-Lewis, Cynthia, 184–85
Williams, Erica L., 224
Williams, Hayes, 19, 22, 28–9, 59, 61–62
Willis, Jonathan, 210

Wilright, Derwin, Jr., 219, 220, 222
Wilson, James Q., 124
Winn Correctional Institute, 99, 105, 107
Women with a Vision (organization), 209, 225, 243
Woods, Clyde, 25, 57, 143
work-release centers, 3, 52–53
wrongful death lawsuit, 133

Yancy, Checo, 89, 93
Yom Kippur War, 30
Youth Study Center jail, 155

Zapatismo, 134
Zimbardo, Philip, 124
Zimmerman, George, 241

www.ingramcontent.com/pod-product-compliance
Lightning Source LLC
Chambersburg PA
CBHW031456161224
19094CB00001B/8